For Theirs Is the Kingdom

For Theirs Is the Kingdom

Inclusion and Participation of Children in the Gospel according to Luke

Amy Lindeman Allen

LEXINGTON BOOKS/FORTRESS ACADEMIC
Lanham • Boulder • New York • London

Published by Lexington Books/Fortress Academic

Lexington Books is an imprint of The Rowman & Littlefield Publishing Group, Inc.
4501 Forbes Boulevard, Suite 200, Lanham, Maryland 20706
www.rowman.com

6 Tinworth Street, London SE11 5AL, United Kingdom

Copyright © 2019 The Rowman & Littlefield Publishing Group, Inc.

All rights reserved. No part of this book may be reproduced in any form or by any electronic or mechanical means, including information storage and retrieval systems, without written permission from the publisher, except by a reviewer who may quote passages in a review.

Portions of chapter 3 originally appeared in Amy Lindeman Allen, "Reading for Inclusion: The Girl from Galilee (Luke 8:40–56)," in *Journal of Childhood and Religion* Vol. 7 (2017), 1–17. Used with permission.

British Library Cataloguing in Publication Information Available

Library of Congress Cataloging-in-Publication Data

ISBN 978-1-9787-0323-0 (cloth)
ISBN 978-1-9787-0322-3 (electronic)

To my children, Becca, Joanna, and William;
To my god-children, Jake and Madeline;
and
To all the children of the congregations of which I've had the privilege to be a part—you have ministered to me far more than I could ever minister to you.

Contents

Acknowledgments	ix
Introduction	xiii
1 Defining Children in Luke's Gospel	1
2 Young Children in the Household of God	23
3 Young Children in Jesus' Ministry	75
4 Child Disciples as Companions of Jesus	123
5 Child Disciples as Hearers and Doers of God's Word	161
6 (Re)membering Children, and Through Them, Christ's Church	203
Bibliography	231
Topical Index	241
Scripture Index	247
About the Author	255

Acknowledgments

This project is one that I could not have imagined when I began my ministry over a decade ago. It is the result of so many influences and encouragements outside of myself and represents my growth, on account of these sources, as both a scholar and a pastor. I am profoundly grateful for all of the institutions and individuals that have helped guide me to this point.

I could not have undertaken my work without the generous financial support of the Vanderbilt Graduate Department of Religion, its Theology and Practice Program, and the Evangelical Lutheran Church in America. I am grateful for both the tangible and intangible resources afforded me by both of these institutions.

For their feedback and encouragement throughout earlier drafts of this work, I am grateful to Fernando Segovia, Daniel Patte, Douglas Knight, Bonnie Miller-McLemore, and Jaco Hamman. In particular, the academic and personal support provided throughout this project by Fernando Segovia is unquantifiable. I am deeply grateful for the example he has set as a scholar and activist, committed to (re)imagining the Church and the world as a more inclusive and welcoming place for *all* people. For empowering me to identify my calling to childist criticism, I owe him a great debt of gratitude. From within the burgeoning field of children and religion, I am especially thankful for the mentorship Bonnie Miller-McLemore and Julie Faith Parker have offered as well as their model scholarship.

The final version of this book as it exists today would not have been possible without the time, encouragement, and inspiration allotted me by the various students, faculties, and staffs that I have had the privilege of working with since its inception. I am grateful to all the students, faculty, and staff at Columbia Theological Seminary in Atlanta, Georgia with whom I was blessed to serve as a teaching extern during the bulk of my writing process.

I am especially grateful to Stan Saunders, Raj Nadella, Beth Johnson, and Christine Yoder for the grace with which they welcomed me into the Bible Department. To the staff of Lutheran Church of the Good Shepherd in Reno, NV, where I served as co-lead pastor after leaving Atlanta—your full and generous spirits have nurtured my faith and my scholarship more than you can know. I am especially to Maribeth Doerr, Deanna Gaunt, Shaun O'Reilly, and Kent Kubista through whom I found the courage to return to this work, submit, and prepare it for publication. Most recently, for the faculty, students, and staff at Christian Theological Seminary, where I presently teach as Assistant Professor of New Testament, I give my thanks. I am grateful for the confidence you have shown in me and the space that you have given me to complete the necessary revisions for this manuscript. For so many other scholars and ministers who have helped me to grow in my scholarship whose names are too many to list—thank you.

For revising my grammar, dear friend Wendy Force is responsible for any semblance of legibility in this book (any remaining grammar foibles are my own). Since the first time we met in college, I cannot think of a paper or an article that I've submitted that Wendy has not first read. As we have grown together, Wendy has not only provided both tangible and intangible support and encouragement for my scholarship, but is the godmother of my youngest child. I would not be the person or the scholar that I am without her.

Along my path of childist biblical criticism, I encountered two child-centered faith formation programs: Godly Play and Catechesis of the Good Shepherd. These programs have kept me grounded and connected with real children in the contemporary church and have fed my own spiritual yearning. To this end I want to also express my gratitude especially to the National Association for the Catechesis of the Good Shepherd for the spiritual formation provided especially by my formation leaders and colleagues, Joanne Williams and Elizabeth Piper.

And finally, I am profoundly grateful to my family for their steadfast patience, encouragement, and support. My parents, Bonnie and Roland Lindeman, and my brother, Tony, have affirmed for me ever since I was a small child that my place, and that of all people regardless of age or any other distinction is important and valuable to Christ in His Church. They paved the foundation for this childist project long before it was ever conceived. And they, together with my grandparents, Roger and Joanne Stecker, have continued to encourage me in its completion along every step of the way.

My husband, Erik, possesses more confidence in me than I have in myself. He has faithfully walked alongside me at every step of this process, even when we didn't know where the next step would lead. His hard-work, patience, and love have enabled me to pursue my passion. And, of course, our children, Becca, Joanna, and William, are the reason for my passion and my work. They have at the same time inspired me to make the church more welcoming and accessible for them, taught me what welcome in the name of Christ really is, and been patient and supportive of me as I completed my writing project.

Soli Deo Gloria.

Introduction

It has long been said, "Children in company should be seen and not heard."[1] Such a perspective both dismisses and devalues the participation of children. Children as a group and the individual children who make up such groups bring unique and valuable contributions to the mixed generational company that such sayings imply. These contributions and often the spirit behind them are lost when children are categorically dismissed and silenced. Unfortunately, in the recent history of biblical scholarship, this has often been the default. In contrast, child-centered biblical criticism of the last decade has sought to return the voices of children to the table. In line with such scholarship, this book is a project in *hearing* children and celebrating the contributions they have brought and continue to bring to the diverse company of people who have considered themselves followers of Jesus over the centuries.

Specifically, this is a project in hearing the children of Luke's gospel account. By listening for the voices of children in and behind the pages of Luke's gospel, my aim is to hear these first child followers of Jesus back into being—or, perhaps hear them into being for the first time.[2] Direct speech attributed to children appears only twice in Luke's gospel: first with the boy Jesus in the Temple (Lk 2:49) and again with the servant-girl in Herod's court (Lk 22:56).[3] However, for the one who has ears to hear, the multiple and teeming voices of the first century children with whom Jesus lived and ministered lie just below the surface.

Already in the prologue to Luke's gospel, the angel Gabriel prophesies that John will "go before [Jesus] to turn the hearts of parents to their children (τέκνα)" (Lk 1:17a). This is the task currently at hand. In an adult-dominated world, this book seeks, with John, to turn from the self-absorbed task of adults constructing, deconstructing, and instructing one another in discipleship toward the child disciples whom Jesus raises up not only as models of that very task, but as proprietors of the entire Kingdom of God (Lk 18:15–17).

Luke recounts John engaging in this prophesied task before he is even born. As an infant in Elizabeth's womb, John already proclaims the good news of God's incarnation in Jesus (Lk 1:41–44). The result of this proclamation turns the heart of Jesus' mother, Mary, to God's mission, as she in turn proclaims the great reversal God has begun through her son (Lk 1:46–55). From the very beginning of Luke's gospel account, children, indeed *infants*, are thus active in both the proclamation of and living out of the Gospel. At this point in Luke's story, it would not be going too far to identify the infant John as Jesus' first disciple, receiving and responding to the miracle of God's Word as he does.

Nevertheless, despite the singular richness of Luke among the gospel accounts in its description of both John's and Jesus' births and Jesus' childhood, Luke's gospel has heretofore received little attention in relation to what it has to say for and about the lives of real children, both then and now.

HISTORY OF INTERPRETATION

Luke's Children in Traditional Scholarship

Traditional scholarship tends to read child characters in Luke's account respectively as prologue to the main narrative and/or metaphor for adult discipleship. Lukan scholarship addresses the lives of children (if at all) almost exclusively within the confines of children's concerns within the broader context of family systems and first century household structure. These discussions rarely distinguish between non-adult children and their adult counterparts who continue to live under the *pater familias* of the eldest generation.[4]

Such adultist tendencies in Western scholarship reflect a broader trend in the humanities to either coddle or protect the idealized image of "the child," with little attention to the contextualized nature of childhood(s) or the personhood of individual children.[5] This can be traced back as early as the previously quoted assertion that "children in company should be seen and not heard"—an assertion that by the time of its writing had already shifted in the minds of the public to aphorism rather than novel idea.[6] Children and their concerns have thus long been marginalized in favor of the more rational and complete adult agenda.

Such an agenda, however, was by no means the novel invention of the Enlightenment. It was, rather, born out of the patristic hierarchy that dominated the first century Mediterranean world. At the margins of society, the adult males who authored most texts did not deem children worthy of explicit or extensive mention. Consequently, non-adult children have all but disappeared from the ancient sources. Even as recent ideological trends in scholarship have sought to uncover other oppressed voices from the margins, children in the first century Mediterranean world continue virtually unseen. For example, Robert Knapp, in his otherwise excellent monograph *Invisible Romans*, turns his eye away from emperors, philosophers, and senators, to the "ordinary" members of society with an impressive list of chapters accounting for the diverse subsections of ordinary life in ancient Rome; however, as he sheds intentional light on these often invisible people, occasionally including children within these groups, children as their own subgroup with unique contributions to offer remain unseen.[7]

Similarly, Luke's gospel and its message of reversal, first proclaimed by Mary at the inspiration of the infant John, has spoken words of hope for those on the margins even as the very child disciples who first inspired and modeled such hope have largely been muted or ignored. The themes of reversal and divine preference for the poor pervade Luke's gospel. These have been and continue to be successfully explored by liberation theologians, postcolonial critics, and others.[8] Luke's gospel has been interpreted, albeit not universally, as a message of hope proclaiming equal dignity for followers of Jesus for those who have been marginalized due to their income, gender, race, and ethnicity.

Although it is valuable and necessary to consider children as members of nearly every other marginalized identity which ideological criticism has taken up, it is also necessary to turn concerted attention to children as a uniquely marginalized group in their own right.[9] This need can be seen in the easy dismissal of children by post-enlightenment figures as well as in the treatment of children in condescending remarks aimed at other marginalized groups. For example, Thomas Jefferson reportedly compared freeing a slave to "abandoning a child."[10] Scholarship has for some time rightly refuted the racism apparent in such an analogy, even while popular sensitivity to the harm of such racism has lamentably not yet reached the needed response of universal repudiation. However, scholarship and the broader public are only beginning to acknowledge and to address the second layer of marginalization that exists in such statements of prejudice.

Acknowledging a second layer of marginalization in such racist statements means addressing the use of children as a negative caricature. Racist remarks like Jefferson's thus not only marginalize the intended targets, in this case nineteenth century enslaved people of color in the U.S., but also the children with whom these targets are compared with the intent to demean, thus doubly marginalizing children of African American descent. Literary theorist Anna Mae Duanne describes this oversight thoughtfully in relation to the expansion of what she describes as the "citizen-subject," which "often stops short of engaging the child figure against which the citizen-subject continues to be measured."[11] With the turn of the century, awareness of the lacuna that Duanne identifies has been growing, beginning with the emergence of an interdisciplinary field called Childhood Studies and continuing into religious studies with movements in both Child Theology and child-centered biblical interpretation.

Childhood Studies

In the early twentieth century, developmental psychology had become the primary voice on childhood—following a Child Theory largely developed by Charles Darwin that asserted childhood as a largely biological category of immaturity and development. This branch of study focused almost solely on the biological nature of children and the study of childhood as a positivistic science, minimizing Darwin's astute observations about the concomitant social character of childhood. As a result, Darwinism as it was embraced by psychology led to the institutionalization of the social category of childhood under the purview of experts. Erik Erikson and Jean Piaget developed a robust field of child psychology and the discrete disciplines of pediatric medicine took root.[12]

Into this climate, French historian Philippe Ariès brought the expertise of the field of historical study to bear on questions of children and childhood with the publication of his landmark work, *Centuries of Childhood* (1960, 1962). Although many of Ariès claims, most notably that the idea of childhood did not exist before the Enlightenment, have justifiably been called into question, his social history largely pioneered the study of childhood as an independent discipline.[13] Newly aware of the constructed nature of childhood as described by Ariès, sociologists and cultural anthropologists in the latter half of the twentieth century began to notice a diversity of childhoods rather than a single structure of childhood in various cultures across time and place. Meanwhile, a growing youth movement in the political sphere, alongside continued developments in the fields of sociology and psychology, led the study of children to expand across the disciplines. Growing out of this, the interdisciplinary field of Childhood Studies began to emerge in the 1980s with a dual emphasis on the agency of children and social constructedness of childhood.[14]

Child-Centered Biblical Interpretation of the New Testament

With this growing emphasis on children in the religious and interdisciplinary spheres, the time was ripe for a renewed attention to children in the biblical texts. In the twentieth century, growing attention began to be paid to the historical place of children in the ancient world as it relates to interpretation of biblical treatments of them. In New Testament studies, this began with Lester Bradner in the early 1920s and continued up to and beyond influential work of well known historical critic, John Dominic Crossan.[15] While this shift shone a much-needed light on the lives of ancient children in relation to the New Testament, emphasis on the social marginalization of children at times runs the risk of obscuring the multifaceted nature of childhoods—including ancient childhoods.

More recently, New Testament critics such as James Francis (*Adults as Children: Images of Childhood in the Ancient World and the New Testament*, 2006), Beverly Roberts Gaventa (*Our Mother Saint Paul*, 2007), and Jennifer Houston McNeel (*Paul as Infant and Nursing Mother*, 2014) have taken up the historical and sociological insights gained through Childhood Studies to present a more tempered view of children and childhood in antiquity. Drawing on material and epigraphic evidence from the first century Mediterranean world, they read New Testament metaphorizations of children, particularly in the Pauline corpus, in light of children as both valued and cultivated resources who are treasured and nurtured members of the household.

Complementing this emerging focus on the complex picture of childhood in Pauline Studies, two landmark surveys of children in the New Testament and the two Testaments respectively marked a coming of age of Child Centered Biblical Criticism. In 2008 Marcia J. Bunge, Terence Fretheim and Beverly Roberts Gaventa, edited a volume on children in the two testaments titled *The Child in the Bible*. The following year, Cornelia B. Horn and John W. Martens published their survey of childhood across the New Testament and early Christianity *"Let the Little Children Come to Me": Childhood and Children in Early Christianity* (2009). Together these volumes introduce a variety of interpretive methods, all with concern for children in and beyond the biblical texts as a centering force.

With respect to the emphasis on children in Luke's gospel account in particular, John T. Carroll's essay, "'What Then Will This Child Become?': Perspectives on Children in the Gospel of Luke" in *The Child and the Bible* stands out as the first chapter-length treatment of children exclusive to Luke. Carroll's essay successfully introduces the reader to the presence of children in Luke's account and the need for further attention to their perspectives. However, the limits of the intentional survey nature of this piece prevent him from going in depth into the particularities of these characters and their perspectives and the implications of their presence for one's reading of Luke's narrative as a whole. Judith M. Gundry's essay in the same volume is worth noting for its focused treatment of Jesus' blessing of children in Mark 10:13–

15 (paralleled in Luke 18:15–17), demonstrating the fruitful possibilities of a child-centered reading of individual synoptic texts. Together, these essays and the others like them in *The Child in the Bible* led the way in foregrounding the needs and concerns of children within biblical scholarship.

Continuing this progression in child-centered readings, A. James Murphy's monograph, *Kids and Kingdom: The Precarious Presence of Children in the Synoptic Gospels* (2013), surveys child characters across the synoptic gospel accounts. Like Gundry, Murphy highlights the needs and concerns of children both as characters within the texts and as real people behind the text. However, Murphy departs from previously positive portraits of children in the New Testament world, such as Carroll's and Gundry's. He performs a deconstructive reading that calls into question the culture of wandering radicalism demanded by early Christianity as harmful to young children, raising important questions about the ways in which the message of the synoptic gospels either match or, as he reads it, fail to match the lived realities of children beneath the texts.

Maintaining a more positive outlook of the role of children in early Christianity, Sharon Betsworth's *Children in Early Christian Narratives* (2015) focuses predominately on the children as literary characters in the gospel texts, thus avoiding Murphy's historical critiques. Betsworth follows Gundry in moving beyond broad surveys of children in Early Christian literature to consider specific children and narratives concerning children as they are treated in discrete New Testament texts. With chapters devoted to each of the canonical gospels and significant apocryphal texts, Betsworth treats each appearance of a child or children within the particular literary framework and theology of each gospel narrative. Betsworth's publication thus contributes the second chapter length child-centered reading of Luke's gospel account with a focus on the "only child" theme that runs throughout.

Most recently, Sharon Betsworth and Julie Faith Parker edited a T&T Clark Handbook of Children in the Bible and the Biblical World (2019). In addition to chapters on the Hebrew Bible, New Testament, and Intertexts, this volume contains chapters on both methodology and history of research for the reader who wishes to more deeply explore the progression of child-centered biblical criticism.

CHILDIST BIBLICAL CRITICISM AS A METHODOLOGY

As a pioneer in child-centered biblical criticism, Hebrew Bible scholar Julie Faith Parker stands alongside many of her New Testament colleagues mentioned above. In her early work, Parker coined her child-centered approach to scholarship: "childist biblical criticism."[16] Although there is still debate about the best label for the discrete child-centered approaches that are emerging in biblical studies (and there may never be just one term), Parker contends that the term "childist" can counteract the objectification and metaphorization of children in adult-centered scholarship, emphasizing "children's active role in shaping culture, instead of seeing them as largely passive or victimized."[17] In this way, a childist approach to the biblical text shines a light on the frequently overlooked agency already present in human beings at infancy and into early childhood.

Distinct from other modes of ideological criticism that rely primarily on the voices of those from the marginalized communities that they represent, such child-centered biblical criticism recognizes in the unique modes of being that make up childhood an interdependence that invites adult readers to read alongside of and with the interests of children at the center. This interdependence (and not simply dependence) is key because in the same way that most children are not readily equipped to engage in the discourse of the academy and thus need adult advocates to speak out on their behalf, so too adults who engage in child-centered readings have found that our understandings of Scripture have been enlarged and enriched by reading texts with concerns for children at the fore. Adults and children need one another. Highlighting this need is at the core of the angel Gabriel's commission to turn the hearts of parents to their children—a task which John himself begins in his infancy but continues throughout the whole of his lifetime.

To this end, I employ a child-centered (hereafter, childist) lens. Following Gabriel's commission of John, my reading seeks to turn the hearts of parents to their children; or, more broadly put, to turn the hearts of this generation of scholarship to the younger generations living, working, and playing amongst us, as well as to those younger generations who lived, worked, and played amongst the first followers of Jesus. Both traditional scholarship and contemporary discourse around children and discipleship in the twenty-first century too often stifle the voices of children with aphorisms such as "Children in company should be seen and not heard," or, more recently and predominately, "Children are the future of the church." By seeing children as the future alone, however, we miss the opportunity to engage children fully in the *present* moments that we share together now. Applied to Luke's gospel account, a view of children that only looks to their future as adults misses the ways in which children lived, moved, and participated in the early Jesus movement as Luke describes it. Moreover, by overlooking Luke's portrayal of children scholars fail to engage and learn with the very people to whom Luke's Jesus declares the Kingdom of God to belong.

HEARING LUKE'S CHILDREN

By hearing the children of these two disparate contexts back into being, my hope is to liberate children inside and outside of Luke's text from the adultist concerns within which they have been entrapped and to invite their renewed participation in the intergenerational community of Jesus followers to which they rightfully belong. To this end, this book explores Luke's depiction of discipleship as emblematic of a broader ethic of *koinonia*, or Christian community.[18] In this community of disciples, both children and adults, interdependent upon one another, proclaim and live the Gospel of Jesus as Christ in which the hearts of parents (and all adults) are turned to children as both subjects and agents of the Gospel that orients their lives.

In the first chapter I begin this task by considering various definitions and vocabulary for children and childhood in the first century Mediterranean context of Luke's gospel. Favoring a multifaceted socio-cultural understanding of childhood, I outline physical, legal, and occupational modes of identity and weigh their role in determining an individual's socially understood role as child or adult. I conclude with a survey of the various vocabulary employed by Luke to speak about children, infants, and youth, highlighting the range of meanings in each term and its relation to the broader socio-cultural understanding of children in Luke's gospel account.

In the next two chapters, I establish the ample presence of children throughout Luke's gospel account. In chapter 2, I establish the presence of children in the background of much of Jesus' ministry: in homes, public places, and among the crowds. I highlight Jesus' specific welcome and inclusion of children in Lk 9:47–50 and Lk 18:15–17 as both in keeping with and an extension of the welcome and inclusion of children in the wider Jewish and Greco-Roman culture of Luke's day. In chapter 3, I establish the presence of children as recipients of Jesus' ministry of healing and reconciliation through the examination of four discrete instances of Jesus healing children in Luke's gospel account, concluding with the uniquely Lukan parable of Jesus' restoration of two brothers to their father. The culmination of these chapters is thus a (re)membering of the presence and participation of many children just beneath the surface of the gospel account.

In the following two chapters, I reach beyond a mere remembrance of children in the backgrounds of Luke's text to argue for children in the foreground of Jesus' ministry as it is described by Luke as active participants in Jesus' ministry and disciples in their own right. In chapter 4, operating from an accompaniment definition of discipleship, I again emphasize Lk 9:47–50 and Lk 18:15–17 as evidence of Jesus calling children to be his disciples. I demonstrate the presence of children among both the sedentary and itinerant groups of Jesus' followers in Luke's gospel account. I conclude with a case study of James and John as potential child disciples among Jesus' core group of Twelve. In chapter 5, I build upon the basis already established, arguing that child disciples do not merely follow along with Jesus, but participate fully in the ministry of the Kingdom, described in Luke as hearing and doing the Word of God. As in chapter 3, I consider here specific instances of children engaged in both discipleship activities of learning from and serving Jesus.

In chapter 6, I conclude by challenging assumptions that vulnerable children were indeed left behind by the first Christians and suggesting instead that the combination of the vulnerability and value of the young children in Luke's discipleship community presents an alternative vision for relational living for all Christians. I do this by extending the remembrance of child disciples in Luke's gospel account to a (re)*membering* of child disciples in the contemporary Western Christian Church as an extension of Luke's ideal audience. Finally, I invite readers as part of this contemporary audience to reimagine *koinonia* in light of this more inclusive picture of Luke's discipleship community.

Such community reimagined is the result of hearing the voices of Luke's children back into being. To this end, Marilou Ibita and Reimund Bieringer powerfully argue, "Inquiry into what scripture says about children leads to ask what the scriptures allow children to say, that is, what we can find as traces of the children's voices which are disturbingly silent at many points."[19] It is to these traces that we now turn.

NOTES

1. John Quincy Adams, *Memoirs* Vol. V, ed. Charles Francis Adams (Philadelphia: J. B. Lippincott, 1875) 165. Up until this publication the proverb was "A maid should be seen, but not heard," originating with Augustinian in 1389 and made popular by John Mirk's *Festial* in 1450 (Stanley J. St. Clair, *Most Comprehensive Origins of Clichés, Proverbs, and Figurative Expressions* [Minnville, TN: St Clair Publications, 2013] 100). This shift from the marginalization of women to female children to all children is at the same time disturbing across the board and a reminder of the appropriateness of applying a feminist hermeneutic to the characters of children in literary and biblical accounts.

2. There is significant debate in scholarship about the identity of the author known as Luke; however, this project is primarily interested in "Luke" as author I will not engage in historical inquiry into the author's specific identity. I use the terms Luke and Lukan author synonymously to refer to the unknown author of the two-volume work that tradition has come to call Luke-Acts.

3. In addition to these two direct quotations, Jesus quotes a child's song in Lk 7:32 and assigns speech to the younger son in the parable of the forgiving father (Lk 15:11–32). The body of this work will argue that several other characters not directly identified as children may also be read as children and some of these characters also speak in Luke's gospel account—most notably Mary the mother of Jesus and Mary the sister of Martha.

4. See David Balch and Carolyn Osiek, *Families in the New Testament World: Households and House Churches* (Louisville: Westminster John Knox, 1997); and Peter Balla, *The Child-Parent Relationship in the New Testament and Its Environment*. (Tübingen: Mohr Siebeck, 2003) 155–156.

5. On these two trends as they developed in the Enlightenment and kept hold into early modernity, see Philippe Ariès, *Centuries of Childhood: A Social History of Family Life*, trans. Robert Baldick (New York: Vintage Books, 1962) 132–133.

6. John Quincy Adams, *Memoirs* (1876).

7. Robert Knapp, *Invisible Romans* (London: Profile Books, 2011).

8. See Loveday C. Alexander, "Luke's Political Vision," in *Interpretation* 66:3 (July 2012) 283–294; Lawrence R. Farley, *The Gospel of Luke: Good News for the Poor* (Chesterton, IN: Conciliar Press, 2011); Joel B. Green, "Good News to Whom? Jesus and the 'Poor' in the Gospel of Luke," in *Jesus of Nazareth: Lord and Christ. Essays on the Historical Jesus and New Testament Christology*, ed. Joel B. Green and Max Turner (Grand Rapids, MI: Eerdmans, 1994) 59–74; Julius Kiambi, *Postcolonial 'Redaction' of Social-economic parables in Luke's Gospel: Bible and Making of the poor in Kenya*. (Saarbrücken, Germany: LAP Lambert Academic, 2011); D. O. López Rodriguez, *The Liberating Mission of Jesus: The Message of the Gospel of Luke* (Eugene, OR: Pickwick Publications, 2012); and John O. York, *The Last Shall Be First: The Rhetoric of Reversal in Luke* (Sheffield: Sheffield Academic, 1991).

9. The only presently known exception being a similarly generationally oriented concern for the elderly taken up by ageist criticism—itself at this time only in a nascent stage of recognition among biblical scholarship.

10. Quoted in Anna Mae Duanne, "Introduction," in *The Children's Table: Childhood Studies and the Humanities,* ed. Anna Mae Duanne (Athens, GA: University of Georgia Press, 2013), 6.

11. Duanne, 6.

12. Pediatric medicine has existed in its most basic form since antiquity, with the acknowledgment that children were particularly vulnerable to certain diseases and needed to be treated differently than adults. However, in light of Child Theory, pediatrics took on a new "institutionalized" status, moving from simply treating illness to ascribing value and meaning to the particular developmental phases of immaturity.

13. Ariès, 128.

14. Allison James and Alan Prout, "A New Paradigm for the Sociology of Childhood? Provenance, Promise, and Problems," in *Constructing and Reconstructing Childhood: Contemporary Issues in the Sociological Study of Childhood*, ed. by Allison James and Alan Prout (Baskingtoke: Falmer Press, 1990); Allison James and Alan Prout, "Introduction," in *Constructing and Reconstructing Childhood*, 2nd ed., ed. Allison James and Alan Prout (New York: Routledge Falmer, 1997); and John

Wall, "Childism: The Challenge of Childhood to Ethics and the Humanities," in *The Children's Table: Childhood Studies and the Humanities,* ed. Anna Mae Duanne (Athens, GA: University of Georgia Press, 2013).

15. Lester Bradner, "The Kingdom and the Child," *Anglican Theological Review* 3:1 (May 1920) 62; John Dominic Crossan, "A Kingdom of Nobodies," in *The Historical Jesus: The Life of a Mediterranean Jewish Peasant* (New York: Harper Collins, 1991).

16. Julie Faith Parker first applied the term childist to her exegetical method in *Valuable and Vulnerable: Children in the Hebrew Bible, Especially the Elijah Cycle* (Atlanta: Society of Biblical Literature, 2013). Although –ism can often carry a negative connotation, as in the case of racism, sexism, heterosexism, etc., Parker claims it as liberative category, following upon its similar use in religious studies by John Wall in "Childism and the Ethics of Responsibility," in *Children's Voices: Children's Perspectives in Ethics, Theology, and Religious Education,* edited by Annemie Dillen and Didier Pollefeyt (Walpole, MA: Uitgeverij Peeters, 2010).

17. Parker, 17.

18. Parker, 86.

19. Marilou Ibita and Reimund Bieringer, "(Stifled) Voices of the Future: Learning about Children in the Bible," in Annemie Dillen and Didier Pollefeyt, *Children's Voices: Children's Perspectives in Ethics, Theology, and Religious Education.* (Paris Walpole: Uitgeverij Peeters, 2010) 91.

Chapter 1

Defining Children in Luke's Gospel

As appealing as a neat and rigid definition of children may seem, the reality is that *childhood is messy*. Experiences of children and childhood differ across multiple intersections of culture, economics, and race, and there is no magic age at which a child becomes an adult. Even within shared social settings, conceptions of childhood vary widely. Such variance only increases when one reaches across the expanse of oceans and millennia that separate North American scholars from the authors of the canonical gospel accounts. Sociologist of Childhood, Chris Jenks, explains that childhood is not a fixed category, but rather, a social construct, "delineated by boundaries that vary through time and from society to society" and, indeed, within societies.[1] What it means to be a child on the Southern Horn of Africa is very different from what it means to be a child in the United States of America. Moreover, such differences don't even begin to account for the added variables of culture, economics, and race. With such multiplicity of childhoods within even this one snapshot in time, it should not come as a surprise that the images of childhood conjured in the predominately Western twentieth and twenty-first century academy often differ widely from the experiences of childhood most likely normative in first century Palestine.

Who and what terms like "child" and "childhood" refer to vary across time and place. No matter how neatly one may seek to define the line between children and adults, society rarely experiences it this way. Thus, while ancient and contemporary definitions of childhood are available in their respective legal and medical texts, such definitions quickly lose the crisp clarity they began with when studied alongside case histories. The most complete understanding of children in Luke's gospel account therefore must weigh contemporaneous technical definitions alongside more fluid social conceptions derived from life transitions typical in first century Jewish and Greco-Roman societies and ranges of meaning in Luke's actual text.

LIFE TRANSITIONS BETWEEN CHILDHOOD AND ADULTHOOD

The historians of antiquity did not typically track age and birthdays with the same precision as those in the modern Western world. When age does appear in these sources it serves more as a guidepost to identifying the range of time around which people experienced major life transitions rather than as a rigid rule or determination of status.[2] Kristine Garroway, professor of Hebrew Bible, observes that in the Ancient Near East: "Both textual and archaeological materials often refer to the minor by a social category: infant, toddler, young man, and so on, instead of giving a chronological age. For the ancient author, this choice may have been made for many different reasons, the chief of which seems to be that ancient societies did not emphasize chronological age."[3] As such, definitions of youth and childhood from both turn of the century Greco-Roman and ancient Near East sources tend to employ age *ranges* rather than definitive years.

Chronological age is not what primarily determines adulthood; rather, a person's position relative to society determines whether they are considered a child or adult. Related to, but not in direct correspondence with stages of biological development, people experience different periods, or categories, of social experience.[4] These categories generally correspond to the way in which a person interacts with the rest of society. Classicist Tim Parkin demonstrates that "the transition to adulthood" is typically marked in the Greco-Roman world with "the emphasis of rites . . . frequently placed on the emerging new roles—social, political, and religious—of the individual, be it as a soldier, active citizen, spouse, and/or parent."[5] In addition to physical maturity, social participation in institutions such as marriage (and procreation), civic and/or religious responsibility, and work thus serve to mark a child's transition into adulthood in these social worlds that undergird Luke's gospel account.

Definitions of Physical Maturity

In antiquity, adulthood, or at least the first stage of adulthood, was often linked to physical—specifically, sexual—maturity. Hebrew Bible scholar Hans Wolff distinguishes "three phases of life . . . from one another" and various sub-phases of childhood based on vocabulary describing physical characteristics and maturity.[6] Similarly, Greek statesman Solon (c. 638–c.

558 BCE) divided human life into symbolic seven-year intervals, dictated later by mental and moral advancement, but in the stages of childhood by physical development. Solon characterizes the first three stages (21 years) as respectively marking "growth of teeth," "capacity to emit seed," and "growth of beard."[7]

Between the time of Solon and the second century CE, a variety of philosophers, lawyers, and doctors similarly systematized the human life cycle. Of these, the system devised by the Greek physician Hippocrates is the most famous. However, Parkin notes inconsistencies in the various accounts of this system, such that ". . . while the basic seven ages remain the same, the year divisions vary. The first two stages are consistently described as ages birth to seven and seven to fourteen years . . . but the third stage, that of the youth, can extend up to the age of twenty-eight years."[8] This haziness in defining the transition into adulthood likely reflects the same shift in Hippocrates' classification as seen in Solon's description of the latter years of life. From adolescence until old age, philosophers observed shifts in the human cycle more visibly through social rather than physical categories. As such, the term νεανίσκος stretches from 21 to 41 years in its *attic* usage. Moreover, the overlapping use of the term with μειράκιον makes a case for the elision of the two terms when the latter drops from common usage in *koine* manuscripts. If this is the case, the chronological boundaries of νεανίσκος, defined in the New Testament and Early Christian literature simply as "a youth," could stretch as far back as 10–14 years.[9]

Amid such fluctuation, though, it is little coincidence that the age fourteen remains relatively consistent as a developmental marker. Parkin explains, "It is worth remarking that the mathematical neatness of the number usefully coincides, approximately, with the age of puberty for males as described by medical and legal writers from ancient times."[10] At the height of Roman law, between 100 BCE and 250 CE, children born into Roman citizenship were defined as "minors at law until they reached the legally defined age of puberty or majority, meaning twelve for females and ca. fourteen for males."[11] By this standard childhood is thus defined as a measurable state of physical immaturity, codified at the age of puberty for the sake of simplicity and the law.

Nevertheless, even with allowances made for windows of development, as in the Hippocratic system of classification, there are drawbacks to defining childhood solely based upon physical growth and change. Garroway illustrates the social deficiency of "lumping all biologically immature persons together" in her critique of an anthropological study that seeks insight into ancient childhood through such classification.[12] She argues that while this study can "responsibly label bones with terms that correlate to specific chronological ages, it leaves out the social age factor—the acknowledgment that, while people may biologically move through chronological ages/stages in a reliable manner, socially, people may reach different stages at different ages."[13] Ancient childhood, just as ancient adulthood, must be defined by a series of biological, psychological, and social categories.

To this end, life cycle classifications by Greek philosophers, rather than physicians, offer a more robust depiction of the boundaries of childhood in antiquity—both the physical and social ones. Specializing in ancient history, Valerie French summarizes these distinctions:

> Plato and Aristotle describe five stages of childhood: (1) Babyhood—birth to two when the child is weaned and can talk; (2) 2 to 3–5, beginning to separate from their mothers or nurses and become more physically active; (3) 3 to 6–7, active and forming their own social networks with friends and games, which often replicate adult activities; (4) 6–7 to 12–14, enter school; (5) late teens—twenties, adolescence (17).[14]

In such a system, while the defining age of puberty does not entirely disappear, it becomes more obscured. Socially defining experiences, which may or may not coincide with a child's physical changes, begin to bracket the definition of childhood. Consequently, marriage becomes more important than the ability to produce semen in determining an individual's place in relation to childhood.

Participation in Marriage and Civic Service

Marriage

In antiquity, a person's marital status often served as a defining social indicator for whether society treated them as a child or an adult.[15] Marriage served as a particularly strong social indicator for female children. In the first century Greco-Roman world, when a girl married, she left her childhood, along with her paternal family, behind and joined the household (οἶκος) of her husband. Similarly, by the time of the Roman Empire, there was significant cultural overlap between Jewish and Roman martial practice. Mary's betrothal to Joseph and her accompaniment of him to his hometown for the census described in the first chapters of Luke's gospel account follows this general pattern (1:26–2:5).[16] Within Luke's cultural context, marriage thus marked an important step toward adulthood.

Despite its social components, marriage in antiquity generally took the shape of a contractual arrangement. As such, using marriage alone to delineate the line between childhood and adulthood remains a legal expedient that does not take into consideration the full social and psychological and picture. The occurrence, albeit rare, of girls marrying well before reaching physical maturity illustrates this complexity. Under Roman law, the legal marriage age for girls was already very low, at the age of twelve.[17] Sarah Pomeroy, a classicist specializing in the girls and women of antiquity, explains that under this Augustan law, "The first marriage of most girls took place between the ages of twelve and fifteen. Since menarche typically occurred at thirteen or fourteen, prepubescent marriage took place."[18] Moreover, in the case of marriages for political alliance, Roman aristocratic and Jewish patriarchal families would not always wait even this long to betroth their daughters in marriage.[19] On the other hand, boys in the Roman world would not typically be expected to marry until the ages of 25 to 30 years old [20] after completing either an apprenticeship or military service (the latter required of all male citizens between the ages of 17–18).[21]

Civic Service

Because it was more typical for males to marry at a later age than females, other markers, such as work and civic service often served to mark a male child's transition into adulthood prior to a marriage contract. Civic service, in particular, is often cited as the ancient transition into adulthood for boys. Roman historian Beryl Rawson explains, "Boys' arrival at the age of adult citizenship was marked by a ceremony in which they exchanged the garb of boyhood (the *toga praetexta*) for that of manhood (the *toga virilis*). There was no fixed age for this: families decided. The usual age was fifteen-sixteen. The age for beginning military service was seventeen-eighteen."[22] Boys typically married after completing this service and thus at an older age than their wives. As such, a Roman boy would often take on certain characteristics and responsibilities of adulthood as a youth, while still not fully entering into his own in society until even decades later. For this reason, Roman historian Thomas McGinn highlights the fluidity of childhood for unmarried males, noting, "Minors should not be confused with young adults, meaning those past puberty/majority but younger (*minores*) than twenty-five, who enjoyed certain legal protections of their own."[23] Much as many adolescents experience in contemporary Western culture today, the transition between childhood and adulthood in the ancient world was not seamless. Political obligations, social status, and legal protections did not always directly align and so there remained a liminal period during which young people were considered neither fully child nor fully adult.

The structure of the Roman household and the power afforded to the eldest male as *pater familias* further enhanced this liminality. On one end of the spectrum, orphaned boys might attain to the role of *pater familias* at an early age, before otherwise granted full legal and financial freedoms.[24] Beryl Rawson describes this liminal period experienced primarily by the elite as "a source of frustration to the young men who were physically adult and already well educated, more than half of them already *sui iuris* through the death of their fathers (Garnsey and Saller 1987: 138), but who were too young for public office and who normally would not expect to marry and establish conjugal families of their own for some years to come."[25] On the other end, grown and even married men would continue in subservient roles under the patronage of their fathers as *pater familias*.

Moreover, like marriage, civic service could also be accorded to the very young—particularly the elite. For example, "At the sage of six, the child Numerius Popidius Celsinus was nominated onto the town council of Pompeii."[26] Similarly, "Alongside one hundred adults members of the town council [of Canusium] are listed twenty-five *praetextati*, or those who wear the childhood toga."[27] This period of transition between boyhood and "young adulthood," while not equivalent to modern definitions of adolescence, thus marks a period of liminality between childhood and adulthood. For the purposes of retrieving non-adult characters from Luke's text, this period, while not the same as young childhood, can be understood as an extension of non-adult childhood as distinct from being an adult.

Shifts in Occupational Identity

While marriage and civic service play important roles in defining the social relationships of the elite in ancient society, work influenced the construction of childhood among slaves, who often could not marry, and the subsistence class more generally. The vast majority of people in antiquity came from the subsistence class of fishing and agricultural workers or were slaves. Given the long hours that these occupations demanded, the daily lives of such workers were primarily defined by their work. For those in the subsistence class, the ways in which individuals participated in the economic welfare of their households thus became primary indicators of childhood or adulthood.

Both adults and children participated in the upkeep of the household at the subsistence level. In this way, children were integral to their household's survival in the ancient Mediterranean context. In the case of children born or sold into slavery, they were put to work according to their abilities at the earliest age possible in order to achieve the greatest economic gain. Cornelia Horn and John Martens observe that "the majority of children in the Roman Empire were involved in work at a young age."[28] The children in Luke's audience would thus have been quite familiar with the labor of work. Rawson extrapolates an earlier end to childhood among poorer children based upon these realities.[29] Such an extrapolation, however, assumes a modern definition of childhood that excludes hard labor. In antiquity work was not treated as a distraction or hindrance to childhood; it was simply a part of everyday life.[30] In addition to serving the immediate needs of the household, a child's work helped to socialize them as an integral part of their household. A person's transition from childhood to adulthood can thus be tracked not by their presence or absence from the workforce, but rather, by attention to corresponding shifts in their occupational identity as their presence evolved.

Few if any jobs were unique to the domain of childhood. Some adults surely continued to perform similar tasks to their younger coworkers either throughout their lives or again as they aged. Nevertheless, the distinction of particular jobs as fitting for children helps to retrieve possible markers of childhood in ancient texts that have often been overlooked. Even at the subsistence level of the economy, many adults engaged in trades or day labor in addition to household and agricultural tasks. It is thus worth noting that in these same households, children seem to have worked primarily at household chores or agricultural labor that kept them close to the home.[31]

Primary sources on Roman agriculture dating both before and after Luke's gospel account confirm the participation of children in agricultural work. Roman scholar Marcus Terentius Varro, writing roughly a century before Luke's gospel account, describes children as engaged primarily in agricultural work.[32] More contemporaneous with Luke and his narrative setting, Lucius Junius Moderatus Columella's *De Re Rustica*, addressed to Roman estate owners in the early to mid-first century adds important details in establishing this practice. Describing tenant farms, Columella reports that these were "rented out to families whose members grew up on the land and who worked the land together with their children. Country estates, therefore, seemed to have employed considerable numbers of child laborers, especially young slaves, who were performing duties alongside adult slaves both in the home and in the fields."[33] According to Lovén and Strömberg, "Other Roman writers express similar views: children were capable of helping with farm work, especially unskilled tasks that needed little or no training or could be undertaken from a very early age."[34] As the economy advanced, adults' jobs—particularly males'—began to vary, but children continue to be listed primarily among the unskilled workers.

Columella describes adults and children working alongside each other with "no distinction regarding age with respect to the work they performed or the time they engaged in it. The single exception pertained to the overseer, who was to be neither too old nor too young (*Rust.* 1.8.3; 11.1.3–6)."[35] To this end, adult workers are seen to have had more options available to them than their youthful counterparts, even when they would sometimes engage in the same work together. Horn and Martens summarize: "That the overseer was to assume the task of running the estate at such a young age indicates his intimate familiarity with the many tasks required of him already from boyhood on (*Rust.* 1.8.3)."[36] Columella's insistence that the overseer be "not too young" assumes the more general existence of child labor quite before the adolescent stage as well as a distinction between the types of labor appropriate to both children and adults. Jobs reserved for particularly young children included keeping charge of fowls, pruning and weeding, shepherding, herding small livestock, apprenticeships, and looking after younger children and infants.[37] The *Infancy Gospel of Thomas*, likely authored within a hundred years of Luke's account, confirms this continuity in children's labor by similarly depicting children in the role of completing certain unskilled household tasks, such as fetching water.[38]

Among slaves, such distinctions not only indicated ability and/or age but also influenced their monetary valuation. Distinctions were made between the values assigned to infants incapable of labor, children capable of lighter unskilled tasks, and adults from whom a slave owner can hope to extract the maximum amount of work. In this context, Hanne Sigismund-Nielsen defines infancy as "the inability to understand one's role and the expectations that one's family or master have of one," adding, "The moment a child gains this ability it is no longer an *infans*. And so they were set to work."[39] To this extent, an individual's intellectual and physical acuity determined their ability to work and therefore relative value to the household.

It is interesting to note that the only clearly defined classification of ages in the Hebrew Bible operates according to similar standards. Leviticus 27:1–8 concerns the redemption price set for people whose lives have been dedicated to service of God in the Temple. To this end the passage divides the human life cycle into four periods, with the first two spanning from one month to five years and five to twenty years of age respectively (v. 5–6). However, Joseph Fleishman emphasizes, "The monetary values were set in accordance with the potential work capacity of the dedicated person,"[40] and thus rejects this passage as a useful measure of an age of accountability to the Torah law. In this rejection, he sees in the passage a greater emphasis on physical maturity and ability rather than social or moral accountability. While such systems of classification are thus unlikely to provide a rigid standard for determining age, they prove more useful in drawing rough boundaries. As such, while these Levitical conventions should not be read in a binding sense, they suggest age ranges around which Roman Jews might have constructed their understanding of childhood in relation to work.

Such a construction of childhood in relation to work capacity, moreover, is in line with Roman definitions of youth (particularly for males) that extends from puberty into the mid-to-late-twenties. Thus, in the overlapping contexts of family, work, and society, a general picture begins to emerge within which childhood is loosely defined as that period within which infants first become aware of the social structures they have been born into to the moment in which they participate to the highest level of their ability in the structures of household, civics, and work. Chronologically, this spans from approximately one month of age to upwards of twenty years or more depending upon individuals and other life circumstances.

WORDS THAT DESIGNATE CHILDREN AND YOUTH

Although physical and social definitions provide a starting point for understanding childhood in Luke's gospel account, they do not take deeply into account the lived experience of the Lukan author and his particular community. To account for these nuances in her study of the Elisha cycle in the Hebrew Bible, Julie Faith Parker applies linguistic theory to her childist interpretation under the premise that "the vocabulary of a given culture reflects its realities."[41] Following this paradigm, drawing on the vocabulary used by the Lukan author to reflect the semantic field of childhood in the gospel account can thus help to narrow what is meant by conceptions of children and childhood in the gospel writer's particular context.

By comparison with the variety of experiences of childhood in antiquity outlined above, the number of terms used to reference children in the New Testament is relatively sparse. However, this paucity is made up for in the range of meanings that the Lukan author assigns to each term. Parker explains, "A word's 'meaning potential' encapsulates a range of interpretation. One word can be used in various ways, even by the same speaker or writer. The meaning of the same word can also change over time. A certain term can carry clear or subtle implications or be used in a nonliteral way."[42] In search of such meaning potential, what follows is thus a brief review of Luke's use of each of the terms related to childhood in his account. These terms include: βρέφος, παιδίον, παῖς, τέκνον, νεανίσκος, υἱός, θυγάτηρ, and μικρός.

βρέφος

This term appears eight times in the New Testament, six of which are in the Lukan corpus, as well as five times in the Septuagint (LXX). The primary meaning in ancient literature encompasses both humans and animals and refers to a "babe in the womb; foetus; new-born babe."[43] In the New Testament and Early Christianity a similar meaning is retained while broadening the timeframe of before or at birth to refer more generally to "a very small child" either inside or outside of the mother's womb.[44]

Twice in Luke and once in LXX βρέφος is clearly used to refer to an unborn child (Lk 1:41, 44; Sir 19:11). Of the remaining ten references, eight situate βρέφος sometime in the first weeks after birth, especially indicated by the Maccabean references to circumcising τὰ βρέφη (1 Mac 1:61; 2 Mac 6:10; 3 Mac 5:49). Marilou Ibita and Reimund Bieringer point out that even when not specifically referring to a fetus, Luke's use of βρέφος is in keeping with the special use of the term in birth narratives. They note that in the prologue, "Luke uses words in a precise, age-specific sense to present Jesus growing in age from newborn baby via an infant of eight days [βρέφος, Lk 2:16–21] to a twelve-year-old child [παιδίον/παῖς, Lk 2:40–43]."[45]

The remaining two occurrences of βρέφος in the New Testament are Luke 18:15 and 2 Timothy 3:15, where the context is less certain. In large part because of the deviation of Luke from Matthew and Mark in the vocabulary used to describe the children being brought to Jesus here, most mainstream translations have preserved the uniquely Lukan reference to βρέφοι as infants or babies. However, the tendency of Western modernity to ascribe "reason," or the ability to know about the teachings of Scripture, to children only after they reach a certain age and developmental maturity has led to a more conservative approach to 2 Tim 3:15. Of the major scholarly translations (NRSV, NIV, NASB, NKJV, ESV), only the NIV translates ἀπὸ βρέφους as "from infancy" rather than "from childhood."

In contrast to this adultist assumption, the clear sense of the word throughout biblical literature, and so I would argue also in Luke 18:15 and 2 Timothy 3:15, is that βρέφος refers to a very young infant, either still in or having just emerged from his or her mother's womb. As such, the βρέφοι are at the most dependent state of human existence, requiring their mothers to carry them (προσφέρω, Lk 18:15) to Jesus. While it is significant that Jesus shows acceptance to even these most vulnerable children, it is also significant that such a high level of dependence is nowhere ascribed to παιδία, whom Jesus summons in the following verse, despite modern tendencies to conflate these words.

παιδίον, παῖς

Grammatically, παιδίον is a diminutive of παῖς, deriving from the substantive form of the adverb παιδιόθεν.[46] Taken separately, the two words have been used to refer to two discrete stages in a child's development. In such use, παιδίον refers more specifically to a "little child," whereas παῖς references a child in what Hippocrates labels as the second plane of development, from roughly seven to fourteen years old.[47] However, the lines between these distinctions are blurry and alternate depending upon the particular classification system being employed. The class of παιδίον is entirely lacking from the systems of both Plato and Claudius Ptolemy, which define παῖς as the stage immediately after βρέφος, ranging from the ages of 4–10 and 4–14 years respectively.[48] Moreover, as highlighted above, this concept becomes further complicated by the lack of direct correlation between chronology and ancient definitions of childhood as such.

More likely, for common people in antiquity, including the Lukan author and audience(s), context reveals more about the meaning ascribed to each word than its use in contradistinction to the other. Forms of the two words are used extensively and often interchangeably in Luke's gospel account. At the youngest extreme, παιδίον overlaps with βρέφος to describe the infant John just after his birth and at his circumcision (Lk 1:59, 66, 76, 80) and again to address the broader group of children among whom the βρέφοι are a part in Lk 18:15–16.

Likewise, in Matthew's gospel account, a form of παῖς is used to refer to all children under the age of two years whom Herod orders to be killed (τοὺς παῖδας, Matt 2:16). This overlap is again seen at the age of twelve years, when Luke's description of the child Jesus (παιδίον) growing in strength (Lk 2:40) is immediately followed by reference to the child Jesus (παῖς) remaining behind in the Temple. Assuming a similar fluidity between the two terms, Luke Timothy Johnson has no problem suggesting that the child whom Jesus uplifts in 9:47 (παιδίον) may even have been the exorcised boy of 9:42 (παῖς).[49]

In any case, with reference to free-born people, both terms seem to refer to non-adult children, with παιδίον stretching at times into earlier stages of infancy that the term παῖς does not as readily describe. Translation is complicated, however, by the additional use of both words to refer to slaves or servants. The definition of παῖς is thus divided into three potentially overlapping relationships: "in relation to Descent, *child*, whether *son* or *daughter*; in relation to Age, *child, boy* or *girl*; in relation to Condition, *slave, servant, man* or *maid* (of all ages)—of slaves and personal attendants, *slave, servant*."[50] While child slaves were common in antiquity, the range of meaning for παῖς in reference to condition can contextually extend to all slaves regardless of their age. This is an ancient instance of the same condescension toward and infantilization of adults based upon external characteristics such as social status and race illustrated by Thomas Jefferson's equivocation between children and adult slaves.

In the LXX παῖς is used to translate both the Hebrew noun עבד meaning "young man" or "servant" and ילד meaning "someone who is young" or in "a kinship relationship."[51] This overlap, however, has more to do with the prevailing Greco-Roman culture of paternalism than it does with the primary meaning of the word. The most common term for a slave in Greek antiquity is δοῦλος. This word occurs 334 times in the LXX, frequently translating the Hebrew noun עבד. It occurs 118 times in the New Testament as well. The occasional use of the term παῖς to refer to adult slaves therefore is not necessitated by a lack of appropriate vocabulary. Rather, it is reflective of the household structure whereby both children and slaves were subject to the rule of the eldest freeborn male in the house—the *pater familias*.[52] Appropriately, one possible definition of the word is as "one who is committed in total obedience to another, *slave, servant.*"[53] Within the structure of the Roman household, however, such obedience would also have described children and women.

Contemporary translations often prefer a subdued translation of "servant" with reference to Jesus' relationship to God. Frederick Danker asserts an explicit preference for "servant" when speaking "of Christ in his relation to God . . . because of the identification of the 'servant of God' of certain [Old Testament] passages with the Messiah (Is 52:13 et al)."[54] Consequently, the entry on this last definition of παῖς in this lexicon is the longest of the three, taking up nearly a column and a half, discussing occurrences in biblical and early Christian literature, whereas the same entry in LSJ occupies only four lines of text—by far the shortest of the entries on παῖς.

Given the common use of παῖς to refer to a child in a more literal rather than paternalistic sense, it bears questioning whether too great a liberty has been taken in translating παῖς as "slave" or "servant" in English translations of the New Testament and early Christian literature. Notwithstanding the legitimacy of the theological claim made by Danker, bringing these New Testament passages into line with Old Testament intertexts is insufficient reason for ignoring the plain meaning of the word. Indeed, the early declarations in each of the synoptic gospel accounts affirms that Jesus' relationship with God is also one of descent (Mat 4:3; Mk 1:1; Lk 1:35; Jn 1:34). So the angel declares to Mary, "The Holy Spirit will come upon you, and the power of the Most High will overshadow you; therefore the child to be born will be holy; he will be called Son of God" (Lk 1:35).

While the relation of subservience certainly applies, there is no reason to assume that the relation of descent is not intended when Luke describes God as raising up τὸν παῖδα αὐτοῦ (Acts 3:26).[55] This is not to say that the translation of παῖς as "slave" or "servant" is never appropriate, but rather that it should be made with care in order to avoid both adultist tendencies to elide children (both slave and free) from the biblical texts and paternalist tendencies to mitigate the atrocities of slavery that have been perpetrated throughout history, particularly in my North American context.

νεανίσκος, νεανίας, νεᾶνις

The term νεανίσκος occurs frequently in the LXX, but only ten times in the New Testament. Fitting with Luke's more frequent use of technical language of childhood, including βρέφος, half of the New Testament occurrences of νεανίσκος are in Luke-Acts. Luke, however, does not seem to use the term in a technical sense. Rather, similar to its meaning in the LXX, Luke's use of νεανίσκος seems to cover the broad range of later childhood, from the onset of puberty to adult.

In Hippocrates' schema, the designation νεανίσκος refers to a male youth who is between the ages of fourteen and twenty-one.[56] It is derived from the term νεανίας, meaning "youth, young man."[57] Generally, though not always, meaning a boy who has passed puberty, these terms represent the transition period between child and adult. Although there is a tendency in contemporary interpretation to see puberty as the line between children and adults, sexual maturity was only one of many facets related to this passage in antiquity.

As a νεανίσκος the male child continues to receive greater recognition in society—as, indeed, he has at each stage of his childhood up to this point—while at the same time retaining certain freedoms and protections not available to adults. This can be seen in rights granted to youth to own and sell property, coupled with legal protections provided to prevent youth from being take advantage of in business deals.[58] To this end, even taxonomies such as that of Diogenes Laertius, which classify a νεανίσκος on the latter end of the age range (as late as 40 years old), maintain that this stage is distinct from that of [adult] maturity: "One remains a child (παῖς) for twenty years, then a youth (νεηνίσκος) for twenty more years, a mature person (νεηνίης) for another twenty years, and an older person (γέρων) for a final twenty years (8.10)."[59]

Likewise, the Hippocratics, in setting a more typical post-puberty age range, count both a child (παῖς) and "young adult (*parthenoi, neaniskoi, meirakia*)" as "distinct from 'those in their prime' (*akmazontes*, a term designating individuals from about twenty-five to forty-five; e.g. *Prorrhetic* II.9)."[60] It is most fitting, therefore, to describe the νεανίσκος or νεανίας as inhabiting a liminal stage between early childhood and adulthood. The tendency to withhold full adult standing for men until long past puberty can also be seen in the Hebrew Scriptures.[61] "Fleishman contends that from Deuteronomy 1:39, "it is possible to deduce that at this age [20 years] a child was considered to have reached full intellectual maturity . . . This verse . . . defines the spiritual-intellectual capacity of those who are under the age of twenty. According to this verse, those under the age of twenty were not punished for sinning because they 'do not yet know good from bad.'"[62]

As such, these terms carry with them, more than a direct chronology, a sense of temperament and status—the state of being a youth. The term νεανίσκος thus conveys "a sense of a *youth* in character, i.e. either in a good sense, *impetuous, active*, or in a bad sense, *hot-headed, willful, headstrong*."[63] The female correlate, not present in Christian scripture, νεᾶνις, likewise refers to a "young woman," including girls in their teenage years.[64] For this reason, I choose to employ the equally nebulous contemporary terminology of "youth" in translation.

τέκνον, υἱός, θυγάτηρ

Often a distinction is drawn between τέκνον and παῖς whereby the former is interpreted as relating to descent and the latter as relating to chronology. In light of the complexities of defining childhood in antiquity, however, such a simplification is incomplete. Indeed, there are points in the New Testament where παῖς seems to point more towards descent and τέκνον is best understood as a reference to chronological age.[65]

In ancient literature τέκνον simply means "*child*; as a form of address from elders to their youngers, *my son, my child*; of animals, *young*; metaphorically [of flowers, birds, frogs, etc.]."[66] Definitions focusing upon the subset of New Testament and Early Christian literature tend to nuance the attribute of descent more explicitly. Such traditions emphasize Hebraisms through which the genitive plural can reference the inhabitants of a city or people with a shared characteristic. However, even those who argue for the word's more generic use in practice still affirm that at its core τέκνον refers to "an offspring of human parents, *child*."[67]

Luke typically uses τέκνον when referencing children in relation either to another person or persons or to a particular trait (e.g. "wisdom is vindicated by all her children" Lk 7:35). Such use does not immediately assume that the child in question is either a young or adult person, but rather leaves this open to the context to determine. So, for example, when the Lukan narrator describes Elizabeth and Zechariah as childless, the reader rightly assumes that they have no descendants of any age—for "Elizabeth was barren" (Lk 1:7).

Similar to τέκνον, υἱός and θυγάτηρ primarily denote relationships. The noun υἱός refers to "a male who is in a kinship relationship either biologically or by legal action, *son, offspring, descendant*; a person related or closely associated as if by ties of sonship."[68] So also, θυγάτηρ designates "a human female in relation of child to parent, *daughter*; someone treated as one's daughter, *daughter*; female members of an ancestral group, political entity, or specific class of persons, *daughters*; something personified as female, *daughter*."[69]

Also correlative to the discussion of τέκνον, these words can refer to a child of any age. So Elizabeth is prophesied to bear Zechariah a son (υἱόν) before John is even born (Lk 1:13), Mary gives birth to her firstborn son (υἱόν, Lk 2:7), and Jesus' lineage is described at thirty-years-old (υἱός, Lk 3:23). Likewise, the noun θυγάτηρ is used to describe both a girl of only twelve years old (Lk 8:42) and Elizabeth and Anna in their old age (Lk 1:5; 2:36). The use of the terms thus alerts a childist reader to the potential for a non-adult child in the text, while not guaranteeing that this is the case. The age of the τέκνον must therefore be verified by context. It is the task of a childist reading not to let previous adultist assumptions slant the interpretation of context in such a way that the potential for reading a younger character in such instances is ignored.

μικρός, νέος

For obvious reasons, the adjectives μικρός and νέος in their substantive forms also fall into the semantic category of terms used to describe children. With relation to size, μικρός can be read as "pertaining to a relatively limited size, measure, or quantity, *small, short*—of stature; of age substantively *the little one, the child*."[70] This term, when used with reference to children, emphasizes their limitations—their shortness or smallness. So τὸ μικρὸν is often taken in translations of Luke 17:2 with reference to those who are literally small, i.e. children.

Yet, given such an origin, it is not surprising that ancient usage also carries μικρός over as "pertaining to being of little import, *unimportant, insignificant*—of persons lacking in importance, influence, power, etc.; *small, insignificant*; The state of being small, *smallness*."[71] Luke has such an emphasis on insignificance clearly in mind in 9:48, with the table-turning effect of making those considered by society to be insignificant the most significant of all. In other places in both Luke and Acts, the context is less clear, such that passages such as Acts 8:10a can be read either as "All of them, from the least to the greatest, listened to him eagerly," or "All of them, from the smallest to the largest, listened to him eagerly," with the latter translation calling more readily to mind the participation of children among the early followers of Jesus and the Church.

With relation to time, νέος means "pertaining to being in existence but a relatively short time, *new, fresh* . . . pertaining to being in the early stages of life, *young*—as an adjective; mostly comparatively; as a substantive; a person beginning to experience something, *novice*."[72] Because this word is used in some of the chronological classification systems, its meaning across the larger corpus of Greek literature is even more specific, defining νέος as "*young, youthful* (of children, youths, and of men at least as old as 30); of all *young creatures*; Rarely of animals and plants; *suited to a youth, youthful*; *new, fresh*; Of events with notion of *unexpected, strange, untoward, evil*."[73]

As such, when Luke talks about new wineskins, he obviously does not have human children in mind (5:37). On the other hand, the newness, or youth, of the wineskins may be akin to the youth to whom Jesus refers in Luke 15:12 or that of the comparably younger brother in Luke 15:12ff. Thus, this term, together with μικρός, serves as a good potential signifier for the presence of people who are not yet adults in the biblical text. Indeed, given the complex definition of childhood, the use of descriptive and/or comparative terms to reference people throughout the various stages of their lives is not only natural, but appropriate.

CONCLUSION: SOCIAL CONCEPTS OF CHILDREN AND CHILDHOOD IN LUKE

A particular word, age grouping, or single marker of identity cannot define childhood in antiquity. Rather, children and childhood are social concepts that occupy fluctuating and overlapping spaces in the mind and imagination of the Lukan author and his readers. This, however, does not mean that Ariès was correct to observe the absence of a concept of childhood in antiquity; the realities of childhood, though vastly different in many other ways, are no more clearly defined in today's world.

The murkiness in defining the concept of childhood, however, does not preclude some basic guidelines for the understanding and use of terms relating to the conceptions of these categories as articulated in Luke's gospel account.[74] Evidence about the roles of children in antiquity combined with careful readings of biblical accounts confirm that children occupy a distinct social category from adults, even when the precise edges of this delineation remain ambiguous. The plurality of classification systems for a child's chronological development in antiquity testifies to the lack of uniformity around any particular moment in a child's attaining adulthood, yet some ages and moments stand out among others. These ages take on particular importance when attached with a social dimension marking transitions between childhood and adulthood, such as sexual maturity, marital status, civic service, and occupational shifts. Social dimensions of childhood thus provide the basis for a child-centered reading of Luke's gospel account.

A particular term or number of years, therefore, does not define a child in Luke's gospel account; rather, a child is defined by their interactions in the world of the text. When an individual aligns primarily with the social and physical relationships having to do with ancient childhood, he or she ought to be read as a child. Luke uses vocabulary related to these relationships in order to signify this. The task of a childist reading is to take note of such vocabulary and to be conscious of the simultaneously simple presence and complex construction of children in Luke's gospel account.

NOTES

1. Chris Jenks, *Childhood* (London: Routledge, 1996) 3.
2. Tim Parkin, "Life Cycle," in *A Cultural History of Childhood and Family in Antiquity*, ed. Mary Harlow and Ray Laurence (London: Bloomsbury, 2010) 103. "These stages occur as new members enter the household grouping, as existing members age and their roles change over time, and as existing members—whatever their age—leave the household to enter another group, perhaps to found their own family or as they leave life itself".
3. Kristine Garroway, *Children in the Ancient Near Eastern Household* (Winona Lake, IN: Eisenbrauns, 2014) 18.
4. While such categories are often called "stages" both in ancient and modern terms I resist this terminology because it implies a developmental "progress" whereby childhood is not experienced as a complete state of being in itself, but rather as an end toward the perfect stage of adulthood. In contrast, I understand each category or period in a person's life as uniquely valuable and productive and therefore as an end in itself, even as each person transitions into different periods.
5. Parkin, "Life Cycle," 103.
6. Hans Wolff, *Anthropology of the Old Testament*, trans. Margaret Kohl (Philadelphia: Fortress Press, 1974) 120: ". . . at least three phases of life are distinguished from one another: children (*yōnēq*, the sucking child, Deut. 32.25; *na'ar*, the boy, Ps. 148.12; *tap*, pattering, not capable of walking; Ezek. 9.6); young but fully grown men and grown-up girls (*bāhūr* and *bĕtūlā*, Deut. 32.25; Ezek. 9.6 and Ps. 148.12); and mature, elderly men and women (*zāqēn*, who wear a beard, Ezek. 9.6; Ps. 148.12; 'īśēbā, the grey-haired man, Deut. 32.25; *'iššā*, Ezek. 9.6)."
7. Solon fragment 27 [West] (as quoted by Philo *de Opif. Mundi* 35.103–104), cited in Parkin, "Life Cycle," 97.
8. Parkin, "Life Cycle," 98–99.
9. BDAG, 667.
10. Parkin, "Life Cycle," 99.
11. Thomas A. J. McGinn, "Roman Children and the Law," in *The Oxford Handbook of Childhood and Education in the Classical World*, ed. Judith Grubbs, Tim Parkin, & Roslynne Bell (Oxford: Oxford University Press, 2013) 342; see Parkin, "Life Cycle," 104.
12. Garroway, 17.
13. Garroway, 17.
14. Valerie French, "Children in Antiquity," in *Children in Historical and Comparative Perspective*: *An International Handbook and Research Guide*, ed. Joseph M. Hawes and N. Ray Hiner, 13-21. New York: Greenwood Press, 1991) 17.
15. See Garroway, 18; Parkin, "Life Cycle," 104.
16. See Margaret Williams, "The Jewish Family in Judaea from Pompey to Hadrian—the Limits of Romanization" in *The Roman Family in the Empire: Rome, Italy, and Beyond*, edited by Michael George (Oxford: Oxford University Press, 2001) 172: For Jews in the early Roman period, "their nuptial practices will already

have been brought broadly into line with those of the Romans through the 'disturbance' to their marital customs in the Persian and Hellenistic periods," attested by a shift in marital practice from Hebrew Bible to Intertestamental literature." See also Shaye Cohen, "Introduction," in *The Jewish Family in Antiquity*, edited by Shaye Cohen (Atlanta: Scholar's Press, 1993): "The Jewish family in antiquity seems not to have been distinctive by the power of its Jewishness; rather, its structure, ideals, and dynamics seem to have been virtually identical with those of its ambient culture(s)."

17. Mary Harlow, "Family Relationships," in *A Cultural History of Childhood and Family in Antiquity*, vol. 1.(Oxford: Berg Press, 2010) 17; Beryl Rawson, "Adult-Child Relationships," in *Marriage, Divorce, and Children in Ancient Rome*, ed. Beryl Rawson (Oxford: Oxford University Press, 1991) 27.

18. Sarah Pomeroy, *Goddesses, Whores, Wives, and Slaves: Women in Classical Antiquity* (New York: Schocken Books, 1995) 164.

19. See Janette McWilliam, "The Socialization of Roman Children," in *The Oxford Handbook of Childhood and Education in the Classical World* (Oxford: Oxford University Press, 2013) 273: "T. Pomponius Atticus, good friend of Cicero, began to look for a husband for his daughter Attica when she was six (Cic. *Att.* 13.21a.4)." For more on young age at betrothal see also Mary Harlow and Ray Laurence, *Growing Up and Growing Old in Ancient Rome: A Life Course Approach* (London: Routledge, 2002) 59–60.

20. See P. R. C. Weaver, "Children of Freedmen (and Freedwomen)," in *Marriage, Divorce, and Children in Ancient Rome*, ed. Beryl Rawson (Oxford: Oxford University Press, 1991) 46.

21. Rawson, "Adult-Child Relationships," 28.

22. Rawson, "Adult-Child Relationships," 27–28; See also Suzanne Dixon, *The Roman Mother* (OK: Oklahoma University Press, 1989) 101–102.

23. McGinn, "Roman Children and the Law," 342 fn 3.

24. "Children whose *paterfamilias* was dead were subject to supervision by a *tutor* ('guardian'). Boys were freed of this supervision when they reached the age of fourteen, but they did not achieve full financial autonomy until the age of twenty-five" (Rawson, "Adult-Child Relationships," 28).

25. Rawson, "Adult-Child Relationships," 28.

26. Ray Laurence, "Community," in *A Cultural History of Childhood and Family in Antiquity*, edited by Mary Harlow and Ray Laurence, (London: Bloomsbury, 2010) 37.

27. Laurence, 37–38.

28. Cornelia B. Horn and John W. Martens, *"Let the little children come to me": Childhood and Early Christianity* (Washington, D.C.: Catholic University of America Press, 2009) 166. On child labor in the Roman family see also Keith R. Bradley, *Discovering the Roman Family: Studies in Roman Social History* (Oxford: Oxford University Press, 1991) 103–110.

29. Rawson, "Adult-Child Relationships," 28: "For those closer to the subsistence level of existence, childhood must have ended early: both boys and girls of quite young ages (less than ten) were associated with adults in the world of work and earning a living."

30. See Lena Larsson Lovén and Agnet Strömberg, "Economy," in *A Cultural History of Childhood and Family in Antiquity,* ed. Mary Harlow and Ray Laurence, (London: Bloomsbury, 2010) 56.

31. Agricultural work was not the only occupation of children. Some children, particularly in the liminal years between childhood and adulthood, may also have engaged as apprentices to a particular trade (Horn and Martens, 167).

32. Varro, *On Agriculture* 1–17.

33. Horn and Martens, 169.

34. Larsson Lovén and Strömberg, 56.

35. Horn and Martens, 168.

36. Horn and Martens, 168.

37. Hanne Sigismund-Nielsen, "Slave and Lower-Class Roman Children," in in *The Oxford Handbook of Childhood and Education in the Classical World,* ed. Judith Grubbs, Tim Parkin, & Roslynne Bell (Oxford: Oxford University Press, 2013) 290, 296.

38. *Infancy Gospel of Thomas* 10:1–2.

39. Sigismund-Nielsen, 290.

40. Joseph Fleishman, "The Age of Legal Maturity in Biblical Law," *Journal of the Ancient Near Eastern Society* 21 (1992) 35.

41. Julie Faith Parker, *Valuable and Vulnerable: Children in the Hebrew Bible, Especially the Elijah Cycle (*Atlanta: Society of Biblical Literature, 2013) 41.

42. Parker, 44.

43. LSJ, 329.

44. BDAG, 183.

45. Marilou Ibita and Reimund Bieringer, "The Beloved Child: The Presentation of Jesus as a Child in the Second Testament." In *Children's Voices: Children's Perspectives in Ethics, Theology, and Religious Education,* edited by Annemie Dillen and Didier Pollefeyt (Walpole, MA: Uitgeverij Peeters, 2010) 122.

46. LSJ, 1287.

47. Hippocrates, *Hebdomades* 5 (as quoted in Philo, *de Opif. Mundi* 36.105), quoted in Parkin, "Life Cycle," 98.

48. Parkin, "Life Cycle," 98–99.

49. Luke Timothy Johnson, *The Gospel of Luke* (Collegeville, MN: Liturgical Press, 1991) 159.

50. LSJ, 1289.

51. Parker, 64.

52. On this basis, Warren Carter argues, "The central dimension of 'becoming as children' is identified in [Matthew] 18.4 as 'humbling oneself'... Jesus has constantly been presented as the Son who submits to, obeys (3.13–4.11), and is instructed by, God (11.27)" (*Households and Discipleship: A Study of Matthew 19-*20 [Sheffield: Sheffield Academic Press, 1994] 96–97).

53. BDAG, 750.

54. BDAG, 750.

55. The ministry of Jesus reference here, however, notably does not refer to God raising Jesus from the dead, but rather, God raising God's child, Jesus, up in hu-

man flesh in order to minister first to the Jews and then to the Gentiles. While the traditional assumption has located this ministry in the adult life of Jesus, apocryphal sources, such as the *Infancy Gospel of Thomas* suggest that at least some tradition(s) within antiquity understood Jesus to begin his ministry to the Jews as a child. When read with this openness to Jesus' role, there does not remain a single reference in Luke-Acts where the term παῖς is translated as "servant" that must necessarily refer to an adult servant.

56. See Lesley Dean-Jones: "According to *Fleshes* 13, a child becomes a *neaniskos* between the ages of fourteen and twenty-one" ("The Child Patient of the Hippocratics: Early Pediatrics?" in *The Oxford Handbook of Childhood and Education in the Classical World*, ed. Judith Evan Grubbs and Tim Parkin [Oxford: Oxford University Press, 2013] 110.).

57. BDAG, 667.

58. See Diogene Laertius, cited in Marvin W. Meyer, "The Youth in the *Secret Gospel of Mark*," in *Semeia* (Jan 1990) 139: Other legal acknowledgments of childhood and youth included the *Lex Plaetoria* (or *Laetoria*) of about 200 B.C., whereby a person over puberty but under twenty-five, if sued for a contracted debt, could claim an *exception* on the ground that his (and, later, her) youthful inexperience had been exploited by the other party . . . by the second century A.D. imperial rulings made it virtually compulsory for people between puberty and twenty-five years to have a *curator* present for most transactions.

59. Diogene Laertius, cited in Marvin W. Meyer, "The Youth in the *Secret Gospel of Mark*," in *Semeia* (Jan 1990), 139.

60. Dean-Jones, 110.

61. Note the distinction here between male and female life stages. Because the full legal status of a voting citizen was rarely if ever conferred upon females in this time period, no direct comparison exists. Instead, girls moved from one dependent relationship (to their father) into another (with their husband), usually at the time of puberty—between 11 and 14 years old.

62. Fleishman, 37. See also, Fleishman, 36: "The age of twenty as the age of adulthood finds expression in the fact that only people twenty years and older pay the half shekel, are counted in the census, and are defined as those going to the army. The Levites also begin work in the sanctuary at this age [at the youngest]." See also: Ex 30:13–14; 38:26; Num 1:2–3, 18, 22; 4:3, 23; 8:24; 1 Chr 23:24, 27; 27:23; 2 Chr 25:5; Ezra 3:8.

63. LSJ, 1163.

64. BDAG, 667.

65. For example, Mary refers to David as a παιδὸς of God in Lk 1:69 and addresses the child Jesus as τέκνον in Lk 2:48. Particularly in the first case, the use of παιδὸς with reference to descent can often be obscured by the translation of "slave" or "servant."

66. LSJ, 1768.

67. BDAG, 994–995.

68. BDAG, 1024–1027.

69. BDAG, 460–461.

70. BDAG, 650–651.
71. BDAG, 650–651.
72. BDAG, 668–669.
73. LSJ, 1169.
74. In support of this task, Julie Faith Parker draws on the work of philosopher David Archard, whom she cites as distinguishing "between the *concept* of childhood (recognizing children as different from adults) and the *conception* of childhood (in which those differences are specified and articulated)" (Parker, 23. See also David Archard, *Children: Rights and Childhood* [London: Routledge, 1993] 23).

Chapter 2

Young Children in the Household of God

In the first century Mediterranean world, the household was at the center of most children's lives whether they were slaves or free. Without the security that their household afforded, however limited in some cases it may have been, these vulnerable people were not able to grow into adults. Their lives and existence were centered around and depended upon their place in their household, which was characterized by hierarchical power relationships.[1]

The early Christian communities described in Luke-Acts carry over this language of household, portraying God as the head of the new Christian household replacing the Roman *pater familias*. The inclusion depicted in Luke's narrative, however, paints a new Christian family no longer bound by exclusive ties (cf. Lk 14:26). Luke's new family extends a wide welcome and reverses the meaning of what it means to be at the "head," such that Luke's Jesus instructs his disciples, "the least among all of you is the greatest" (Lk 9:48b).[2] This represents a significant break from the conventional Roman household.

On account of this break, together with the strong demands of discipleship that pull away from familial obligations, A. James Murphy concludes that the Church portrayed by the synoptic authors is hostile to family life and the interests of children. In these texts, he highlights the reality that children, particularly those very young and consequently dependent upon the provisions and security of their household, are presented "with challenges of household and disruption and alienation as a consequence of the in-breaking of the kingdom of God."[3] Such challenges existed for every member of the households impacted by Jesus' ministry; however, they would have been especially felt by those in the most dependent positions of the household (e.g. young children, the disabled, widows, and slaves) when and if key providers for the well-being of the household (e.g. the *pater familias* or mothers of children under the age of five) joined Jesus' itinerant followers. Such difficulties, including the fact of judgment itself, are too often glossed over by those in the Christian church who wish to paint a rosy picture of Jesus' reception of the children and need to be addressed. To the list of potential dangers for children in the Jesus movement that Murphy enumerates, later in this chapter I add Luke's vision of inclusive judgment. However, an overemphasis on such hardships does not paint the full picture of the effect that discipleship likely had on children either.

In a more tempered depiction, John Barclay aptly describes the early Christian movement as "ambiguous in its attitude to family life."[4] This ambiguity can be seen by the juxtaposition of Jesus' admonition that: "Whoever comes to me and does not hate father and mother, wife and children, brothers and sisters, yes, and even life itself, cannot be my disciple" (14:26) with his later calling for the little children to come to him in Luke 18:15–17. While Murphy sees this as an example of the dissonance between the gospels' proclaimed message of care for children and lived reality of abandonment of children, Barclay leaves space for a more moderate approach.

To this end, it is helpful to understand the full socio-cultural impact of itinerant discipleship on the households left behind. In a detailed study of household economics in first century Palestine, anthropologist Adriana Destro and historian Mauro Pesce conclude that Jesus' itinerant followers would have been composed almost entirely of members of the intermediate generation—adult children of the *pater familias* who may or may not have children of their own.[5] Destro and Pesce unfortunately follow adultist trends, dismissing non-adult children of the youngest generation from among Jesus' itinerant followers with little justification. However, their rationale behind the stability/mobility of the older two generations remains sound and provides a window into the lives of those children who did not join parents or other family members in the itinerant following of Jesus.

As in the case of Luke's parable of the welcoming father, the impact of the departure of members of this intermediate generation upon the household and its dependents would not have been as significantly felt as the departure of the *pater familias*. Although non-adult children would have been disrupted by the departure of certain members of the intermediate generation, particularly their parents, the household and its livelihood would not have been significantly impacted as long as the *pater familias* and sufficient workers remained to care for them. The most damaging loss in this scenario would have been the departure of nursing mothers to follow Jesus. While this is not to be minimized, however, even the effect of young mothers leaving their families may have been mitigated, depending upon the class and social situation of the family, with the practice of slave women or even other family members nursing and rearing the very young.[6]

Such nuancing is not meant to overshadow the very real dangers and vulnerability of children in the ancient world, particularly those who may have lost the valuable protections and provisions of family members who chose to join Jesus in his itinerant ministry. Most Jewish families in first century Palestine lived on the precipice of economic ruin and any decision, including the decision of certain household members to leave home and follow Jesus, could have pushed them over the edge. However, complete abandonment or economic and social ruin were by no means a guarantee. By reading Jesus' warning that one must hate one's children alongside his welcome of children, one does not erase the sting of the former, but rather contextualizes it as one part of a larger picture—the picture of discipleship life. Reading these passages as two parts of the same whole, child disciples need not be mere victims of the difficult life of discipleship, but rather, part of it.

Membership in God's household, as described by the Lukan author, is challenging and demanding—it demands sacrifice and commitment. Nevertheless, Luke's depiction of God's household calls for all of its members—presumably regardless of status, gender, ethnicity, or age—to hold all things in common (Acts 2:43–47; 4:32–35).[7] In the process, this new household actually reverses the structure of the first century Mediterranean household itself. In particular, in this chapter I demonstrate the inclusion of non-adult children among the children of God's household and its consequent effect on the household as a whole.[8] I do so by exploring the experience of the young child (τὸ βρέφος, τὸ παιδίον) as one of God's children (τὰ τέκνα θεοῦ) who has received grace as described in Lukan narratives of welcome, nurture, and healing.

Cultural circumstances of the Lukan author, his redactors, and interpreters leave an adultist imprint according to which no children are mentioned as such by name. However, despite the paucity of literary evidence of their presence, the experiences of such children and, indeed their inclusion in larger society, can be culled from the shadows of Luke's text. This re-imagining of children in Luke's narrative world occurs through a re-examination of the narratives that mention nameless children in groups or as individuals and narratives that implicitly include children within larger social groupings. Each group of text is examined first in terms of the experience of welcome and then in terms of the experience of grace and healing in order to trace the theme of inclusion of children that runs throughout the Lukan narrative.

WELCOME AND INCLUSION IN FIRST CENTURY PALESTINE AND SURROUNDING CULTURES

That a child would have been included among those following Jesus in Roman-occupied Palestine should not be surprising given the often understated but pervasive presence of young children in Jewish and Greco-Roman societies of the first century. Although these early followers were Jewish, the lack of documentation around the lives of children in the first century make it necessary to look beyond specific ethnic groups for a broader understanding of the cultural milieu. Surveying the written and material witness, Reidar Aasgaard concludes that "ethnic and cultural differences for children in antiquity were small: Greek, Roman, and Jewish children had to cope with the same basic conditions."[9]

There is little doubt that childhood was a difficult time in antiquity. Children in the first century Mediterranean context suffered a greater susceptibility to disease and bore a lower, subservient status. However, recent research has shown that children were nevertheless valued within the sentimentalities and infrastructures of their time. This value, as will be seen, extended into the welcoming and celebration of infants, the accepted presence of children in the public sphere, the attendance of children at communal celebrations and commemorations, and the presence and participation of children in religious rituals.

Welcome and Celebration of Infants in the Greco-Roman World

Even from infancy, non-adult children were understood to be a part of society in antiquity. Such inclusion was marked in different ways among the classes, including their presentation at specified ages in both Roman and Jewish religious ceremonies. A child's acceptance within a household began at the moment of birth, when, as historian Suzanne Dixon describes, "The newborn child, once pronounced fit to live . . . would then be placed on the ground for the *pater familias* to raise up ritually as his indication that he accepted his paternity of the child and wished to rear it."[10] Such ritual acknowledges paternity but, more basically, acknowledges the role and status of the child *as child*. Implicit in a father's acceptance of a child is acknowledgment of that child's place in the family and so the commitment that the family will provide and care for the child.

Another example of early inclusion at the societal level was the legal registry of free, Roman-born children into an official registry thirty days after the child's birth.[11] Although these infants were not understood as full citizens at this age, their social stratification would have been no different than the stratification between adult sons and fathers, freed men and slaves, men and women, foreign visitors, and so forth. Stratification itself was a part of life in first century Palestine.

Not only were children were present and included in the fabric of ancient social and public life, they were welcomed into it. From birth, the child, while often viewed as not yet complete, was greeted with joy and merriment. Roman historian Janette McWilliam observes, "The birth of a Roman child was celebrated both within the *domus* and among the wider community."[12] In the Roman household, upon which the later Christian household was modeled (at least in form), the birth of a child was an occasion for revelry, despite the looming reality of high infant mortality rates.[13] Seneca even includes such an occasion among his narration of events commonly thought to bring joy (Letters 59.2). Such celebrations included the public acknowledgment of the child—and his or her official entry into the *familia* in both Greek and Roman families. This ceremony, called *lustratio* in Latin, took place when a baby was eight-days-old (nine days for girls).[14]

In a similar manner, babies born into Jewish families were welcomed into their individual families and into the family of God, the covenant community. This happened through the circumcision of baby boys on the eighth day (Gen 17:10–14; see also Lev 12:3). Indeed, procreation was the primary aim of the ancient marriage. As a result, children were welcomed into the ancient families into which they were born from birth.

Presence of Children in the Public and Religious Sphere

By virtue of necessity, as these young children grew they did so within the public sphere.[15] Children spent their days in the very houses, markets, synagogues, riversides, and villages where Jesus' ministry took place, with little to no differentiation between adult and child-oriented space. Cultural expectations welcomed and encouraged the public presence of children as a part of daily life. Numerous ancient documents and funerary monuments testify to the affection felt by parents in antiquity for their children—even when such affection does not always match contemporary western sensibilities about parental love.[16]

Children were cared for and cherished by their parents; however, at the same time, parents, whether Greco-Roman or Jewish, maintained a strict view of the place of children in the household, their obligations to obedience, and expectations of participation in the ongoing wellbeing of both their home and society. Consequently, the view of children in the first century world was complicated. Warren Carter describes the delicate balance: "Though occupying a subordinate position in the household, and though regarded as a threat to the social order unless properly trained, the child is also an object of affection and value."[17] First century Mediterranean children played an integral role in their households and broader society, but that role was strictly defined by the hierarchies and household structures that governed much of the rest of life for adults and children alike.

The public presence of children in the ancient world is seen particularly in regard to their home life, work, public celebrations, and religious rituals. In Luke's gospel, households and home structures of various sizes are indicated by descriptions of intimate family conflicts (indicative of the more typical small size of a single conjugal family) and intricate receptions and banquets (indicative of wealthy landowners and estates and reflecting a multi-generational, extended family). In each of these households, children played an important and integral role. This can be seen with particular attention to child slaves and *delicia* in the larger Roman households. However, for the purposes of understanding the background of Luke's narrative, a closer look at the roles of children in these middle and small-size households is most appropriate.[18]

With several notable exceptions, such as Levi and Zacchaeus, it is generally assumed that most of Jesus' followers came from lower class, largely subsistence families. Such families would have lived in modest homes in the country or apartment blocks in larger towns, generally with very little private space. Roman historian Mary Harlow notes that "in the smaller dwellings or apartment blocks of larger towns it is hard to locate a space that would fit the modern sense of family life—for instance, rooms that might allow for privacy. Here the space must have been multipurpose and served as sleeping, working, eating, and general living quarters."[19] Crowded living spaces and shared daily tasks necessitated that adults and children lived and worked closely side-by-side. Much of children's (and, indeed, adults') day-to-day activities in these households would likely have been conducted outdoors in the public sphere of either the city or the fields.

Children, sometimes from as young as five years old, were present and active participants in the agricultural work of the first century. Varro's writings on *Agriculture* illustrate the close relationship between children and adults in such contexts: "All fields are worked by human beings, whether slaves or free men or both; they are worked by free men either when these people work their own land, as many poor people do with the help of their children, or when they are hired laborers . . ." (Varro, *Agriculture* 1, 17.2).

Young children in Jesus' day were not shielded from the realities of life. Indeed, children, particularly in the lower classes, participated as much as they were able in the work of the parents and their household, and as they grew, their responsibilities grew with them. Beryl Rawson describes this process of socialization:

Children were constantly exposed to the public spaces of their hometowns. If they were already working for a living, their occupation and often their residence were located in and above shops, and there were many errands to be run through the streets. Slave children came and went with their masters or ran errands or did the shopping. And there was much time spent as spectators or participants in public festivals, celebrations, processions, and performances.[20]

Due to their lower social status, there is less written about the presence of children (as well as poor people) in the cities and villages—the Christian gospels being no exception. However, the evidence that does exist suggests that children were both present and active in the public and social worlds in which they lived.

One source of evidence for the presence and participation of young children in family and public life are funerary monuments. Lena Larsson Lovén, a specialist in Roman archaeology, observes: "For more than three hundred years, from the late Republic to the later third century CE, Roman children appear as regular subjects in various commemorative contexts."[21] Although initially such depictions only show children within their family groups, by the first century CE children begin to appear with more regularity as "individuals in their own right."[22] Such commemorative altars show children with toys and other instruments of childhood, pointing to a growing recognition of children as independent agents active and present in public life in their own unique ways.

In connection with this acknowledgment of the individuality and contributions of young children, it is not surprising that one facet of public life where significant evidence of children does exist is that of state and ritual celebrations. Often children were included in such celebrations specifically because of their young age and special capacities associated with youth. At the state level, Roman historian Janette McWilliam explains, "Emperors continued to allow their sons to ride in the chariot or on race horses," thus "permitting children of the imperial family . . . to participate and become part of the history of Roman achievement."[23] Nor was such pomp reserved for the royal families, since children across a variety of ages and socio-economic backgrounds attended such parades with their families.[24] In the ancient Mediterranean world, when something major was going on or a public figure was visiting their city or village, children, along with most of the rest of the population, would show up. The inclusion of children in such public moments grew not only out of the closeness of public space that necessitated the presence of children, but also out of the connection to posterity that children carried. In this way it answered the familial desire in the ancient world for children to experience and be able to speak about important figures and events.

In the religious sphere, children participated in ordinary religious life and were also called upon to perform special services in the respective rituals of Roman and Jewish cultures. As evidence of the participation of children in first century Jewish synagogues, Wayne Meeks cites Josephus' record of "Roman authorities in Sardis granting the right for 'Jewish citizens living in our city' to 'come together and have a communal life and adjudicate suits among themselves, and that a place be given them in which they may gather together with their wives and children and offer their ancestral prayers and sacrifices to God.'"[25]

Such inclusion should not be surprising given the biblical mandate for Jews to educate their children in the scriptures. Indeed, in this instance, Jewish culture may deviate slightly from their Greco-Roman neighbors in its strong emphasis on the inclusion of, as well as the intrinsic value of young children. While the Greco-Roman practice of exposure and infanticide is often over-emphasized compared to actual practice, the concept itself was prohibited in Jewish law. Bonnie Miller-McLemore attributes such prohibitions to the covenant promise, explaining:

> Children . . . not only represented the promise, sign, and guarantee of the covenant; they were also participants in it, to be included in religious observances, educated in the covenant, and routinely brought into and formed by the rich practices and believes of love of God and neighbor. The commandments to teach the love of God "to your children and your children's children" steadfastly, diligently—"when you are home and when you are away, when you lie down and when you rise" (Deut. 6:2, 7)—stands at the very heart of Jewish law.[26]

Just as Roman citizens were concerned with socializing their children to celebrate and participate in the Roman government, Jewish parents were concerned with socializing their children to celebrate and give service to the God of Israel.

Participation in the life of Israel naturally meant attention to religious education and attendance at religious events for children. Jews were unique in the intrinsic valuation of children as signs of God's covenant; however, the socialization of children into their parents' religion extended across antiquity. McWilliam notes that Roman children both attended and participated in religious observances.[27] Translating these Roman practices to the cultural context of the New Testament, Carter elaborates on the unique value of children in religious roles:

> Children are thought to be effective in intercessory roles for several reasons. Because of their weakness and marginal status, children are "dear to the gods"

and merit favor and protection. The absence of sexual activity or awareness is also a factor . . . Hence here . . . the child's present power and significance are valued and recognized precisely because the child is not an adult.[28]

As participants in religious rituals, children were acknowledged and welcomed into an intergenerational community that recognized and valued their unique place within it. This place was marked both by their present and future capacities, as youth who would yet become adults. While the unique abilities that children contributed were drawn from their youth, another factor in their parents' desire to expose them to such rituals was drawn from their preparation to become adults. The presence of children at public and religious events in antiquity was not only assumed, but likely encouraged or even mandated.

Parents who wanted to raise their children according to their own values and view of the world—a major goal of parenting in antiquity—naturally wanted their children to witness to and participate in the public events that shaped their values. For Roman parents this would have included the baths, races, and victory parades. For Jewish parents, it would have included Temple festivals and learning in the synagogues. For nascent followers of Jesus, this naturally extended to listening to and learning from the sermons of Jesus and his apostles (cf. Acts 2:1–17; Acts of Thomas 28:1). Indeed, in the Jewish family, because of their inclusion in the covenant, children "were regarded as an essential part of God's blessing," seen throughout the Hebrew Bible and again in Luke's gospel in Mary's Magnificat.[29]

Overall, children in the first century, from whom Jewish children were no exception, continued to maintain a marginal status in society and to were expected to give abject obedience to the head of their household (the Roman *pater familias*). Nevertheless, to say with Crossan that "To be a child was to be a nobody," is overstating the case.[30] To be a child in first century Palestine was a difficult and marginalized existence to be sure. However, to be a child was also to be woven into the very fabric of society, included in both the daily and celebratory going-ons of public life, as an essential and valued participant in the twin institutions of household and community.

To be a Jewish child in particular was to be a part of the covenant community and thus the extended family of God known as the Children of Israel. In short, such children, while not necessarily coddled or cosseted, were welcomed and included in their families, households, communities, and society at large. Luke's narrative describes such an experience of welcome and inclusion for the young child within both the broader Jewish community of which Jesus was a part and the specific community of those following Jesus.

WELCOME AND INCLUSION IN LUKE 9:47–50 AND 18:15–17

The welcome and inclusion of young children among Jesus' followers can be seen most vividly in Luke 9:47–50 and 18:15–17, in which Jesus exhorts his disciples to welcome little children (τὰ παιδία) and infants (τοί βρέφοι). In these exhortations the character of Jesus shows more than a sympathetic soft spot for cuddly children, as popular culture often paints these encounters. Rather, in these texts, Luke is clarifying the equal place of children among adult disciples in the Kingdom of God. While most explicitly stated in these texts, the full inclusion of the young child is assumed throughout Luke's narrative from the angel's prophecy about John in 1:11–17 (esp. 1:17) to Jesus' predictions of the end times (see also 7:31–35 and 21:34–35) and finally as a part of the community of disciples to whom Jesus grants understanding and blessing before he ascends into heaven (24:45–53).

Luke 9:47–50

Luke first openly deals with the place of little children in God's Kingdom in 9:47–50. In response to an argument among the disciples about who is greatest among them, Jesus brings a little child (παιδίον) to his side and urges those who are arguing: "Whoever welcomes this child in my name welcomes me, and whoever welcomes me welcomes the one who sent me; for the least among all of you is the greatest" (9:48). This is significant first because it establishes the location of a concrete non-adult child among Jesus' followers and second because it plainly instructs those who are arguing to welcome both the literal child and those who, like her,[31] are considered "the least *among*" the disciples (9:48, emphasis added).

In response to a presumably adult disagreement, these intimations combine to speak powerfully to the presence of young children among Jesus' followers. While such a presence is not independently recorded in the narrative, most likely due to the low place of children within the social structure of society at that time, texts such as this one shine a light on the shadows of children in the background of the Lukan narrative and reveal their persistent presence, which was likely assumed throughout by Luke's first century audience (as it would have been in society at large).

Luke 9:48 confirms the presence of at least one non-adult child among the community of Jesus' followers while at the same time implying a more extensive presence of children in their midst. This encounter with a real child is narrated in all three of the synoptics; however, it is Luke's account that, through the use of the demonstrative pronoun, makes most evident the presence of the young child as a real individual previously present among Jesus' disciples. Luke Timothy Johnson notes, "The demonstrative is deliberate. It is not any child, or 'all children,' as though this were a moral lesson."[32] Luke's Jesus here interacts with a real, individual child. In contrast, Mark's account more quickly distances the audience from the real child in her individuality by exhorting the disciples to welcome "one such child" (Mk 9:37). While Matthew, despite keeping the real child in focus at first, turns this child even more readily into a metaphoric example by exhorting the disciples to take "the lowly position of this child" (Matt 18:4). Luke's specific reference to "this child" (τοῦτο τὸ παιδίον) as the object of welcome compared to these more metaphoric treatments shows even more clearly the real person behind the narrative account. Only after establishing this literal layer of the story does Luke subsequently generalize from the real child to the greatness and implicit welcome of all children in the discipleship community as "the least among all of you" who are to be seen and treated as the greatest (Lk 9:48).

The place of this child among the discipleship community in Luke comes into focus most clearly when compared to the more ambiguous place that this child is given in Matthew and Mark. In Matthew's account Jesus "calls" and "places" the child among his disciples (Matt 18:2–3). In Mark's account, the group with whom Jesus is speaking is specifically limited to the Twelve[33] (Mk 9:35) among whom he places the child (Mk 9:36). Significantly, Luke diverges from each of these accounts by describing the instigating conversation among a broader community of Jesus' disciples (9:43, 46)[34] from whom Jesus takes a child (implicitly already present among this community) and places the child "by *his* side" (Lk 9:47).[35] Since Luke sees no need for Jesus to call to the child in this instance (as he does to the children and their caregivers in Lk 18:16) it can be inferred that this child is already among those to whom Jesus is addressing himself—his disciples.

This is further confirmed by the location in their midst in which the little child is placed. For Mark and Matthew, the primary emphasis is on Jesus placing this child (perhaps an outsider or sort of spectacle object) *in the middle* of the disciples (ἐν μέσῳ αὐτῶν); however, for Luke, Jesus places the child at his own side and emphasizes instead the child's preexistent place within the broader community of disciples already established, making of this child an example of the least *among all* of the disciples (ἐν πᾶσιν ὑμῖν). By this gesture, Jesus places this child in community with him—signaling his solidarity with her on her own terms.[36] François Bovon even goes so far as to suggest that "this proximity to Jesus has a particular meaning, since it expresses a choice and a privilege, just as being a Christian does in itself (cf. 10:21–22)."[37] This child, and by extension other children, are already understood by Luke's Jesus to be a part of the Kingdom—valued children of God.

In this way, a child's inclusion in the community brought about in God's Kingdom is presumed. The new revelation in the passage is that this representative of the "least" among them is actually to be treated as the greatest and thus welcomed enthusiastically. On the meaning of "welcome" (Δέχεσθαι) in v. 48, Bovon elaborates, "Δέχεσθαι means here a caring 'acceptance,' perhaps even an enduring 'welcome,' because both Jesus and God want to be 'welcomed.'"[38] To welcome this child—and any child—is more than a simple act of human compassion, but rather, is a broader gesture towards this child's acceptance and inclusion *in Christ's name*.

Bovon highlights the significance of this phrase, 'in my name,' which was already in Luke's source at Mark 9:37, [and] is frequently encountered in the Third Gospel" as connected to Luke's literary style and "his theology of relationship."[39] Jesus' followers stand in relation to one another on account of their common familial identity established not in the line of a traditional *pater familias*, but rather in the name of Jesus, God's son. By the same token, Johnson traces the use of this term throughout Luke's narrative, concluding, "In biblical parlance, the 'name' (*onoma*) defines identity. The name with which Christians are associated in their mission is that of Jesus (9:48–49; 10:17; Acts 2:38; 3:6, 16; 4:7, 10, 12, 30; 8:12, 16; 9:27, 28; 10:43, 48; 16:18; 19:5; 22:16; 26:9) and it is for this same name that they will experience suffering (21:8, 12, 17; Acts 4:17–18; 5:28, 40; 9:14, 16)."[40] Thus, to receive a child in Jesus' name means to recognize that child's relationship with and identification through Jesus as a follower of Jesus and a part of God's Kingdom that Jesus is proclaiming.

It is important to note that this final statement of the Lukan Jesus regarding who is the greatest is exclusive, unlike in the Markan and Matthean parallels. It is directed specifically at the internal dispute. Jesus is not concerned here about who is the greatest in society at large, but rather, is referring to only those in the immediate group of his followers (as per the initial dispute). That the young child signaled out at his side is to be understood among this group is made clear by the initial demonstrative purpose, the specific exhortation to welcome her, and her implicit place among "the least" to whom Jesus refers at the end of his exhortation. Moving away from this one specific, concrete child to a general sense of those considered "least" in this social group, moreover, opens the grounds for a reasonable assumption that other non-adult children would also fit into this category. The exhortation is addressed in the plural, and there is no other reasonable explanation given for why this one child would be considered an exception to the group dynamics as a whole or an expression of surprise on the part of the other disciples at her presence.

Luke 18:15-17

Second, Jesus builds on this expression of the welcome and inclusion of young children in Luke 9:47-50 by explicitly including and welcoming young children, including infants, into his midst in 18:15-17. On this most interpreters of the synoptics are agreed: at this narrative moment, and, indeed, in God's future kingdom, children are welcome. Often this important point is overshadowed by the predominately metaphorical treatment of the passage in contemporary scholarship.[41] Such readings generally apply the phrase "as a child" either to the disciples as those who receive the Kingdom or to the Kingdom itself as that which is to be received. These divergent readings stem from an ambiguity in the Greek syntax of the original text. Frederick Schilling delineates the two possibilities:

> The word *paidion* (child) is, of course, singular as is the subject of the verb and as is the object. It could be subject in apposition to the subject of the verb 'whoever receives,' or object in apposition to *tain basileian*. This could throw the comparative *hos paidion* ('as/like a child') to the subject of the verb, 'whoever' (third person singular) or to the object, the noun, 'kingdom.' The two meanings would then be 'as though he were a child,' or 'as though the Kingdom were a child.'[42]

Grammatically, the comparison "as a child" can be applied to either the subject(s) of Jesus' address—the disciples—or to the object of their receipt—the Kingdom of God. Which of these two translations scholars choose dramatically influences the attributes of childhood to which they contend the metaphor refers. In the first case of a child as a metaphor for Jesus' disciples, or more generally discipleship, interpreters generally emphasize the humility and other (often active) idyllic qualities of childhood. Conversely, in the latter case of a child as a metaphor for God's Kingdom, the emphasis tends towards the more passive qualities of children such as their smallness, social status, and potentiality—qualities that have more to do with how the disciples might treat them as objects, rather than how they themselves behave as disciples and subjects.

The most common academic interpretation of Luke 18:15-17 understands the little child as a metaphor for discipleship.[43] While such an interpretation has a long history in interpretive tradition, it has become particularly enticing in Western scholarship in recent times alongside growing idealizations of children in Western culture. Since the Renaissance and within the last century in particular, the contribution of children to the maintenance of the household in Western European and North American countries has receded. This has resulted in a need to preserve the value of children within their households by placing an increasing value on the intrinsic worth of children regardless of their contributions.⁴⁴ Thus, Ronald R. Clark observes, "Children today are seen as innocent, humble, trusting, and pure."⁴⁵ As the value of children within a household has become less apparent externally, Western culture has sought to transfer this value to such internal qualities such as innocence and morality that the adult population, clearly subjects of the Fall, can be seen to benefit from.

An alternate reading of the Greek text allows for the possibility that the object of the metaphor is not the one who is to receive God's Kingdom (the disciple), but the Kingdom itself. Clark advocates for this interpretation, reading the noun παιδίον in the accusative rather than nominative case, which shifts Kingdom to the role of object in the sentence.⁴⁶ Following this line of reasoning, Clark and others have proposed a reading of Luke 18:15–17 in which the little child serves as a metaphor for God's Kingdom.⁴⁷ As when children are read as a metaphor for discipleship, however, the question must still be asked, what does Jesus' teaching reveal about God's Kingdom through the metaphor of the child?

To answer this question, it remains necessary for scholars to unpack the meaning of "the child" in Jesus' metaphor. As in the previous instance, a variety of different approaches have been used to go about this task, often drawing on similar tools and traditions. However, by treating a child as the object to be received rather than the subject who receives the Kingdom, these inquiries have yielded slightly nuanced results. Instead of emphasizing the moral character of the child as an example to follow, those who translate ὡς παιδίον in the accusative case tend to emphasize a child's low standing and helplessness.

Such a turn away from the agency of the child toward the way in which she is received is particularly appropriate in Luke's account, where the children initially received by Jesus are described as βρεφή (infants) rather than the more generic παιδίους (children). Daniel Patte observes that translating the child of Lk 18:17 in relation to the Kingdom "would fit the description of the children as 'babies' who, as infants, are not in a position to perform acts such as 'receiving the Kingdom,' but are indeed received (as in Matt 18:5)."⁴⁸ Whatever the age of this child, however, when she is placed in relation to the Kingdom the concern shifts from her action to the way in which she is acted upon.

In contrast, foregrounding actual children and families combats the systems of adult domination that have plagued previous interpretations of Luke 18:15–17 and its parallels, as well as New Testament scholarship more broadly. Recent research into the first century context(s) of childhood(s) in the Greco-Roman world and child-centered readings of the same texts performed more recently by Cornelia Horn, John Martens, Judith Gundry, John Carroll, and Sharon Betsworth illustrate this point. Cornelia Horn and John Martens affirm that the "place [of children] in the kingdom is by virtue of their being simply children of God."[49] There is no need to read an additional rationale into Jesus' valuing of children as the above metaphorical readings assume. The simplest reading, in this case, is the clearest—in this text and throughout Luke's gospel, children are simply valued *as children*.

Such a reading is consistent with first century Jewish beliefs about the place of children within God's Kingdom as indicated above in the language of covenant. While exclusivist claims were present in first century Jewish and Christian expressions of God's Kingdom, the question of the day was not whether children were included, but rather, *which* children were included in the Kingdom. A dispute between Rabbi Gamaliel II and Rabbi Joshua illustrates this point: "Gamaliel forbade foreign children who were born in Israel to enter to the kingdom of God, whereas Joshua granted entry to them."[50]

While much scholarly inquiry has been devoted to determining what qualities of children recommend them for inclusion in God's Kingdom, the simplest answer remains that absent any particular quality, children have simply always been and will always be a part of the household of God. Moreover, lest any human authority attempt to dictate the exclusion of children (or anyone else) from God's Kingdom,

> The maxim [in v. 16 not to hinder the children] attributed to Jesus redefines the notion of limits. The negative imperative means that no human authority can or must regulate access to Christ or God. If there are to be any limits to the community, they will be neither exterior nor formal. They will depend on the One who calls each person—here, using a living metaphor, who invites the "children."[51]

God is in control. Children are included in the Kingdom not because the disciples choose to invite or allow them to be included, nor even because they have traditionally been included—though they have. Rather, in Lk 18:16, Luke's Jesus makes clear that it is God who will decide who is a part of God's Kingdom. And God, through Jesus' call, chooses children.

Thus, rather than focusing on what about children makes them worthy of a place in God's Kingdom, Judith Gundry turns the tables to consider instead why God chooses to include children in the Kingdom despite their apparent unworthiness. She observes, it is "not any particular quality of the child, but 'the child's littleness, immaturity and need of assistance, though commonly disparaged, [that] keep the way open for the fatherly love of God.'"[52] God includes small children in God's family because such children need God's care and protection.

In this respect, God's household functions in much the same way as the first century Greco-Roman household—held together by a common kinship tie, each person has their place, not on account of their particular virtues, but rather, on their common need and dependence upon one another. Carroll puts it eloquently in his essay on Luke in the same volume as Gundry's work cited above:

> If you want to know what God's reign is like, how God's household is constituted, then you need look no further than these children! Indeed, any who wish to have a place in God's realm should look to these vulnerable, low-status children as the model to be emulated. One enters God's realm by embracing it without pretension to status or power.[53]

Children, and adults too for that matter, are a part of God's Kingdom because God wants them there.

That a place in God's Kingdom cannot be earned by the possession or emulation of childlike virtues or any other positivistic act is only further highlighted by Luke's use of βρέφοι ("infants").[54] Supporting this shift as an indication of Luke's deviation from works as a motivating factor, Robert Tannehill cites such infants as "too young to do much at all."[55] Tannehill overreaches, missing the many ways in which infants just after birth are able to seek out basic needs such as security and milk. However, he accurately captures the dominant adult view of infants' abilities for both Luke's first century audience and most twenty-first century audiences today, describing infants as "powerless" and possessing "no right to claim attention in the public world dominated by adult males."[56] Within this notion of patriarchy, the audience would have understood infants as unable to positively earn their place in God's Kingdom on their own. To this end, Luke's replacement of the more general term παιδίον ("small child") used in the other synoptics emphasizes what Luke portrays as a lack of human involvement in determining one's place in God's Kingdom. Describing this theme as it recurs throughout Luke's narrative, Luke Timothy Johnson concludes, "The kingdom proclaimed by Jesus is entirely about the power of God at work to heal and liberate and empower, not about humans accomplishing things for themselves."[57] The inclusion of children is a shining example of this. Such an innate inclusion of children is seen throughout Luke's narrative when one looks behind the shadows of the adult characters given center stage.

Even more, the Lukan author goes further than a mere toleration or even acknowledgment of the place of children in God's Kingdom by signaling their explicit welcome through Jesus' unambiguous call (προσεκαλέσατο) that they come (ἔρχεσθαι) to him (Lk 18:14). As noted above, Jesus' call overrides the power of the disciples (or even the children and their parents) to decide who is welcome in his presence and, correspondingly, God's Kingdom. That determination rests solely on Jesus, who clearly and definitively chooses to call these children to himself (προσεκαλέσατο, v. 16)—into the divine presence. "By calling the children to him," New Testament commentator

François Bovon observes, "Jesus demonstrated to his listeners God's method of making the welcoming of infants with open arms a priority. He explained what approach to adopt in order to 'enter' the kingdom of God. The apothegm says: God welcomes children."[58] There can be no mistaking that Jesus' call represents a positive response to these infants and children.

With Jesus' summons in Lk 18:16, the focus of attention turns from the adults who dominate the action of v. 15, either by bringing children or by preventing them, to the gathered children themselves. Bovon notes, "The *auta* makes clear that it is the children and not the parents or disciples that he [Jesus] calls to himself."[59] It would have been easy, given the initial attribution of action to the parents bringing their children, to continue this line and depict Jesus as calling the parents to bring their children to him. Such a call would have closely paralleled Jesus instruction to the disciples regarding the children. However, instead, Jesus' focus is entirely on the gathered children. Luke's Jesus highlights the place of children in God's Kingdom by actively welcoming them as human agents, capable of coming or allowing themselves to be brought to his presence by their own power.[60] With his invitation, Jesus both welcomes and empowers these small children, even the infants, as recipients of his grace, members of God's Kingdom, and children in the household of God.

The significance of Jesus' welcome of these children whom he calls to himself can be particularly seen in light of the first century context of hospitality. Hospitality was a central societal expectation in antiquity, which was generally extended to those of one's own cultural group or kin, but could occasionally be extended to strangers as well.[61] This usually involved welcoming another person into one's home—a cultural expectation on which Jesus and his followers relied. However, for Jesus who claims no home (Lk 9:58), hospitality is symbolically extended in his very person. Inviting another person or group of people to oneself becomes itself an extension of hospitality.

In this way, Jesus permits children to enter his presence in a parallel form to that with which he prohibits the adult disciples from preventing them. Jesus extends hospitality to these children. By physically extending welcome to them, Jesus is acting toward these children in much the same manner as the woman whom he praises for taking the time to anoint his feet (Lk 7:44–46).[62] Moreover, by inviting these children, whom the disciples sought to relegate to a lesser place, unto himself Jesus enacts the kind of hospitality he has previously commended to his disciples in which those who cannot repay are the very ones who are to be invited to God's banquet table (see Lk 14:7–14). By extending hospitality to children and inviting them to approach him, Jesus welcomes them into the eschatological Kingdom, but more importantly, into an immediate experience of God's Kingdom personified by his acceptance and blessing of them in the flesh.

This is significant because the children whom Jesus welcomes, particularly the infants cannot be expected to return Jesus' hospitality with any sort of reciprocal response—an hallmark that Jesus makes central to welcome in the Kingdom of God (cf. Luke 14:15–24).[63] The welcome that God extends to children through Jesus is not simply a rhetorical or eschatological sense of belonging, but rather a physical and embodied inclusion experienced within and thereby reframing their cultural frame of reference.

Combined, Luke 9:47–50 and 18:15–17 powerfully verbalize what has otherwise been implicit throughout Luke's narrative—children are included and welcome among Jesus' followers as a part of the proclaimed Kingdom of God.[64] This has been demonstrated through attention to the immediate of presence of children among Jesus' followers, Jesus' intentional actions and invitations to bring children close to him, and the maxims that include specific, real children as representatives of the Kingdom of God.

While such maxims are often interpreted metaphorically with an emphasis on how the concept of child might serve as a model for how adults are to achieve status in the Kingdom of God, 9:47–50 and 18:15–17 make it abundantly clear that Jesus' concern is not with human achievements or status. Rather, Jesus is concerned with the relationship that God establishes with both children and adults first through the Abrahamic covenant and now also through the Kingdom and new household of God that Jesus proclaims. In this household, while they may not always be prominently seen, children were and are expected to remain welcomed and valued participants.

WELCOME AND INCLUSION THROUGHOUT LUKE'S NARRATIVE

The welcome and inclusion of children as valued participants in God's Kingdom is not always as readily apparent throughout Luke's gospel account as it is in Luke 9:47–50 and 18:15–17 or some of the healing narratives to be discussed in the next chapter. However, when one peels back the layers of first century adult-centered narrative and twenty-first century adultist assumptions, the presence and welcome of children within the community of Jesus' followers as Luke describes it begins to emerge with new clarity. Luke's gospel account begins with a heavy emphasis on the inclusion of children in God's Kingdom, signaled by the expectation and celebration of John and Jesus' births, and through their infancies, a glimpse into the ritual welcome and inclusion of all infants in the covenantal community through circumcision, purification, and Passover celebration. As Luke shifts into his description of the adult ministries of John and Jesus, young children become less visible but no less present in the account.

The continued welcome and inclusion of children becomes apparent when one re-reads Luke's gospel account with an awareness of the already established presence of children in first century homes, religious spaces, and marketplaces. Such a reading highlights the impact on and participation of children throughout Jesus' teaching, healing, and judgment. In addition, the full inclusion of children in the experience of Jesus' ministry comes to light when one adds the experience of children at public celebrations connected and often central to Jesus' teaching and ministry, such as funerals, weddings, trials and executions, and again, the Passover Meal.

Welcome and Celebration of Infants as Experienced in Luke 1–2

The first two chapters of Luke's gospel account, commonly set off as a prologue, put highlight the inclusion of children within the Jewish covenant community as seen specifically through the births and infancies of John and Jesus. The Psalter expresses well the value that Jewish families placed in the birth of children: "Sons are indeed a heritage from the Lord, the fruit of the womb a reward" (Ps 127:3). Like the ambient cultures that surrounded them, first century Jewish families expected and celebrated the birth of children within a marriage relationship.

For this reason, Zechariah, like Hannah and many others before him, prays for the birth of a child (1:13–14) and Elizabeth celebrates "what the Lord has done for me when he looked favorably on me and took away the disgrace I have endured among my people" (1:25). Before they knew the special purpose to which their son John was destined, Zechariah and Elizabeth longed for a child. When they learned of Elizabeth's pregnancy they welcomed and celebrated their child as a long-awaited blessing. Likewise, the angel describes this announcement as "good news" and when Elizabeth's "neighbors and relatives heard that the Lord had shown his great mercy to her . . . they rejoiced with her" (1:19, 58). This joy at the baby's birth comes solely from the arrival of their child, apart from any special status, as demonstrated by the fact that the community is portrayed as completely unaware of the expectations placed on John.

This is illustrated by Zechariah's inability to speak in order to explain the angelic message he received prior to John's naming and by the initial objections of the neighbors and relatives to the name chosen for the infant (cf. 1:22, 59–63). This narrative, with the primary purpose of showing fulfilled prophecy and the divine nature of John and Jesus' birth, also reveals the shadows of an ethos of welcome and inclusion for infants that was woven into the culture into which John and Jesus were born.

This ethos of welcome and inclusion of children, particularly infants, continues in the first two chapters of Luke's narrative with the accounts of the naming and circumcisions of both John and Jesus. Here the inclusion of children within the Jewish community through the Abrahamic covenant takes on flesh in the artfully related examples of these two infants. At this point in the narrative miraculous interventions and angelic announcements have made it clear to the reader that God has something special in store for John and Jesus; however, their circumcisions are described as simply a matter of course (1:59; 2:21). Circumcision in the Jewish tradition ritualistically welcomed male infants into the covenant community at eight days of age. Members of the community frequently attended these celebrations alongside the family, highlighting the importance of the event. Since John's and Jesus' circumcisions followed this pattern, Luke's narration of their circumcisions offers a glimpse into some of the ordinary actions of inclusion in which first century Jewish families engaged.

Turning the spotlight away from John, Luke continues to describe Mary and Joseph's observance of Torah with reference to their travels with their child to the Temple. The family first travels to Jerusalem when Jesus is a baby in order to perform a rite of purification and thereafter for annual Passover observances. Immediately after mention of Jesus' circumcision, Luke describes a trip to the Temple with an infant Jesus "to present him to the Lord (as it is written in the law of the Lord, 'Every firstborn male shall be designated as holy to the Lord')" (2:22–23). There is some confusion about whether the Torah law Luke references is the purification of mothers after childbirth or the ritual dedication of the first born. Luke's interpretation of the tradition here likely reflects a conflation of the two obligations; however, in either case, the clear inclusion of infants in the covenantal and religious life in the community is brought to the fore.

When Jesus later calls for his followers to receive (δέξηται, 18:17) the Kingdom of God as a little child, it is possible to see in this invitation an allusion to the same welcome that Simeon extended to the infant Jesus when he received him (ἐδέχατο αὐτὸ, 2:28) into his arms on his first trip to the Temple.[65] In this way, the welcome of the infant Jesus at the Temple indicates his welcome *as an infant* and foreshadows the later welcome he will extend to infants (βρέφοι, 18:15) himself. Whatever the purpose of his visit, then, it is clear the infant Jesus at just one-month of age is clearly welcomed and accepted in the Temple environment.[66]

Luke continues and extends this welcome in his description of the family's annual visit "to Jerusalem for the festival of the Passover" (2:41). In the highlighted account, Jesus is twelve years of age, described as still a "child" (παιδίον, v. 40, 48), expected to show obedience to his earthly parents (v. 51), and continuing to grow in years and wisdom as expected of a child (v. 52). Bovon elaborates, "Unlike a girl, a twelve year old boy is not completely grown, but is indeed at least a παῖς. Whoever places Jesus here at the stage of adulthood misses precisely the point: even as a child, Jesus possesses the wisdom of the great ones."[67] Bovon is accurate in assessing the likely intention of the Lukan author; however, when examined with an aim toward locating the place of children in the text, the shadows of a likely unintentional, but even more basic point begin to peek through. That a child, even of twelve, takes part in the Passover celebrations, is welcomed in the Temple, and is listened to long enough for the teachers to notice his remarkable understanding (v. 47) speaks to the typical inclusion and acceptance of children in Jewish religious life.

Jewish children were present at and accepted in the Temple.[68] The Temple teachers' amazement at what Jesus knows, of course, suggests that the typical child would not have been expected to possess his degree of religious knowledge. However, that these teachers accept Jesus' presence as a child points to this presence as a norm. Moreover, that the teachers proceed to listen to Jesus long enough to note his exceptional knowledge demonstrates an openness to at least some contribution from children. The Temple teachers are able to marvel at Jesus' wisdom because they are first open to hear the voice of a child.

What is more, Luke's narrative never implies that such inclusion should be thought of as unique to children twelve years or older either. Older commentaries, such as Joseph Fitzmyer's, based upon later Mishnaic traditions set down far after Luke's gospel, focus on the twelfth year as a coming of age for Jesus. From this emphasis it is possible to infer that this may have been Jesus' first pilgrimage to Jerusalem, representing a coming of age within his Jewish community as he began to assume covenantal responsibility. However, even Fitzmyer recognizes that since "there was no obligation for women or children to participate in this pilgrim feast (see *M. Hagiga* 1:1) The fact that Luke depicts Mary and Jesus together accompanying Joseph to Jerusalem is part of the Temple piety that pervades the infancy narrative in general."[69]

Law did not require the pilgrimage of women and children to Jerusalem for the Passover; however, it did not forbid it either. Hagith Sivan, an expert in Jewish Antiquity, goes even further to suggest without specification of gender that during the time of the Second Temple, "Jewish children were initiated into Temple cult and ideology during one of the annual pilgrimage festivities."[70] Given the connection that Sivan later draws between such initiation and the later initiation of children into post-Temple Judaism through synagogue participation, it is likely that she also assumes a much younger age of first exposure. In this broad sense, participation in the Temple ritual can be understood as an integral part of what it meant to be socialized in as a Jewish child in the Second Temple period.

The close company that young children kept with their nurses and mothers as their primary caregivers may also have necessitated such early inclusion at the Temple. Courtyards reserved solely for women architecturally attest to the common participation of women in Temple life. The participation of women in the Passover pilgrimage is further indicated by the "women who were beating their breasts and wailing for him [Jesus]" (23:27) and the presence of "the women who had followed him from Galilee" (23:49) at Jesus' crucifixion, which occurred during the Passover festival. The presence of both women and children in Jerusalem for festal celebrations can also be inferred, despite Peter's patriarchal address to the Jewish pilgrims in Acts 2:5–36, by his citation of Joel's prophecy that "your sons and your daughters shall prophesy, and your young men shall see visions . . . Even upon my slaves, both men and women, in those days I will pour out my Spirit; and they shall prophesy" (Acts 2:17–18). And, indeed, by Peter's baptismal assurance, "For the promise is for you, for your children, and for all who are far away, everyone whom the Lord our God calls to him" (Acts 2:39).

While it is not clear what age range Jesus means to specify, when one takes a broader understanding of Jesus' disciples to include small children, Jesus' reproach to his disciples while in Jerusalem that "the greatest among you must become like the youngest" can also be read to confirm the presence of children in Jerusalem for the Passover (Lk 22:26). Indeed, Fitzmyer's justification of Mary's presence in light of Temple piety seems to suggest a continual participation of Mary and the child Jesus in Temple festivals. This is highlighted by the infant Jesus' presence at his mother's purification in the Temple when he is only a month of age, despite the fact that this ritual was not even directly required by the law. That their presence does not draw any special note only serves to highlight the likelihood that, albeit not required, the presence of women and children during festal pilgrimages was not uncommon.

Removed from assumptions drawn from later regulations and tradition, the casual narration of the annual pilgrimage as Luke presents it assumes that the boy Jesus would have been present with his parents on their previous Passover pilgrimages to Jerusalem as well. Nothing in the narrative sets this pilgrimage up as unique, giving no indication that this year was to be understood as special or Jesus' first pilgrimage.[71] This can be inferred from the distributive use of κατα and the corresponding iterative force of ἐπορεύοντο v. 41 that point towards this family journey as a routine action.

That the Passover celebration itself is a family affair is apparent from the Torah appointment of the festivals for all the people of Israel (Lev 23:37–38) as well as later traditions of observance. Fitzmyer explains that the feast of

Passover "was the feast when the Passover lamb, slain in the late hours of 14 Nisan (i.e. in the afternoon), was roasted and eaten in a family circle at sundown."[72] As such, women and children who did not complete the Jerusalem pilgrimage were still expected to celebrate the feast. The book of Exodus records, "That was for the LORD a night of vigil, to bring [the people of Israel] out of the land of Egypt. That same night is a vigil to be kept for the LORD by *all the Israelites* throughout their generations" (12:42, emphasis added). The Passover is prescribed as a celebration for "the whole congregation of Israel" to eat together in their homes (Ex 12:43–50).

While familial piety may have dictated who made the pilgrimage to Jerusalem, it is clear that the Passover was a family event in which children were included. Moreover, the Temple piety of Jesus' family, established earlier in Luke's account, suggests the regular participation of Jesus in the Temple pilgrimage from a young age. Given the unremarkable nature with which Luke narrates such piety, it is not a great leap to further assume that Jesus would have been accompanied by other children in this trip. Indeed, such an assumption is confirmed by the need for Joseph and Mary to search for Jesus among the traveling group, within which, given his status as a child, it would not have been unusual for him to have been separated from his parents, walking with his peers instead (Lk 2:44).[73]

In a typical adult-centric pattern, Luke 2:41 narrates only the journey of Jesus' parents to Jerusalem and were the boy not mentioned in v. 43, it would make both grammatical and logical sense to understand the subject of the verb ἀναβαινόντων ("they went up") as referring solely to Jesus' parents. Bovon expounds: "from the beginning Luke neatly keeps parents and child separate: until v. 43b, only Mary and Joseph are active. Of course, Jesus has traveled with them, but he attracts attention as an individual only through his desire to stay in Jerusalem."[74] In line with the overlooked and ubiquitous presence of children in the first century world, the presence of a child on the pilgrimage only becomes worth noting when that child deviates from the expected obedient norm. The norm, then, to be assumed is that children of various ages, while not required to do so, would have been among the men and women traveling to Jerusalem for the Passover, if for no other reason than that for those for whom it was possible, the Passover was a celebration intended to be observed as a family. Indeed, if their mothers made the journey, very small children in particular would have needed to remain in their care.

Hence, within the first two chapters of his narrative, Luke sets up an ethos around children that assumes their presence and participation in the general daily life of their families and in the particular religious observances of the Jewish community. Male infants are circumcised at eight days old and are so welcomed into the covenant community. This community is together expected to observe Torah laws and festivals as the whole people of Israel—children and adults. The acceptance of children in such observances, even within the Jerusalem Temple itself, are highlighted in the two vignettes that Luke tells, first of Jesus' journey with his family to the Temple at one-month-old for Mary's purification (and perhaps his own dedication) and second of the family's annual pilgrimage to the Jerusalem Temple, including the child Jesus in every fabric of this event. While the authorial focus is on the novelty of Jesus' reception in these stories—by Anna and Simeon as an infant and by the teachers and elders at the age of twelve—the narrative set up invokes an expectation of a general acceptance of and participation of all children in such rituals as well.

Invisible Presence of Children Throughout Jesus' Adult Ministry

Entering into the broader body of Luke's narrative, such celebration of children quickly shifts into the inclusion of children as recipients of the adult ministry of Jesus. This reading requires greater inferences than in the first two chapters in which one infers the presence and activity of ordinary children from the descriptions of the extraordinary childhoods of John and Jesus who were biologically still children. Retrieving the shadows of children present throughout Luke's narrative in the remainder of the gospel account requires greater attention to not simply the vocabulary of biological immaturity, but to the activities and contexts in which first century children lived their lives.

Children in the Home (οἶκος)

First, the ubiquitous presence of children in the household itself points to their attendance at and consequent reception of the teaching and acts of power that Jesus performed in local houses. Through Jesus' instructions to the apostles whom he sends out ahead of him, as well as through Jesus' practical actions, the Lukan author makes clear that the home (οἶκος) is a primary locus for Jesus' ministry within the narrative.[75] The word οἶκος can be used to refer to both a dwelling structure and those who dwell in it—a household or family. When using it in a locative sense, however, the Lukan author clearly intends the latter. As already established, first century—particularly peasant—homes consisted of very tight living corridors. It would have been impossible to exclude children from these venues, even if they were expected (as they surely were) to primarily serve and be silent when a guest was invited into the house.

Luke's gospel alludes to the close presence of children in Galilean homes through the first example Jesus gives regarding perseverance of prayer: "Suppose one of you has a friend, and you go to him at midnight and say to him, 'Friend, lend me three loaves of bread; for a friend of mine has arrived, and I have nothing to set before him.' And he answers from within, 'Do not bother me; the door has already been locked, *and my children are with me in bed*; I cannot get up and give you anything'" (Lk 11:5–7, emphasis added). Due to the size of homes and cultural expectations, especially with regard to infants prior to weaning, parents and children would frequently sleep together in the first century Mediterranean context. Indeed, it was not uncommon for whole families to share a bed. Similar constraints applied to other living spaces as well, such that children and adults were rarely segregated in the ancient family home. Given the close quarters of these living arrangements, children would have been among those who heard and witnessed Jesus' ministry from within the home.

In the context of their household, children were used to hearing stories performed for both education and entertainment.[76] Dwelling in close quarters with the rest of the household, first century children were accustomed to listening to stories that foregrounded their own interests and those that foregrounded the interests of the adults in the household. Storytelling, far from mere entertainment, was the main vehicle for cultural transmission. As a result, children, who were expected to carry on their household's cultural practices, were exposed frequently to stories. Remarking on the ubiquity of storytelling in the ancient world, Aasgaard observes that families told stories during "family dinners and hours of leisure," "children's bedtime," and even "at places of work."[77] In all of these activities, the boundaries between adult and child space would have overlapped—even with regard to slave children—creating what Aasgaard describes as "multi-age settings, in which stories would float back and forth."[78] Stories with this sort of broad appeal continue in the twenty-first century in wide ranging forms. For examples, traditional fables are still passed on from generation to generation in rural settings, with adult morals embedded in children's stories. In more urban environments, adult humor is hidden in animated movies in order to maintain the interest of multiple generations. Within the multi-age context of the first century household, Jesus' teachings, while primarily directed to the adults in the household, would have been received within this range of experience. For households who welcomed Jesus, the transmission of his message to their children would have been vital to their long-term support of both his message and ministry. In this context, Luke's audience would have assumed that the teachings and stories of Jesus recounted in the gospel would reach and connect with the children dwelling alongside the adults. Such children, in turn, received Jesus' message in their own ways and through their unique means of perceiving and understanding.

Even when they are not explicitly mentioned, the presence of children can be assumed in much of the ministry that Jesus and his apostles conduct within the home (οἴκος). To begin with, on Jesus' first venture outside of his hometown of Nazareth (where it would have been expected that he stayed in his family home) to Capernaum, Luke gives attention to the detail of where Jesus stays after teaching in the synagogue—at Simon's house (4:38). While the people of Capernaum may have first been made aware of Jesus' presence through his teaching and healing at the synagogue, it is to Simon's house that "all those who had any who were sick" bring their friends and family to be healed (Lk 4:40).

In a similar manner, when Jesus sends apostles out to proclaim the message of God's Kingdom he assumes that their ministry will also be located in the context of a family dwelling, or house (οἶκος). This occurs first with the sending of the Gerasene demoniac, whom Jesus instructs, "Return to your home, and declare how much God has done for you" (8:39) and later on a broader scale with Jesus' sending of first the Twelve and then the Seventy (9:1–6; 10:1–20). To the Twelve, Jesus commands, "Whatever house you enter, stay there, and leave from there" (9:4) and to the Seventy he elaborates, "Whatever house you enter, first say, 'Peace to this house!' And if anyone is there who shares in peace, your peace will rest on that person; but if not, it will return to you" (10:5–6). Such a greeting would not have been directed solely at the adult householder, but rather, at the entirety of the household—including its non-adult children.[79] This would have held particularly true for small children who would have been assumed to be in the care of their mothers and female domestic servants within the household and/or expected to perform simple household tasks depending upon their place in and the status of the household.[80] Thus, children would have been at the very nucleus of Jesus' ministry and the proclamation of the Kingdom of God as it spread across Galilee, Judea, and even the Gerasene countryside.

Luke describes this ministry, as experienced in the house (οἶκος), to have consisted primarily of healing and teaching. In his first recorded visit to another's house, Jesus first heals Simon's mother-in-law of a fever, followed by a plethora of healings as the people of Capernaum bring their sick and demon-possessed to Jesus at Simon's home (4:39–41). Given cultural norms for families and households in the first century Mediterranean world, Luke's audience would have likely assumed the presence of children in this and other homes. Indeed, the social and practical value of children combined with high infant mortality rates in antiquity led to an increase birth rate, such that Amram Tropper, studying the demographics of Jewish antiquity, concludes, "the young . . . were the largest segment of the population" and "greatly outnumbered the elderly."[81]

Thus, it is a likely inference that children, either from Simon's marriage or his extended family, would have resided in his home and witnessed this healing. Moreover, even if Simon's house conspicuously lacked children, the fact that Luke emphasizes that *all* who had *any* sick came to Jesus suggests that children, considered particularly vulnerable because of the propensities for childhood illness (contributing to the high infant mortality rates mentioned above) would have been among the totality of the sick described in this verse. Lacking any clear indication of their absence, the Lukan author thus seems to have assumed the presence of children—and likely in great multitude—among many of the first people whom Jesus healed, taught, and from whom he cast out demons in Capernaum.

Nor are Jesus' healings in Capernaum an isolated event. As residents and guests of the houses that Jesus visits, children continue to show up behind the adult-centered narrative that Luke weaves up through the very end of the narrative. Most obviously, the theme of Jesus' ongoing ministry based out of the home (οἶκος) resurfaces at the homes of Martha and Mary (10:38–42), Zacchaeus (19:1–10), and the disciples on the road to Emmaus (24:29–31). In each instance, although these narratives are commonly read with the assumption that the residents of these homes are limited to the named individuals in the account, this would have been exceedingly unlikely given the economy of first century Palestine.

In contrast, Santiago Guijarro draws upon literary, historical, and sociological evidence from first century Galilee to suggest that depending upon social status and wealth, a typical household would be classified as large, multiple, nucleated, and scattered.[82] Based on Luke's description, Guijarro extrapolates that at least five of the twelve apostles would have belonged to this type of larger household. These consisted of a greater number of relatives, potentially with closer socio-economic ties.[83] However, whether large or small, Guijarro concludes that "family was the basic reference of the individual and channel through which he or she was inserted into society."[84]

As such, even smaller homes, providing dwelling for either a nucleated household, consisting of a conjugal couple and their offspring, or a scattered household, consisting of a looser grouping of relatives often due to the loss of the nuclear family from death (fathers, being much older at the time of marriage, frequently left widows and children) or divorce, would have provided shelter for a handful of people, likely of varying ages. Hence, the presence of children would have been assumed to continue to be norm. Moreover, there are narrative clues that suggest Mary herself may be a child in this episode, including: the designation of the home as belonging to a woman (γυνή) Martha (10:38); mentioning Mary only as her sister, with no indication of ownership or maturity; and Mary's seated stance before Jesus, calling to mind the boy Jesus in the Temple seated among the elders (Lk 2:46).[85]

In addition, to these direct references to Jesus' ministry within the home, or household (οἶκος), it is likely that Jesus' healing of a paralytic man lowered down by friends through a roof occurred in a home as well (Lk 5:18–19). Since Luke does not specify the kind of dwelling Jesus was teaching in when this man and his friends approached, it is possible that the locale might have been a synagogue or other public gathering place. However, given the centrality of homes in Jesus' ministry, the preponderance of open-air public gatherings (even for synagogues) in first century villages, and the typical structure of multiple-storied homes with access to the roof from the outside, it is likely that here as at Simon's house, a multitude of people have sought Jesus out at the home in which he has made his base of ministry in this city. In such a household setting, children from the hosting household itself as well as from the surrounding cities and countryside would have had the opportunity to witness and participate in Jesus' ministry.

Children in the Temple and Synagogues

Second, attention must be given to the place of children in religious gathering places, such as the Temple and synagogues that Jesus visited. Although the house served as the home base of Jesus' ministry, Luke's gospel contains the most abundant references to Jesus teaching and healing in religious gathering places—the Jerusalem Temple and community synagogues. Jesus' presence at the Temple "among the teachers, listening to them and asking them questions" when he was twelve years old (Lk 2:46) has already been noted above. Given the teachers' acceptance of the boy Jesus in this capacity and the welcome of children in the Temple, it is likely that there may have been other children among this group—listening to the teachers together with Jesus, albeit not asking questions or offering answers that conveyed the same understanding about which the people were amazed (2:47).

After this youthful experience at the Temple, although Jesus' family's tradition of an annual pilgrimage would suggest that Jesus visited the Temple many more times in the intervening years, Luke jumps ahead to describe Jesus' interactions in the Temple during the last days of his life and ministry. Luke first places the adult Jesus in the Temple again after entering Jerusalem for the Passover festival in an aggressive scene in which "he entered the temple and began to drive out those who were selling things" (19:45). Once more, the social context suggests that children in the Temple would have borne witness to these events, especially in the exterior courtyards of the Temple where commerce took place. Given the role of children helping their parents in the marketplaces, it is likely that child merchants were among those whom Jesus drove out of the Temple.

After this, Luke reports that Jesus was "teaching the people in the temple" (Lk 20:1) and again, "Every day he was teaching in the temple . . . And all the people would get up early in the morning to listen to him in the temple"

(Lk 21:37–38). It is significant here that the word used for "people" is λαὸς, which defined as "people, in a general sense; the mass of a community as distinguished from interest groups; a body of people with common cultural bonds and to a specific territory" and, in more specific use, "people of God."[86] Luke's choice of words make no patriarchal allusion to a male-only gathering, for example, of "brothers," but instead, emphasizes in hyperbole the presence of the *"all"* the populace (πᾶς ὁ λαὸς) at the Temple—a social and cultural grouping that would certainly have included children. This is a theme that continues in Acts, where the Lukan author describes the early Christians (many of whom converted by the households which typically included children) to have "spent much time together in the temple" (Acts 2:46). Luke depicts the Temple and its courtyards as a communal place of gathering—one that had no reason to exclude children, but rather, would have welcomed them out of necessity and as a means of socialization in the Temple cult.

Nor does Luke assume that this mass of people just happens to be milling about at the Temple such that they overhear Jesus' teaching. Instead, the action of the sentence is placed with the people themselves—all of whom are said to get up early in the morning to listen to Jesus. Although Luke does not intend to signal any particular member of this populace out, a reader with an eye for the remnants of children in Luke's telling might begin to picture a small boy or girl enthusiastically rising before the break of dawn to complete his or her morning chores—perhaps fetching water for the family—in order to hurry, just a little bit behind the grown-ups who have left already in order to hear what new words this strange teacher, Jesus, might have to share that day. In the courtyards of the Temple, therefore, children of first century Jerusalem—and those who joined their parents in the Passover pilgrimage there—begin to emerge from the shadows of Luke's adult-centered narrative as eager and active participants, exposed to Jesus and his teachings and, at times, actively seeking him out.

A similar transformation occurs when one examines Jesus' teaching ministry in the synagogues. The life of the first century Jewish community was centered on the synagogue, which encapsulated "the political, liturgical, social, educational, judicial, and spiritual" aspects of life within a single gathering.[87] Not surprisingly within this context, Luke tells us that Jesus' custom was to go to the synagogue of whatever town or village he was in on the Sabbath day (Lk 4:15). Throughout Luke's gospel account Jesus is found teaching and healing in synagogues throughout Galilee and Judea (see Lk 4:31–37; 4:43–44; 6:6; 13:10; and possibly 5:17–19). What is often overlooked in contemporary readings of these encounters, however, is the presence of the whole of the Jewish community—adults and children—at the synagogue as this social center.

Josephus describes this communal aspect of the synagogue in his record of the decree of the Sardinians regarding the Jews, "that a place may be given them where they may have their congregations, *with their wives and children*, and may offer, as did their forefathers, their prayers and sacrifices to God" (emphasis added).[88] In this way, the local synagogues served a central role in the maintenance of Jewish identity and culture across generations.[89] Describing the function of the synagogues in the period immediately following the destruction of the Second Temple, in which Luke-Acts was composed, Sivan explains,

> A book (the Bible), a congregation, and an assembly house (the synagogue) provide a primary scheme that frames Jewish childhood in antiquity . . . Together they account for the social experience and acculturation of children into a society governed by communal prayers, festivities, synagogal gatherings, and rules harking back to Scripture.[90]

Children in this period learned what it meant to be Jewish through their affiliation with their Jewish household, as described in the previous section, but also by attending a synagogue with their household.[91] Hence, Sivan continues, "As centers of sociability, these synagogues played a role that was far from trivial in determining Jewish identity from infancy via adolescence to adulthood."[92] Because culture is shared across generations and parents desired to socialize their children into their culture, children were introduced to and incorporated into the life of the synagogue from a very young age.

The synagogue was the primary place to which Jewish children were brought to learn the Law of God, and, in all likelihood, accounted for the majority (if any) literacy education that a common Jewish child would receive as well. "One late rabbinic tradition speaks of 480 synagogues in pre-70 Jerusalem, each of which had a primary school and an advanced school."[93] Although this number is likely formalized and exaggerated, the fact that Jewish children, especially boys, were educated in the Torah is well attested—often with the expectation that both parents would attend synagogue with their children.[94]

This expectation comes straight from Jewish Scripture with many commandments summarized in the exhortation of Deuteronomy 11:19 to "Teach [the laws] to your children, talking about them when you are at home and when you are away, when you lie down and when you rise." In his letter to the Romans, Paul affirms the continued commitment among Jewish communities to teach children as a part of the faithful living out of the law, critiquing those who may not always live out the law in its fullness themselves and yet call themselves a "teacher of children," literally, διδάσκαλον νηπίον—teacher of *infants* (Rom 2:20).[95] The religious education of children was in many ways central to the Jewish life and as such children were embedded in the communal framework of the synagogue.

Moreover, children were not simply expected to attend the synagogue or to receive a specialized separate instruction apart from the adults. Children were expected to pay attention and participate in the Sabbath services. Philo recounts, regarding the Sabbath: "For that day has been set apart to be kept holy and on it they [all the Israelites] abstain from all other work and proceed to sacred spots which they call synagogues [συναγςγαί]. There, arranged in rows according to their ages, the younger below the elder, they sit decorously as befits the occasion with attentive ears."[96] In each of these synagogues that Jesus visited and proclaimed the message of God's kingdom, often performing healing signs of God's reign, Jewish children would have been there, receiving and internalizing his words and actions along with their adult counterparts. Indeed, as members of the covenant community and the people of God, children actively witnessed and participated in the synagogue service.

A second century account speaks to this when it "notes that the synagogue community of Tarbant dismissed one R. Simeon when the latter proved unwilling to comply with their requests: "The villagers said to him: 'Pause between your words [either when reading the Torah or rendering the *targum*], so that we may relate this to our children.'"[97] Likewise, Tractate Soferim relates:

> If he [the reader of Lamentations on Tish'a b'Av] knows how to translate it, this is preferred, and if not, he gives it to someone who knows how to translate it well, and he translates so that the rest of the people [i.e., the men] and women and children will understand. . . . And that is the reason it was said, "He who recites the blessing must raise his voice for the benefit of his sons, his wife, and his daughters."[98]

The presence of children in the synagogues was not enough. Their understanding was sought and expected. Levine further signals an alternate translation of this same text in which the request was made "so that they [i.e., our children] may recite this material to us."[99]

This attention to children in the life of the synagogue reflected the status of children in the covenant community as well as the commands of the Torah to educate children in the Law. Josephus prescribes, "Again the Law . . . orders that they [i.e., the children] shall be taught to read and shall learn both the laws and the deeds of their forefathers, in order that they may imitate the latter, and, being grounded in the former, may neither transgress nor have any excuse for being ignorant of them."[100] Given the perennial presence of children in the synagogues, that a similar expectation that such children be given opportunity to understand the happenings of the synagogues would have also existed in the first century during Jesus' lifetime seems a likely conjecture. Children played an active role in the life of the synagogue.

Such activity even extended to verbal participation in the service. "Regarding the question as to who should respond 'Amen' in synagogues where all the men were priests and therefore recited the priestly blessing, it was decided that it should be answered by the women and children present."[101] Although the formal practice of communal prayer in the synagogues was not fully established at the beginning of the first century, the rapid movement into such practice by all in attendance again indicates the deep-rooted place of children of all ages in the community synagogue.

More formally, this could be seen in the participation of Jewish boys in the central part of the service—the reading of the Torah. The Mishnah records that "a child could read from the Torah or the prophets at the synagogue service."[102] When Jesus reads from Isaiah in Luke 4:16–20, therefore, it is likely this is not the first time that the people of his hometown have heard him read in the synagogue. This may have been a regular activity of his as a child—the young person they knew to be "Joseph's son" (v. 22).

What is unusual, of course, comes later in Jesus' proclamation that this prophecy of reversal is now fulfilled—a theme that will be revisited in chapter five. In the meantime, for the purpose of bringing the role of children in the synagogues out of the shadows, it is worthwhile to pause on this first recognition and to recognize in it a broader awareness and acceptance of the participation of ordinary children in the life of the synagogue. With this image in mind, the synagogues in which Jesus preached come to life not as stale gatherings of old men and religious leaders, but as bustling centers of life and activity within the communities he visited. These communities would have been naturally populated by the faithful of all ages, with youth serving at the *bima*, reading from the scrolls, and even the smallest children gathered to hear the words of the teachers.

Children Among the Crowds and in the Public Sphere

Third, children can be seen in the streets, outdoor marketplaces, and other public venues in which the proclamation of God's Kingdom was spread by the testimony of John, his disciples, and Jesus' own acts of healing and preaching. The public presence of children in first century cities and villages has already been elaborated above. In light of archaeological and literary evidence, McWilliam summarizes, "Children were very much a part of public life in Rome and in their local towns and communities. They attended the baths [and] experienced life in and around the forum and other public buildings."[103] Children were present in the towns, at the docks, and in the markets, sometimes accompanying their parents and often in groups of other children or on their own. They performed such actions as observing, working, and even playing in this public space.[104]

Although the portrait of children's life in the first century certainly indicate, "Children here may have had less time to play and spent more time generally helping the household survive," based on the presence of toys in various arenas, Mary Harlow concludes, "In all these [public and private] spaces, and on streets and in fields, children presumably played."[105] Children in first century Palestine were ubiquitous—present in nearly every venue of life.

Luke's gospel confirms the known presence of children in the marketplace, recounting Jesus's lament, "To what then will I compare the people of this generation, and what are they like? They are like children sitting in the marketplace and calling to one another, 'We played the pipe for you, and you did not dance; we wailed, and you did not weep'" (7:31–32). Veiled in biting critique of the current generation's (ironically, not excluding children themselves) failure to respond to the ministrations of either John the Baptist or Jesus, this lament inadvertently shines a light into a lived activity of real children as Luke and his intended audience would have known them.

Children could be found amusing themselves, and perhaps others, in the public marketplaces either "with parents nearby selling their wares or with the children being alone, calling out to their friends."[106] Such a picture is not intended to supply an idyllic image of children's lives as careless and free in the first century, or of any particular sentimentalization of the children who performed such activities, but rather, to present a realistic picture of the visibility children would have had in the public sphere in Jesus' society.[107] In fact, returning again to the demographic estimates, children may have even dominated certain public spaces.

In first century Palestine, as in other societies with a high infant mortality rates and increased vulnerability for sickness and death during early childhood, a greater number of births were necessary in order to sustain and grow an adult population. As a result, person for person, there were many more children among the crowds of people whom Jesus met than one might typically encounter in a public crowd today. Demographer Tim Parkin estimates that "in an ancient society roughly one-third of the population would have been under the age of fifteen years at any one time; the comparable figure today in the developed world is more like 19 percent."[108]

Although adults may not have written or spoken much about children, they could not have avoided recognizing their presence. In order to account for the increased likelihood of death throughout childhood, it was not uncommon for one couple to have multiple children in hopes that one or more would survive to adulthood. As a result, children outnumbered adults in the first century Mediterranean world. Amram Tropper writes,

Although the magnitude of the children's population did not necessarily translate into a higher public visibility for children, the sheer numbers of young people must have influenced society in various ways. Children in urban areas probably enjoyed large peer groups consisting of many potential friends while adults would have been forced to constantly consider the needs of the younger generation as well as the challenges they might pose to the traditional order.[109]

Children were, in short, a silent, yet constant presence. Parkin elaborates on the implications of this increased presence by drawing on the reflections of social historian and demographer Peter Laslett, about whom Parkin writes, although he describes a later era,

> ... his words bring to my mind, inter alia, scenes from Roman sarcophagi or even the Ara Pacis (cf. Dixon 1992: 177, plate 16; Huskinson 1996: 140, plate 4.4; see also Larsson Lovén in this volume): "In the pre-industrial world there were children everywhere; playing in the village street and fields when they were very small, hanging around the farmyards and getting in the way, until they had grown enough to be given child-sized jobs to do . . . ; forever clinging to the skirts of women in the house and wherever they went and above all crowding round the cottage fires . . . The perpetual distraction of childish noise and talk must have affected everyone almost all the time."[110]

Taking a step back from the adult-centric view of Jesus' ministry, influenced by authorial bias, a vision of an ancient world teeming with children begins to emerge.

Moreover, these children were not simply playing games and relying on their parents for their every need, as contemporary children and youth are often caricatured by the media. Rather, children then (as now) were a part of every aspect of society—concomitantly passive receivers at the margins of adult status and volition and active participants, forming their own alliances and abilities. Their parents provided them the necessary means and training to work according to their skill, loosely supervised their games within the space of the community, and accepted their presence as necessary and active members of the farms and towns in which they lived.

Children did not simply loiter in the public sphere, their presence carried meaning. From a child's perspective, such meaning may have been perceived more indirectly—in terms of their relationships and activities themselves. From an adult perspective, however, parents, employers, and slave owners all had clear expectations about what the children under their charge would accomplish, ranging from helping with simple tasks at the market, learning a craft by apprenticeship, running errands, providing a service, and/or receiving socialization into their role and place in society.

One of the most ready, though distasteful, examples of this is the case of child prostitution. Reflecting on the practice of child prostitution, Werner Krenkel notes, "Slave boys were sent out to attract customers, especially in harbor towns where they swarmed the dock like flies (Plautus, *The Little Carthaginian [Poenulus]* 688–691): they roamed cities (Seneca the Younger, *Dialogues* 1.5.3) and infested baths (Pliny the Elder, *Natural History* 33.40)."[111] Such slaves, present to serve the clear aims of their masters, were at the same time interacting with, learning from, and in their own ways changing the environment and community with which they came into contact. Children, even slave children, were not merely passive receivers of society, but active and members (albeit marginally) of it.

As Krenkel's description so vividly paints, children were everywhere. The sheer demographic numbers discussed above make certain of this. More innocuously than the presence of child prostitution, children were an assumed part of everyday aspects of public life in the early Christian Mediterranean world.[112] In *Acts of Paul and Thecla* 2:2 the children of Onesiphorus are mentioned by name as Simmias and Zeno and later addressed alternately as τέκνοις (2:2; 23:4) and παῖδες (23:2, 3, 5) indicating their youth. In this text, Simmias and Zeno are depicted as participating in a fast with Paul and their father and participating in the marketplace when they are sent to buy bread (23:4). In the same apocryphal text, other children are depicted as resisting Paul's message when "boys and maidens brought wood and hay to burn Thecla" (παῖδες και αἱ παρθένοι, 22:1). In the apocryphal acts νεανίσκοι figure prominently as messengers and laborers (*Acts of John* 19:7; 48:2; 49:1; 50:3; 53:1; 54:2–5; 71:1; 73:1, 4; 75:1–2; 76:3; 79:3; 86:2; 111:3–6), as sailors (*Acts of Andrew and Matthew* 6:1; 7:10; 22:8), as well as recipients of miraculous healing (*Acts of John* 47:1–3; *Acts of Philip* 4:2; 5:3; 29:1) and even teachers (*Acts of Philip* 143:2; *Acts of Thomas* 154:11). Jesus is even mistaken himself for a little child (παιδίον, *Acts of John* 88:4) and appears in the form of a small child (μικρῷ παιδίῳ, *Acts of Andrew and Matthew* 18:5; 43:1; παιδίῳ, *Acts of Peter and Andrew* 2:1; 16:1). In these early Christian communities, the presence of children was ubiquitous. Even from the margins, unable to participate in the Roman senate or join certain associations, children were both influenced by and themselves influenced the communities in which they lived. In short, children—slave and free, at work and at play—permeated the towns and spaces in which Jesus moved and preached as (limited) agential individuals included in them.

Consequently, when the Lukan author refers to Jesus teaching as "the crowd was pressing in on him" (Lk 5:1) or "with a great multitude of people from all Judea, Jerusalem, and the coast of Tyre and Sidon" (6:17), it is justifiable to assume that there were children thronged among them. John's interpretation of the synoptic feeding narratives (cf. Lk 9:1–7) brings this assumption to light by recounting the acquisition of the loaves from "a boy with five small barley loaves and two small fish" (Jn 6:9). Here, as in the Lukan reference to children in the marketplace, the emphasis is placed not on the child, but on how this child and his ordinary activities might provide an opportunity for the extraordinary revelation of God's Kingdom. However, John's passing reference to this child, together with Matthew's clarification to the Markan and Lukan accounts that "The number of those who ate was about five thousand men, besides women and children" (Matt 14:21) clearly indicates a culturally assumed presence of children in such crowds.[113] This combined witness leaves little doubt to the fact that a Lukan audience and the Lukan author himself, coming from a similar point of cultural reference, would have assumed, if not counted on, the presence of children among the crowds in the feeding account. And if children are assumed in this crowd, then they would have been similarly expected elsewhere when the multitudes flock to and surround Jesus as he heals and teaches.

In light of this unspoken presence, one can and should read again varied accounts of Jesus' activity in the public sphere in a new light—recognizing the dynamic composition of each crowd as including, indeed, teeming with children of all ages.[114] Although often the "crowds" are defined simply as such, the significance of those places in which Luke refers in exaggerated measure to "all the people" or "all the surrounding country" (Lk 3:21; 4:14; 7:29; etc.) as moments where the shadows of children begin to peek through should not be dismissed too lightly.

Indeed, in Lk 7:23, Jesus sends John's disciples with the message, "And blessed is *anyone* who takes no offense at me" (emphasis added), and given the blessings that Jesus bestows on the infants and small children later brought into his presence in 18:15–17, there is no reason to believe that such blessing—as with the blessings bestowed upon the crowds at various other points in Jesus' preaching (notably the beatitudes, again as a replication of the blessing given to children in 18:15–17)—is not intended for children as well as adults. In this context, when Jesus concludes his critique of the present generation, begun with a reference to the play of young children (παιδίοις) in 7:32, with the aphorism of 7:35: "Nevertheless, wisdom is vindicated by all its children" (πάντων τῶν τέκνων) the "all" preceding τῶν τέκνων as a non age-specific term for children, or descendants, takes on particular meaning in pointing to *all* the children of wisdom included in the generation to whom Jesus is preaching and ministering—whatever their age.

Luke's intertextual use of the prophet Jonah[115] provides another opportunity to glimpse the hidden children behind an otherwise adult-centered presentation of the crowds. In Luke 11:29–32, Jesus says, again to the crowds, "This generation is an evil generation; it asks for a sign, but no sign will be given to it except the sign of Jonah. For just as Jonah became a sign to the people of Nineveh, so the Son of Man will be to this generation" (Lk 11:29–30).

While interpreters might argue for ambiguity in Jesus' intended audience (adult or otherwise) with regard to such proclamations, the author of Jonah leaves no room for ambiguity in the definition of the people with whom Luke's Jesus compares his audience. After Jonah brings the word of God to the people of Nineveh, the book continues:

> And the people of Nineveh believed God; they proclaimed a fast, and everyone, great and small (קָטָן), put on sackcloth. When the news reached the king of Nineveh, he rose from his throne, removed his robe, covered himself with sackcloth, and sat in ashes. Then he had a proclamation made in Nineveh: "By the decree of the king and his nobles: No human being or animal, no herd or flock, shall taste anything. They shall not feed, nor shall they drink water. Human beings and animals shall be covered with sackcloth, and they shall cry mightily to God. All shall turn from their evil ways and from the violence that is in their hands. Who knows? God may relent and change his mind; he may turn from his fierce anger, so that we do not perish" (Jonah 3:5–9).

With even the animals included in the fast, there is little question as to whether or not every resident of Nineveh, from the oldest to the youngest, also partook.

The Hebrew root word קטן that the NRSV translates as "small" literally means "small" or "insignificant." Typically in the Hebrew Bible this term applies to those who are insignificant in terms of social status, often the poor or socially marginalized. However, the term also appears occasionally with reference to youth, used frequently to "indicate the youngest child in the family or comparative smallness" and "can suggest a child by modifying age-ambiguous nouns."[116] Together with its antonym גדול, as it is presented in Jonah 3:5 is frequently translated "young and old." No serious interpreter of Jonah suggests that it is only those short in stature who participate in the king's fast. One rather, reads in these verses the intended inclusivity, which expresses a complete participation of the entire city of Nineveh—from the lowliest to the most important.The LXX translation, ἀπὸ μεγάλου αὐτῶν ἕως μικροῦ αὐτῶν ("from the greatest of them to the smallest of them"), confirms this. The root word μικρόν here being the same word used in Luke 9:45, again in comparison with the greatest, but here with a clear reference to small children (cf. Lk 17:2; Acts 8:10; 26:22).

Although these social categories are generally applied solely to adults, there is no reason to assume that they did not include children as well. Moreover, the use of a term that can be translated with reference to children, combined with the indication of *complete* participation of the whole city, suggests the inclusion of children within these categories. This is especially the case since ancient cities, including Nineveh, were teeming with children.

According to this text, children, therefore, regardless of their volition, would have been included in God's judgment—the destruction of the city—just as they participate in the King's fast and repentance and so are included also in God's grace.[117] With reference to Luke's use of this text a similar inclusivity across ages ought also to be assumed.

Applying the wrath of God's judgment to small children feels less comfortable than dwelling on the little children who Jesus calls to himself (Lk 18:15–17) or even allowing for the seemingly innocuous presence of children among the crowds. Nevertheless, this step is just as necessary in removing the characters of children—in their full personhoods—from the shadows of Luke's account and recognizing their *full* inclusion in the mission and ministry of Jesus.

Here the intertexts serve as a helpful bridge. The children of Nineveh were included in the fullness of God's activity among them: receiving judgment, enacting repentance, and ultimately experiencing grace through the forgiveness God offers. It is within this experience of God that Jesus encourages those to whom he is preaching—adults and children—to find themselves. There remains hope that they may yet repent from their wrongdoings and be included in God's grace. In less optimistic portrayals, however, Luke's Jesus goes onto compare the "days of the Son of Man"—the coming judgment—to "the days of Noah" (17:26) and "the days of Lot" (17:27–30). In each of these instances, (all but) complete destruction leaves no question that the non-adult children of these towns and countrysides were included in the divine judgment and destruction.

In the case of Noah, Jesus describes how "the flood came and destroyed all of them" (Lk 17:27). The hope-filled part of the narrative tends to center around the compassion that God shows for Noah and his family: "Then the Lord said to Noah, 'Go into the ark, you and all your household [LXX: οἶκος], for I have seen that you alone are righteous before me in this generation" (Gen 7:1). Although not specifically mentioned one way or another, the description of Noah's household here suggests that any grandchildren (his sons are already adults, as inferred by the presence of their wives) would also have entered the ark at the same time as "Noah with his sons and his wife and his sons' wives" (Gen 7:7). Indeed, the mention of Ham as the father of Canaan (Gen 9:18) and the assumed presence of Canaan given Noah's curse (Gen 9:24–27) following the events that transpire immediately following the family disembarking the ark suggest that at least one non-adult child, Canaan, accompanied Noah and his family onto the ark. The failure to mention him in the formulaic description of their loading and unloading likely reflects a lack of cultural concern for explicitly naming such non-adult children until, as in the case of Canaan, it becomes pertinent to the story—much as is continued in the synoptic gospel accounts. In any case, while the children (either born or unborn) of Noah's nuclear family are included in the experience of God's grace on the ark, the majority of children of all ages who had come to populate the earth in the days of the Nephilim (cf. Gen 6:1–4) are clearly included in what God judges to be "the wickedness of humankind" (Gen 6:5), God's consequent regret "that he had made humankind on the earth" (Gen 6:6), and God's ultimate decision: "I will blot out from the earth the human beings I have created—people together with animals and creeping things and birds of the air, for I am sorry that I have made them" (Gen 6:7). Here, as later in the case of Nineveh, the full inclusion of every living thing on the earth leaves little room to doubt that young children number among them.

Hence, young children died as a part of God's inclusive judgment of humanity when God "blotted out every living thing that was on the face of the ground, human beings and animals and creeping things and birds of the air; they were blotted out from the earth," such that "Only Noah was left, and those that were with him in the ark" (Gen 7:23). Such extreme inclusivity leaves little room to object that children are thus also included in the judgment about which Jesus prophesies in the coming days of the Son of Man. Indeed, few interpreters would suggest that this is not the case.[118] Instead, they simply fail to comment on the fate of children in God's judgment one way or the other.

With regard to Lot's story, Jesus calls to mind the destruction of Sodom (and Gomorrah), similarly comparing the potential to be included in either God's grace or God's judgment on the coming day of the Son of Man to God's provisions for Lot (cf. Lk 17:28–31). In Genesis 19, the ages of Lot's daughters are unnamed. The fact that they "have not known a man" (Gen 19:8) combined with a traditionally early marriage age for females could imply that these girls have not yet reached adulthood. Indeed, the omission of the designation בתולה, a term generally associated with young women who have reached puberty, in describing Lot's daughters might suggest a younger age.[119] If the girls had not yet reached puberty when the Lord rescued them from the destruction of Sodom (cf. 19:15–16) then this would be a clear example of God's mercy extended to Lot's (non-adult) children. Indeed, God extends this mercy to the girls despite their human father's earlier willingness to sacrifice them in favor of the wellbeing of his two biologically mature guests (cf. Gen 19:7–8).

Even if the Lot's daughters are of marriageable age, however, the invitation of Lot's visitors to bring to safety all who are in Lot's household remains an inclusive one—"Then the men said to Lot, 'Have you anyone else here? Sons-in-law, sons, daughters, or anyone you have in the city—bring them out of the place" (Gen 19:12). While not specifically highlighted within the narrative, the children of Lot's household are definitively included in the mercy extended him. In appropriate juxtaposition, then, God's judgment on the inhabitants of Sodom, the men of whom—both "young and old," "small and great" (Gen 19:4, 11)—instigate the initial offense, are summarily consumed in destruction.[120] "Then the Lord rained on Sodom and Gomorrah sulfur and fire from the Lord out of heaven; and he overthrew those cities, and all the Plain, and *all the inhabitants* of the cities, and what grew on the ground" (Gen 19:24–25, emphasis added). As in Nineveh and in the days of Noah, the destruction of every living thing—including all that grew on the ground—make it plain that the non-adult children of these cities were not spared. Children—even the youngest and the smallest—in the days of Lot are portrayed as capable of committing sin, receiving God's mercy, and suffering God's wrath. In every aspect of the covenantal life, children are included. As with the former intertext in Jesus' prophecy, so here children ought to be taken as part and parcel of the judgment Jesus pronounces.

Not surprisingly, the Lukan Jesus' later warnings about eschatological judgment do not exclude children either. When Jesus weeps for Jerusalem in Luke 19:44, he laments that the city's enemies "will crush you to the ground, you and your children [τέκνα] within you." This sentiment reflects the tenor of total annihilation in the previous Scripture references. As such, the more general term for children here includes adult and non-adult children (descendants) of Jerusalem alike. Jesus' warning in Luke 21:35 that the Day of the Lord "will come upon *all who live* on the face of the whole earth" (emphasis added) likewise echoes the inclusivity of the intertextual judgment accounts already brought to mind. No one, not even young children, is excluded from God's judgment on the earth.

The two judgment statements that Jesus addresses specifically to mothers further highlight the complete inclusivity of God's judgment with regard to the young. Prior to his summation about the judgment of all those who live on the face of the earth, Jesus proclaims in the same teaching, "Woe to those who are pregnant and to those who are nursing infants in those days! For there will be great distress on the earth and wrath against this people; they will fall by the edge of the sword and be taken away as captives among all nations; and Jerusalem will be trampled on by the Gentiles, until the times of the Gentiles are fulfilled" (Lk 21:23–24).

Likewise, in the last words of Jesus for the women of Jerusalem prior to his crucifixion, Luke brings the plight of non-adult children into surprisingly sharp sight (this given Luke's shadowy depiction of their presence throughout the bulk of the rest of the gospel account). Luke narrates, as Jesus was carrying his cross toward his execution,

> A great number of the people followed him, and among them were women who were beating their breasts and wailing for him. But Jesus turned to them and said, "Daughters of Jerusalem, do not weep for me, but weep for yourselves and for your children. For the days are surely coming when they will say, 'Blessed are the barren, and the wombs that never bore, and the breasts that never nursed.'" (23:27–29)

Here, despite the use of the age ambiguous term τὰ τέκνα ("children" or "descendants"), the intended inclusion of infants and young children is clear given the imagery of barren wombs and empty breasts.

These verses have often been interpreted as proof-texts for early Christian asceticism. However, when read in the context of Jesus' consistently inclusive judgment announcements, they reflect the broader inclusion of non-adult children in the complete experience of divine mercy—including prerequisite divine judgment from which to contrast it. In this way, these texts stand out as yet another affirmation of a tradition within the Jewish Scriptures that supports the full inclusion of all of God's children, whatever their age, in God's eschatological future.[121]

The canonical gospel accounts were principally intended for adults and composed with this audience in mind.[122] Yet in spite of this, the crowds who thronged around Jesus were just as certainly populated by a large number of children. Consequently, it would be naïve to assume that Jesus' ministry did not impact these children as well.[123] Children lived in the households from which Jesus and his apostles centered their ministry. They attended the synagogues and traveled to the Temple where they heard Jesus proclaim the advent of God's Kingdom. Children, even when not explicitly named, were among those healed, forgiven, taught, and critiqued by Jesus as he moved from town to town and throughout the countryside. When children emerge from the shadows in which Luke and the other synoptic writers, readers, and interpreters have banished them for centuries, a vital and complex picture emerges of the young people with whom Jesus' associated throughout his life.

CONCLUSION

The inclusion and welcome of children in Jesus' circles and among those to whom he ministered is concomitantly unremarkable and monumental. Despite attempts by some Christians to highlight Jesus' welcome of children (particularly in Lk 18:15–17 and its synoptic parallels) as a distinctly Christian act of inclusion, the welcome of children in Jesus' circles is unremarkable in the sense that written and archaeological evidence point rather to a general acceptance of and celebration of children in the first century institutions of family and society.

Nevertheless, recognition of this acceptance among Jesus' first followers and within later Christian circles remains monumental given the virtual invisibility of children in both the gospel accounts and cultural memory of the first century Greco-Roman world at large. It is this invisibility, particularly in the canonical texts, which I would posit has limited the full inclusion and participation of young children in certain contemporary Christian religious activity.

Such invisibility, however, is the result not of a cultural distaste or even ambivalence toward children, either by the first century Greco-Roman world or Jesus' followers. Rather, this invisibility is the symptom of a cultural valuing of the adult experience as primary, resulting in a general passing over of children as independent subjects in narrative treatments.[124] In other words, children were an interwoven part of the fabric and life of society in the first century Greco-Roman world—pagan, Jewish, and Christian—however, due to the social practices of the time, authors rarely thought to mention them.

In the first century Mediterranean world in which Luke's text was composed, the presence of children was assumed and generally ignored. As time passed, children's presence in the gospel narratives consequently proceeded from the marginalized shadows in which they already dwelt into the silence and invisibility to which they are subject in many Christian reading communities today. Through the preceding investigation into the background of children in these cultures and Luke's gospel account—as they are specifically named and voicelessly inferred—my aim has been to (re)claim a voice and vision for children in Luke's narrative and through them, for those children who continue to be impacted by it today. In the following chapters, the place of children will be subsequently (re)claimed through attention to the constructions of childhood and voices of children hidden in the narrative on account of adult dominance and time.

NOTES

1. See Halvor Moxnes, "What is Family? Problems in Constructing Early Christian Families," in *Constructing Early Christian Families: Family as Social Reality and Metaphor*, ed. Halvor Moxnes (London: Routledge, 1997) 2–3: "Since ancient language did not have a word that is equivalent to the modern '(nuclear) family,' it is necessary when studying early Christian texts about 'family' to use various perspectives: household, kinship, marriage, inter-relations between members."

2. This is in contrast to both Pauline and Petrine understandings of the Christian household, wherein a human hierarchy continues, frequently with Paul painting himself in a parental role (See Moxnes, 36).

3. A. James Murphy, *Kids and Kingdom: The Precarious Presence of Children in the Synoptic Gospels* (Eugene, OR: Pickwick Publications, 2013) 34.

4. John M. G. Barclay, "The Family as the Bearer of Religion in Judaism and Early Christianity," in *Constructing Early Christian Families: Family as Social Reality and Metaphor*, ed. Halvor Moxnes (London: Routledge, 1997) 63.

5. Adriana Destro and Mauro Pesce, in "Fathers and Householders in the Jesus Movement: The Perspective of the Gospel of Luke," in *Biblical Interpretation* (January 2003).

6. On nurse maids, see Beryl Rawson, "Children in the Roman *Familia*," in *The Family in Ancient Rome*, ed. Beryl Rawson (New York: Cornell, 1986) 191 and Keith R. Bradley, "Wet-nursing at Rome: a Study in Social Relations," in *The Family in Ancient Rome*, ed. Beryl Rawson (New York: Cornell, 1986) 201–229.

7. Despite prudent historical-critical questions about the feasibility of the Acts community of common good, or even the Lukan author's intent to convey such a community as a standard, from a literary perspective, such an inclusive and encompassing community remains the ideal.

8. See chapter 1 for an in-depth discussion of the language for childhood and markers of childhood in Luke and its surrounding cultures. In what follows, references to children assume non-adult children as defined in this discussion of the Concepts of Children and Childhood in Luke unless otherwise noted.

9. Reidar Aasgaard, *The Childhood of Jesus: Decoding the Apocryphal Infancy Gospel of Thomas* (Eugene, OR: Cascade Books, 2009) 94. See also Ross Kraemer, "Typical and Atypical Jewish Family Dynamics: The Cases of Babatha and Bernice," in *Early Christian Families in Context: an interdisciplinary dialogue*, ed. David Balch and Carolyn Osiek (Grand Rapids: Wm. Eerdmann's, 2003) 131: "Evidence from two Jewish women living within about a century of Jesus suggests that this evidence is generally, if not entirely, consistent with the overall evidence for non-Jewish families in the same period."

10. Suzanne Dixon, *The Roman Mother* (Norman, OK: Oklahoma University Press, 1989) 101.

11. Beryl Rawson, *Children and Childhood in Roman Italy* (Oxford: Oxford University Press, 2003) 111.

12. Janette McWilliam, "The Socialization of Roman Children," in *The Oxford Handbook of Childhood and Education in the Classical World* (Oxford: Oxford University Press, 2013) 267.

13. Rawson, *Children and Childhood in Roman Italy*, 106–108.

14. McWilliam, 268.

15. Even the home itself was not a private sphere in the same way we would consider it according to modern Western sensibilities. For the lower classes, homes were small and crowded and nearly all activities were conducted outdoors and in common in a communal setting. For upper classes, the home was expected to be a

place to receive callers, conduct business, and socialize (see Rawson, *Children and Childhood in Roman Italy,* 269).

16. See Lena Larsson Lovén, "Children and Childhood in Roman Commemorative Art," in *The Oxford Handbook of Childhood and Education in the Classical World*, ed. Judith Evans Grubbs and Tim Parkin (Oxford: Oxford University Press, 2013) 302–321.

17. Warren Carter, *Households and Discipleship: A Study of Matthew 19-20* (Sheffield: Sheffield Academic Press, 1994) 108.

18. See Destro and Pesce, 227–228.

19. Mary Harlow, "Toys, Dolls, and the Material Culture of Childhood," in *The Oxford Handbook of Childhood and Education in the Classical World*, ed. Judith Evans Grubbs, Tim Parkin, and Roslynne Bell (Oxford: Oxford University Press, 2013) 323.

20. Rawson, *Children and Childhood in Roman Italy,* 275.

21. Larsson Lovén, 316.

22. Larsson Lovén, 317.

23. McWilliam, 280: The young age at which children participated in such events is illustrated by "Commodus, aged five, and Marchus Annius Verus, aged four, [who] joined Marcus Aurelius in 166 CE in this Parthian triumph" (280).

24. McWilliam, 280.

25. Wayne A. Meeks, *The First Urban Christians: The Social World of the Apostle Paul* (New Haven: Yale University Press, 1983) 34.

26. Bonnie Miller-McLemore, *Let the Children Come: Reimagining Childhood from a Christian Perspective* (San Francisco: Jossey-Bass, 2003) 99.

27. McWilliam, 228.

28. Carter, *Households and Discipleship,* 112.

29. Miller-McLemore, "Jesus Loves the Little Children?" in *Journal of Childhood and Religion* 1:7 (October 2010) 10.

30. John Dominic Crossan, *The Historical Jesus: The Life of a Mediterranean Jewish Peasant* (New York: Harper Collins, 1991) 269.

31. The pronoun "her" is consciously selected here in order to emphasize the personhood—male or female—of the child as a real individual in the disciples' midst. Grammatically Jesus refers to a specific real child, the term for which happens to take a neuter pronoun in the Greek language. The personhood of this child is consequently diminished by English translations that render the neuter pronoun as "it," a translation which perhaps aid in the ready turn to metaphorical readings that move too quickly from the person of the child to the traits of children that adults who wish to be great in God's Kingdom might seek to emulate.

32. Luke Timothy Johnson, *The Gospel of Luke* (Collegeville, MN: Liturgical Press, 1991) 159.

33. Although the rapid and abbreviated nature of Mark's gospel leaves room the possibility that there are moments when the Twelve are addressed, but a larger discipleship community may be presumed to be listening in without directly mentioning them.

34. In contrast to Mark and Matthew where the term disciple is applied to the Twelve and apostle is reserved for a point after Jesus' resurrection, in Luke, as early as 6:13 the narrator clearly designates the difference between the Twelve, whom Jesus calls apostles, and the larger group from which they were called out of and with which they continue to interact—the disciples. This more expansive use is especially evident in 14:26–33, 19:37, and Jesus' teaching directed to the disciples in Luke 9:18–27, moments which Luke 24:6–8 confirms that the women in Luke 8:1–3, who were not a part of the Twelve apostles, were privy to. More accurately, in Luke the term "disciples" is used to refer to any grouping of more than one of Jesus' followers. In general, the core group of Jesus' disciples are called "the Twelve" or "apostles," while both members (including the Twelve) and the entirety of the larger, more fluid group of people who accompany Jesus in his ministry are referred to as "disciples." Thus, I concur with Green that in Lk 9:1–50, "The fluidity of 'disciples' for Luke is marked here . . . Even though the twelve come in for special development [at points, including 9:47–50], then, we are reminded that they are representative of a larger group who will also be involved in the instruction and formation this narrative unit anticipates" (Joel B. Green, *The Gospel of Luke* [Grand Rapids, MI: Eerdmans, 1997] 354).

35. While some have argued that this divergence indicates a distancing of Luke's Jesus from the child by omitting the more intimate actions of "placing in the midst" or taking "into his arms," I concur with François Bovon that "The reason for this is not a rejection of Jesus' expression of emotion, but rather that Luke is describing a child who can stand, not an infant who must be carried (as in Mark)" (François Bovon, *Luke 1*, trans. Christine M. Thomas [Minneapolis: Fortress Press, 2002] 392).

36. See Sharon Betsworth, *Children in Early Christian Narratives* (London: Bloomsbury T&T Clark, 2015) 123–124; James L. Bailey, "Experiencing the Kingdom as a Little Child: A Rereading of Mark 10:13–16," in *Word and World* 15:1 (Winter 1995) 63.

37. Bovon, *Luke 1*, 394.

38. Bovon, *Luke 1*, fn 45, 395.

39. Bovon, *Luke 1*, 395.

40. Johnson, 107.

41. One significant exception to this practice was the interpretation spearheaded in the mid-twentieth century by scholars such as Joachim Jeremias and Oscar Cullmann. These scholars suggested that Jesus' insistence that one must enter the Kingdom of God "as a little child" is an argument for the place, and indeed, priority of infant baptism. Although the connection between this text and the rite of baptism had been made in liturgical practice since the Reformation, these men brought it to scholarly attention, employing historical critical methods that allowed them to envision an (albeit faint) baptismal vestige. Their claims, however, were too ambitious in scope and have largely been dismissed. Given the preponderance of evidence for adult conversion and believer's baptism in both the early Church synoptic traditions respectively, it is unlikely that such a literal reading is in line with the gospel writer's (or Jesus') original intent. See Joachim Jeremias, *Infant Baptism in the First Four Centuries* (trans. David Cairns; London: SCM Press, 1960) 54–55; Oscar Cullmann, *Baptism in the New Testament* (trans. J. K. S. Reid; London: SCM Press, 1950), 78;

David Wright, *Out, In, Out: Jesus' Blessing of the Children and Infant Baptism* in *Dimensions of Baptism: Biblical and Theological Studies* edited by Stanley E. Porter and Anthony R. Cross (London: Sheffield Academic Press, 2002) 193.

42. Frederick A. Schilling, "What Means the Saying about Receiving the Kingdom of God as a Little Child" in *Expository Times* 77:2 (Nov 1965) 56.

43. See Hans-Ruedi Weber, *Jesus and the Children: Biblical Resources for Study and Preaching* (Atlanta: John Knox Press, 1979); Joseph A. Fitzmyer, *The Gospel According to Luke X–XXIV* (New York: Doubleday, 1983); John T. Carroll, "'What Then Will This Child Become?': Perspectives on Children in the Gospel of Luke," in *The Child in the Bible*, edited by Marcia Bunge, Terence Fretheim, and Beverly Roberts Gaventa (Grand Rapids: Wm. B. Eerdman's, 2008); and Cornelia B. Horn and John W. Martens, *"Let the little children come to me": Childhood and Early Christianity* (Washington, D.C.: Catholic University of America Press, 2009).

44. The notion of children as valuable in themselves is not an innovation of Western culture or of Christianity, but has its roots in the Hebrew Bible itself. What has changed in recent times, however, is the accent that is placed on this value over and against the relative drain that a child would be on the average Western household otherwise.

45. Ronald R. Clark, "Kingdoms, Kids, and Kindness: A New Context for Luke 18:15–17." *Stone-Campbell Journal* 5 (Fall 2002): 240.

46. Clark, 236.

47. See Lester Bradner "The Kingdom and the Child," in *Anglican Theological Review* 3:1 (May 1920); Frederick A. Schilling, "What Means the Saying about Receiving the Kingdom of God as a Little Child." *Expository Times* 77:2 (Nov 1965); Daniel Patte, "Jesus' Pronouncement about Entering the Kingdom Like a Child: A Structural Exegesis" in *Semeia* 29 (1983); Clark; and Horn and Martens.

48. Patte, 34.

49. Horn and Martens, 259.

50. Cited in François Bovon, *Luke* 2, trans. Donald S. Deer (Minneapolis: Augsburg, 2013) fn 40, 559.

51. Bovon, *Luke* 2, 558.

52. Judith M. Gundry, "Children in the Gospel of Mark, with Special Attention to Jesus' Blessing of the Children (Mark 10:13–16) and the Purpose of Mark," in *The Child in the Bible,* ed. Marcia J. Bunge, Terence Fretheim, and Beverly Roberts Gaventa. Grand Rapids: William B. Eerdmans, 2008) 152.

53. Carroll, 190.

54. For use of this term in Luke in correlation with its dictionary form to mean real, non-adult infants under the age of 2 years old, see also: Lk 1:41, 44; 2:12, 16; Acts 7:19. Bovon notes, "The question has been raised as to whether the term 'newborn children' (βρέφη) might not have been a title used for themselves by a group of Christians, for example, some itinerant prophets. According to that theory, the 'disciples' (μαθηταί) stood for ministers of the Great Church, or of the majority community, anxious to maintain their authority and their privileges" (*Luke 2,* 557). While an interesting theory, and one worth exploring on the level of what it would

have meant for adult Christians to place the dependent—or, as I will argue in my conclusion, *interdependent*—label of child upon themselves, it remains at this point solely conjecture. Therefore, in the interest of uncovering the shadows of real children both from behind such possible labels and more immediately, Luke's text as it stands, I read v. 15 to refer to actual, non-adult infants. Further, given the use of the verb προσέφερον and the context of the rest of the passage, I am inclined to agree with Bovon's conclusion that "This would not appear to be the hermeneutical level on which the Gospel writer operated" (*Luke 2*, 557).

55. Robert C. Tannehill, *Luke* (Nashville, Abingdon Press, 1996), 267.
56. Robert C. Tannehill, *Luke* (Nashville, Abingdon Press, 1996), 267.
57. Johnson, 281.
58. Bovon, *Luke 2*, 559.
59. Johnson, 276.
60. This goes further than Bovon who, while reading the text as ultimately referring to the place of children within God's Kingdom, reads Jesus' address to the disciples as a teaching solely intended for adults. Bovon likely does not envision children in Jesus' intended audience because he fails to understand children as a part of Luke's discipleship community from the start. As a consequence, Bovon notes that in this passage "Luke himself runs the risk of neglecting children, whose worth he brings out in other respects" failing to direct Jesus' teaching to the children and instead treating the children as "moving examples" (*Luke 2*, 559). Given my assessment of children within the discipleship community, alluded to already above and explained in depth in chapter three, I avoid this conundrum and suggest that while Luke, in line with the cultural values of the first century, fails to highlight the invisible place of children in the discipleship community, neither does he exclude this possibility. Thus, Lk 18:15–17 remains a consistent example from which readers can reclaim the presence of children within and among the first followers of Jesus.
61. See Destro and Pesce, 228.
62. See Green, *Gospel of Luke*, 651.
63. See Destro and Pesce, 229.
64. Indeed, following Luke's inclusive definition of discipleship, children can and should be read as disciples themselves. I have touched on this point briefly above, but will return to it at length as the topic of chapter three.
65. See Bovon, *Luke 2*, 559, fn 43.
66. For Jesus' age see Leviticus 12:2–4.
67. Bovon, *Luke 1*, 111.
68. See Tannehill, 75.
69. Joseph A. Fitzmyer, *The Gospel According to Luke I-IX* (New York: Doubleday, 1970) 440.
70. Hagith Sivan, "Pictorial *Paideia*: Children in the Synagogue" in *The Oxford Handbook of Childhood and Education in the Classical World*, ed. by Judith Evans Grubbs, Tim Parkin, and Roslynne Bell (Oxford: Oxford University Press, 2013) 532.
71. See Betsworth, 108.
72. Fitzmyer, *Luke I–IX*, 439.

73. Fitzmyer explains, "The noun *synodia* is found only here in the NT; it is used by Epictetus (*Dissertationes* 4.1,91), Josephus (*J. W.* 2.21,1; *Ant.* 6.12,1), and Strabo (*Geography* 4.6, 6) of a group of people traveling together" (*Luke I–IX*, 441).

74. Bovon, *Luke 1*, 111.

75. See Destro and Pesce, 226. Although the role of children is not their focus, it is significant to note that with the possible exception of banquets (at which children while not themselves guests, may still have been present in service positions), each of the categories that Destro and Pesce cite involve at least one child-centered narrative.

76. Aasgaard, 196.

77. Aasgaard, 196.

78. Aasgaard, 196.

79. See Destro and Pesce, 227: "The disciples shall say 'Peace to this οἶκος,' in other words to the group of people who live in the οἰκία." Although they don't specifically deal with the presence of non-adult children, such would be assumed in their three-generation model of the typical household.

80. On the care of Jewish and Greco-Roman free children in the household up to the age of seven, see Horn and Martens, 24; On the typical work of Roman slave children in or near the household, see Nielsen, 288.

81. Amram Tropper, "Children and Childhood in Light of the Demographics of the Jewish Family in Late Antiquity," in *Journal for the Study of Judaism* 37:3 (2006) 342.

82. Santiago Guijarro, "The Family in First century Galilee," in *Constructing Early Christian Families: Family as Social Reality and Metaphor*, ed. Halvor Moxnes (London: Routledge, 1997) 58.

83. Guijarro, 63.

84. Guijarro, 62.

85. See Chapter 4 on Discipleship for an in depth elaboration of this thesis.

86. BDAG, 586.

87. Lee I. Levine, *The Ancient Synagogue: The First Thousand* Years (New Haven: Yale University Press, 2000) 172–173. See also Levine, 144, 169.

88. Josephus, *Antiquities* 14.24, trans. William Whiston.

89. This takes an interesting shape in post-second Temple Judaism, in which several synagogues have been discovered that depart from the austere appearance described above, in which "Within the sanctified space of the synagogue, children were cast as visual archetypes of obedience to parental and divine precepts, reinforcing an orthodoxy anchored in the commonality of language and liturgy. Synagogal pictures of foundational moments featuring children reflect a dialectical relationship with an environment in which Greco-Roman educational practices aspired to groom the young . . . Sounds, images and Scripture engulfed the young within a protective envelope of family and community that came regularly together in the synagogue" (Sivan, 552–553).

90. Sivan, 533.

91. For more on the inclusion of children in the synagogues and their relative availability to the masses, see Horn and Martens, 28.

92. Sivan, 533.

93. Levine, 144. See also Seder Eliyahu Rabbah 11 (pp. 54–55), cited in Levine, 384: "[Regarding] a small town in Israel, they [the townspeople] built for themselves a synagogue and academy and hired a sage and instructors for their children. When a nearby town saw [this], it [also] built a synagogue and academy, and likewise hired teachers for their children." See also Horn and Martens, 34.

94. Levine, 289, citing Gafni: ". . . in speaking of mothers who bring their children to study [in the synagogue], it is the Bavil which notes that their husbands were studying in the academy at the same time." See also Levine, 377–378.

95. See Horn and Martens, 137.

96. Philo, *Every Good Man is Free* 81.

97. Levine, 383.

98. Levine, 502. Tractate Soferim 18.5 (pp. 316–17).

99. Levine, 383, fn 9.

100. Josephus, *Against Apion* 2.204, cited in Levine, 145.

101. Levine, 502; See also Ginzberg, *Commentary*, IV, 279 and Levine, 527.

102. *m. Megillah* 4:5–6, cited in Horn and Martens, 28.

103. McWilliam, 278.

104. Horn and Martens, 169–173, 195.

105. Harlow, "Toys, Dolls, and the Material Culture of Childhood," 323.

106. Horn and Martens, 170; See also Carroll, 191.

107. See William Strange, *Children in the Early Church* (Cumbria, UK: Pater Noster, 1996) 50–51: "Jesus was . . . a realist about human nature; he was equally realistic about the nature of children . . . he knew how children, in their play, act out roles in which they exercise power over others . . . There was . . . no sentimentality in Jesus' view of children."

108. Tim Parkin, "The Demographics of Infancy and Early Childhood in the Ancient World," in *The Oxford Handbook of Childhood and Education in the Classical World*, ed. Judith Evan Grubbs and Tim Parkin (Oxford: Oxford University Press, 2013) 41.

109. Tropper, 330.

110. Parkin, "Demographics," 42.

111. Werner Krenkel, cited in Horn and Martens, 169–170.

112. See Horn and Martens, 181.

113. See Horn and Martens, 264.

114. See units as varied as: Lk 3:3–21 5:1–3, 15; 6:17–7:1; 7:1–10, 11–17, 18–35; 8:1–21, 26–39, 40–56; 9:6, 10–17, 37–43; 11:14–28, 29–36; 12:1–13:9; 13:22–45; 14:25–15:32; 18:35–42; 19:1–27, 36–44; 22:47–23:49; 24:9–11, 13–35, and potentially others. In each of these, children are never named, but can easily be assumed. The agency of the swineherds in 8:34–36 deserves particular consideration in light of the parallels with the young son who is similarly employed feeding pigs in Jesus' parable (15:11–32) discussed below.

115. Here it is necessary to offer a word about intertextuality and how I understand Luke's use of this rhetorical device. Intertextuality is a term that was coined by poststructuralist Julia Kristeva in the 1960s, and as such, it would be anachronistic to say that the Lukan author intentionally employs "intertextuality." At the same time,

the ancient text (along with other texts of its time period) employs references to other texts with a presumed knowledge that such references possess the ability to deepen the experience of the reader by calling this common background to mind. In the broadest sense of the term, Michel Foucault describes the interrelationship of every text with all those texts that have come before it: "The frontiers of a book are never clear-cut: beyond the title, the first lines and the last full stop, beyond its configuration and its autonomous form, it is caught up in a system of references to other books, other texts, other sentences: it is a node within a network" (Michel Foucault, *The Archaeology of Knowledge* (London: Tavistock, 1974) 23. Everything that is written can and does call to mind within individual readers that which they have read or experienced as text before. While I philosophically agree with Foucault's description of the broad sense of interrelation between texts of all kinds, for the purposes of the narrative analysis that I apply to Luke's text, when used within this book, I mean by "intertext" and "intertextuality" the narrower category of pre-extant literary documents either implied, referenced, or directly quoted by the author. In particular, I draw attention to narratives within the Hebrew Bible as intertexts intentionally used by the Lukan author throughout the gospel account as a common document that would have been familiar to much of his ancient audience and continues to be familiar to a large section of his contemporary audience today. Understanding of these texts enables a deepened understanding of Luke's narrative and in some cases presents the reader with feasible options by which to fill the gaps in the gospel narrative itself, with particular attention to how this relates to one's understanding of children within each text.

116. Parker, 52.

117. It is worth struggling with the concept of small children, especially infants "fasting" here. Given the dependence of children on the household as a provision of security and food, it may not be fair to describe what would likely have been, for them, a deprivation of food by order of the head of the household and executed by its women and servants as a conscious religious activity. This deserves particular caution in light of present day situations of child abuse and neglect perpetrated in the name of religion. At the same time, however, it is worth questioning the degree to which the entire city—under a parallel order of the patriarchal king—was truly able to exercise volition in this fast. Consequently, the example of Nineveh remains for me an example (albeit a troubled one) of the interdependent experiences of both adults and children together in relation to the judgment and grace of an almighty God.

118. A notable exception to this is proponents of a rapture theology. Such scholars typically acknowledge that the Bible is unspecific on this point, but based upon a belief in God's grace, argue for an age of accountability at which point a child is able to accept Christ, and before which, small children—whether of believers or unbelievers—would be included among the raptured in God's judgment.

119. Although the translation of this term has been the cause of some controversy due to its connection with prophecies about Jesus' birth from a "virgin," some translators to continue to render it thusly. Peggy Day argues "that a בתולה may have had sex since the explanatory qualifier 'did not know a man' accompanies the designation of בתולה in Gen 24:16 and Judg 21:12 (see also Gen 19:8; Judg 11:39). Day further posits that a בתולה has reached puberty but has yet to become a mother" (Peggy L. Day,

"From the Child is Born the Woman: The Story of Jephthah's Daughter," in *Gender and Difference in Ancient Israel*, ed. Peggy L. Day [Minneapolis: Augsburg Fortress, 1989], cited in Parker, 58.) See Parker, 58 for a discussion of the merits of translating the term as a young woman of marriageable age. A counter argument against a pre-pubescent age, however, could be made based upon the subsequent pregnancies of both daughters, although a precise timeline of their stay in the cave is not given (see Gen 19:30–38).

120. It should be noted, however, that while there is more age ambiguity with regard to the daughters, and the overall meaning of the narrative indicates the total destruction of all the inhabitants, those who came to Lot's door may more likely have been assumed to have already reached puberty. The LXX renders 19:4: ἀπὸ νεανίσκου ἕως πρεσβυτέρου ἅπας, with νεανίσκος in Philo's hierarchy of ages indicating a "young man" who has already reached puberty. This all makes narrative sense given the insinuations of gang rape that this scene implies.

121. Note, such a tradition stands as one among many within the Hebrew Bible as a text that was written over hundreds of years and by many hands. Without the appropriate background or research into the theme of children in the Hebrew Bible as a whole, my intention here is not to make a sweeping generalization, but rather to note a theme that stands out within the specific texts quoted by Luke, as the Lukan author has presented them.

122. For a compelling argument on the intended audience of the *Infancy Gospel of Thomas* as being young children, see Aasgaard, *The Childhood of Jesus*.

123. Indeed, Murphy affirms this point, noting the potential negative impacts given the "precarious presence of children" in his book by the same name, *Kids and Kingdom: The Precarious Presence of Children in the Synoptic Gospels*. While I concur that Murphy is right to highlight the obvious impact of Jesus' whole ministry (not just the two blessing scenes) on children, for reasons elaborated elsewhere (see chapter 3), I challenge his conclusion that this impact would have been any more negative for children effected by Jesus' ministry than for adults.

124. This conclusion relies upon the past 25 years of childhood studies in opposition to Philippe Ariès' thesis that childhood was invented during the Renaissance.

Chapter 3

Young Children in Jesus' Ministry

That young children were present among those with and to whom Jesus ministered in first century Palestine has been demonstrated above with regard to the near continual inferences of their presence alongside oft-cited specific texts (Lk 9:47–50; 18:15–17). The full welcome and inclusion of such children by Jesus, however, is more unmistakably seen in those moments in which Luke recounts the specific healing or reconciliation of a child.[1]

Thus, Warren Carter contends that by the time Matthew (and so too Luke) reaches the account of Jesus welcoming children, the audience already expects an inclusive and welcoming response from Jesus, "since children have been presented as recipients of divine presence, protection and mercy."[2] Through Jesus' provision of healing and description of acceptance, Luke models the inclusion and welcome of children at several key points throughout Jesus' ministry, leading up to the ultimate statement of the place of children in the Kingdom made in Luke 18:15–17.

This chapter seeks to lay the groundwork for such inclusion by exploring each of the scenes in which Jesus extends the restorative power of the Kingdom, either through healing or reconciliation, to specific children who cross his path, including: Jesus' healing of a young slave (7:1–10), raising of a youth at Nain (7:11–17), raising of a girl in Galilee (8:40–56), expulsion of a demon from a boy (9:37–45), and parabolic use of two brothers to describe God's forgiveness (15:11–32) in turn.[3]

A contemporary audience may be surprised to note the presence of several of these texts in relation to Jesus' ministry to children. Here Horn and Martens' insightful assessment of difficulties that modern translations present in retrieving child narratives from the ancient texts is key. They note that there exists within biblical scholarship a "methodological problem that in translations of ancient texts children may at times be concealed by inattentive renditions of a given phrase or expression into the target language."[4] Consequently the exact age of the children in some of these texts is unclear, again, owing to the cultural invisibility of children established above, and may in some cases even be obscured or misrepresented by overly definitive translations. Nevertheless, taken together, these children's general experience of healing and acceptance at the hand of Jesus comes through as a testimony to the inclusion of young and adolescent children—those who are not yet adults—in Luke's description of Jesus' earthly ministry of restoration.

JESUS HEALS A YOUNG SLAVE (7:1–10)

The Slave as Child

As aforementioned,[5] the word παῖς is used with reference to both a child, especially a young child, and a slave in ancient literature. Context determines the difference. In the case of Luke 7:7, παῖς has been consistently rendered in English translations as either "servant" or "slave" on account of the narrator's previous description of the ill person as the centurion's "slave" (δοῦλος) in 7:2 and again in 7:10. As a result, at the literary level, the status of the person in question within the centurion's household is unquestionably as a slave.[6] However, as attention to the pervasive presence of children in the public sphere has demonstrated, one does not necessarily exclude the other. Indeed, Marianne Bjelland Kartzow suggests that "one of every three children" in the first century Mediterranean world "would have been a slave."[7]

In the first century world, many children were subject to slavery either as a result of having been found as infants after their parents exposed them at birth, being sold due to family debt, or being born into this station in their master's house.[8] As such, the ill person's status as a slave does not exclude the possibility that this slave is also a child. Rather, the question, from a childist perspective, is whether there is anything in the text to indicate that this slave could or should be read as a child, and thus an example of Jesus' healing ministry (and the centurion's empathetic concern) being extended beyond adults.

To answer this, it is helpful to consider the use of the term παῖς across the Lukan corpus. Modern translations render forms of this root either servant or slave three times in Luke's narrative—first here, again in Lk 12:45 in the parable of the faithful and unfaithful servant, and finally in Lk 15:26 with reference to a group of slaves preparing the festivities at the return of the lost brother in Jesus' parable of the prodigal son. In each case there is little direct indication of the age of the slave(s). With attention to the intersectionality between slavery and childhood in the ancient world, Kartzow goes even further than this to suggest that every time δοῦλος as the more general word for slave is mentioned that one should consider the possibility that the individual in question may be slave child.[9] While it is impossible to assign an age to any one of these characters with certainty, attention to the context opens up interpretive possibilities. In both parables, the παῖδα are described within the household system. In Lk 15:26, the παῖδα are described as being near the house—a position generally reserved for child and female slaves, while older men worked in the fields. That such a position also likely applied to the centurion's slave when he was well may be inferred by his close relationship with his master, indicated by the narrator's description of the slave as "a slave whom he [the centurion] highly valued" (ἔντιμος, Lk 7:2).

This word, used in the New Testament only by Luke, carries the connotation of value in terms of honor and preciousness (cf. Lk 14:8).[10] It refers not so much to the slave's monetary value as to the slave's prized position in the household of the centurion. Since it is unlikely, given his occupation and status, that the centurion himself would have engaged in the more manual outdoor work assigned to grown men, the slave's position of value may indicate that he worked more closely within the house itself, a position that, when held among males, was occupied by children. This favored status and the centurion's extraordinary efforts in seeking help for his ailing slave suggest that this individual was more than just a servant in the centurion's household, but likely qualified as a quasi-family member about whom the centurion cared on more than a solely pragmatic level. After all, the expense itself of maintaining a slave who is described as "close to death" would necessitate some level of concern beyond just how useful the slave is to the centurion.

Nor was this type of relationship uncommon in the Roman world. Slaves who were born into the household were called *vernae*, and there is evidence that they may have been treated better than a typical slave. In particular, Hanne Sigismund-Nielsen, classical philologist, observes, "Young *vernae* are frequently commemorated affectionately as 'dear small children.'"[11] If the centurion's slave held such a position in his household, his affection and value for the slave begins to make sense in the larger context, including the efforts that he would go through in order to secure Jesus' healing on account of this young slave.

Moreover, the high value that the centurion holds for this slave, causing him even to reduce his honor in order to seek healing from Jesus, a Jewish Galilean, suggests that this was a child of particular value to the centurion, perhaps even in the Roman category of a *delicia*. Although the treatment of *delicia* children has been the subject of some debate among classical historians, at its most basic level, classicist Hanne Sigismund-Nielsen explains, "The word *delicium* can be used as a term of relationship about a young child, frequently of slave status . . . a relationship of quasi-familial character."[12] In the context of the centurion in Luke's account, the centurion's affection for his slave may indicate the slave's role in the household and even special status in the eyes of the master, in keeping with a broad understanding of *delicia*—a role reserved for children. The legitimacy of such a reading of the centurion's slave as a child is further confirmed when one moves from a survey of the term παῖς in Luke's gospel to a more inclusive study of the use of the two related terms παῖς and δοῦλος in Luke's use across the gospel and Acts.

Luke uses the more general term δοῦλος extensively throughout both works, especially in the gospel.[13] Notably, in this unit itself, only the narrator himself uses the term in reference to the ill person. While the centurion uses the term δοῦλος in his message to Jesus (Lk 7:8), he does so not with reference to the παῖς in quesiton, but rather, as a more general illustration of the command which he carries over all of his slaves. This then accords with the suggestion that παῖς means something more than just "slave" in Luke's account. Indeed, most interpreters concur with this, suggesting that the term in relation to the statement about the slave's special status in 7:2 reflects a close and trusted relationship between the centurion and the slave.[14]

However, when one examines Luke's more fastidious use of this term, especially in Acts, that this special relationship reflects a familial status (as implicated by the connections with a Roman *vernae or delicia*) becomes clear. When the Lukan author employs the term παῖς in Acts in connection with servitude, as he does here and in 15:26, it is always as a double reference to an individual's special status before God as both slave *and child*. This is true especially in relation to Jesus in Acts 3:13, 26; 4:27, 30 but also of David in Acts 4:25. Although in these instances, for theological purposes, the author plays more on the meaning of child as a descendant rather than a youth, the understanding of the term as carrying a primary meaning in relation to childhood is clear.

Thus, while there is no definitive way to judge whether the centurion's slave was a loved adult or child, socio-cultural and textual indications point towards the reading of this slave as a young child, perhaps even *delicia*, as plausible and legitimate. Indeed, in light of a childist perspective that seeks to bring to light instances where children may have faded into the adultist background of writing and interpretation, this becomes a prime account for retrieving a vulnerable slave child from the background and observing Jesus' care in including this child in his ministry of healing and well-being.[15]

Experience of Inclusion

While the narrative places the emphasis of the healing on the centurion's faith (Lk 7:9), the attention directed at the young slave both by the centurion and by Jesus should not be overlooked. The value that this child holds in the eyes of the centurion has already been discussed at length above. The fact that Jesus never directly encounters this child slave comes about at the bequest of the centurion rather than Jesus. This need not indicate that this child is of any less value to the centurion so much as it is intended to show the centurion's deference to Jesus as a person of authority.

Based on rabbinic law, Tannehill suggests that it is likely that the centurion may have been concerned about the presumption of inviting "a Jewish holy man to defile himself by entering the dwelling of a Gentile."[16] Notably, then, despite any purity concerns that may have existed, Jesus responds to the messengers and sets off toward the centurion's house *for the sake of the child* immediately (Lk 7:6). Only after Jesus comes near to the house does the centurion send word for him not to enter, and Jesus affirms the centurion's faith. Therefore, one should not read Jesus' initial act of compassion toward the slave child as having anything to do with the centurion's faith, which has not yet been established, but as a locus of action directed toward an ailing child.

Just as the centurion receives Jesus' affirmation by means of his faith, the child in illness is also included in Jesus' affirming and, indeed, healing actions. Tannehill concludes, "Gentiles in the Lukan audience would rightly understand this scene to be an invitation to share in the community of Jesus and the reign of God."[17] To this, it seems appropriate to add that children—even slave children of Gentiles—would also rightly understand this scene to be not just an invitation, but in fact, an act of inclusion, embracing them through Jesus' attentiveness in the healing power of the Kingdom of God.

JESUS RAISES A YOUTH AT NAIN (7:11–17)

The Youth as Child

Of the specific instances of Jesus healing children in Luke's gospel account, this is the most tenuous one.[18] Given the tendency of several English translations to render the perfect participle τεθνηκώς (v. 12, 15) as "dead man" (NKJV, NASB) or "man who had died" (NRSV, ESV) rather than the more literal "one who has died," it may seem puzzling that this unit is even included in a discussion of children. Moreover, even when one accepts the ambiguity of this first designation, the second and only textual indication of the dead son's age, which occurs by way of Jesus' address to him, continues to point to this son's identity as an adult in English translation. In 7:14, Jesus' addresses the individual lying on the funeral bier with the imperative, νεανίσκε σοὶ λέγω, ἐγέρθητι ("Young man, I say to you, get up!").

However, such translations are less an indication of a known age of this youth and more another example of the methodological problem named earlier with regards to translating the ancient text in a way that can, at times, conceal the presence of children (or the possibility thereof).[19] While the rendering "young man" is technically accurate and appears in nearly every English translation, it can be misleading if taken as the sole indication of the dead person's maturity.

The end of childhood is nebulous in definition. While marriage can serve as a somewhat clear marking point for females in antiquity, setting a bright line for males, who tended to marry later in life is even more difficult. To begin with, there is no one Greek word the equivalent of which could be rendered "[non-adult] child." The closest the Greek language comes are the terms παῖς and παιδίον. However, even together these terms fail to include the whole range of childhood. They focus on the youngest age groups and can, in certain contexts, be used either metaphorically or to indicate servile status instead. In practice, the ancient world utilized a whole range of vocabulary to designate the various stages in child development, much like today (e.g., "infant," "toddler," "preschooler," "young child," "adolescent," "teenager," etc.). Moreover, while for the purposes of certain legal and medical classifications, various taxonomies were proposed, in common usage these words for childhood remain ambiguous and overlapping. This is particularly the case when it comes to defining the last stage of childhood and, correspondingly, the first stage of adulthood—the point on ancient taxonomies where the designation νεανίσκος falls.

In technical terms, although the range varies somewhat across sources, Lesley Dean-Jones, specialist in ancient medicine and philosophy, defines νεανίσκος as a youth who is generally thought to be between the ages of fourteen and twenty-one.[20] In Luke's corpus, the term recurs again in Acts 2:17 together with πρεσβύτεροι with reference to Joel's prophecy that the LORD "will pour out my spirit on all flesh; your sons and your daughters shall prophesy, your old men shall dream dreams, and your young men shall see visions" (Joel 2:28). As noted above, in the broader context of God's judgment and salvation, indicated by the pouring out of God's spirit on *all flesh*, νεανίσκος here can, and for the sake of a childist reading, should be read in a more inclusive sense as a youthful contrast to old age, rather than as a delimited timespan.

In similar fashion, the remaining three references in Acts assume individuals with some freedom and capacity to act for themselves, while at the same time, emphasizing their youthfulness. In Acts 5:10 οἱ νεώτεροι discover and bury the body of Sapphira—an action that requires strength of body and speed. While in Acts 23:17 Paul refers to his nephew as a νεανίας, and later the tribune refers to the youth as a νεανίσκος (v. 22) after the boy overhears and informs them of a conspiracy against Paul. Here it is possible that the boy's youthfulness excludes him from further deliberation and inclusion in the covert actions of the tribunal. In any case, in each instance, no specific age range for the νεανίσκοι is assumed, although it is clear the term does not denote a very young child.

To begin to understand this ambiguity, one need only begin by considering the common usage of the term "young man" in English today. This phrase can be used to designate a male's newly acquired "adult" status, but it is perhaps just as frequently used to refer to a male, particularly a young male child, at any number of points of development. Consider, for example, a mother's reproach to her juvenile son, "Young man, you stop that this instant!" So, too, in Greek, the term νεανίσκος and its root νεανίας can be translated as "young man," but also frequently carry with them "a sense of a *youth* in character, i.e. either in a good sense, *impetuous, active*, or in a bad sense, *hot-headed, willful, headstrong.*"[21]

Given Jesus' call for this youth to return from the dead, a return to the active and lively existence to which his subject previously belonged seems obvious. Given the lack of attention to childhood as a developmental stage throughout the rest of the narrative, that either the character of Jesus or the Lukan author has any intention in this address of defining the son out of such a stage seems unlikely at best. Instead, Luke's Jesus, recognizing the youth of the boy on the funeral bier, addresses him as such with a conveyance of force and authority as he returns this child to the previous vitality he had lost in death.

This attention to the vitality of the newly resuscitated son is paralleled in the resuscitation accounts of the Elijah-Elisha cycles (1 Kings 17:17–24; 2 Kings 4:18–37), with which the Lukan author and his audience would have been familiar. While there is difference of opinion among interpreters regarding the degree to which Luke 7:11–17 parallels one or both of these previous accounts, there is a general assent that some similarity exists.[22] In each of these accounts, a boy in the mid to latter stages of childhood—capable, when living, of acting for himself, and yet still residing in his family home and dependent upon his mother's care—can be inferred.

In the LXX in each case the boy is referred to as both a υἱός ("son," as in Lk 7:12) and παιδάριον (diminutive of παῖς meaning "child" or "youth").[23] As with νεανίσκος, these terms cover a large time span, although παιδάριον has been traditionally associated more frequently with children who have not yet reached full maturity, e.g. adulthood. Indeed, this is the same word for children (παιδίοις) that Luke uses later in the chapter to refer to children playing in the market (7:31–32). These children are clearly not yet fully grown, or they would not have the leisure to play at music and dance. However, in the Septuagint itself, the term generally takes on a bit older age range—referring most frequently to older teenagers, such as Joseph at 17 years old (Gen 37:30) and Benjamin at age 19 (Tobit 6:3).

Without anachronistically imposing an upper (or lower) limit to the first century experience of childhood based on contemporary sensibilities about which stage of life (adolescence or "young adulthood") one becomes an "adult," it is perhaps most useful to think in terms of the social status conferred at each age. While it is clear that with each progression along the life cycle a child is awarded greater status, it is not until he or she passes youth or young adulthood, the period designated by νεανίσκος, that one is considered in his or her "prime."[24] To this end, even taxonomies such as that of Diogenes Laertius, which classify a νεανίσκος on the latter end of the age range—as late as 40 years old, maintain that this stage is distinct from that of [adult] maturity: "One remains a child (παῖς) for twenty years, then a youth (νεηνίσκος) for twenty more years, a mature person (νεηνίης) for another twenty years, and an older person (γέρων) for a final twenty years (8.10)."[25] Likewise, Dean-Jones notes that the Hippocratics, in setting a more typical post-puberty age range, count both a child (παῖς) and "young adult (*parthenoi, neaniskoi, meirakia*)" as "distinct from 'those in their prime' (*akmazontes*, a term designating individuals from about twenty-five to forty-five; e.g. *Prorrhetic* II.9)."[26]

It is perhaps most fitting to describe the νεανίσκος as inhabiting a liminal stage between early childhood and adulthood. For this reason, the contemporary terminology of "youth," with its precedence in earlier interpretations of ancient texts, seems most appropriate for this passage. In the aforementioned cases of Joseph and Benjamin, even as older teenagers, they nevertheless continue to reside in their family homes. They maintain a sense of dependence even as they continue to move further into independence with regard to their parents and kin. Likewise, the youth in Luke 7:11–17 continues to reside in his mother's home. This is indicated both by the lack of mention of any other family (adding to the tragedy of the mother's loss) and by the action of Jesus giving the youth, once resuscitated, back into his mother's care (v. 15). Indeed, while it is evident that the widowed mother is dependent upon her son for the hope that he brings to her future, that hope is not yet fully realized.

For this reason, Dixon describes the death of such a youth as reflecting the greatest tragedy in the ancient Roman world from a social perspective because such a child "had survived long enough for parents to form expectations that the child would outlive them."[27] In a society where infant mortality rate was high, that a child died young was a cause for mourning. In a world where disease and danger were a constant, that a child predeceased his or her parents at any age was likewise to be lamented. However, the greatest tragedy, in perhaps both emotional and economic terms was the death of a child who survived the most vulnerable years, only to die before reaching his or her prime.

In such a liminal state, it can be assumed that the relationship of dependence between mother and son in this narrative is indeed a mutual one. For as much as the mother needed her son, for the time being, at least, the son, handed back into the arms of his mother, remains also dependent upon her.

This liminal in-betweenness of youth in the Greco-Roman world is further illustrated by both social and legal precedent.

Socially, males tended to enter into a first marriage later than their female counterparts due to family and military obligations.[28] Thus, most boys experienced a liminal period transitioning into adulthood. The νεανίσκος, in this transitional stage continues to receive greater recognition in society—as, indeed, he has at each stage of his childhood up to this point—while at the same time retaining certain freedoms as well as protections not available to adults, such as the expectation of a curator to oversee his legal transactions.[29]

Within this context, it is significant that after the age of twelve, Luke tells us that the boy Jesus returned home to Nazareth with his parents "and was obedient to them" (2:51), where he "increased in wisdom and in years, and in divine and human favor" (2:52). After this report, it is not until Jesus is roughly thirty years old, past the upper limits of a νεανίσκος that Luke resumes narration with a fully mature Jesus encountering John and beginning his adult ministry.

The final objection, then, that could be made to the youthful character of this young man at Nain has to do with the funerary procession itself. The question could be raised, would a funeral procession, such as the one described in Lk 7:11, have been conducted for a youth not yet in his prime? Dixon's reflections above regarding the degree of tragedy experienced at the death of a child, particularly a male child, in this age range may begin to give indication of the answer itself. While it is true that very small children, particularly infants in the first weeks and months after birth, were not always mourned or buried with the same pomp, by the time a youth reached the age of ten-years-old, their allotted mourning period was the same as that of an adult. Plutarch describes different mourning practices for children between the ages of birth through three years, with the length of mourning increasing proportionate to the age of the child.[30] By the teenage years and into their twenties, the mourning of children was both officially recognized and comparable to the mourning of the loss of any member of the family. However, even before the age of ten, children were buried and commemorated in Roman funerary art, as noted earlier.[31]

There remains no formal record of the exact age or manner in which children (or, for that matter, adults) were included in funerary processions. However, Dixon notes that extant evidence suggests, "This ceremony, like the grouping of family remains in tombs or of the names on memorial tablets, marks the family as a unit and reminds all kin that kinship is an affiliation that cuts across other social groupings and transcends divisions between the generations and even between the living and the dead."[32] While the exact social and religious details might vary, in general, just as they were celebrated in life and included in family gatherings in between, so too, children were commemorated in death.

In short, the youth resuscitated in Luke 7:11–17 is not an adult. As a νεανίσκος he does not possess the same rights or responsibilities as an older man. His social status is not the same. He continues to reside in his mother's home; he is dependent upon her. Indeed, this is the parallel that Luke draws between the two clearly dependent children in the Elijah and Elisha narratives. Nevertheless, traditional scholarship and Bible translators, reading as they do through an adultist lens, when they give any mention to age at all, anachronistically read this "young man" to be in his prime of life.

Despite any remaining ambiguity, therefore, my decision to interpret this νεανίσκος as a youth—a non-adult child—and so to include him among those children whom Luke explicitly names as recipients of Jesus' healing ministry is a decision of resistance. It is a conscious move to bring discussion of children across the age spectrum into the center of the text. This move of conscientization, however, is not done blindly, but rather, with the support of both fluid descriptions of age and adulthood, socio-historical support, intertextual parallels, and a plausible and legitimate reading of the text.

Experience of Inclusion

Having established the social position of the youth at Nain vis-à-vis his age, the next point of inquiry becomes the extent to which Jesus' resuscitation represents a point of inclusion for youth and children in Jesus' ministry. The mother seems to be the focus of Jesus' attention in Luke's account (e.g. "When the Lord saw her, he had compassion for her . . . " Lk 7:13; "Jesus gave him back to his mother," 7:15). To this end, Robert Price concludes, the "healing is done not for the son, but for the widow."[33] This is not a surprising conclusion given the adult-centric cast of Luke's gospel and its interpreters. Moreover, such a reading has a place when considering, as Price does, Jesus' compassionate treatment and inclusion of widows in God's Kingdom. Indeed, the healing *is* done for the widow; however, this is only one side of the story.

The fact that interpretations tend to focus on the experience of the mother with little regard for the son further emphasizes the qualification of this story for consideration among Luke's narratives of child healings. If the youth had been a fully-grown man or an important citizen, one would suspect, as is the case with the attention given to both the healed servant *and* his centurion master in the scene previous, that the fate and experience of the son might be given at least passing notice.

However, Luke focuses hardly any attention at all on the youth except to note that he "sat up and began to speak" (v. 15), which serves as proof of the efficacy of the miracle more than anything else. Just as his widowed mother was counted among the outcast and the marginalized, so this not yet grown youth is himself marginalized by Luke's account. Behind Luke's adult-centered cloak, Jesus' concern for and inclusion of the youth *as a youth* can be seen in the attention that Jesus gives to him in the scene, the youth's own agential action, and the response and actions of those who witness the miracle.

To begin with, despite the indisputable fact of the grieving mother as the first object of Jesus' compassion, attention is still given to the youth himself. Short of a direct statement to the contrary, there is no reason to assume that Jesus' compassion must be limited to one person. Indeed, in John's account of the resuscitation of Lazarus, Jesus' compassion seems equally placed between the grieving sisters and his dead friend, Lazarus (John 11:1–44). Likewise, while Jesus' sight first falls on the mother, were his concern only for her, there are any number of other ways that the problem of her economic loss may have been resolved without the resuscitation of her son.

Indeed, this would be in keeping with the relativization of traditional gender and family roles that the Jesus of Luke's gospel seems to promote. Turid Karlsen Seim elaborates, "Gender determined family relationships in Luke are neither maintained nor promoted, but are dismissed as irrelevant, being redefined as categories of discipleship, as a new criterion for membership of the fictive family is established."[34] Thus, a move to redefine this widowed mother by her youthful son's ability to provide would run counter to the pattern in Luke of supporting the independence and even ascetic life of widows who so choose this path. Alternately, Jesus might have called the dead youth's mother to join with him, where she would later be cared for in the fellowship of believers (Acts 2:44–45) and by the community's provision for widows (cf. Lk 20:46–47; Acts 6:1–6). He might have called down the Spirit to her that she conceive another son, helped to arrange a new marriage for her, placed her into the care of a prominent member of the community, or any number of other options some of which may have guaranteed more immediate return.

Amidst many alternative means to help the widow, Jesus chooses to return her youthful son, a boy not yet married, not yet the head of his own home, and not yet financially independent in his own right. In other words, his actions, while magnanimous, do not entirely solve the widow's problems. She has, once again, a hope for the future and, of course, the precious life of her son. However, both mother and son's futures remain far from secure. In light of this, there must be something more going on in Jesus' actions than mere concern for the economic future of a widowed mother who has lost her only son. While noting the economic repercussions of the youth's death for the widow, Bovon provides a more balanced view of the subject of Jesus' miracle, noting on the basis of Jesus' direct address to both mother (Lk 7:13) and son (Lk 7:14) that his "attention is turned to both mother *and* son."³⁵ Just as both of their futures remain insecure, both mother and son have something to gain in Jesus' action.

Upon resuscitating the youth, Jesus "gave him" (ἔδωκεν αὐτον) to his mother. While this verb can imply the simple act of bestowal, in connection with a mother-son relationship, it can more fully be translated as the action of putting something, or someone, in the care of another—to *entrust*. This is true in Luke, particularly with regard to Jesus' teachings about stewardship—e.g. a nobleman entrusting his money to his stewards while he is away (Lk 19:13–15; cf. also 12:48). The son is not the mother's rightful possession that Jesus *returns*; rather, this youth, restored to life, is a precious child of God, the care of whom Jesus *entrusts* to his mother.

The relationship is two-sided. The unhappy reality is that many parents in the first century Middle Eastern world found themselves, like the widow in Luke 7:11–17, prematurely burying their children. With reference to ideal contemporaneous Roman practices, Dixon explains:

> *Pietas* laid down certain claims within the family which ideally governed relations between the generations: "It was natural that parents should beget, rear, and educate children, and it was natural that children in return should honour and obey parents, give them material and psychological support, including grandchildren, comfort in old age, and burial."³⁶

Families, even one as small as just these two individuals, were interdependent of one another. The son is expected to care for the mother, just as the mother is expected to care for him.

In this story lies much more than the typical return to fortune that traditional interpretations would point us to. A childist interpretation allows us to see the much deeper, restorative power of relationship in Jesus' recognition of *both* mother *and* son. Only when the parent-child dyad is reunited together is the healing of either complete. As such, the healing that Jesus performs is for both parties—an experience of the radical inclusion both of widows and youth in the healing, indeed life-giving reality of the Kingdom of God.

The inclusive power of Jesus' healing action can further be seen in the active response of the youth himself. Typical of the patriarchal, adult-centered narrative as a whole, Luke does not record the name of either mother or son. Neither does Luke directly report what the youth says when he is resuscitated; however, Luke *does* report that the youth speaks. This significant action ascribes agency to the unnamed youth. From there, it is left to the reader to fill in this gap in the Lukan narrative. Does the youth, in following with the manner by which it is proven that a person has been raised from the dead, ask for something to eat? (cf. Lk 8:55; 24:40–41) Does he express confusion? Or his thanks to Jesus? Or does he, in fact, instigate Jesus' next action, by *asking* for his mother?

Imagining the first response of a scared or injured child—even a teenager—today, often calling out for a parent or loved one who brings security and peace, I conjecture that it is the latter. Indeed, if this is the content of the boy's speech, then it transforms our reading of what may otherwise seem an abrupt movement of Jesus' attention away from the child and toward the mother to a tender acknowledgment that one cannot give attention to one without also acknowledging the other. Parker acknowledges this with regard to the parallel attention given to mother and son in the Elisha narrative:

> The anonymous child says and does little, while arguably remaining the center of attention. The stories of his birth and revival focus primarily on the mother and the prophet. . . . While the child is still through most of the narrative, he is important even in his passivity. Concern for his life steers the plot.[37]

Although inferences can be made about the economic status of the widow in Luke's gospel and the consequent value of the son for her future, such a direct connection is never made. Even when one assumes such implications, a genuine care for her son and sorrow at the loss of his life *as a loss* seems also, if not primarily, to motivate this mother's weeping (Lk 7:13). While her concern for herself may follow later, in this moment of her grief, it is possible, if not likely, that care for her son remains this woman's primary purpose. Indeed, if finances were the sole factor for her grief, she may not have invested in the expense of the funerary procession that Jesus witnesses, accompanied as she is by such a large crowd, preferring instead to save for her uncertain future. In her mourning, this mother shows genuine concern for her son.

Thus, even in his death, this youth influences the actions of his mother. This is an example of what Cristina Grenholm calls the co-creative love of motherhood: "It is not merely about procreation; it is about the coming into being of human beings in communion with others. We co-create each other. Pregnancy, child birth, and continuing care are important aspects of this act of creation."[38] This describes both the affection and mutual dependence that the mother and son in Luke's story have for one another.[39] When they are returned to one another in life, such mutuality can and should be expected to continue.

Finally, the response and actions of those who witness the miracle testify to the youth's experience of healing as one of divine inclusion. This can be seen first in the witness of the large crowd of mourners accompanying the youth and his mother from the start (Lk 7:11) and later in the testimony about Jesus' actions by the disciples of John who, immediately following this scene in Nain, are said to have "reported all these things" to John (Lk 7:18).

With reference to the immediate crowd of mourners, it bears recalling the predominance of children in crowds and cities of the first century world. Since children were not and could not be shielded from death, so much an ever-present reality in their lives, the crowd accompanying a funeral procession would have been no different. The "large crowd" (Lk 7:11) and the funeral procession would have involved children. These children, then, bear witness to Jesus' miraculous actions for one of their own. They see Jesus step forward and dare to touch the ritually unclean funeral bier belonging, as it were, not to an important state official or religious leader, but a simple youth (Lk 7:14). It is possible that one or more of those carrying the bier may have been a youth or young child him or herself. McWilliam observes, "Children attended religious festivals and games, triumphs, and funerals. . . . Some children were able to participate, perhaps singing at a funeral or state ceremony or walking processions."[40] Far from hiding in the background of this story, the children of the community are woven into its very framework. In Jesus' attention to the youth and his mother, children both surround and are surrounded by the power of his presence. The inclusive attention that Jesus gives to this youth—the lowly son of a widow—would not have been lost on them.

When Jesus subsequently returns the youth to the home and care of his mother, the comfort and security so crucial to children, particularly at a young age, would thus be connected in their minds in a real and tangible way with Jesus' announcements of the advent of God's Kingdom. Through the resuscitation of the youth at Nain, children in the crowds and among Jesus' followers experience the inclusive and secure invitation to the Kingdom of God—extended to all of God's children.

Such attention to the youth at Nain is then tacitly acknowledged and confirmed by the reports to John by his disciples. After they convey "all these things" to John (Lk 7:18), John, presumably amazed by what he has heard, sends two disciples to speak with Jesus. In this conversation, the emphasis of the healing event is clearly removed from the widowed mother and placed squarely on the experience of the youthful son. Jesus "answered them, 'Go and tell John what you have seen and heard: the blind receive their sight, the lame walk, the lepers are cleansed, the deaf hear, *the dead are raised*, and the poor have good news brought to them'" (Lk 7:22, emphasis added). Affirming through his actions his identity as Messiah, Jesus does not dwell, with regard to the healing at Nain, on his action for the widowed mother—who quite likely could be numbered among the poor or even the oppressed. Instead, he *adds* the prophetic expectation of the raising of the dead to this paradigmatic statement of Luke 4:18–19.

This is the only resuscitation miracle that Luke has so far recounted and, indeed, is unique to Luke among the synoptics. As a result, there is little doubt that the reference here has most specifically to do with the resuscitation of the youth at Nain. The experience of *this youth*—not his mother—therefore provides key testimony to Jesus' identity as the Messiah. He is included not just in the experience of the Kingdom of God, but also now in the proclamation about Jesus as it brings others to believe.

From a simple account of healing and restoration, then, attention to this child opens for one an experience of God's grace extended to children and their parents through a restored relationship, the provision for trust and security, concern for the outcast and neglected, and inclusion of such ordinary people as the youth at Nain in the proof and proclamation of God's Kingdom. The inclusive grace and welcome extended at Nain, therefore, moves beyond the experience of one mother or one son to encompass more broadly God's plan for the salvation of all of God's children through the life, death, and ministry of God's own son—Jesus. The healing of this youth is more than one moment of gratuitous inclusion. It is not an incidental experience at the margins of Jesus' ministry. Rather, for the Lukan author and his audience, this experience of healing both embodies and testifies to the radical nature of God's Kingdom as one of mutuality and relationship for all of God's children—reversing fortunes and including those otherwise forgotten and rejected by society, or, as in the case of children, too often simply ignored.

JESUS RAISES A GIRL IN GALILEE (8:40–56)[41]

The Girl as Child

In contrast to the previous narrative, there is no reason to guess at the age of the child whom Jesus returns to life in Luke 8:40–56. The narrator tells us that Jairus' daughter is "about twelve years old" (v. 42). While Roman law permitted girls to be legally married at the age of twelve,[42] they typically married much later. P. R. C. Weaver estimates "the *average* age gap between first husband and first wife is at least ten years, probably more," with girls marrying between 15–20 years old and boys, on average, ten years later than that.[43] This average, gathered from analyses of funerary inscriptions and other extant evidence, is generally affirmed across scholars of antiquity, with the notable exception of "elite girls" who "may have been married early in their teens."[44]

Thus, rather than assign twelve as the blanket age at which a girl became an adult in first century Mediterranean society, the consideration of her actual marital state among other social factors provides a more nuanced perspective.[45] In contrast to boys whose transition to adulthood was frequently marked with a series of public rituals, "There was no comparable civic rite of passage for girls, as they never became full citizens in the political sense of voting and standing for office, and they were never eligible for military service."[46] In place of a public transition to citizenship, a girl publicly attained adulthood through marriage and childbearing.[47] When a girl married, she left her childhood, along with her paternal family, behind and joined the household (οἶκος) of her husband. Because the girl in this unit lives in the home of her father (cf. Lk 8:41, 49, 51), she is to be understood as not yet married. Thus, with respect to her status in the household, she is a child.

The girl's status as child is further confirmed textually by the narrator who refers to her as a "child" (ἡ παῖς) twice in Lk 8:51. And, again, by Jesus' character using the same term in her resuscitation itself when he calls out, "Child, get up!" (Lk 8:54). While there are times when some interpreters argue for a broader translation of the term παῖς, the girl's stated age (which Luke moves to the forefront of the story relative to the other synoptic accounts) and the overall context confirm here an unquestionable reference to her as a non-adult child.

Experience of Inclusion

The narrator immediately links this girl's encounter with the previous account of the resuscitation of the youth at Nain, both with the theme of children who have died (or are close to death) and the mention that these children are, in fact, only children (μονογενής, 7:12; 8:42).[48] In light of these connections, an attentive reader may begin to expect, despite the narrative detour, an experience of healing and reception for the girl. The girl's inclusion in Jesus' healing ministry is seen in a similar light to that of the youth at Nain.[49] However, the introduction of the theme of faith in the combined narrative of the restored girl and the healed woman add a further element of inclusion to consider. Ultimately, a close reading of the text from a childist perspective show the girl's receipt of God's grace, as mediated through Jesus, in both her primary resuscitation and Jesus' imperative that faith saves this child.

At the most basic level this girl is included in Jesus' ministry as a recipient of his healing power. It is worth noting that while the narrative interruption of the girl's healing in which Jesus attends to a hemorrhaging woman before a child could imply a hierarchy of needs, I choose rather to read both healings as consistent with Jesus' ministry of restoration and inclusion. As humans, we tend to act as though everything in our world must be zero sum, such that if Jesus helps one person another person is necessarily neglected. However, throughout Scripture God consistently chooses a different path. God doesn't operate with a zero sum.

In this unit, the urgency of *both* individuals—the girl and the woman—is downplayed by Jesus, with the narrative effect of giving the impression that regardless of chronological order, *neither one* is given priority with regards to Jesus' attention. The chronology of the narrative necessitates that one person's needs are met first; however, the narrator uses this chronology to demonstrate that chronological time no longer dominates in Jesus' Kingdom.

Bovon elaborates, "Luke emphasizes, almost in Pauline fashion but with Johannine accents, that it is never too late for God, because God uses even situations in which—humanly speaking—everything is far too late, in order to reveal the glory of his Son."[50]

God works in *kairos* rather than *chronos* time in such a way that brings relief in the current moment while at the same time always treating the moment as a larger whole. Such a *kairos* orientation looks both before and after the moment to bring about God's restorative grace. Thus, Jesus' attention to the woman and the girl does not need to be an either/or in terms of restoration or inclusion. Rather, it is a both/and through which Jesus brings the hope of God's eschatological Kingdom into the present, embodied in the paired vulnerable persons of a suffering woman and a young girl.

Within this *kairos* time, the young girl's experience of Jesus' power and God's inclusion is heightened by the narrative comparison of her healing alongside that of a grown woman.[51] Despite their different assumed roles in their households and community, fraught with as they were with their respective experiences of vulnerability and marginalization, both women are received as *subjects* through Jesus' healing power of touch.

In the case of the woman, "She touched the fringe of his [Jesus'] clothes, and immediately her hemorrhage stopped" (Lk 8:44). In the case of the girl, "Jesus took her by the hand and called out, 'Child, get up!'" Her spirit returned, and she got up at once" (vv. 54–55). The woman is able to approach Jesus more directly. This is due to her status as an adult and the degree of her illness such that she was not confined to home like the girl. However, the story does not let the girl's position (even in death!) define her into passivity.[52] Jesus does not simply touch the hem of her garment and declare to the father that his daughter is well; rather, Jesus takes the girl *by the hand* and demands action *of her*: "Child, get up!" (v. 54).

In both instances, through the emphasis on touch, "Luke stresses the personal character of the healings."[53] The experiences of these two people are not merely paradigmatic of Jesus' healing power, as in summary statements at other points of Luke's narrative, but rather, reflect a deeper and personal connection that Jesus extends to each one of them. Bovon reflects,

> Jesus the wonder-worker did not play the only significant role. Both the women [*sic.*] are relevant, especially in their relationship with Jesus. Sociologically, the account does not concern merely the crescendo from healing to resurrection, but also Jesus' acceptance of two women, that is, their acceptance by the early Christian community.[54]

Bovon fails to recognize in this the significance of the girl's inclusion not simply as a female, but as a child, referring to both characters at this point as "women," despite his acknowledgment of the recipient of the latter miracle as a child in his more text-critical remarks.[55] Nevertheless, he correctly notes the significance of this passage for establishing the inclusion of these characters, and by extension their demographic groups, within the Kingdom of God and later the early Christian community.

This inclusion can be further seen in Luke's description of Jesus as having taken the girl "by the hand," an expression which, while used more frequently by Mark and in the LXX, is used with reference to healing by the Lukan author only in this unit. Uniquely, then, among his healing narratives, Luke uses the expression "by the hand" to link the girl's experience to that of the people of Israel, whom God is spoken of as taking by the hand (cf. Isa 41:13; 42:6; Ps 73:23).[56] In this way, the girl's clear inclusion as a child of Israel, and so a child of God, is affirmed. At only twelve-years of age, she is just as much a part of God's salvation as anyone else.

Nor is God's gracious act for this child limited to a single moment. Still more profoundly, the woman and the child in this narrative are linked by the saving effect of faith. To the woman Jesus comforts, "Daughter, your faith (πίστις) has made you well (σέσωκέν σε); go in peace" (8:48). To the girl's father, Jesus commands, "Only believe and she will be saved" (μόνον πίστευσον, καὶ σωθήσεται, 8:50). Although the NRSV translates each phrase with different words, the same roots are present for each in Greek—πίστις can be rendered as either faith or belief and σώζω comprehensively conveys the action of making one well and salvation, terms which were linked in early Christian understanding. Fitzmyer notes, "In the Gospel, 'salvation' often denotes deliverance from such evils as sickness, infirmity, or sin; and its relation to 'faith' (*pistis*) is often noted (e.g. 7:50; 8:48, 50; 17:19)."[57] Both the woman and the girl experience such deliverance as subjects of Jesus' healing in 8:40–56.

Moreover, both the woman and the girl participate as active agents in their own salvation. Johnson notes that "these two women [*sic.*] joined by the isolation of sickness, death and impurity, are addressed as daughter, and saved by faith (8:40–56)."[58] Like Bovon, when he moves from textual analysis to a more theological reflection, Johnson inadvertently falls into an adultist treatment of both characters as women—presumably, grown. However, perhaps because of this lapse, Johnson moves beyond the broader contemporary question of whether a child can have faith, to envision both characters as representative of saving faith. Johnson does not specifically name whose faith saves each character. Indeed, on first reading, it appears as though the girl's salvation may be dependent upon her father's faith in v. 50 since his imperative to have faith is addressed to Jairus.[59] Yet, the broader context of faith and salvation as they are described in Luke's narrative suggests another possible reading.

Faith and salvation in Luke's gospel are not about intellectual affirmations, nor are they preceded by human initiative. Rather, they are linked by the common experience of hearing the word of God and responding. Take, for example, the woman who "stood behind him [Jesus] at his feet, weeping, and began to bathe his feet with her tears and to dry them with her hair. Then she continued kissing his feet and anointing them with the ointment" (Lk 7:38). Although this woman never speaks once, Jesus says to her, "Your faith (πίστις) has saved you (σέσωκέν σε); go in peace" (7:50). These are the exact same words that he speaks to the hemorrhaging woman in 8:48. Yet, both women have *already* experienced the magnitude of God's grace *before* Jesus announces their salvation. Jesus is acting in *kairos* time.

In the first case, Jesus tells the Pharisees that the woman is acting with great love *because* "her sins, which were many, have been forgiven" (7:57). In the case of the second woman, "immediately her hemorrhage stopped" (8:44) before she is even acknowledged by Jesus. The reader is to understand, therefore, that neither of these women have contributed to their own salvation anymore than the passive child lying dead in her father's home.

Rather, in his explanation of the parable of the sower, which transects these two accounts, Jesus makes clear that salvation (8:11) belongs to "the ones who, when they hear the word, hold it fast in an honest and good heart, and bear fruit with patient endurance" (8:15). As such, faith, or more accurately translated, faithfulness, remains about each person's openness to the movement of God in their life. In the words of the Lukan author, it is to respond with open ears and obedient action to the word of God.[60] The Galilean girl in this unit embodies her faith by resting her hand in the palm of Jesus as he guides her up.

So, while on first reading it may appear as though the girl's salvation is dependent upon her father's faith, in terms of faithful openness she actually outperforms her father Jairus in Luke's account. In contrast to Mark's present imperative, "Do not fear, only believe (πίστευε)" (Mk 5:36), which could imply a continuation of the faith that Jairus already has, Luke's use of the aorist πίστευσον suggests that Jairus does not already have faith. Nor does the narrative give any reason to believe that Jairus' state of belief changes prior to his daughter's healing. In fact, the ambiguity of the Greek, which does not distinguish the mourners from Jairus and his family in vv. 52–53 in terms of who was "weeping and wailing" for the girl and "laughed at" Jesus "knowing that she was dead," may actively suggest that Jairus *does not* believe before Jesus heals his daughter.

In contrast, when Jesus "calls out" to the girl (v. 54), she responds by getting up "at once" (v. 55). In its most basic formula, this child, despite the doubts of her father and those in his household, hears the word of God—

through Jesus' call—and obeys it. Even when the narrative diminishes her role by failing to grant either voice or name to this child who responds to Jesus' call, her single-minded faithfulness shines through.

In their interpretation of this same sequence of events in Mark's account, Horn and Martens note that despite her silence, this child, like the other children in Mark's healings whom they describe, accepts Jesus' healing. Consequently, they reason that "silence should not be read as indicating indifference. Their silent acceptance of healing is a lesson to the adult readers and hearers. To accept Jesus is to accept divine intervention as it might occur."[61] The efficacy of the girl's resuscitation gives silent testimony to her inclusion in the saving power of Jesus through her faith. Or, to put it more simply, this Galilean girl, like the hemorrhaging woman, in her hearing and responding to the Gospel, experiences *wholeness* as a child of God.

Moreover, this wholeness further extends to the inclusion of both the girl and the woman in their communities.[62] In the first century, whether a person was pagan or Jewish, there existed no separation between religious and secular life. Therefore, the woman, who had been ceremonially unclean due to her hemorrhage for twelve years, had been excluded from the religious life of her community due to this ailment. Likewise, this child, in so much as she was considered to be a part of God's covenant with Israel was also considered to be a part of the corpus of the community. To be restored to life in one sphere was to be restored to life in the other. Thus, the girl's salvation from her death-causing illness indicates, at the same time, her inclusion both among her family and community as well as among the broader people of God (of whom, as a daughter of Israel, she would have also previously been a part).

Applied further to the early Christian context of Luke's presumed readers, Bovon adds, "The significance of πιστεύω ("to believe") and σώζω ("to save") are initially limited to the case of the girl who has died, but the reader sees beyond this to understand that it also means everyone's death and resurrection, and the Christian faith as such."[63] Such an inclusion implicitly links the belief and salvation to the girl herself (rather than her father) and, from there, suggests that the faith of this child indeed models a response for all Christians in light of Christian teachings about a shared death and resurrection with Christ. The claim, while theologically significant in its own right, from a childist perspective makes visible in one more way the continuity of place for children across Jewish and Christian receptions of Luke's narrative as *included* and *made well*, indeed, *saved* as individuals among all of God's children.

Here Jesus' action in time reaches across time once again to bring both the initial recipients of his grace and through them, their whole communities to wholeness and completion. The girl's salvation from her death-causing illness indicates, at the same time, her inclusion among her family and community in time, as well as among the broader people of God across time—an experience of *kairos*.

Once again, comparing this girl's experience to that of the male youth revived in Nain, the thread of wide-sweeping inclusion of the young continues to expand across Luke's narrative. As will be taken up later, this narrative strand follows suit with the broader theme of inclusion of the outcast, and, indeed, reversal of fortunes in Luke's narrative. However, while contemporary scholarship sees such acceptance drawn primarily in relation to gender and class, the childist lens applied above opens the possibility for a reading that also includes the acceptance of all people—child or adult—among the community of Jesus' followers. Indeed, the case of the young girl and her father, Jairus, makes clear that the quality of one's relationship with Jesus is in no way dependent upon physical maturity or age.

JESUS CASTS A DEMON FROM A BOY IN GALILEE (9:37–45)

The Boy as Child

The story of Jesus casting out a demon from a boy whom his disciples have previously attempted to help unsuccessfully marks the third in Luke's stories involving children and their parents. This account in 9:37–45 is also the third clear description of Jesus extending his healing powers to a young child. Here again, no clear indication of age is given except for the narrator's comment towards the end of the account that Jesus healed the "boy," literally, "child" (παῖδια, v. 42). This puts the boy in the same age category as the twelve-year-old girl in 8:40–56, as well as the twelve-year-old Jesus who traveled with his parents to Jerusalem (2:43).[64] Johnson even goes so far as to suggest that within the story's structure, the small child (παιδίον) whom Jesus places among his disciples in 9:47 "could even be the exorcised boy."[65] If the narrative is read as such, the upper limit of the boy's age drops significantly further. In any case, the designation of παῖς, combined with the clear connection with the preceding two parent-child narratives,[66] clearly signals to the reader that another non-adult child is involved. Further narrative clues also help to establish the youth of the boy—both his continued presence in his father's house and his illness itself.

As with the sick girl who continues to reside in the home of her father, Jairus, the clear presentation of the boy in this story under the care of his father may point toward his youth and familial dependence. He has not yet been apprenticed to a particular trade, nor has he married and begun a household of his own. While it is also possible that the boy's condition has influenced these factors, it is worth noting that his father has not, as yet, cast him out of the household either (contrast Lk 8:27). The father's continued commitment to the welfare and well-being of his son indicate a boy at least relatively young in age—fitting with the narrator's description of him as a παῖς in Lk 9:42.

Finally, the boy's affliction, which Luke has the father describe in some detail, is typical of a child in the ancient world. The father describes the cause of the boy's trouble as "a spirit" (πνεῦμα, Lk 9:39), while the narrator later labels it both "a demon" (τὸ δαιμόνιον, v. 42) and "an unclean spirit" (τῷ πνεύματι τῷ ἀκαθάρτῳ, v. 42). Yet, there is no reference to sins on the part of either the father or the child that might have brought upon such a spirit. Instead, the account of the demon should be read as a protological explanation for a sickness that was still shrouded in mystery in the ancient world. Modern medicine assigns the boy's symptoms to epilepsy, specifically, *grand mal seizures*;[67] however, the conventional wisdom of antiquity was not so precise and ascribed such ailments to forces of evil.[68]

Those familiar with the boy's symptoms would likely have ascribed them to a supernatural origin, as Luke does. Nevertheless, it was not a completely unknown affliction. Rather, it was a condition known to exist of which the causes and treatment were unknown. As such, it is reasonable to expect that Luke and his audience would have been aware, as modern medicine is today, that such epileptic attacks generally begin in childhood or puberty.[69] As such, Jesus not only receives and responds to a young boy, perhaps at the age of puberty or just below, but does so in the context of the boy's suffering from a known childhood condition that happens to be attributed to a demon.

Experience of Inclusion

The most obvious way in which Jesus extends God's power to this boy possessed by a demon is expressed succinctly as the second of three actions in Luke 9:42 "and Jesus healed the boy" (καὶ ἰάσατο τὸν παῖδια).[70] As in the first two child healings addressed, through his miraculous power of healing, Jesus now extends God's grace and power to this young boy as an experience of inclusion. Moreover, again in parallel to the accounts of the youth at Nain and the girl in Galilee, the boy in this account experiences Jesus' act of inclusion at the familial and communal level as well. Through Jesus' action, the boy is recognized for his humanity and restored to full status as a valued member not just of his household or God's coming Kingdom but also of the covenantal community in which he resides.

This trifold inclusion is signaled in Jesus' three actions in relation to the boy in 9:42. Within Luke's narrative framework, the effect of the boy's healing beyond the exorcism itself becomes clear. Jesus' next move after commanding the demon out of the boy is to address his disciples. This can be taken as a completion of the boy's restoration. Jesus does not stop at curing the disease (in this case, demon possession), but rather, restores the boy to wholeness in community. He does this by addressing *all* those involved: the demon, the father, the boy, and the witnesses, that is, the disciples and the crowd. In light of the effect of Jesus' address both to the demon and the disciples, the boy's restoration to community is actually affirmed twice by the narrative, sandwiching the more personal experiences of restoration between Jesus and his father. Such an emphasis on community makes clear the place of inclusion and welcome that Luke's Jesus intends for this boy to enjoy among God's people as a whole.

First, Luke signals the boy's inclusion in his community at large through Jesus' removal of his demonic stigma. While any illness may be somewhat debilitating, the stigma of this boy's particular condition is emphasized at several points in Luke's description. First, it is attributed to supernatural powers—a point of general mystery and concern in the ancient world. Although their conditions are not identical, the description of the Gerasene demoniac living among the tombs in Luke 8:27 provides a bleak picture of what this boy's life might entail if his affliction continues.

Second, as a part of the Jewish community, regulated by standards and rituals to determine "clean" and "uncleanness," to have been afflicted by an "unclean spirit" (τῷ πνεύματι τῷ ἀκαθάρτῳ, Lk 9:42), as this boy is, would have had immediate consequences (cf. discussion of the hemorrhaging woman in Lk 8:43 above). Finally, as a more general experience of this latter point, the honor/shame culture of Roman antiquity would likely also have come into play in ostracizing the boy and his family from their broader community. Bovon summarizes these points in relation to the boy's father:

> The possession of his son by demons would not only cause the father emotional suffering, but would also stigmatize him in ancient society. It endangers both his descendants and his current reputation. His suffering is rooted in his fear of the unpredictable attacks, in his grieving over his son, and in his own shame (cf. the similar ὄνειδος, 'shame,' of Elizabeth in Luke 1:25).[71]

When one moves beyond the adult-centric focus that motivates Bovon to focus on the experience of the father here, it is easy to see how similar stigma would have been experienced to the same degree, if not greater, by the child himself. Thus, the expulsion of the demon, effected by Jesus' rebuke in 9:42 achieves restoration for both this child and his father at a communal level, even apart from the physical effects.

Second, Luke signals the boy's inclusion in Jesus' mission through Jesus' personal connection with and healing of him. Such connection, indeed, is what the boy's father appeals so passionately for in the first part of the narrative. Despite the commotion going on around Jesus—the crowds welcoming him (9:37a), the father imploring him (9:37b), and the demon resisting (9:42)—until after the healing is complete, Jesus' focus is on the young boy. Only after the boy is healed (9:42) does Jesus return his attention to the disciples and the crowd, elaborating on the brief rebuke of 9:41. And, indeed, this is what the father has requested from the start—that Jesus "look at my son" (ἐπιβλέψαι ἐπὶ τὸν υἱόν μου, 9:37). Here the repetition of ἐπί ('to,' 'at') makes clear that the object towards which Jesus is to direct his attention is not the spirit or the father, but, in fact, the son—the boy.[72] While Jesus' miracle-working action in v. 42 is directed toward three different objects (demon, child, and father), the purpose for his activity, and as such the focus of all that he does, remains centered on the boy.

The quality of such action can be further seen in the father's plea and Jesus' response. The verb ἐπιβλέπω adds a degree of emphasis or focus to the more basic βλέπω ("to look"). It can be translated "to look intently," "to pay close attention to," "show special respect for," "gaze upon," or "look attentively at, with the implication of personal concern for someone."[73] This is the same verb that Luke uses of God's compassion for Mary in her celebration of Jesus' conception in 1:48.[74] It is used only one other time in the New Testament, in James 2:3, where the meaning conveys a special respect or attention given to people of special status.

In line with the theme of reversal in Luke, it is fitting that such respect, when it is noted in his gospel account, occurs not for the wealthy or high in status, but for the "lowly" (1:48), those toward whom society does not traditionally pay such heed—indeed, to the child in the midst (cf. 9:46-48 for Jesus' more explicit acknowledgment of this reversal in God's measure of greatness). In this way, the father shows a strong compassion and concern for his child; and Jesus, honoring the father's request, mirrors this same compassion and concern—indeed, looking upon the boy with favor and grace.

Following the pattern of the previous two child healings, Luke continues to describe the child in this account as silent. Nevertheless, such silence should not be mistaken for complacence or lack of agency. Rather, it is both a symptom of the adult-centric narrative in which the story stands and a severe malady that afflicts the boy within it. With reference to the latter, Bovon reflects, "The condition that we today call epilepsy is one of the most cryptic of diseases. The loss of consciousness for a time would have meant in antiquity that the afflicted person was possessed by a superhuman power. What could anyone, either the shocked spectator or the sick person, do to stop it?"[75] The boy does not approach Jesus on his own account not for lack of will or lack of faithfulness, but, quite simply, because he is afflicted—so much so that even when Jesus calls for his father to *bring him*, "the demon dashed him [the boy] to the ground in convulsions" (Lk 9:42). Undeniably, it is the very dependency of this sick child—just as, it should be noted, an epileptic adult would also have been dependent upon the good will of another—that highlights the power and compassion of God through Jesus. The boy may not be able to request his own healing, but he remains the focus of his father and Jesus throughout the account.

This singularity of focus is highlighted by Luke's emphasis on the healing as one of compassion and not of faith (*contra* Mark 9:23–24; Matt 17:19–20). In the face of the boy's suffering, Luke's Jesus is not primarily concerned with using this child to teach adults a lesson—neither the disciples who could not heal the child nor the boy's father himself. Biblical interpreters of texts involving children could take a cue here. Instead, Luke is interested in highlighting the compassion and power of God.[76] Consequently, "Jesus does not examine the father's guilt—which would have corresponded to a possible doctrine of retribution in contemporary Judaism—but has only the future of the possessed boy in view."[77] From the father's request, Jesus' reaction, and his ultimate healing, the boy remains resolutely at the center of this scene.[78]

Third, Luke signals the boy's inclusion in his father's household through the father's impassioned plea and Jesus' subsequent return of the child to his father. Jesus' action of returning the boy to his father (9:42) recalls Jesus' previous encounter in which he gives the resuscitated youth to his mother at Nain (7:15).[79] The verbs, however, reflect a significant, while nuanced, difference between the two exchanges. The youth at Nain is already dead; his mother has lost him. Therefore, Jesus "gives him" (ἔδωκεν αὐτὸν) in the simplest sense of the English term. In contrast, the boy in 9:37–45 is not dead, nor has his father yet counted him as a loss.

The impassioned appeal that the father makes for his son marks the value of the child in his household. Tannehill notes, "The father's request for help is long in comparison with other elements of the story. It contains vivid description of his son's suffering."[80] Throughout the narrative, before and after Jesus heals the boy, the words and actions of the father testify to the inclusion of the boy in his father's household. Although his father may be stigmatized by his inability to work in the household in the expected way, or potentially, to produce heirs, the father remains steadfastly committed to this boy as a valued part of his family and home.

Thus, it would be inappropriate for Jesus to "give" this child back to the father, who already squarely "possesses" him as such. Instead, Luke relates, Jesus "gave him back to his father" (ἀπέδωκεν αὐτὸν τὸν τῷ πατρὶ αὐτοῦ, 9:42). The prefix ἀπό added to the main verb changes the sense from a one-sided gift to the return of the object, in this case, a child, to the original possessor. Hence, it is translated as "give back," "return," or even "restore."[81] In this instance, the child enters into Jesus' custody temporarily when the father brings him to Jesus (vv. 41–42); however, the boy's place in the household is never fully lost. Nevertheless, the shift from describing the boy solely by his relationship ("son") to the more independent signification of "boy" or "child" after he is healed in v. 42 may indicate that Jesus returns to the father not just a son, which he has always had, but a *child*, who is now able to fully participate in the household to which he has always belonged.

Finally, Luke again signals the boy's inclusion in the broader community by dislocating the confidence of those who might have previously condescended toward him, while at the same time locating the boy himself among the crowd. This final point, which points to Luke's emphasis on the significant inclusion of the boy within the broader community, hinges largely on the demarcation of the unit. Form critics such as Fitzmyer and Bovon[82] tend to describe the section as complete at v. 43b, with the rationale that "the unit 9:37–43a forms a complete healing miracle."[83] Narrative critics such as Tannehill and Johnson, however, take a more holistic approach, reading 9:37–50 as a single scene.[84]

Apart from the unity seen most simply in the narrative indicators of continuous time (e.g. "While everyone was amazed . . ." v. 43b; "[and][85] an argument arose among them . . ." (v. 46), both Tannehill and Johnson identify in this larger unit a common emphasis on the inabilities of the disciples.[86] Narratologically, I agree with this demarcation; however, for the purposes of this chapter, I end the scene dealing specifically with the healing of the boy at v. 45, since I have already dealt significantly with the final segment (9:46–50) above.

In terms of the boy's restoration to community, moreover, it is this section (vv. 43b–45) that most explicitly applies. Johnson notes, "Luke intentionally joins this second passion prediction (cf. 9:22) to the previous story by the participle, 'while they were all marveling' (v. 43b), rather than the more general introduction used by Mark 9:30 and Matt 17:22."[87] Such a joining fits with the Lukan theme of inclusion, allowing the crowds who have just experienced the strength of God's power to listen in on the future surrender of this power upon which Jesus is about to embark.[88]

"Disciples" rarely signifies the Twelve assumed adults in Luke's narrative, referring instead to the broader group of Jesus' followers among whom there likely were children.[89] Moreover, the "great crowd" (Lk 9:37) itself, given the demographics and social makeup of first century Galilee, would have almost certainly included children. Therefore, the boy's return to and inclusion among this group would not be atypical, but rather an indication of his restoration to his community at large. Furthermore, to the extent that these two groups—the disciples and the crowd—are included in Jesus' teaching,

Jesus implicitly addresses the boy, along with other children as a part of the larger audience.

What, then, does this crowd—including its children—hear? To begin with, within the core healing story itself, Jesus exclaims, "You faithless and perverse generation, how much longer must I be with you and bear with you?" (Lk 9:41). Given their identified emphasis on the inabilities of the disciples, Tannehill and Johnson see the disciples as the primary audience of this rebuke.[90] Alternately, Fitzmyer suggests, "The 'all' of v. 43b [*sic.*] would seem to indicate that Luke was referring to both the disciples and the others."[91] Despite a possible priority given to the disciples' hearing of this message, taken in its broader context I am inclined to agree that it is not intended to be heard solely by them.

The general reference to the entirety of the present "generation" (γενεὰ, Lk 9:41), combined with the presence of the crowd described in v. 37, and with the inclusive "all" (πάντες, v. 43a) to which Fitzmyer refers, points to the possibility of a correspondingly inclusive reading of the audience. Nevertheless, it is disappointing that both Fitzmyer, in his affirmation of an extended audience, and Tannehill, in his rejection of the same, focus on the possible audience as limited to the father, the disciples, and the crowd, without giving specific reference to the boy himself, or, not unexpectedly, his peers among the crowd.[92] I propose that, while the disciples' shortcomings seem to be the motivation behind Jesus' lament, his words are directed more generally towards all those with ears to hear. That children could and would have been included in such a judgment of "this generation" has already been shown in relation to the sign of Jonah (11:29–32) and the days of Noah and Lot (17:25ff.).

Assuming the presence of children in the intended audience of this lament, however, one also hears a veiled reference to their presence, as part of the crowd and disciples, "with Jesus," who is compelled to "bear with" the present generation despite their faithlessness and perversity (Lk 9:41).[93] Indeed, resignation to such a calling—bearing with humanity in all of its failures—may be indicated by Jesus' shift from his communal lament to the singular command, "Bring your son" (v. 41b). If this is so, then the inclusion of the boy, and likely other children as well, in the initial audience becomes even more probable. Despite humanity's faithlessness, Jesus continues to extend God's power and mercy to those, like the boy, who are in need.

Such encompassing inclusion is further experienced when one considers the remainder of the narrative (v. 43b–45, and v. 46–50) as an extension of this first scene. In v. 43b, Jesus returns his attention to his disciples, but again, with the crowd, the father, and the child still in earshot. Not coincidentally, then, his address revolves, as it does throughout the Lukan narrative, on the ability of his followers to hear and understand (9:44a). Jesus addresses the disciples, but they do not understand. On the other hand, the possibility remains that others in the crowd might respond differently. Regardless, however, all have equal opportunity to hear this second announcement of Jesus' passion as he prepares to embark on the road towards Jerusalem. All—including the boy and his peers—are privy to the unfolding of Jesus' ministry in their generation and in their lives.

Moreover, returning to Johnson's suggestion that the boy in Lk 9:47 might be the same boy from v. 42, it is possible to infer that there is already one in the midst of the disciples and the crowd who is prepared to respond at Jesus' directive. Expounding on this possibility, Johnson points out, "Jesus could pick *anybody* to do what he has picked [the Twelve] to do."[94] Johnson sees the ordinariness of the child as serving to drive home Jesus' point. Not only could Jesus have picked *any adult*, but even a child is capable of the tasks laid out for the Twelve. Johnson explains, "The very powerlessness of a child makes the point dramatically."[95] Although Johnson's goal is to emphasize Jesus' critique of the disciples, implicitly he lifts up the possibility that within Jesus' framework for the Kingdom, children qualify as disciples by all the same criteria as the Twelve.

Their individual identities notwithstanding, the boy of 9:42, the child of 9:47, and indeed each one of the disciples themselves, do not earn their place in the Kingdom of God or achieve their individual greatness. Instead, just as the boy is healed from his demon possession by God's great power and compassion, so too are the disciples made "great" in the Kingdom of God by God's great power and compassion. So much so that, even when they behave poorly and disappoint (cf. 9:41), God continues to extend a welcoming hand, welcoming all of God's children—child and adult—into Jesus' ministry for the sake of God's Kingdom.

JESUS' TALE OF THE RESTORATION OF TWO BROTHERS TO THEIR FATHER (15:11–32)

The Brothers as Children

In each of the healing accounts discussed so far, it has become clear that Luke's primary concern is not the dissipation of a particular illness, but the demonstration of God's power and grace. As the narrative moves from these initial demonstrations of God's power, Jesus takes on an increased teaching role. Notwithstanding, the themes of God's power and grace—and, indeed, of the inclusivity of these experiences—continue to predominate.

It is difficult to distinguish specific addressees of Jesus' teachings beyond general audiences such as the disciples and crowds discussed above. It is correspondingly difficult to weigh whether such audiences may have included children among them; however, themes of the teachings can provide some clues. In particular, children respond to stories about other children with whom they can identify.[96] Establishing among Jesus' parables, then, stories that involve children's experience of inclusion points to this as a broader theme in Jesus' teaching and as a potentially lived experienced by children among Luke's imagined audience, to whom the parables are addressed.

The difficulty of determining approximate ages of characters in Luke's gospel account, which is itself conveyed as story, is amplified in determining the ages of characters in the parabolic accounts contained therein. It is entirely possible, in fact probable, that the characters in these parables in their earliest forms were never conceived with a specific age. The advantage and disadvantage of this is that it leaves the reader to fill in this literary gap with a plausible and legitimate estimation. Furthermore, to suggest that elements of this parable can appeal to the experience of children is not to suggest that children were its sole or even primary audience. As Aasgaard notes, "the boundaries between tales for children and adults were probably far from distinct."[97]

Instead, I suggest that this parable contains a message that would be applicable to children as well as adults and that the child audience is equally included in the experience of grace offered by the forgiving father; unfortunately, a childist perspective of this text has been dormant for far too long. The question, therefore, in relation to Luke 15:11–32 is not so much whether the brothers *must* be understood as children—indeed, this cannot be known and may never have been intended to have been known. Instead, the question is, from a childist perspective, whether these brothers *can* feasibly be understood as children. Contextual clues in the text help to determine this.

Most interpretations of this parable do not specifically address the age of the brothers in the story. Nevertheless, the adultist trend in biblical scholarship comes out subtly through commentators' typical references to the younger brother as a "young man."[98] Such a moniker, while not specifically ascertaining the character's maturity, seems to lean in that direction; still, it is important to note the room for interpretation that even this appellation gives. Alternatively, Ibita and Bieringer use a similarly ambiguous moniker on the other end of the spectrum, suggesting that the "Parable of the Prodigal Son gives voice to both an erring and (self-)righteous child."[99] Although they do not elaborate further on their reasoning for reading the younger son as a child, the context of Ibita and Bieringer's essay suggests a reading that understands this character in a youthful way.

Similarly, artistic depictions of the parable range the spectrum from Leonello Spada's rather youthful portrait in *Return of the Prodigal* (ca. 1680)[100] in what appears to be adolescence or early teenage years to Pieter Coecke van Aelst's likeness depicting a much older son, surrounded by prostitutes and bearing full facial hair in *Scenes from the Life of the Prodigal* (ca. 1530),[101] with all manner of more ambiguous representations in between that skate the boundary between adolescent and young adult.[102] Following this pattern of treating the sons' ages as a relatively malleable construct, I project a portrait of the younger son in early to mid-adolescence, drawn from socio-cultural background about and textual inferences within the parable itself.

Socio-cultural study of the place of children in the first century Roman world suggests that at as young as five years old, children began to take a significant place in the household ecosystem. Boys in particular frequently began work in the fields around this age, either as the free sons of modest landowners or as slaves or day workers on larger estates. In small estates, such as the one described in Luke's parable, the landowner, his children, and their slaves are said to have worked side-by-side to harvest the land (see Lk 15:25, 29).[103] Thus, Horn and Martens are led to conclude, "Whether or not the [younger] son was still a child, the work he did was identical with the kind of work which children performed on large estates."[104] The agricultural context of the parable thus allows the possibility that one or both brothers are not yet adults.

Other means of distinguishing between boys and men in the ancient Mediterranean context included marriage and civic service. In the Roman context the years between the beginning of civic engagement (between 15 and 17) and marriage (between 25 and 30) marked a liminal pre-adult period. With relation to the outer edge of this period, neither brother in Luke's parable appears to be married. In particular, the younger brother is said to have left home with no other attachments. One contemporary Mediterranean mother reflects anecdotally on this absence, noting "that as a parent she can understand the father's generous forgiveness of the younger son, but she would not have understood this before becoming a parent. 'That's why the older son cannot experience' the father's reaction."[105] Likewise, the younger son, if he had a family for which he was responsible, would not have had the luxury to behave so irresponsibly. Both brothers seem to be missing a part of the generational puzzle.[106] As such, the assumption can reasonably be made that the brothers are to be understood as a part of the youngest generation in the father's household—as still themselves *children*. Similarly, with relation to the former period of civic engagement, neither brother appears to have left home for military service or to anticipate the future imposition of such a role, which suggests that these Roman categories are not applicable to them. Lacking such formal recognition of a change in civic responsibility, and with no indication of the presence of wives or children for either brother, Luke gives no indication of the attainment of adulthood with regard to either brother.

Further textual clues bolster this interpretation of the two brothers as (likely adolescent) children, including the place of each youth in his father's estate, possible intertextual parallels within the Hebrew Bible, and the broader context of Luke's narrative in which the parable is told. To begin with, the most ostensibly apparent clues as to the position of each brother within the household have to do with the distribution of the estate. In Lk 15:12 the younger brother asks for "the share of the property" (μέρος τῆς οὐσίας). Much ink has been spilt on determining the legal or contractual particularities of the inheritance that this request describes. Given the parabolic nature of this story, however, I concur with the strand of scholarship that sees less need in ascertaining the specific origin and legal ramifications of the practice so much as determining its narrative place and function.

As for the plausibility of such a practice as the distribution of one's estate before one's death, while the Jewish law does not specifically account for it, the intertestamental texts of Tobit and Sirach point to the practice, if not the wisdom, of such an act. In Tobit, Raguel's gift of half of all he owns to Tobias at the marriage for Tobias and Raguel's daughter (an only child) sets a precedent for the division of inheritance while the head of the household is still living (Tobit 8:19–21). Likewise, explicit heed against such practice in the book of Sirach suggests that such a practice was known to exist among the Israelites (see Sir 33:19–23). Further, while Raguel's gift occurs at the marriage of his daughter, understood as her entry into adulthood, the description in Sirach places no such restrictions on the breadth of the practice—broadly advising against the distribution of one's property to anybody before one's death. Indeed, the parable fits better the generalities of this context given the evidence against the marriage of either brother as discussed above.

In this light, the brazenness of the younger brother in asking for such a distribution of his father's wealth can be read less as an indication of his own maturity to receive such a gift and more as an indication of his youthful impudence. Neither son has a legal claim on the property of which the young son makes his demand. The claim the younger son makes upon his father is phrased in the future tense in Lk 15:12. Thus, the distribution of the wealth is at the sole discretion of the father as *pater familias*. This would have been the case in the ancient world regardless of the ages of the brothers.

This relationship of subservience of the brothers to their father is further indicated by the older son's continued status within the household below his father, even after the younger son receives his share. Bovon notes that in Lk 15:22–23, "It is evident that for Luke the father remains in control of that part of his estate that he has not already given to his younger son. The older son does not complain about that fact."[107] Given the structure of the ancient household, such subservience would have existed between the *pater familias* and his sons for the entirety of the father's lifespan, regardless of the age of his sons. In contemporary sensibilities, however, the deference that the older son shows to his father speaks again to a perception of youthfulness more than anything else. The older son does not complain about his role because he, just as his younger brother will once he is restored to the family, remains in a position of dependence in relation to his father. Such dependence can, though it need not, indicate the youth of the brothers involved.

Moreover, the use of language and themes within the parable call to mind more specific intertexts within the Hebrew Bible, which while not explicitly mentioned, would have been familiar to the Lukan author and his audience and so readily called to mind. These texts, in addition to bolstering the theme of forgiveness and acceptance at the heart of the parable,[108] also link the figure of the young son with other well-known youths in the Israelite tradition.

First, Bovon suggests that reference to a famine in Lk 15:13 can be read as a formulaic element that "recalls Joseph's saga, or the story of Tobias."[109] To this, one could also add the "travel to a distant country" (v. 13) as reminiscent of both these accounts. Moreover, Bovon compares the father's gift of the ring and shoes to Pharaoh's gifts to Joseph in Gen 41:42, suggesting an overall strong link to the Joseph narrative.[110] While, obviously, Joseph's narrative in the Hebrew Bible spans the entirety of his life, his journey to the distant country of Egypt begins when his brothers sell him into slavery at the age of seventeen (Gen 37:2–28)—within the period of adolescence as it is loosely defined. Similarly, while the book of Tobit does not so distinctly define Tobias' age, with nearly half of the narrative occurring prior to his marriage (Tobit 1:1–6:18) and spanning itself a fair number of years, it can be assumed that when Tobias begins this account of his life it is at a relatively early age.

Hence, the characters with whom the Lukan author and his audience, and indeed, the Jewish audience within the narrative context of Jesus' parable itself, would most readily have identified with the younger brother would have been youths at the intersection of childhood and adult responsibility, who had not yet themselves become fully men in the social sense of the term.

Lastly, the broader context of Luke's narrative teeming as it is with children just beneath the surface supports a reading of the two brothers in the parable as themselves children. The father's exclamation in Luke 15:24a, "For this son of mine was dead and is alive again," while it has connections to the broader resurrection of Jesus and all of the saints, is most immediately associated with the two resuscitation accounts already discussed (Lk 7:11–17 and 8:40–56). In each case, the person restored to life has been shown to be a child or young adolescent, not yet possessing the full social integration characteristic of an adult.

The restoration of this third child to "life" in the eyes of his father should not be lost as a part of the broader narrative of restoration, which the Lukan author is spinning through the narration of these stories. Ultimately, through Jesus' resurrection, this is made complete as the relationship between humanity itself and our creator God are restored (cf. Lk 24:46–47). In the meantime, however, the Lukan author lays the groundwork for this conclusion by carefully retelling the restoration of dependent children to their parents in the persons of the youth at Nain and his mother, the girl in Galilee and Jairus, her father, and now, finally, with a parabolic connection to God's self, this young brother and his forgiving Father.

Even within the parable's more immediate literary context, a connection to children can be seen. The parable of the two brothers occurs within the larger literary unit of parables of "lost and found" in Luke's gospel, beginning with a shepherd who loses his sheep (15:1–7), continuing with a woman who loses her coin (Lk 15:8–10), and culminating in the longer narration of a father who loses his son (Lk 15:11–32). Turid Karlsen Seim sees in these first two parables an example of what she terms "gender pairs"[111]—"a dual witnessing in the sense of a duplication of testimonials to address an audience composed of men and women . . ." By this logic, the Lukan author tells a stories of restoration respectively centered on a male and a female in order to appeal to his larger audience.

However, beyond perhaps an unstated assumption of the Lukan author's patriarchal preference, Karlsen Seim does not explain the presence of the third and final parable about two brothers and their father that follows this gender pair. While not negating the value for a feminist reading of noting gender pairings in Luke's text, it is possible to read this grouping of parables in a different way, through the lens of the ancient household. To this end, the model of the ancient *Haustafel*, or "household code" lends an interesting parallel.

The traditional structure of such a household code involves instructions for husbands and wives, parents and children, and masters and slaves—the three primary relationships in the traditional household.[112] To this end, the owner of an estate—for example, one that possessed one hundred sheep—would not likely have been found directly tending the animals himself. Instead, the role of "shepherd" was often given to the slaves and the children in the family. In the case of a large estate, this role would have fallen to a slave or hired worker.[113] As such, in addition to presenting male-female counterparts, this literary unit presents images from all spheres of household relations—the sphere of service/work in the person of the shepherd as represented in the *haustafel* by the relationship of a master and a slave; the sphere of domesticity/marriage in the person of the woman searching within her house, as represented in the *haustafel* by the relationship of a husband and a wife; and, finally, the sphere of child-rearing in the persons of the two brothers and their father, most explicitly defined, as represented in the *haustafel* by the relationship of parents to their children.

The proper management of God's household, by this measure, is one of grace and inclusivity—even in the face of offense. Such advice runs counter, of course, to most judicious codes of household conduct that one would expect either in antiquity or today. Indeed, Carolyn Osiek and David Balch note, in ancient agrarian society, the parable of the prodigal son would be "an alienating, offensive, implausible, potentially transforming metaphor of the kingdom of God clashing with centuries of domestic, didactic wisdom."[114] However, it is just such offense that leaves room for Luke's depiction of the radical grace and inclusion extended by God. Indeed, the former two parables also place the traditional *haustafel* on its head, focusing on the agency of the lesser party (slave or woman) and celebrating small returns; however, it fits seamlessly with Luke's message of inclusion and forgiveness.

Thus, more than just bringing out the gendered nature of Luke's audience as Karlsen Seim rightly observes, the attention to all spheres of the household structure in this unit of parables in fact can be understood to point to the diversity of ages and genders, not just among the crowds who followed Jesus, but among the first audiences who heard and read Luke's gospel as well. Such a reading lends even greater weight to this combination of parables as Karlsen Seim describes it, "a literary device by which the author seeks to capture the attention of a mixed audience."[115] In this way, not only does the text of the parable point to the identity of the brothers (or at minimum the younger brother) themselves as children, but it opens the way for a more inclusive understanding of Luke's audience as well.

The Young Slave as Child

The brothers need not be the only children uncovered in this text. As with the servant of the centurion (7:1–10), a group of slaves is again referred to as τῶν παιδίων in Luke 15:26. Although this term can be understood more as a form of diminutive address rather than of actual age when used in reference to a worker, several conditions in Luke's parable suggest otherwise in this circumstance.

To begin with, parallels with first century agricultural estates suggest an analogous atmosphere to that described in the parable.[116] Horn and Martens observe these parallels, suggesting that given the lack of distinctions seen in the age of agricultural slaves, "among these slave workers there were also children."[117] Thus, the presence of workers who were both slaves and children would have been common and expected in the audience's frame of reference (with respect to the audience of the parable and that of the gospel itself). Once again acknowledging that, given the storied nature of the narrative, there is no real fixed age for the characters in the parable, such possibility allows room for a plausible and legitimate reading of the servant as a child slave. Moreover, the likelihood that the group of slaves in Lk 15:26 are children is increased by their proximity to the house (see Lk 15:25 ". . . and when he came and approached the house . . ."). As demonstrated above, child slaves, particularly the very young, were frequently assigned to duties within the house—just as the young children of the household also were. Thus, the probability is raised that this slave, who is referred to by the common term for a young child, is indeed a young child.[118]

The value of such a reading can be seen in that, unlike in Lk 7:1–10, here it is the narrator and not any of the other characters who refers to the slave who the elder brother summons as a παῖς. This term is frequently used in ancient literature with reference to (presumed) adult slaves as a specific term of relationship, for example, referring to a close or trusted status of the slave.[119] However, since it is employed here with reference to a group of slaves about whom the parable gives no other indication of special status and is used as an objective description rather than a personal address, such connotations seem to be missing. The neutrality of the narrator's use of the term (contrast with Lk 7:2–3, 10), then, taken together with the expectation of child slaves among the estate, suggests a valid reading of the slave whom the elder brother summons as a young child.

Given use of the more general term δοῦλος throughout the gospel and Acts already detailed in relation to the slave in Lk 7:1–10, it is evident that the term is well known by the Lukan author and preferred, in general, to the more exceptional use of παῖς, used only here and at Luke 7:7. As such, παῖς, should not be understood as a neutral synonym for δοῦλος within the Lukan author's vocabulary, but rather as an indication of special status, or, more simply age. This is corroborated by the exclusive use of παῖς as a term of servitude by the Lukan author in Acts as a double reference to an individual's special status before God as slave and child.

A childist reading therefore legitimately understands the slave with whom the elder brother converses as a child. Moreover, the fact that this child slave is clearly portrayed as knowledgable about the events of the household lends further credence to the inclusion of children in the household, at work, and even in celebratory events—all places where children, slave and free, whose families came into contact with Jesus through his ministry would themselves be likely to encounter Jesus.

Experiences of Inclusion

Luke's parable in 15:11–32 presents not one but three child characters through whom to learn about Jesus' extension of God's grace and welcome to children in his midst. Indeed, each character experiences this inclusive grace in a different way, which will be explored in turn. Before moving to these individual analyses, however, it is worth noticing that in this fundamental teaching about God's relationship with God's people, unique to Luke, every character who is given a speaking role, with the exception of the father who is to be understood as personifying God, is portrayed as a *child*.

Such a cast of characters cannot help but recall and deepen the reader or hearer's understanding of Jesus' words in 9:48: "Whoever welcomes this child in my name welcomes me . . . for the least among all of you is the greatest," and, indeed anticipate Luke 18:17: "Truly I tell you, whoever does not receive the kingdom of God as a little child will never enter it." However, before Luke brings his audience to contemplating how, in fact, children receive God's Kingdom, through the parable of these two brothers, he lays out the abundant grace with which God first receives such children into God's Kingdom God's self.

God's gracious inclusion of even wayward children in the Kingdom is first revealed through the father's treatment of the younger son in the parable. This son demonstrates arrogance and disrespect early in the parable, beginning with his imperious demand of his father (Lk 15:12). Certain socio-cultural models even suggest that the manner with which the boy leaves his household would have necessitated the father ceremonially declaring him "dead" to him, thus explaining the father's words in 15:24, 32 and necessitating the restorative acts of 15:22. In any case, the son has clearly used up all of his inheritance (Lk 15:13) and returns to the family with his previous sense of entitlement stricken (cf. Lk 15:18–19 ". . . and I will say to [my father], ". . . Father, I am no longer worthy to be called your son.").

This boy, who once thought so highly of himself and his independence, has now reached his ultimate low. Jewish purity traditions about swine already set the stage for the young man's ostracization. When this parable is heard following the story of the Gerasene demoniac (Lk 8:26–39) in which Jesus allows unclean spirits to enter into a heard of swine, the ante is upped. Within this context, Johnson concludes, "To tend the pigs of a Gentile is about as alienated as a Jew could imagine being."[120] This son has nothing left to offer and returns to his father not as an idealistically innocent youth, but rather as a child who has known and been known by the world and seeks now in the household of his father the security and provision (v. 17) that he has lost.

Luke's depiction of this repentant boy (v. 17)[121] contrasts sharply with many contemporary notions of what it means to receive the Kingdom of God as a child. In their place, Luke makes room for the more realistic person of the "knowing child"[122]—one among the many children stricken by war, famine, prostitution, hunger, and all other kinds of hardship and abuse. It is such a child (and readers and hearers might also infer, such an adult,) who comes to God of their own free will and agency. The son himself is the subject of the first two verbs in Lk 15:20 "set off" (ἀναστὰς) and "went" (ἦλθεν), as well as the turning action of coming to himself (ἐλθὼν, v. 17), just as he was the subject of the verbs leading to his temporary alienation—when he first "gathered" (συναγαγών) all that he had, then traveled (ἀπεδήμησεν) to a faraway country and "squandered" (διεσκόρπισεν) it (v. 13).

This child is not only included in God's grace and mercy by the forgiveness of his father, but the need for forgiveness also shows his inclusion in the whole course of human sin that first carried him away from his father. Carroll concludes, "Indeed, if the father in the parable of the two sons is viewed as a positive character, perhaps an image of the extravagantly compassionate, merciful God (15:11–32), then even wayward, disappointing, and rebellious children do not forfeit the loving care of their fathers (parents)."[123] Neither Jesus nor the narrator excuses the son's actions on account of his youth. Rather, through his example, God extends forgiveness and mercy to the young son not because of the boy's childishness or even in spite of his childishness, but rather, the boy is restored to relationship solely on account of *God's* graciousness.

Likewise, inclusion in God's Kingdom is also extended to the elder son on the same grounds of paternal graciousness. So Johnson observes, "It is his [the father's] even-handed compassion and concern that extends to both children."[124] Although the actions of this elder boy remain unresolved at the end of the parable, he too is granted the liberty to act for himself. Even after their tense exchange regarding the father's reception of his brother in Lk 15:28–30, the father maintains their relationship both by calling him by the endearing relational term of "child" (τέκνον, v. 31) and by reminding him, in the present tense, "you know that all that is mine *is* yours" (σὺ πάντοτε μετ' ἐμοῦ πάντα τὰ ἐμά σά ἐστιν, v. 31 emphasis added). Here again, a reading that foregrounds the boy's youth foreshadows Jesus' more well-known saying about children in Luke 18:15–17: "For it is to such as these that the kingdom of God *belongs*" (Lk 18:16b emphasis added). Even before the boy moves to enter the party or accept his brother, his father reminds him of his own ongoing inclusion in his household as a member of the family.[125]

Finally, there comes the less extreme, but nonetheless meaningful expression of inclusion extended toward the child slave in Luke's parable. As noted above, this child is well integrated into household, being readily able to summarize for the elder son the events that have taken place while he was in the field: "Your brother has come, and your father has killed the fatted calf, because he has got him back safe and sound" (Lk 15:27). This child, even as a slave, is thus included in the activities and celebrations that the father—the landowner—has set about. Furthermore, as a member of the more general class of δοῦλοι in the estate, the young slave also counts among those whom the young son reflects, "How many of my father's hired hands have bread enough and to spare . . ." (Lk 15:17). The young son's lament reveals that slaves, including child slaves, are provided for in this father's household and given more than enough. Indeed, it is likely to such slaves that the boy compares himself when he imagines a better lot back home. Such a comparison parallels his own youth and his role as a hired worker feeding pigs, a job often associated with children.

Just as the young son returns seeking security in the father's household, so this security is already present for the young slaves to whom the elder brother calls. In this way, albeit given the disparities of slavery and status that cannot and should not be ignored, the young slave is also extended by the parable a place in the household of God.

CONCLUSION

Taken together, these five narratives—one healing, two resuscitations, one exorcism, and one reconciliation—represent far more than individual testimonies to the presence of children in Luke's gospel account or the receipt by such children of Jesus' ministrations. Rather, these narratives tell of this and much more. This string of stories, largely within the broader section of Luke's gospel dealing with the restoration to God of the lost, form a narrative pattern by which one experiences time and time again through very different circumstances and very different children the extent of God's inclusive and restorative grace.

Children are not simply rhetorical shorthand for humility or innocence to the Lukan author. Each child who experiences restoration at the word of Jesus in these narratives is a distinct individual. Their accounts are highlighted in the text among the many children whom Jesus healed who are not mentioned explicitly (see Lk 4:40–41) in order to illustrate the breadth and depth of the restoration and renewal that God is bringing about through Jesus. Recall the words of angel Gabriel's prophecy about John to Zechariah, "With the spirit and power of Elijah he will go before him, to turn the hearts of parents to their children, and the disobedient to the wisdom of the righteous, to make ready a people prepared for the Lord" (Lk 1:17). Through Jesus, children and adults together experience restoration.

In Luke's theology, the Lord has come to bring about a Kingdom that reaches out to the outcast and celebrates the return of the lost. Although in all but one of these accounts of restoration the voices of the children themselves have not been preserved, the power of Jesus' intervention for them remains. By re-imagining the place of these children in Luke's narrative, Horn and Martens remind us that Jesus' actions are "not simply for the sake of the parents, but for the children's own well-being."[126] Through Jesus, children are included in the restoration that God is bringing into the world.[127]

Such inclusion of children in the ancient world was not, of course, unique to Jesus or to Christianity.[128] The concern and action on behalf of children by the adult members of their household, both Jewish and Gentile, illustrate the valued place that children held as a part of their communities and their families. The message that emerges from attention to child characters in Luke's gospel, then, is neither one that demands of adults a caricatured "child-like" response to Christ nor one of Christian moral superiority with regard to Christ's response to children. Instead, through Jesus' encounter and interaction with these children, Luke includes them within a broader narrative of restoration and grace that brings hope to the lost and renewal to the marginalized and afflicted.

NOTES

1. In what follows I specifically avoid the typical labels given to these characters (Widow's son, Jairus' daughter, son, and prodigal son respectively) as resistance to the adult-centric narrative in which their stories are preserved. By naming these children on their own terms, even when proper names are not given, I seek to emphasize the personhood of the children in these accounts as specific characters and not merely in relation to the adult characters given primacy of place in Luke's narrative.

2. Warren Carter, *Households and Discipleship: A Study of Matthew 19–20* (Sheffield: Sheffield Academic Press, 1994) 97.

3. This list differs slightly from a similar list that Horn and Martens provide, focused more exclusively on healings as opposed to the above broader definition of the receipt of God's grace (thus excluding parabolic representations, such as the latter listed here). Their Markan focus also omits the youth at Nain, recorded only in Luke, while adding the account of the Syro-Phoenician's daughter, not present in Luke's account.

4. Horn and Martens, 93.

5. See chapter 1.

6. Note that at the level of tradition, Horn and Martens call this into question, suggesting in light of similarities between Lk 7:1–10 and its Matthean parallel (Matt 8:5–13) with the healing of a royal official's child in John 4:46–54 that "Perhaps the slave was a child, and that detail was lost in the synoptic authors, except for the use

of *pais* (Mt 8:6, 8; Lk 7:7)" (264). While such a conclusion could simply refer to the age of the slave, if one accepts a connection between the three accounts, it may also reflect a possibility that in a separate tradition (from which John draws), the ill person was understood not as a slave at all, but as the child of the official. So also Fitzmyer understands παῖς as "servant boy" in light of a form critical tradition in which he relates this scene to both John's account and, following Bultmann, as a possible variant of the healing of the Syro-Phoenician woman's child (Matt 15:21–28; Mark 7:24–31) absent in Luke (Joseph A. Fitzmyer, *The Gospel According to Luke I-IX* [New York: Doubleday, 1970] 648).

7. Marianne Bjelland Kartzow, "Slave Children in the First-Century Jesus Movement," in *Childhood in History: Perceptions of Children in the Ancient and Medieval Worlds*, edited by Reidar Aasgaard, Cornelia Horn, and Oana Maria Cojocaru (London: Routledge, 2017) 111.

8. See Hanne Sigismund-Nielsen, "Slave and Lower-Class Roman Children" in *The Oxford Handbook of Childhood and Education in the Classical World*, edited by Judith Grubbs, Tim Parkin, and Roslynne Bell (Oxford: Oxford University Press, 2013) 287–293.

9. Kartzow, 115; cf. her compelling case for the potential youthfulness of the servants in Luke 12:41–48, pp. 116–118.

10. This is further emphasized with the textual variant τίμος in MS D.

11. Sigismund-Nielsen, 294.

12. Sigismund-Nielsen, 298. While this term has been connected by some historians with relationships of a sexual nature, recent scholarship has begun to call such a direct relationship between the known use of child slaves as sexual playthings and the relationship indicated by the term *delicia* into question (see Sigismund-Nielsen, 298; Christian Laes, "Desperately Different? *Delicia* Children in the Roman Household," in *Early Christian Families in Context: An Interdisciplinary Dialogue*, ed. David Balch and Carolyn Osiek (Grand Rapids: Wm. Eerdmann's, 2003) 298-326, esp. 320.

13. See Lk 2:29; 7:2–3, 8, 10; 12:37, 43, 45–47; 14:17, 21–23; 15:22; 17:7, 9–10; 19:13, 15, 17, 22; 20:10–11; 22:50; Acts 2:18; 4:29; 16:17.

14. See François Bovon, *Luke 2*, translated by Donald S. Deer (Minneapolis: Fortress Press, 2013) 261.

15. The presence of a child in this narrative may also be supported, though loosely, by the intertextual connection to Elisha's healing of Naaman, which occurs at the intercession of a young Jewish girl (cf. Luke Timothy Johnson, *The Gospel of Luke* [Collegeville, MN: Liturgical Press, 1991] 120; Robert C. Tannehill, *Luke* [Nashville, Abingdon Press, 1996] 123–124) for the parallels between the two accounts.

16. Tannehill, 125.

17. Tannehill, 126.

18. See John T. Carroll, "'What Then Will This Child Become?': Perspectives on Children in the Gospel of Luke, " in *The Child in the Bible*, edited by Marcia Bunge, Terence Fretheim, and Beverly Roberts Gaventa, 177–194 (Grand Rapids: Wm. B. Eerdman's, 2008) 180–181: "Typically, in Lukan healing stories, the children Jesus aids are their parents' *only* children (this is also the case for the only son of the widow

at Nain in 7:11–17, although the age of the dead son is unknown." For precedence on including this story among Luke's child healing accounts, see also Carroll, 171.

19. See Horn and Martens, 93.

20. See Lesley Dean-Jones, "The Child Patient of the Hippocratics: Early Pediatrics?" in *The Oxford Handbook of Childhood and Education in the Classical World*, edited by Judith Evan Grubbs and Tim Parkin, 108–124 (Oxford: Oxford University Press, 2013): "According to *Fleshes* 13, a child becomes a *neaniskos* between the ages of fourteen and twenty-one" (110).

21. LSJ, 1163.

22. See Tannehill, 127.

23. While the original Hebrew maintains a bit more variance in terminology, the general sense remains the same—the boys are certainly not infants, given their ability to carry themselves; however, neither are they full grown. See Parker, 144–155 for a detailed discussion on the Shunammite's son of 2 Kings 4, with the conclusion that "the boy appears relatively young since a servant lifts and brings him to his mother (v. 20) and she carries him out of the prophet's chamber at the end of the story (v. 37)" (Parker, 145). See also Parker 61–64 for in depth word study on the Hebrew words נער and ילד for "boy" and "child" used in these narratives in 1 and 2 Kings. She notes, "As with נער, the ages of characters described as ילד vary significantly. A ילד can be as young as a fetus (Exod 21:22), but more often suggests a newborn child (e.g., Gen 21:8; Exod 2:3-10; 2 Sam 12:15; 1 Kgs 3:25; Isa 9:5 [Eng 9:6]; Ruth 4:16). Young boys and girls appear designated by ילד and ילדה in Joel 4:3 (Eng 3:3) and Zech 8:5. Noticeably older are the accomplished young men . . . brought from Israel to Babylon (Dan 1:4). After the seventeen-year-old Joseph (Gen 37:2) has been sold into slavery, Reuben describes him as a ילד (Gen 37:30), and uses the same term later when referring to this incident (Gen 42:22)" (Parker, 64).

24. Note the distinction here between male and female life stages. Because the full legal status of a voting citizen was rarely if ever conferred upon females in this time period, no direct comparison exists. Instead, girls moved from one dependent relationship (to their father) into another (with their husband), usually at the time of puberty—between 11 and 14 years old.

25. Diogene Laertius, cited in Marvin W. Meyer, "The Youth in the *Secret Gospel of Mark*," in *Semeia* (Jan 1990) 139.

26. Dean-Jones, 110.

27. Suzanne Dixon, *The Roman Mother*. Norman, OK: Oklahoma University Press, 1989) 100.

28. Dixon, 101–102.

29. Dixon, 106–107.

30. Plutarch, *Numa* 12.2 Cf. *Fragmenta Vaticana* 321 for the legal use in this context of the Latin verb *sublurgere* (to half-mourn), cited in Parkin, "Demographics," 48.

31. Larsson Lovén, 304–309; see also chapter 2 on the inclusion of children.

32. Dixon, 135–136; see also Janette McWilliam, "The Socialization of Roman Children," in *The Oxford Handbook of Childhood and Education in the Classical World* (Oxford: Oxford University Press, 2013), 282: "They [children] would have

been affected by the deaths of adults and other children, attended their funerals, and visited their burial sites in graveyards housing remains of the dead."

33. Robert M. Price, *The Widow Traditions in Luke-Acts: A Feminist Critical Scrutiny* (Atlanta: Scholar's Press, 1997) 85.

34. Turid Karlsen Seim, *The Double Message: Patterns of Gender in Luke-Acts* (Nashville: Abingdon, 1994) 186. See also Karlsen Seim, *The Double Message*, 185: "Marriage and childbirth, which was normally women's primary possibility in life and their legitimation, is dismissed as irrelevant in the community of Jesus as Luke describes it. As concrete expressions of this, we have met independent women among Jesus' followers who appear by virtue of their own story and identity. Women have charge over their own houses and their own resources, while household duties cannot be used to draw them away from devotion to the word of the Lord."

35. François Bovon, *Luke 1*, translated by Christine Thomas (Minneapolis: Fortress Press, 2002) 267.

36. Dixon, 157–158.

37. Parker, 144.

38. Cristina Grenholm, *Motherhood and Love: Beyond Gendered Stereotypes of Theology*, trans. Marie Tåqvist (Grand Rapids, MI: Wm. B Eerdmann's, 2011) 31.

39. The dependency of the mother in this account, therefore, should not be seen as a sign of weakness. In contrast, the strength of her mutual relationship with her youthful son can be brought to bear in support Karlsen Seim's claim for the independence of women in Luke over against those of feminist exegetes who have found in Luke a limited, passive view of the women. For a more complete review of these diverging feminist perspectives, cf. Claudia Janssen and Regene Lamb, "Gospel of Luke: The Humbled Will Be Lifted Up," in *Feminist Biblical Interpretation: A Compendium of Critical Commentary on the Books of the Bible and Related Literature*, ed. Luise Schottroff and Marie-Theres Wacker, (Grand Rapids: Wm. B. Eerdmann's, 2012) 645–661.

40. McWilliam, 280.

41. This section was previously published as Amy Lindeman Allen, "Reading for Inclusion: The Girl from Galilee (Luke 8:40–56)," in the *Journal of Childhood and Religion*, Vol. 7 (2017). Used with permission.

42. Mary Harlow, "Family Relationships," in *A Cultural History of Childhood and Family in Antiquity,* vol. 1. Oxford: Berg Press, 2010) 17; Rawson, "Adult-Child Relationships," 27.

43. P. R. C. Weaver, "Children of Freedmen (and Freedwomen)," in *Marriage, Divorce, and Children in Ancient Rome*, edited by Beryl Rawson (Oxford: Oxford University Press, 1991) 176.

44. Eve D'Ambra, *Roman Women* (Cambridge: Cambridge University Press, 2007) 46. See also Robert Garland, "Children in Athenian Religion," in in *The Oxford Handbook of Childhood and Education in the Classical World*, ed. by Judith Evans Grubbs, Tim Parkin, and Roslynne Bell (Oxford: Oxford University Press, 2013) 214; Harlow, "Family Relationships," 17; McWilliam, 273; Weaver, 175.

45. See Chapter 1 for definitions of children in the first century Mediterranean context.

46. Rawson, "Adult-Child Relationships," 27–28.

47. Harlow, "Family Relationships," 17; see also D'Ambra, who describes this transition vividly as a still liminal time, despite the definitive moment of marriage: "The adolescent girl, often represented in the visual arts as part child, part woman on the brink of growing up, was domesticated by marriage" (12); This transition was often marked by a ritual sacrifice of the girl's childhood dolls, see Mary Harlow, "Toys, Dolls, and the Material Culture of Childhood," in *The Oxford Handbook of Childhood and Education in the Classical World*, ed. by Judith Evans Grubbs, Tim Parkin, and Roslynne Bell. Oxford: Oxford University Press, 2013) 332, 334–335.

48. While most translations render the term in Lk 8:42 "only daughter," it is actually a gender-neutral term, thus increasing the stakes of what Jairus has to lose at the loss, not just of his only daughter, but, indeed, his only child.

49. While there is every reason to assume that other children would have been present among the crowd that initially welcome Jesus, observe the woman's healing, and hear Jairus' request, and, indeed, among the mourners, this presence is not explored at length here since the unit makes clear that those who observe the actual healing of this child are limited to her parents, Jesus, Peter, James, and John (Lk 8:51).

50. Bovon, *Luke 1*, 339.

51. For more on the narrative links between these two healings, see Johnson, 143: "More than a mechanical sandwiching links the raising of Jairus' daughter and the healing of the hemorrhaging woman. Both women are called 'daughter.' The girl is twelve years old, an age traditionally associated with menarche (*Protoevangelium of James* 8:3); the woman has had a 'flow of blood' (obviously gynecological in origin) for twelve years . . . The situation of both seems hopeless . . . [Moreover,] The stories are joined most explicitly by the healing power of Jesus and the saving response of faith."

52. It has been noted that even before her death, "[t]he sick girl does not appear, but rather her father" (Bovon, *Luke 1*, 335); however, neither should this be taken as indicative of her status as a child, so much as an indication of how sick she already was such that she was unable to approach Jesus, as the hemorrhaging woman does, on her own. For parallels of adults or people of uncertain age whose requests are likewise brought by a representative see Lk 4:40; 5:17–26; 7:1–10 and those approached directly by Jesus 6:8–10; 7:11–17; 7:21; 8:26–39; 13:10–13; 14:1–6.

53. Johnson,143.

54. Bovon, *Luke 1*, 335.

55. See also Bovon, *Luke 1*, 336: "If one is aware of the extent to which the vocabulary of resurrection was used in the early Church to describe Christian existence, could one not see in the daughter of Jairus the experience of young Christian women?" in contrast to Bovon, *Luke 1*, 334, 337, and 340–341 (esp. fn 61).

56. See Bovon, *Luke 1*, 340; Fitzmyer, *Luke I-IX,* 749.

57. Fitzmyer, *Luke I-IX,* 223.

58. Johnson, 144.

59. The ambiguity of the Greek leaves possible (but unlikely) the messenger from Jairus' house as an alternative object of Jesus' command. The context, however, seems to suggest the father. In any case, the girl who is not present at the scene

does not make sense either contextually or grammatically as the subject of Jesus' imperative.

60. For more on this as the qualification of discipleship and the role of children in fulfilling it, see chapters 3 and 4; Cf. Johnson, 143.

61. Horn and Martens, 263.

62. See Johnson, 143: "In both stories, we notice, the person who is saved is restored to community. The girl is returned to her family. More impressive still is the woman with the hemorrhage who for twelve years was excluded from the common life of the people because of purity regulations."

63. Bovon, *Luke 1*, 340.

64. The term παῖς may also be used to convey the meaning "servant" or "slave" (see Lk 7:7; 15:26); however, given the clear description of this boy as the father's "son" (τὸν υἱόν μου), and his only child (μονογενής) at that, the context clearly indicates a reference to a non-adult child (Lk 9:38).

65. Johnson, 159.

66. See Johnson, 158; Tannehill, 163. Fitzmyer also sees in the disciples' initial inability to effect a cure a possible connection to Gehazi's inability to help the boy resuscitated in 2 Kgs 4:31 (*Luke I–IX*, 809). For more parallels to this child healing account, see the above discussion of the youth at Nain.

67. Fitzmyer, *Luke I–IX*, 808; Johnson, 158.

68. See Bovon, *Luke 1*, 386.

69. Fitzmyer, *Luke I–IX*, 808.

70. The term "healing" is uncommon here, but given the coalescence of ancient understandings of demon possession and disease, not entirely out of place. See Fitzmyer, *Luke I–IX*, 810: "In most cases the verb *iasthai* is used of healing diseases (as in 5:17; 6:18–19; 7:7; 8:47; 9:2, 11; 14:4; 17:15; 22:51; Acts 9:34; 28:8), but here it is said of an exorcism (cf. Acts 10:38). This is another indication of 'demon-sickness' or the failure to distinguish clearly between a healing and an exorcism." See also Fitzmyer, *Luke I–IX*, 545.

71. Bovon, *Luke 1*, 385.

72. See Bovon, *Luke 1*, 385.

73. BDAG, 368.

74. See Fitzmyer, *Luke I–IX*, 808; BDAG, 369.

75. Bovon, *Luke 1*, 388.

76. See Bovon, *Luke 1*, 384; Fitzmyer, *Luke I–IX*, 807; Johnson, 186.

77. Bovon, *Luke 1*, 386.

78. Indeed, the centrality of the child in Jesus' response becomes even more apparent if one imagines, with Johnson, that he may be the same child placed into the center of the disciples' dispute in the parenesis that follows (Lk 9:47).

79. See Fitzmyer, *Luke I–IX*, 810; Johnson, 158.

80. Tannehill, 163.

81. BDAG, 110.

82. Although he does not directly engage in form-critical analysis, cf. Carroll, 177, 180.

83. Bovon, *Luke 1*, 382.

84. See also Ulrich Busse, *Die Wunder des Propheten Jesus: Die Rezeption, Komposition, und Interpretation der Wundertradition im Evangelium des Lukas* (Stuttgart: Katholisches Bibelwerk, 1977) 252–253.

85. Johnson translates vv. 45b–46, "'And they were afraid to ask him about it. Instead, they entered into a discussion concerning who might be the greater among them.' . . . The translation takes the conjunction *de* seriously. Luke intends a real contrast between the disciples' unwillingness to discuss Jesus' suffering and their eager participation in a debate about their rank" (Johnson, 157, 159).

86. Johnson, 157; Tannehill, 163.

87. Johnson, 158.

88. See Tannehill, 164: "There is a sharp shift of mood here. Everyone else is rejoicing in amazement, but Jesus turns to his disciples and says with vehemence, 'Let these words sink into your ears,' then indicates that the Son of Man whose deeds are so powerful will have no power to escape his human enemies."

89. See chapter 3 on Discipleship.

90. Johnson, 160; Tannehill, 163.

91. Fitzmyer, *Luke I–IX,* 809.

92. See Fitzmyer, *Luke I–IX,* 809; Tannehill, 163.

93. This theme will be expanded upon in the following section with regard to the restoration of the two brothers to their father in what is traditionally called the parable of the prodigal son.

94. Johnson, 160.

95. Johnson, 160.

96. Aasgaard, 202. For more evidence on the practice of telling stories to children in antiquity, see also Aasgaard, 198–202.

97. Aasgaard, 193.

98. A notable exception to this tendency is Fitzmyer, who alternates between referencing the younger son as a "young man" and, more frequently, "young son;" even referring to him at one point in relation to his employment with the Gentile pig farmer as a "Jewish boy" (*Luke X–XXIV,* 1088). Unfortunately, because he does not address the issue of age specifically, it is impossible to know whether this is a lapse in language or whether Fitzmyer himself imagines the younger son as a young boy. Setting aside previous presuppositions about the age of the characters, his commentary can be read to support either interpretation.

99. Marilou Ibita and Reimund Bieringer, "(Stifled) Voices of the Future: Learning about Children in the Bible," in *Children's Voices: Children's Perspectives in Ethics, Theology, and Religious Education,* ed. Annemie Dillen and Didier Pollefeyt (Walpole, MA: Uitgeverij Peeters, 2010) 93.

100. Lionello Spada, *The Return of the Prodigal Son,* 1608, oil on canvas, 160x119cm, The Louvre, Paris.

101. Pieter Coecke van Aelst, *Scenes from the Life of the Prodigal,* 1530, pen and brown ink and gray wash, over traces of black chalk, 19.2x51.4cm, The J. Paul Getty Museum, Los Angeles.

102. See Bovon, *Luke 2,* 431–438 for a "History of Interpretation" that includes a brief survey of artistic treatments of this parable in the literary and dramatic genres.

Notably, an adaptation Burkhard Waldis in 1527, "A narrator introduces the action, then comments on it at the end of each of the two acts of the play," while "A *child* reads the Gospel at the beginning and pronounces the benediction at the end" (Bovon, *Luke 2,* 428 emphasis added).

103. See Bovon, *Luke 2,* 428: "That he himself [the older son] works the land—an observation mentioned in passing [v. 24c–25]—is an indication that the father is not a large landowner of a great landed estate (*latifundia*) but someone who exploits an estate of medium size."

104. Horn and Martens, 177.

105. Carol Schersten LaHurd, "Re-viewing Luke 15 with Arab Christian Women," in *A Feminist Companion to Luke,* ed. Amy-Jill Levine and Marianne Blickenstaff (London: Sheffield Academic Press, 2002) 265.

106. Some interpreters might be tempted to argue for the sexual maturity of the younger brother, despite his unmarried status, in light of tradition that suggests he spent his inheritance on prostitutes (see the older brother's complaint in Lk 15:30). Two points must be clarified here. First, while the older brother makes this suggestion, presumably with no previous knowledge of his brother's whereabouts or activity, the phrase translated as "dissolute living" (ζῶν ἀσώτως, v. 13) from which the term "prodigal" comes indicates that the younger son spent his inheritance wastefully, or profligately, but does not by itself suggest any sexual excess (see also Johnson, 236). Further, the likelihood that a boy at or even below puberty in the ancient world might partake in sexual encounters with a prostitute should not be overlooked. Prepubescent children were sold into sexual slavery and worked as prostitutes, slave children could be treated as *deliciae* or sexual playthings by their masters, and free boys may even enter into receiving sexual relationships in order to curry favor and respect among older men. The sexual freedom and activity of post-pubescent adolescents and teenagers would have been even more common and assumed, especially considering androcentric adultery laws that defined the crime only in terms of the violation of a married woman. Thus, while artistic depictions that imagine such licentiousness tend to lean towards an older portrait of the prodigal, this is neither called for by the text nor the ancient context from which it originates.

107. Bovon, *Luke 2,* 427.

108. See Bovon, *Luke 2,* 426–428.

109. Bovon, *Luke 2,* 426.

110. See Bovon, *Luke 2,* 428.

111. Turid Karlsen Seim, "The Gospel of Luke," in *Searching the Scriptures: A Feminist Commentary*, ed. Elisabeth Schüssler (New York: Crossroad, 1994) 730.

112. See Betsy J. Bauman-Martin, "Women on the Edge: New Perspectives on Women in the Petrine Haustafel" in *Journal of Biblical* Literature 123:2 (2004) 265.

113. Consider also the marginalized status attributed by Luke to the shepherds who attend Jesus' birth in Lk 2:8–20.

114. Balch and Osiek, 139.

115. Karlsen Seim, "The Gospel of Luke," 731.

116. See "Shifts in Occupational Identity" in chapter 1, especially Columella's description of agricultural life on a larger estate.

117. Horn and Martens, 177–178.

118. This is also the position of Bovon, although he gives no support for his reading other than a reference back to the parallel in Lk 7:7, about which his commentary is silent on the age of the centurion's slave. Cf. Bovon, *Luke 2*, 428: "We should probably group the 'servants' (παῖδες) (v. 26) with the 'servants' (δοῦλοι) of v. 22; all of them are the master's servants, except the ones in v. 26 (παῖδες) are probably the younger servants (cf. 7:7)."

119. See Lk 7:7; Gen 24:2ff LXX; Appian, Iber. 27, 107

120. Johnson, 237.

121. On this religious interpretation of the phrase "came to himself" (εἰς ἑαυτὸν δὲ ἐλθών), see Bovon: "For Hellenistic Judaism and early Christianity it expressed a decisive step of 'conversion' (μετάνοια), a return to God" (*Luke 2*, 426).

122. Miller-McLemore, *Let the Children Come: Reimagining Childhood from a Christian Perspective* (San Francisco: Jossey-Bass, 2003) 18–23; See also Anne Higonnet, *Pictures of Innocence: The History and Crisis of Ideal Childhood* (New York: Thames and Hudson, 1998).

123. Carroll, 181.

124. Johnson, 240.

125. Anecdotally, this is fitting with contemporary Middle Eastern notions of family. In LaHurd's interview with five Arab women about this parable, contrary to models that present the structure of the Middle Eastern household in strict terms of honor and shame, these Christian Arab women affirmed, "when asked whether any part of the father's behavior was unexpected in the light of their experience of the Middle Eastern family, all answered negatively and provided stories about how the family serves as location of unconditional care" (259).

126. Horn and Martens, 93.

127. This is not intended to reflect an idealistic vision that ignores the pronouncements of judgment and division that Jesus brings. These are dealt with elsewhere in Ch 2 with relation to children's inclusion in God's judgment and Ch 4 with relation to the Lukan costs of discipleship for all Jesus' followers, inclusive of children. However, it should not be lost on the reader that Jesus' mission is not division for the sake of divison, but rather, for the sake of a broader restoration in the household of God (see Lk 15:11–32).

128. See chapter 2 on the welcome and inclusion of children in the first century Roman and Jewish world.

Chapter 4

Child Disciples as Companions of Jesus

Children and their causes are often touted within Christianity as important with the rationale that children are "the future of the church." This, however, is not the only way to understand the relationship of children to religion—either in first century Judaism or twenty-first century Christianity. Before they become the future of the church, children *are* the church of their day and age. Or, at least, children are *as much* a part of the church as any other demographic group.

The apostle Paul asserts that every believer, or disciple, is as much a part of the body of Christ as any other individual member (1 Cor. 12; Rom. 12:3–8). The open question, of course, remains whether for Paul and the early church children were considered to be disciples, or members of Christ's body, in the first place. While the biblical texts can be read in a number of ways, this chapter demonstrates that the inclusion of children as disciples in Luke's gospel account is a plausible and legitimate way to read the text and, indeed, holds value for the sake of child disciples in the church today.

Participation in Jesus' earthly ministry, of course, would not yet have been referred to as being a part of the "body of Christ" in the gospel accounts. The closest parallel to this later Pauline language comes when Jesus' disciples are invited to partake of Christ's body, given for them, as they share Jesus' last supper with him (Lk 22:19).[1] Rather, these first followers of Jesus were identified not by their membership in Christ's body, so much as by their physical presence with him (σὺν αὐτῷ)—following Jesus and participating in a shared proclamation of the advent of the Kingdom of God. This, for Luke, is what it means to be a disciple. Such a definition contrasts with the conflation of the category of disciples (οἱ μαθηταί) with the special status of the Twelve (Jesus' inner circle) as described in Matthew and Mark and draws a wide net of who is intended by the Lukan use of the word "disciple."

In Luke, a broad inclusivity among Jesus' disciples is clear from the first mention of the Twelve by name, at which point Luke describes Jesus as addressing "a great crowd of his disciples" (ὄχλος πολὺς μαθητῶν αὐτοῦ, Lk 6:17) from among whom he has just selected Twelve, "whom he also named apostles" (οὓς καὶ ὠνόμασεν ἀποστόλος, Lk 6:13). This inclusive definition of discipleship as a larger group among whom the twelve apostles are a part is carried throughout Luke, magnified upon Jesus' entry into Jerusalem.

As Jesus rides into Jerusalem with his disciples accompanying him, Luke describes "the whole multitude of disciples" (τὸ πλῆθος τῶν μαθητῶν) as praising Jesus (Lk 19:37), after two of the disciples are sent ahead to prepare the way for them (Lk 19:29ff). So too, Luke's association of the disciples with a large group or community is assumed in Acts when "the twelve called together the whole community of the disciples" (προσκαλεσάμενοι δὲ οἱ δώδεκα τὸ πλῆθος τῶν μαθητῶν, Acts 6:2a).

From the beginning to the end of Jesus' ministry, the disciples are thus understood by Luke as a large group accompanying Jesus while he is on earth and even continuing to increase after his ascension (Acts 6:7; 14:21), from among whom Jesus occasionally selects particular representatives for specific tasks. The role of Jesus' disciples in Luke's gospel overlaps with, while remaining distinct from, the apostleship of the Twelve as Jesus' inner circle of followers.

While Luke's Jesus clarifies the specific responsibilities of discipleship at particular points, there are other points when it is clear that Jesus refers to people as disciples who are not yet living up to the term as he has defined it. Hence, while Jesus twice defines his family, or those serving God's Kingdom, as "those who hear the word of God and do it" (Lk 8:21; 11:28),[2] his disciples still fail to "hear" with the sense of understanding (e.g. Lk 9:43–45) and "do" the work of God without stumbling (e.g. Lk 9:37–43).

Likewise, while Jesus says, "Whoever comes to me and does not hate father and mother, wife and children, brothers and sisters, yes, and even life itself, cannot be my disciple." (Lk 14:25–26, see also v. 33), and again, "Whoever does not carry the cross and follow me cannot be my disciple," (Lk 14:27), his disciples—even Peter—fail to follow him to the cross (Lk 22:31–34, 54–62). Therefore, the broadest definition of Jesus' disciples as portrayed by Luke seems most simply to be that Jesus' disciples are those who follow or accompany Jesus. They are the ones who are with Jesus along his way—listening, though not always healing and striving, though not always succeeding to do the word of God that Jesus proclaims.

In relation to children this means several things. First, Luke's broad definition of discipleship leaves room for the presence of children not just among the crowds who hear Jesus' teachings and receive healing and restoration through Jesus' word,³ but indeed among the close followers—the disciples of Jesus themselves. Second, in order to determine whether the category of disciple could or should be applied to children, Luke gives us three criteria to consider: accompaniment, hearing, and doing the word of God.⁴

Moreover, each of these criteria, particularly the latter two, are presented by Luke as a work in progress for Jesus' disciples rather than as immediate and unconditional demands swiftly met.⁵ Therefore, in as much as children in Luke's gospel can be seen to meet, or more accurately be striving to meet, these criteria, such children can and, for the sake of the church, ought to be understood as a part of those named disciples who accompanied Jesus in his earthly ministry.

In this chapter, I explore the first criterion of accompaniment and its application to children as they are portrayed whether implicitly or explicitly in Luke's narrative. This sets the stage for a more thorough application of the latter two criteria to children in chapter 5.

ACCOMPANYING JESUS AS A CRITERION FOR DISCIPLESHIP

Beginning with the call of Simon, James, and John in Luke 5:1–11, the reader is aware that there are those who have "left everything and followed" Jesus (Lk 5:11). These are the people whom the contemporary reader typically associates with disciples; however, the first reference to Jesus' companions as "disciples" does not occur until later at 5:30 (τοὺς μαθητὰς). Even then, the term does not initially come from Jesus or the Lukan narrator directly. Instead, the narrator employs the label "disciples" in reference to the scribes and the Pharisees' complaint against Jesus (5:30). Jesus then compares his companions to their own disciples and those of John the Baptist (5:33) as like communities who engage in different practices.

Although the term "disciple" later comes to take on special meaning within some Christian circles and is often associated with Jesus' inner circle of twelve (including Simon, James, and John), for the Pharisees and John the Baptist the term consistently refers to the broader group of people associated with their particular set of views.⁶ Thus, Luke never distinguishes an inner circle from among the broader group associated with John in the gospel account. Reference to Jesus' disciples by the Pharisees, then, should be assumed to have such a broad group in mind. Indeed, since Jesus has not yet formed the inner group of the Twelve, this is the only logical meaning.

After this point in the narrative, the narrator picks up the designation of disciples as a general description of those who are with Jesus again in Lk

6:1. Throughout the rest of the narrative, the term disciple is used frequently to designate the large group of people accompanying Jesus in his ministry,[7] particularly as the direct recipients of certain teachings.[8] Moreover, not only is Luke's discipleship community larger than the twelve named apostles of 6:12–16, but the narrative also clearly acknowledges its inclusion of women. Such inclusion is especially evident in the multitude of Lk 19:37 and Jesus' teaching in 9:18-27, a teaching which Luke's later narration of 24:6–8 assumes that the women following Jesus since Galilee (Lk 8:1–3) were privy to. That this group includes both men and women is made clear when Mary, Joanna, and the other women are said to have "remembered" (24:6–10) what Jesus said to the disciples in 9:18–22.[9] Later, in Acts 9:36 Tabitha is also directly named as a disciple (μαθήτρια).

The manner in which the Lukan author depicts the transition of the community between Jesus' arrest, crucifixion, resurrection, and ascension helps to illustrate the centrality of accompaniment as a criterion of Lukan discipleship both in the gospel and, carried over by means of the Holy Spirit, in the Acts of the Apostles as well.

Up until Jesus' arrest at Gethsemane, the disciples are portrayed as being almost continually with Jesus. They follow Jesus in his travels through and away from Galilee, near to him also in his private moments (Lk 9:18; 10:23; 11:1; 22:39, 45). Even when they are not directly named, the narrator assumes the disciples' presence with Jesus. Thus, the narrator returns Jesus' attention easily to the disciples without noting where they have come from after significant narrative gaps, such as when Jesus addresses his disciples in the midst of a crowd in 12:1, after they have not been formally named as a group since one of the disciples asked Jesus to teach them to pray at a different location in 11:1.

However, from the moment of Jesus' arrest, the disciples as a group are noticeably absent from Luke's narrative. While several known disciples and apostles are mentioned by name or in smaller groupings, such as "the women" from Galilee (23:49, 55; 24:22) or "the eleven" (24:9, 33), the community as a whole is referenced only in relation to one another (e.g. "the eleven and the rest," 24:9; "some women of our group," 24:22; "the eleven and their companions," 24:33) or simply as Jesus' acquaintances (πάντες οἱ γνωστοὶ αὐτῷ lit. "all those who had known him," 23:49). Indeed, even after Jesus' ascension, accompaniment becomes a key measure of status, if not exclusivity, in the community of believers, such that a replacement for Judas among the apostles is selected from among "one of the men who have accompanied us during all the time that the Lord Jesus went in and out among us" (Acts 1:21).

Nevertheless, while Luke almost immediately resumes use of the term "apostles" (ἀποστόλοις) in Acts 1:2 to designate the Twelve, he continues to associate them with the larger community of Jesus' followers. Such association is made by the dual means of relation and proximity. Luke writes that the apostles were "together with certain women, including Mary the mother of Jesus, as well as his brothers" (Acts 1:14) and that "Peter stood up among the believers (together the crowd numbered about one hundred twenty persons)," (Acts 1:15). Similarly, he describes Judas as "numbered among us" (Acts 1:16–17) and recounts that the believers "were altogether in one place" until after the coming of the Holy Spirit on Pentecost (Acts 2:1ff). In each case, before the coming of the Holy Spirit the sub-group of apostles are grouped together with the larger community of believers—a continuation of the disciples of Luke's gospel account.

Following the giving of the Holy Spirit, Acts tells us that "about three thousand persons were added" to the community who had accompanied Jesus (2:41) and that this group continued to grow in "great numbers of both men and women" (5:14). That this group of believers is the same community previously identified as the disciples is made clear in 6:1–2 when "the twelve called together the whole community of the disciples." That the qualification of accompaniment has now been extended to the whole community of those who believe in Jesus as the Christ is further affirmed throughout the rest of the narrative (Acts 9:26; 15:10; 19:1, 8; 21:16). Significantly, then, the term disciple is extended throughout Luke's gospel and Acts to all of those who live in relationship with one another for the sake of Jesus' mission—the proclamation and embodiment of the Word of God in the world.

CHILDREN AMONG JESUS' COMPANIONS

Although most ancient texts, including Luke's gospel account, tend to obscure children, textual and funerary evidence point to the plentiful presence of children in the public sphere of the first century Mediterranean world. Within this context, children can and should be assumed to have been an ample part of the crowds and households among whom Jesus moved and taught. In this sense, there are, of course, children present "with" Jesus throughout the Lukan narrative.

However, the Lukan author consistently distinguishes between the "crowds" (οἱ ὄχλοι) of people who follow Jesus and the community of his "disciples" (οἱ μαθηταὶ) who are also with him.[10] In light of this, Rosalie Ryan infers that to be "with Jesus" in these terms "means much more than physical presence."[11] As "a technical expression of discipleship (8:28; 9:18; 22:56),"[12] to be "with Jesus" means to accompany him in his proclamation and in his mission. Barbara Reid characterizes discipleship life among Jesus' followers in Luke and in the Acts as "life together in community, characterized by corporate mission, shared decision-making, accountability to one another, networking and hospitality among the communities, and sharing of material possessions.[13] The ministry that Jesus conducts in Luke-Acts relies upon and builds a corporate community. Those who are Jesus' disciples, above everything else, are those who form a part of this *koinonia* community—who *accompany* him, participating given their various capacities in his proclamation and ministry. While children have been shown to be physically proximate to Jesus throughout Luke's narration of his ministry (chapter 2) and even to have been recipients of this ministry (chapter 3), the question remains whether young children are both capable of and included in actual *participation* in Jesus' ministry according to Luke.[14] This participation and thus the inclusion of children within the discipleship community portrayed in Luke will be seen through attention to the Jesus' explicit call of children, the social structure of the discipleship community, and the ability of children to meet the demands of itinerancy that such a call requires.

Jesus' Call to Children

The presence of children close to and even among those who followed Jesus is insufficient to warrant the claim that children themselves either believed in or acted out of their own volition to follow Jesus—in other words, that they willfully accompanied him. In the ancient Mediterranean world children were concomitantly included in the daily life and workings of their families and communities and excluded from positions of prominence, rank, and power. In many cases their very inclusion was with the intention of socializing them to pre-established adult conceptions of household and society, and thus, their bodies were simultaneously included in public functions while their state of *being as children* was excluded from these same practices and concerns.[15] That children were physically proximate to Jesus' ministry and even recipients of it thus does not alone indicate that Jesus desired them to accompany him or that these children actively participated in the ministry of which they were recipients. To substantiate these claims it is necessary to consider both Jesus' call, or invitation, to children to accompany him and their subsequent responses.

In Luke's telling, Jesus' verbalizes his desire for children to be among those who accompany him by extending a specific call to them. Luke's Jesus extends such an invitation to children at first indirectly in his instruction to his disciples to "welcome this child (παιδίον) in my name" (Lk 9:48) and later directly in Lk 18:15–17. In Lk 9:48, by physically aligning the child with himself, Jesus welcomes this child not just as a part of the crowd but as a valued participant in his discipleship community. Horn and Martens infer from this welcome, narrated in all three synoptic texts, the inclusion of children in Jesus' call to discipleship, thereby establishing a precedent for understanding children as part of the discipleship community.[16]

Even more directly, Jesus' explicit call to young children can be seen by the language that Luke uses in Lk 18:15–17. Here Jesus calls (προσεκαλέσατο) for the infants (βρέφη) to come to him, further instructing those who would have hindered or prevented their response, "Let the little children (παιδία) come to me (ἔρχεσθαι πρός με)" (Lk 18:16). The meaning of the verb προσκαλέω is "to call to or notify in order to secure someone's presence" and connotes the sense of a summons or invitation.[17] It is used exclusively in the middle voice in the New Testament (and predominately in the LXX and other Greek literature as well) with the implication of calling or summoning another person to one's self. Thus, in Lk 18:15–17, Jesus does not simply permit, but in fact, invites small children into his presence. So Bovon writes, Luke's Jesus "calls, even summons, the very small children. The verb 'call to oneself' (προσκαλέομαι) is carefully chosen and is a felicitous replacement for the banal 'say' in Mk 10:14."[18] Jesus' specific and personalized action makes it clear that he is addressing the children who were being brought to him and not the objecting disciples (who are already in his presence). Such direct address creates a clear and personal connection between Jesus and these children.

Moreover, for the contemporary reader, this language of "call" creates an immediate connection between Jesus' relationship with the children in Luke 18:15–17 and with the twelve apostles, many of whose call stories are individually narrated. Such a connection stems from the conception of the disciples as those most intimately connected with—accompanying—Jesus and thus those who, one infers, Jesus has called to himself. At this thematic level, emphasizing the role of proximity to Jesus, the connection is a legitimate one. However, one must be careful not to take the linguistic connection too far.

In English, "call" or invitation is frequently attached with the assembly of Jesus' first disciples, such that the subheadings of these narratives in the *New Interpreter's Study Bible* indicate "Jesus Calls the First Disciples" and "Jesus Calls Levi."[19] Such headings are typical of most mainline printings that include this convention. Nevertheless, none of the evangelists employ either the term προσκαλέω or the related προσφωνέω ("to call out, address"; in the middle voice: "to call to oneself, summon") with relation to these accounts.[20] Rather, the call is more implicit, manifested in individual disciples' actions and response. Thus, Luke describes Jesus as telling Simon, "Do not be afraid; from now on you will be called fishers of people" (Lk 5:10), after which Simon, James, and John "left everything and followed him" (5:11). Likewise, though in a somewhat more direct manner, Luke's Jesus says (εἶπεν) to Levi,

"Follow me," (5:27) and "he got up, left everything, and followed him" (5:28). In each instance, then, the focus is not on a specific verb of vocation, but on the invitation of Jesus extended in various forms (declaration in 5:10; summons in 5:27; call in 18:16) followed by an affirmative response by the individuals to whom it is directed.

The children in Lk 18:15–17 can be understood to fit into this tradition of call to discipleship, then, in so much as they respond positively to Jesus' invitation. While the responses of the disciples in Lk 5:11 and 5:28 are clearly narrated, in 18:15–17 Luke leaves his audience to fill in the gap.[21] While it is possible to thus assume that these children never actually continue toward Jesus after the disciples' initial reproach, this seems unlikely given Jesus' subsequent use of children as a positive example of discipleship following his personal invitation. Jesus states, "Truly I tell you, whoever does not receive the kingdom of God as a little child will never enter it" (18:17). Since it seems unlikely that Jesus would suggest that the proper way to receive the kingdom of God is by, in fact, shying away from it, it can be inferred that following Jesus' invitation, the children whom he has beckoned do in fact draw near to him—an action more explicitly stated in both Mark and Matthew's accounts (Mk 10:16; Matt 19:15).

Moreover, in terms of volition, it is notable that by not narrating the children's approach as either directed by Jesus or their caregivers, the Lukan author leaves room for the willful action of these children themselves to come to Jesus. That such a response is anticipated is implied by the placement of children (παιδία) as the main subject of the verb in Lk 18:16.[22] It is these children, not himself, his disciples, or any other adult, whom Jesus invites into action. Indeed, these children respond in such an appropriate way that Jesus uplifts them as examples for how everyone ought to behave when approaching the mission and ministry of God's Kingdom.[23]

The little children in Luke's gospel are not only allowed to respond to Jesus, but it is reasonable to infer from the text that their response is one of approaching Jesus, subscribing to his Word, and accompanying him on his path of ministry. Jesus invites the children in Lk 18:15–17 to accompany him in discipleship and, at least some of them, follow.

The connection between children as exemplars of discipleship, however, begins much earlier in Luke's narrative than this. In Lk 9:48, the child whom Jesus places alongside himself is signaled out both in terms of her proximity to Jesus, as one accompanying him, and at the same time, assumed to have been there all along. Bovon notes this continuity: "The subject [of the discussion in 9:46] was who would be the greatest among the disciples, not who would be greater than the disciples, as the answer in v. 48b finally makes clear."[24] In this context, the child (παιδίον) whom Jesus draws to his side is meant to illustrate "the least among all of you" (v. 48b), thus at the same time affirming this child as a disciple—accompanying both Jesus and those in the dispute—and making this child representative of what it means to be an ideal disciple—to be great (v. 48b).[25] Although an active response of this child is not recorded, Jesus' attention to her nevertheless sets the scene for the children in Lk 18:15–17 to act as active examples of discipleship. Moreover, in each case, it is clear that the inclusion of children among Jesus' followers reflects their inclusion *qua* children.

Children are not welcomed into this group of followers in hopes that they will be socialized according to the activities of their adult companions, but for the sake of their already active and valid participation in Jesus' ministry in their own right. Indeed, in a typical Lukan reversal, the adults are instructed to welcome these children (Lk 9:48a) and receive the kingdom as a little child (18:17), in fact socializing themselves according to the manner of their child companions instead. This theme can also be read in Jesus' warning to his disciples in 17:2, "It would be better for you if a millstone were hung around your neck and you were thrown into the sea than for you to cause one of these little ones to stumble." The term for "these little ones" (τῶν μικρῶν τούτων), while not exclusively reserved for children, has been seen to apply to them.

In Luke 17, Jesus' concern points to the possibility that the "cause of stumbling" represents those in community causing others among them to sin. In the immediate context, following Jesus' response to the Pharisees, Jesus' words can be read equally as rebuke of the Pharisees for being guilty of such action and warning to the disciples not to be like the Pharisees. So Bovon concludes, "This presupposes the setting of a community: the disciples (perhaps considered as ministers) shock other believers (called 'little ones' in v. 2) by their scandalous behavior; by taking advantage of their power, embezzling funds, betraying conjugal fidelity, giving up serving God alone, and so on."[26] However, while the warning certainly calls for a community of believers (those who are accompanying Jesus) as its setting, Bovon's identification of "disciples" as ministers and "other believers" as little ones goes against the picture of discipleship in the rest of Luke's gospel.

If this were the intent, it would have been better for Jesus to address his lesson to the "apostles" rather than the "disciples" in Lk 17:1. Instead, the term "little ones" more appropriately looks back to Luke's reference to a child as one of "the least among you" in 9:48 and turns the disciples' attention to the dangers inherent in the socialization of the young. Consequently, one can read Jesus' lesson as an instruction for the adult disciples to be cautious that they not cause their younger counterparts (and those who seek to emulate them by "being the least") to stumble from the right path they are already following by training them according to the adult standards of the world instead.

While it is dangerous to make broad generalizations about any group of people that connote "all" behave or behaved in a uniform way, it is nevertheless possible to at least state that some children within Luke's narrative can be read as having been called into accompaniment by and responding to Jesus in such a way that bespeaks discipleship. What is even more radical is the purpose of such inclusion. Luke's inclusion of children as disciples contrasts with the typical Greco-Roman inclusion of children in public and religious rituals for the purposes of socialization intent on forming children into adults. Instead, Luke places value on what these children might bring to the community *as* children, indeed even forming or re-forming adult disciples in the process.

Such a reversal of common expectations is in line with Luke's new conception of God's household and what it means to be in community with one another as depicted throughout Luke-Acts. In Luke's gospel Jesus places young children at his side and summons them to participate in *koinonia* community with him. The life of discipleship may not be an easy life for youth and small children, but it is one to which Jesus calls them and to which at least some children in Luke's account willingly and actively respond.

The Demands of Itinerancy

Destro and Pesce divide Lukan discipleship into the categories of itinerant and sedentary followers of Jesus.[27] The most demanding life of discipleship in Luke's gospel is itinerancy. This is true whether a disciple is a child or an adult. While discipleship takes on a narrower definition in some of the other accounts, Luke's Jesus identifies his family and, one can infer, his disciples, quite broadly with those who hear the word of God and do it (8:19–21; 11:27–28). Thus, itinerancy, while the most highlighted way of performing God's will in Luke's gospel, is not the only option that Luke presents. Illuminating Luke's portrayal of sedentary disciples as well, Destro and Pesce observe, "Jesus and his movement need the household structure because they have to find somewhere to lodge."[28] They thereby conclude, upon analysis of Luke's household parables, that Jesus has both itinerant followers *and* "sedentary followers who have to open up their houses."[29]

This sedentary life would have allowed such disciples to retain and, indeed, capitalize upon the protections of their household in ways that itinerant disciples could not. Citing the examples of Zacchaeus and the rich man and Lazarus (the latter as a counter example), Destro and Pesce maintain, "Only itinerant followers, in Luke's view, must sell everything, whereas sympathizers may adopt a less radical attitude . . . *providing* hospitality."[30] Sedentary disciples provide a necessary service to Jesus and his itinerant followers in need of hospitality in the various places where they travel. Such sedentary disciples exercise their discipleship not by following Jesus in his itinerant ministry, but by ministering to Jesus and his itinerant disciples as members of the same new household of believers wherever they might find themselves.

While Destro and Pesce portray this with reference to the *pater familias* who would be able to provide familial protection, it follows that others in their household, including young children due to their increased dependency upon such family leaders for protection and socialization, would have followed suit. Although child disciples could not on their own accord open up their homes as such, their service through the routine tasks of the household remained indispensable. Thus, sedentary discipleship provides a vital lens through which to view and investigate the role of children among Jesus' disciples.

Children Among the Sedentary Disciples

Luke's inclusion of children in Jesus' discipleship community on account of their association with Christian households has long been argued by proponents of infant baptism in relation to texts that describe the baptism of entire households.[31] To the extent that such inclusion of children in the later Christian community is accepted in relation to their role in the οἶκος, it is reasonable to read a similar inclusion among the earliest followers of Jesus due to their same household positioning. Moreover, as happened through infant baptism, the presence of these child disciples in sedentary households would have promoted the growth and perpetuation of the Lukan community.

Luke's parable in 15:11–32, often dubbed either the "Prodigal Son" or "The Forgiving Father," with its range of child characters, also elucidates the role of children among Jesus' sedentary disciples. In this parable of the restoration of two sons to their father, through the magnanimous invitation of the father to the eldest son to join in the celebration, Luke makes clear that the role of welcoming the lost, poor, and marginalized (in this case, the younger son) does not rest solely upon the householder, in this case the father, but is extended across the entire household structure—including children. Indeed, it is child slaves (παίδων, v. 26) who enact the celebration that the father declares. In this story that Luke's Jesus tells, children across generations and socio-economic roles thus participate in a display of hospitality that Luke then sets up as paradigmatic of hospitality in God's Kingdom. True to the parabolic form, such hospitality is to be expected—or at least hoped for—throughout the discipleship community.

Due to the strong participatory role that children had in household tasks, the successful reception of Jesus and his itinerant followers by sedentary disciples would have been effectually impossible without the participation of the young. This, however, raises serious questions about the difference between participation by personal assent or by power-driven coercion. Given the heavy role of the household, as represented by the will of the *pater familias*, in socializing children (both slave and free) it is difficult if not impossible to entirely separate these two motives. As a child was socialized in the first century atmosphere, the will of the *pater familias* became his or her will. Nevertheless, characters such as the eldest son in Luke's parable suggest that this was not always the case. Indeed, childhood as a transitional moment in development may offer the largest window into social resistance at the household level available in antiquity. The dissent of children who were still learning the ways of the household and their society would have been excused in ways that were not possible for adults.[32] While such questions will be taken up in the concluding chapter as a path forward in the re-construction of children as followers of Jesus, for now the conflation of these two motives—free and coerced—must remain in tension as an opportunity to see the lived role of children both within individual households and Jesus' discipleship community more broadly conceived.

Children Among the Itinerant Disciples

Notwithstanding the potential room for reclaiming the place of children in these household narratives, the primary group of disciples to whom Jesus addresses himself in Luke's gospel is, by virtue of proximity, those disciples who have followed Jesus from Galilee and beyond. Even while including children among the sedentary followers of Jesus, to exclude children from participation among the itinerant followers would be to exclude them from a significant experience of and participation in Jesus' ministry as relayed by Luke. Such an exclusion severely limits (re)construction of the place and role of children in Luke's gospel account, given the nature of Luke's text as largely a travel narrative.

Moreover, if the absence of children among the itinerant disciples of Luke's account continues to be assumed despite an allowance for their presence among sedentary household disciples, the harmful neglect caused by the metaphorization and allegorization of children within Luke's travel account is merely softened at best. Only when the lived realities of children are read holistically as a part of Jesus' mission and ministry—both sedentary and itinerant—can scholarship move beyond such adultist approaches and thus read the welcome extended to children in texts such as Lk 18:15–17 truly in a liberating and empowering way.[33]

Therefore, while acknowledging the existence of children and youth among Luke's sedentary disciples of Jesus, it remains necessary to consider the feasibility of their participation among the itinerant disciples of Jesus as well. To do so moves children from hapless victims of the family division described in Lk 12:49–53 and 14:25–26 to active participants in it for the sake of the gospel. Moreover, it looks beyond mere consideration of a child's smallness as a vulnerability and hindrance within an itinerant lifestyle to a holistic view of children as children that, while not overlooking their particular needs and dependencies, at the same time sees children for their potential to enrich the itinerant community in their own right.

To begin with, the agency of itinerant child disciples in Luke's gospel who *choose* to follow Jesus has been illustrated in the above discussion of children's response to Jesus' call in Lk 18:15–17. A. James Murphy disputes this assumption on the grounds that Jesus' statements about leaving family and hating *even sons and daughters* prove disruptive to children left in a would-be [adult] disciple's wake.[34] Indeed, if the history of the early church is any indication, Luke's itinerant disciples can be plausibly assumed to have left many family members—including non-adult children in their wake.[35] Nevertheless, it is equally reasonable to assume that in Luke's vision, such non-adult children themselves were, in some cases, the cause of such division.

The terms "sons and daughters" or "children" (παιδία) themselves do not indicate age so much as relationship and are, in fact, two among a whole list of relational identities disrupted by a life of discipleship.[36] Destro and Pesce posit that in Peter's response to Jesus in Lk 18:28–30, "Luke puts forward a series of alternative cases that defines the intermediate generation: he who abandons his wife, or his brothers or else parents or children."[37] While each of these alternatives certainly can apply to the intermediate generation, there is no reason to assume that each case applies for every disciple. On account of the itinerant disciples' self-described abandonment of either parents or children, Destro and Pesce argue that such disciples must come from an intermediate generation with both living parents and (non-adult) children to leave behind. However, the either/or character of this statement also leaves room for the possibility that while some disciples fit into this intermediate category, other (older) disciples may have had solely children to leave behind and younger (non-adult) disciples correspondingly may have had solely parents to leave behind. Horn and Martens agree: "It is not clear whether this [leaving behind of family] means that all of [the disciples] were married and had children, or whether it means that a widowed mother may have followed her young son on the road in his itinerant ministry. This, too, would be a 'family.'"[38] The only clear affirmation in these descriptions of disruption is that for Luke's Jesus, and indeed, across the synoptics, one's commitment to discipleship must come before one's personal family ties.

The use of such relational terms is thus aimed directly at those family members who would object to or stand in the way of a disciple following Jesus. This role, in fact, is less likely to apply to a young child (or any non-adult child) given their dependent and impressionable place in the family. This role would make them unlikely to forcibly exercise such an objection in relation to their caregiver. Moreover, Luke never states that *all* child-parent dyads must be separated by an affirmative response to discipleship. Given their particular dependencies, combined with the absence of any specific directive that they must be left behind, it is likely that many children responded to this call *together* with at least one of their primary caregivers.

Nevertheless, some children, just as some adult family members, were left behind—either from their own choice, the choice of their caregiver, or a combination of the two. These are the sons and daughters, of all ages, to whom Luke's Jesus refers as those for whom the disruption must occur.[39] Indeed, the very fact that Luke's Jesus describes this division in terms of disruption rather than abandonment, as assumed by Murphy, implies a choice for the non-adult children of adult disciples as to whether or not to follow Jesus with their parents as disciples themselves.[40]

As discussed in relation to children's participation in sedentary discipleship roles of hospitality, however, such autonomy for non-adult children in Luke's world was not the norm. In light of this, Murphy goes so far as to call the distance between the synoptic depictions of itinerancy and social-cultural realities of household obligation "a bewildering gap."[41] Indeed, the autonomy to choose to leave one's household such as that assumed in Luke's parable of the two sons was not the cultural norm even for adult children in the intermediate generation, members of which are widely attested in Luke's discipleship groups (see Lk 5:10; 6:15–16). The gap to which Murphy refers between the synoptics and surrounding culture can thus best be understood as the very disruption that Luke's Jesus both acknowledges and counters across generations in Jesus' insistence that disruption is a component of discipleship (see 12:49–53; 14:25–26).

Moreover, the relative autonomy seen in children working and playing in first century Mediterranean culture suggests that a decision to join in the crowds following Jesus may well have been in keeping with the general autonomy of children in this culture. Thus, the major cultural barrier that would have prevented non-adult children from committing to follow Jesus would not have been their youth. Rather, such children would likely have been hindered only in so much as adult children were also hindered by the overarching control of a *pater familias* who did not also accept the call to discipleship.

While many child followers behind the Lukan text can thus be accounted for as joining the discipleship band together with another family member, it remains important to note the possibility and, indeed, likelihood that at least some of these child followers—particularly as they grew older in age—would also have answered the call to follow Jesus on their own. As early as the second century, such independent discipleship of the young, while perhaps not the norm, seems to be taken for granted.

Summarizing Celsus' second century description of the education of children in the Christian faith, John M. G. Barclay concludes, "Even children may be converted without the acquiescence of their parents," citing Celsus' description of "children being instructed by Christian 'cobblers' not to listen to their fathers."[42] Horn and Martens cite a young flute girl recorded in the *Acts of Thomas* as an example of such a child who, separate from any clear familial connections, joins the itinerant fellowship of the early disciples. In this account, a Hebrew flute-girl (*auletria*) who "is presented as an associate of the young [οἱ νεώτεροι] . . . seems to have been attracted by Thomas's youthful beauty and joined the young married couple [for whose wedding she played] when they assumed a life of asceticism, eventually going with them to India to meet Thomas."[43] Although the young girl's age is never given, her identified association with the young in combination with known evidence for child entertainment in the ancient world, leads Horn and Martens to conclude that "it is quite likely that this flute player still was a relatively young girl"—perhaps as young as five-years-old.[44]

In each instance that Barclay cites, children, while clearly welcomed into the fellowship of disciples, remain ancillary to the goals of the texts that contain them. In the first place, the question is one of education; in the second place, the narrative is centered on the young couple who marry and then follow Thomas into a life of asceticism. Consequently, the relative silence of ancient literature on the lives of children remains, and it is impossible from these texts to know how common or exemplary these instances of child discipleship are apart from others in their families who would have been in the early Christian communities.

In each case, these child disciples do not enter into the life of discipleship alone—even when they leave their family to do so. Instead, they follow and are instructed by other adult disciples. This is the very essence of the new family that Luke's Jesus describes for those who leave their families for the sake of the gospel: "And [Jesus] said to them, 'Truly I tell you, there is no one who has left house or wife or brothers or parents or children for the sake of the kingdom of God, who will not get back very much more in this age, and in the age to come eternal life" (Lk 18:29–30).[45]

Disciples who leave their families on account of the disruption that their discipleship might cause are not promised a new family in the age to come, but rather in the *present* age. This new and abundant family (including the homes where they might stay among non-itinerant disciples) is the discipleship community itself, the *koinonia* described in Acts. Luke makes this clear in the beginning chapters of Acts, describing all of the things that the disciples held in common. Hence, child disciples need not worry about leaving the care and security that their previous households afforded them because through their discipleship Luke effectually incorporates them into the wider family of disciples—the new household of God.[46]

Moreover, such agential participation of children as itinerant disciples of Jesus serves as an asset, not a liability to Luke's community. Although the life of itinerancy itself was undoubtedly difficult, it is likely that some of the demands of such discipleship would have been easier for children to meet. The Roman household system that dominated the first century ambient cultures of Luke's gospel account valued children for their contributions to the household but granted them no legal stake in the household itself.[47] As such, children—even children of the very wealthy—would have had little or no possessions to leave behind. The value of wealthy children existed in what they stood to inherit, not in what they actually possessed.[48] As such, the task of estimating one's ability to follow through with an abandonment of personal property in Lk 14:25–33 would have been easy for children who possessed little to nothing of their own.

Such a point is further made when Jesus comments on the difficulty for the rich of entering the Kingdom of Heaven in Lk 18:18–24. Indeed, this text follows immediately upon Luke's description of Jesus receiving young children, whom he cites as models for the adult disciples. It cannot be—and has not been—taken for a coincidence that this mandate of dispossession follows immediately after Jesus' command to be like a little child in order to enter into the Kingdom of Heaven. Itinerant discipleship demands that one no longer be a slave to wealth or cling to possessions as though they were one's source of security or social position, and that one give precedence to the family of God and especially to those in need. In this regard, young children—on account of their unique status within the household system—can take the lead.

In short, nothing within the social structure of the discipleship community in Luke precludes the participation of children. The interdependent and egalitarian nature of the first communities of Jesus' disciples described by Luke highlights and supports the ways in which children were already active in their individual households and communities. Luke's characterization of such a community may even suggest a model—albeit one which has been neglected by Christians throughout history—in which the place and autonomy of children within the community might even have been thought to be elevated.

Contribution of Children to the Discipleship Community

Accepting that, in Luke's narrative, Jesus calls children to accompany him in discipleship and that this call is met with a positive response, one must then (re)vision the composition and social structure of the discipleship community during Jesus' earthly ministry. Of what groups was such a community composed? How did they interact with one another? How did they interact with the larger community around them? And, of course, how did children fit in? The most obvious place to begin such an inquiry, as insinuated by already given attention in Luke's narrative to the prominence of the οἶκος, is from the point of view of the household. In many of Jesus' teachings and healings, the structures and relationships of the household provide not only a physical setting, but a cultural grounding. This can be seen in, but is not limited to Luke's depictions of the youth at Nain and his mother, the young servant and the centurion, the dying girl and her father Jairus, and the boy with the demon and his father.[49] Household, thus, serves as a primary reference point (both positively and negatively) for Jesus, even as he reforms the ideal of household among the community of his disciples.

For those who follow Jesus, the new community of disciples supplants the previous households of which they each had been respectively a part. So Jesus concludes his blessings and woes directed to the "great crowd of his disciples" (Lk 6:17) and others in the crowd with the admonition, "But love your enemies, do good, and lend, expecting nothing in return. Your reward will be great, and you will be children (υἱοὶ) of the Most High; for he is kind to the ungrateful and the wicked" (6:35). Continuing in his Jewish tradition of identifying the Israelites as the children of God (Deut 14:1), Luke's Jesus affirms that relationships in the Kingdom of God are not defined by biology, but by participation in community.[50]

Luke magnifies the centrality of relationships within the household of God for the present generation, however, when Jesus identifies his own family as those who hear the word of God and do it. For Luke's Jesus, such identification was no longer tied to descent from Abraham or viewed as an eschatological promise lived out primarily in conjunction with conventional household responsibilities. Rather, it is with relation to the imminent demands of God's Kingdom that such membership in God's household takes priority (cf. Lk 9:60).[51]

Thus, following shortly after Jesus' longest exposition on discipleship in Luke (the parable of the sower and its explanation [Lk 8:4–15]), Jesus is informed that his mother and brothers have come to see him (Lk 8:20); he affirms the priority of a different kind of household. While not denying a place in the new household to these members of his biological family (cf. Acts 1:14; also possibly Lk 24:10), Luke's Jesus' response makes it clear that community, indeed family, is now defined in terms of discipleship. He states, "My mother and my brothers are those who hear the word of God and do it" (Lk 8:21).[52]

Likewise, when a woman in the crowd calls out a blessing to "the womb that bore you and the breasts that nursed you!" (Lk 11:27), Luke's Jesus replies, "Blessed rather are those who hear the word of God and obey it!" (Lk 11:28). In God's household, as embodied by the discipleship community, one's response to the Kingdom is more important than one's kinship. Turid Karlsen Seim explains, "The relationship to the word of the Lord is constitutive for the family of Jesus and the community of the disciples and transforms the obligations and relationships presupposed by the biological family."[53] Households and families thus exist in service to the Kingdom.

While such a transformation might relativize Jesus' relationship with his biological family, it also places the power of agency in their hands (and the hands of all Jesus' disciples) to determine the extent to which they participate in God's household. Membership doesn't depend upon her reproductive capacity or biological lottery, but upon God's grace and individual response to it. Such relativization of the biological family and of women's reproductive capacities in particular has led some feminist scholars, including Karlsen Seim, to conclude that the women who follow Jesus disavow any maternal roles or capacities. Karlsen Seim continues, "For women, this means that their reproductive functions cease, and the women who follow Jesus are portrayed precisely as women with an autonomous mobility; they do not seem to be subordinated to family obligations."[54] The cessation of such reproductive function presumes that the women who follow Jesus, if not already childless, intend no longer to bear any (further) children of their own. In some cases, such an understanding may also lead to the assumption that the women who follow Jesus in Luke's account, if they may be presumed to already have had young children in their household, have abandoned these children in order to do so.[55] However, such conclusions are necessarily speculative. The maternal status of the women who follow Jesus in Luke's gospel remains open—a literary gap for each reader to fill responsibly.

In contrast, Luke explicitly names several of female disciples as mothers, such as Mary the mother of Jesus (Lk 8:20–21) and Mary the Mother of James (24:10). Although it is generally assumed that James, like Jesus, at this point in the narrative is grown, this may not be the case. Moreover, the absence of the direct identification of young mothers in a narrative that rarely identifies women or children as a general rule should not be taken as reason enough to dismiss them from the discipleship community as a whole.

Luke's narrative provides striking reason why such statements by Jesus about household ties being related to hearing and action rather than kinship ought not to be taken as a negation of the blessing on Jesus' mother or others in his biological family. Jesus' statements about household, instead, reflect a reorientation in terms of the source of blessing. Mary is not blessed because she bore a special son; she is blessed because of her faithfulness to the word of God.[56] To this end, Jesus' response in Lk 11:27-28 is actually a confirmation of Elizabeth's words in Luke 1:45, "And blessed is she who believed that there would be a fulfillment of what was spoken to her by the Lord." Mary is not "blessed among women" *because* of the "fruit of her womb" (Lk 1:42); she is blessed because she *believes*—with hearing ears—what had been spoken to her regarding her unborn child and *acts* accordingly. In Luke 8:21, then, Jesus does not exclude Mary and her children from the household of disciples, instead he reorients the crowds' view of the means by which they might find their inclusion. Thus, Luke 8:21 and Luke 11:27 serve simultaneously as a paradigmatic definition of discipleship and an inclusive invitation into God's household.

Consequently, one should not exclude the possibility—indeed, the likelihood—that not only individuals, but also families or portions of family groups were among Jesus' disciples. With an emphasis on gender inclusion, Talvikki Mattila persuasively argues:

> ... it is possible to imagine that families were the ones following Jesus. If there were sons and mothers, it is likely that there were daughters too. In the feeding miracles in Matthew (14:21; 15:38), it is said that many men shared in these meals "to say nothing of women and children." In the crowed following Jesus there were men, women, and children. The inner circle of disciples might have consisted of families, in which there were twelve men who afterwards were chosen as the symbolical group for the new Israel.[57]

In Luke in particular, it is clear that the inner circle called the Twelve does not reflect the discipleship community as a whole. Even to the extent that they do, that this group may have had other family members together with them in the broader discipleship group need not be excluded.

The passage most frequently cited as evidence that these disciples left their families is Peter's declaration in Luke 18:28. The NRSV translates this verse, "Then Peter said, 'Look, we have left our homes and followed you.'" The NIV translates the same verse, "Peter said to him, 'We have left all we had to follow you!'" In Greek, the word translated respectively as "our homes" and "all we had" is τὰ ἴδια, which means literally "our own things." It is in the context not of Jesus' statements about the divisions of family, but in response to Jesus' parenesis to the rich ruler who sought to live out all of the commandments. Jesus replied, "One thing you still lack; sell all that you possess and distribute it to the poor, and you shall have treasure in heaven; and come, follow me" (Lk 18:22). Thus, the things that Peter replies he and the other disciples have already left ought most closely to be associated with material belongings rather than family members.

Jesus responds to Peter's material claim by raising the stakes and assuring the disciples, "Truly I tell you, there is no one who has left house (οἰκίαν) or wife or brothers or parents or children (τέκνα), for the sake of the kingdom of God, who will not get back very much more in this age (ἐν τῷ καιρῷ τούτῳ) and in the age to come eternal life" (18:29–30). However, this is less a confirmation that every disciple has left all of these things and people, and rather an affirmation that whatever (or whoever) they left in their previous household for the sake of the Kingdom, they have already received again in plenty in the new household of God—and, indeed, they will receive in the age of eternal life to come.

That the cost of discipleship was not the same for everyone in the community is made clear by the use of the conjunction "or" (ἤ) rather than "and" (καὶ, δὲ) in Lk 18:29.

Relativisation of family ties, clearly demanded by Luke's Jesus, need not be understood as abandonment of one's family. Indeed, that all of the disciples left even all of their material things remains unlikely, given the background in Lk 8:1–3 that the women with Jesus "provided for [Jesus and the twelve apostles] out of their resources" (v. 3). What is necessary to follow Jesus, as with contemporary Jewish and Greco-Roman religious associations that required sacrifice, is not that disciples abandon everything, but that they value God before everything else. To the extent that maintaining family ties did not conflict with Jesus' mission, it can be expected that many disciples traveled with their family as they followed Jesus from Galilee.

The expectation of the presence of family members, especially children, among Jesus' discipleship group is validated in Luke 11:1–13. In response to the request of one of his disciples that he teach them how to pray (v. 1), Jesus instructs his disciples in words and illustration. First Jesus says to the disciples, "Suppose one of you has a friend (φίλον), and you go to him at midnight, and say to him, 'Friend (Φίλε), lend me three loaves of bread, for a friend of mine (φίλος μου) has arrived, and I have nothing to set before him.' And he answers from within, 'Do not bother me; the door has already been locked, and my children (τὰ παιδία μου) are with me in bed; I cannot get up and give you anything" (vv. 5–8). Here, although it is not stated whether the imagined friend is a disciple or not, Luke's Jesus describes a community of mutual concern (φιλέω) in which friends provide for one another and parents look out for their small children. Moreover, in order for such an illustration to carry the intended meaning for Jesus' disciples, it is necessary that they understand and relate to this sort of mutual concern—whether in the role of friend or in the role of parent.

That at least some of the disciples could, indeed, relate to the concerns of parental affection expressed in 11:6 is confirmed in Jesus' next illustration.

He adds, continuing to address his disciples, "Is there anyone among you who, if your child (ἐξ ὑμῶν τὸν πατέρα αἰτήσει ὁ υἱός) asks for a fish, will give a snake instead of a fish? Or if the child asks for an egg, will give a scorpion? If you, then, who are evil, know how to give good gifts to your children (τοῖς τέκνοις ὑμῶν), how much more will the heavenly Father give the Holy Spirit to those who ask him!" (vv. 11–13). The age of the child in vv. 11–12 is less clear; however, it may be inferred in relation both to the reference to small children (τὰ παιδία) in v. 7 and the implicit dependence of the child, literally "son," asking for a fish or an egg from his father (πατέρα).

More significantly, with regard to the question of family groups among Jesus' disciples, however, is the reference to the disciples to whom Jesus addresses himself in relational terms—in the illustration, as a father and son. Furthermore, as with the first illustration, in order for this teaching to carry the intended meaning, the disciples would need to still understand and experience such a relationship in positive terms. The point of the teaching is not to depict the heavenly Father as a parent who abandons their children, but rather as a parent who is affectionately concerned for the little ones under their care. Jesus' statement implies here that at least some of the disciples themselves have children.

This is in keeping with Destro and Pesce's description of Luke's "typical disciple" in light of the *logions* of Lk 12:52 and 14:26.[58] Specifically with relation to 14:26, they describe the "typical disciple" as "a male who has a father and mother, who is married with children and who has brothers and sisters."[59] The broader community of Jesus' disciples is therefore expected, in Luke, to have personal experience with parent-child relationships on either side of this dialectic, and for many of them, in the intermediate position of both parent and child.[60] Moreover, in order for the comparison between a loving parent and the heavenly Father to make sense in the way that Luke seems to intend it to, the disciples must retain a positive conception of the parent-child relationship. They would not be able to relate to God as an affectionate parent if they had all (or even most) abandoned their own children for the sake of discipleship. Instead, Jesus assumes that many disciples continue to be able to provide for their children within the discipleship community; children are thus established as a valued part of the discipleship group.

This presence is not surprising: it has already been seen in Lk 9:47, when Jesus, aware that an argument about status had arisen between the disciples, takes a little child and puts it by his side in an act of solidarity. It is again implied in the presence of children in Lk 18:15–17 whom Jesus calls to himself. As already demonstrated, the primary context of dialogue in Lk 9:43b–49 centers around Jesus and his disciples. Therefore, the child whom Jesus places by his side is most likely to have originated from amidst the community of disciples to whom Jesus addresses himself.[61] Yet, more to the point, in this text and even more clearly in Lk 18:15–17, children are not merely acknowledged as present in the vicinity of Jesus and his disciples, but are held up as archetypes of discipleship. By placing this child at his *side,* it has been noted that Jesus demonstrates a stance of solidarity with this child—his ministry is not simply *for* or *about* children in a paternalistic sense, it is *alongside* them.[62]

With reference to the parallel of Luke 18:15–17 in Matthew 19:13–15, Carter writes, "At the literal level, it affirms the importance of children in the alternative households of the kingdom. At a metaphorical level, it identifies disciples as children and children as a model for discipleship."[63] Child disciples provide the ideal model for discipleship according to these texts and their synoptic parallels. Most contemporary interpretations, however, place so much emphasis on what adults might be able to draw from such a model that they miss the apparent reality that such a comparison assumes the discipleship of children themselves.

The significance of such modeling moves one from merely establishing the place of children among Jesus' disciples to considering what it is that children as children uniquely bring to the community of disciples. James Francis, albeit primarily focusing on the metaphorical use of children in these texts, brings this contribution to light. He writes,

> In the metaphorical significance of the child as an image of discipleship, whilst the NT shares a culture critique of childishness, a remarkable emphasis is placed on childlikeness whereby it is not only the role of the child to be taught by the adult but that the adult may learn lessons of faith from the child, and indeed must become as a child in trustful dependency and in the discovery of God in the marginalized.[64]

Whereas children were traditionally valued as members of households, cultural and religious groups, and societies, as productive participants, capable of being socialized according to the dominant values, Luke's Jesus supposes something different.[65]

Rather than seeing children only as sponges to be taught to become adults and assist in adult tasks, the Lukan author presents children as capable of *teaching* adults. Beyond affection, service, and future potential, Luke's Jesus affirms that children *as children* have something uniquely valuable to contribute to the discipleship community. Francis names this as "trustful dependency," a theme also emphasized by Gundry who describes the defining characteristic of children in this context as "not any particular quality of the child, but 'the child's littleness, immaturity and need of assistance, though commonly disparaged, [that] keep the way open for the fatherly love of God.'"[66] Both of these scholars draw attention to the gospel writers' portraits of real children as active contributors to the dialectic within the discipleship community.

Affirming the spirit in which they bring children to the fore, I would nuance Francis' use of the word "dependency" with the term "inter-dependency." Inter-dependency better reflects the quality that both Francis and Gundry seem to describe of children, who by their nature of littleness and immaturity, continue to need assistance from their adult counterparts, while at the same time, being portrayed by the synoptic authors as *giving* assistance to these adults by way of modeling a posture of discipleship. So Carter writes,

> The metaphor underlines that discipleship is an egalitarian existence. All disciples are children. In the Matthean household code, in contrast to the Aristotelian tradition, there is no reference to the duties of parents. In the prevailing household organization parental status betokens power over others, and this is denied to the disciples . . . Equality among disciples and not hierarchy is to pervade the kingdom's households. The hierarchical distinctions are abolished, to be replaced by an anti-structure existence, an egalitarian way of life in which all disciples are obedient to the will of God their Father.[67]

Similarly, the authority of parents over children is not emphasized in Luke's gospel because the single authority in Jesus' new household is understood as God. However, the *relationship* between parents and children within God's household is not abolished. Instead, as in Jesus' teachings in Lk 11:1–13 and 18:15–17, this dialectical relationship of interdependency is recast as a model for the relationship between *all* disciples (young and old) and God as their caring parent.

Moreover, in Luke's account, this model of the household as a bastion of care and support, both among disciples as equals and in their relations to God as the heavenly Father, goes further. Luke suggests that God not only welcomes and supports those disciples who perfectly follow the demands of discipleship, or even demonstrate their need and dependency on God, but also extends a consistent welcome to those who fail and return. This is most profoundly represented in the restoration of Jesus' disciples after their abandonment of Jesus at the cross. It can also be seen the depiction of the forgiveness extended by father to son in the aforementioned parable in Lk 15:11–32. It may be expected that children and youth may not always be able to live up to the demands of discipleship. Children likely sometimes failed in the same way as their adult counterparts, and other times in ways unique to their unique identities as children. Nevertheless, God as a loving parent intends for such children to remain a part of the community and thus continually receives them back even as they continue to strive towards this end.

In like manner, Francis notes the significance that Lk 7:31–35 "does not contain a criticism of the children that their game failed, nor serve necessarily as an example of foreboding which children's games could sometimes have for adults, but points to a lesson which is drawn from observation of the game."[68] Discipleship is not about perfect performance either of games or of rules and standards—a feat that Luke's gospel makes clear is inaccessible both to children and adults—but is rather a continued commitment and a willingness to recognize the interdependence of all of God's children upon one another.[69]

CHILDREN AMONG THE TWELVE: THE CASE OF JAMES AND JOHN

Up until now, this chapter has attempted to retrieve a memory of children in Luke's community from their absence in his literary description. However, when Luke's account is read through a childist lens, otherwise hidden child characters may also exist within plain sight. The combination of Luke's adult bias along with assumptions about his audiences' shared knowledge may have led to the omission of details identifying certain characters as children when they do appear in the gospel account; nevertheless, the shadows of such details remain.[70]

On this basis, I suggest that reading the characters of James and John among Jesus' disciples as non-adult children in Luke's text is both plausible and legitimate. Furthermore, such an understanding of James and John as children ought to be pursued in a childist reading such as this one because it holds value for readers concerned with the wellbeing of children in the present-day church. Identifying with James and John as child disciples offers a positive model for the full inclusion of children in the Christian community and illustrates the ability of at least some children to thrive among Jesus' itinerant disciples.

Jesus' disciples are rarely explicitly identified according to their age. For the majority of common people in the first century, including Jesus' disciples, it is unlikely that anyone—even the disciples themselves—would have known such a detail with precision.[71] The lack of attention to age is illustrated in two of the three cases in Luke's account in which an age is mentioned: a girl whom Jesus heals and Jesus himself. In both cases, the age that is given is not an exact number so much as a reasonable approximation. Luke states that the girl and Jesus were "*about* [ὡσεὶ]" twelve and thirty years old respectively (8:42; 3:23). Given the attention to detail elsewhere in Luke's narrative and the stated goal to provide an "orderly account" (1:1), one would expect precise ages to be given as it is in Lk 2:42. Since birthdays were not commonly celebrated in the ancient world as they are today, it is reasonable to infer that Luke did not have access to more precise ages. Notably, this information remains missing even for the main character of his account! As a result, it can be assumed that Luke's failure to mention age should neither indicate the youth or the maturity of his subject. Instead, the age of each character must be inferred from details elsewhere in the account.

Even in the later apocryphal *Acts of John*, where some indication of the brothers' ages are given, exact years are not the concern. Rather, the brothers are identified according to their facial hair, John with "beard thick and flowing" and James as "a young man (νεανίσκος) whose beard had newly come" (*Acts of John*, 89:2). Moreover, writing as John, the author locates John's first call to discipleship earlier than this moment at the seashore, in his own youth (νεότητι) when God appeared to him (*Acts of John*, 113:1). Although the ambiguity of the term *youth* in each case could imply either a child/adolescent or a young man, the latter interpretation (and the specificity around James' age) could also be read as an adultist attempt to refute potentially popular traditions among the early Christian communities that James was a child himself when he answered the call to follow Jesus. The very fact that the apocryphal author finds the need to address the ages of these two brothers so specifically and does not mention the ages of Peter and Andrew suggests an awareness or sense of wondering about the youth of James and John among the early Christian community (*Acts of John*, 88:3–89:2).

Within Luke's gospel itself, one detail that can help to discern a disciple's relative age is the place of that individual in his or her household. At least four of the Twelve who form the core group of Jesus' disciples are located within a family unit. These include James son of Alphaeus (Lk 6:16), Judas son of James (6:15), and James and John sons of Zebedee (5:10).[72] Luke also identifies Jesus both as "Son of God" and as "Joseph's son" (3:23) and John as the son of Zechariah (1:57–80; 3:2). However, especially for Jesus, this identification through sonship is carried past his genealogy and infancy into his youth and adult ministry.[73] This is a result of the household structure previously described.

The Roman practice of *pater familias*, some form of which seems indicated in the typical Mediterranean Jewish households with which Luke engages, leaves open the possibility that a "son" or "daughter" of a household could range in age anywhere from a newborn to an older adult, caring for children of his or her own. The qualifying factor seems to be not the individual's age, but his or her place relative to the oldest living family member. Consequently, one's place as a son in a household can at most tell the reader that such an individual is not (yet) the patriarch of his household. This leaves open the possibility that such disciples are still children, but by no means assumes it.

A next step in determining the age of Luke's characters is to search for additional literary clues. For example, because Luke mentions Simon's mother-in-law, the readers know that Simon is married. Based on his home ownership, Simon can be identified as the head of his house (4:38). Both of these details point to Simon as an adult. Likewise, Simon appears established in his industry given the account in 5:3 that he owns the fishing boat that Jesus boards. This again points to a rank and status within the fishing industry attributable to an adult.

On the other hand, James and John are not identified according to their own holdings (house or boat). Rather, these disciples are identified by their relationships with Simon (their partner) and Zebedee (their father) (5:10). In a positive sense, such identifications do not imply the age of James and John as either a juvenile or an adult.[74] However, in a negative sense, in contrast to Simon, the details connected with James and John do not rule out their youthfulness either. That neither one is the head of their house nor their fishing cooperative is clear from their connections with Zebedee and Simon. This, at minimum, leaves the possibility open that one or both of the sons of Zebedee is in fact still a non-adult child.

A proper exploration of the plausibility of James and John as child characters requires a reconstruction of the power relationships in first century Mediterranean fishing associations with which Luke and his audience would have been acquainted relative to these characters' stations vis a vis Zebedee and Simon in the fishing cooperative described by Luke. Absent direct records from such associations, K. C. Hanson provides a useful model, derived mainly from parallel associations evidenced in Egyptian and Syrian societies of the same time period.[75] According to this model Hanson conjectures that Luke has crafted Simon and Zebedee's families as a part of "a small-scale collective cooperative."[76] Hanson reaches this conclusion based upon the interaction between these characters as described in Luke's text.

Similar to the operation of fishing guilds and cooperatives in Hanson's regions of study, Luke describes these fisher families as working with partners in nearby boats whom they signal to assist with a large catch. Additionally, they appear to be family businesses, which, assuming Luke knows Mark's narrative, may occasionally hire day workers to help with their load.[77] Detailing this Galilean fishing economy, Hanson explains, "The largest part of the population was composed of peasant farmers, and the family functioned as both a producing and consuming unit. This means that relatives normally worked together, and that kinship ties were fundamental for 'guild' or trade relations."[78] Luke's description of the characters and action align closely with this model, placing James and John as younger family members in Zebedee and Simon's fishing cooperative.

Moreover, the position and interaction of James and John within this cooperative suggest that Luke's audience can plausibly understand them as non-adult children of Zebedee. The participation of such children in first century Mediterranean fishing cooperatives is affirmed by Tønnes Bekker-Nielsen in "Fishing in the Roman World," when he describes the interaction of a slightly larger scale cooperative fishing endeavor.[79] Bekker-Nielsen bases his description on comparisons between ancient depictions of the fishing industry and contemporary observations of modern fishermen using casting nets cooperatively.

To illustrate this practice, Bekker-Nielsen refers to two figures that depict "the casting-net being used from a boat . . . in a manner closely corresponding to similar images from the Roman period."[80] While the figures in the third century Roman mosaic are neutral enough to make it difficult to discern the ages of those in the boats, it is certainly plausible that at least some of the shorter figures may have been intended to portray children. Moreover, the modern photographs that Bekker-Nielsen describes as "closely corresponding" clearly depict young boys, both prepubescent and adolescent.

At minimum, such visual depictions confirm the physical ability of youths to perform the work of fishing as described in Luke's narrative. More broadly, the application of Bekker-Nielsen's observations together with Hanson's model for fishing cooperatives make it not only conceivable, but likely, that Luke and his audience would have expected young boys to participate in the fishing industry. As such, they may also have understood the characters of James and John as representatives not of the intermediate, but rather of the youngest generation—children.

In opposition to the participation of this youngest generation among Jesus' disciples, Destro and Pesce return again to the son of the widow of Nain, reasoning that "the young man does not show any desire to follow him, nor does Jesus ask him to, perhaps precisely because he is very young (νεανίσκος)."[81] My discussion of the youth at Nain in chapter 3 explicitly calls this into question, arguing that without any explicit label to the effect, the young man's actions still qualify him as a disciple. The case of James and John, among others, further problematizes Destro and Pesce's heavy reliance on this episode in dismissing the younger generation as a focus of attention among Jesus' disciples in Luke. Even if it were the case that the youth at Nain should not be considered a disciple (a point I contest above), this does not preclude the participation of other youths in Jesus' discipleship circle. Indeed, this is certainly not the case when it comes to women (contrast the youth's mother with the women in Lk 8:1–3).

Destro and Pesce's use of the Nain episode in particular is helpful in understanding possible perceptions of James and John since they ground their dismissal of the "very young" on the response of a νεανίσκος.[82] Likewise, in describing the fishing operations in Asia Minor in the second century, which seem not to have changed much from Luke's first century description, Aelian writes that "each boat has six youths [νεανίας] a side."[83] The term νεανίας, from the same root as νεανίσκος is an adjective meaning "youthful," used here by Aelian as a substantive. Although Bekker-Nielsen translates the same term to mean "young men,"[84] the maturity understood in contemporary English by the term "men" in such a translation is nowhere implied in the original text. It is more appropriately translated in parallel with the term "youth" used previously to translate νεανίσκος in Luke 7 in order to show the correlation between the two terms. The Liddel-Scott-Jones Greek Lexicon describes the adjective νεανίας as one used "frequently with the sense of *a youth* in character, i.e. either in good sense, *impetuous, active* or in bad sense, *hot-headed, willful, headstrong*."[85] In short, those manning fishing boats not only could be among the younger generation, but were typified by such youth—likely because of their strength and stamina.

Such an age difference fits with Hanson's description of those who mind the nets as lower in the hierarchy of the fishing organization than boat owners—whom one may infer are often their fathers, as in Luke's narrative. Thus, the role that the two sons play in the fishing cooperative combined with their relationship with Zebedee suggests that, while Luke never uses chronological language to describe their characters, it is a valid reading to understand their characters as νεανίσκοι, or youth.

Such a relation in the hierarchy of the fishing organization can be further extrapolated from the use of the more general term κοινωνοί to describe James and John in their relationship with Simon (5:10), rather than the technical term μέτοχοι used to describe Simon's relationship with those in the other boat in 5:7.[86] If analogies between agriculture and fishing can be drawn, the technical term μέτοχοι should be understood as a financial partner in funding the lease of fishing rights for the association—a householder with financial means.[87] The former term, closely related to κοινωνία, used later by Luke to describe the common fellowship of the entire community of believers in Acts 2:42, 44, suggests a relationship between the three men of community—specifically, in this case, the fishing association. In contrast, the latter term suggests a more technical relationship between Simon and Zebedee as partners in the ownership of the same fishing organization. That Luke does not repeat the term μέτοχοι in 5:10, instead using κοινωνοί, a term used nowhere else in his corpus, suggests that the move to distinguish James and John from Simon's business partners in v. 7 is intentional. James and John are associated with Simon but are not in rank (or, it seems feasible to assume, in age) his equals.

In contrast to the assumptions of authors such as Murphy, Destro, and Pesce, Horn and Martens suggest that the infrequent mention of offspring of Jesus' disciples might stem not from an abandonment of such children at home by a group of followers made up largely of the intermediate generation, but rather by the fact that these disciples are made up in part (if not in majority) by just such children of the younger generation themselves. Reaching across the synoptic accounts, Horn and Martens highlight the relationships between James and Joses and their mother (Mk 15:40; Mt 27:56; Lk 24:10) and the sons of Zebedee and their mother (Mt 20:20–23; 27:56). Neither pair of brothers is ever identified with a wife or children and the care and concern of their mothers seems to remain a central theme. Drawing on these examples, Horn and Martens conclude, "We should consider that youths, without a wife or children, were precisely the age group who followed teachers like Jesus."[88]

The role of James and John as sons and associates in their father's fishing organization in Luke's description leaves space to read these brothers as non-adult children from this youngest generation. While this is not the only possible reading of these characters in Luke's account, their location among the Twelve—the inner circle of Jesus' disciples in Luke's narrative—makes such a reading valuable in ascertaining the pervasive presence and participation of children among the disciples more broadly. When read with this lens, Luke's narrative does not paint children at the margins of discipleship. Through a childist reading of Luke's account, children emerge right at the center—active participants at all levels and in all manners of following Jesus.

CONCLUSION

The lack of specialized vocabulary to indicate the presence of children at each turn in Luke's narrative should no more be taken as a sign of their absence than the lack of explicit reference to women between Lk 8:1–3 and the crucifixion narrative should be taken as a sign that women did not follow Jesus consistently from Galilee. Lk 23:55ff confirms that, despite the evangelist's relative silence on their presence, the women disciples were with Jesus throughout. The same can be said about child disciples, despite their similar recurrence primarily as minor characters in Luke's narrative.

Moreover, this chapter has shown the plausible and valid reading of children as present not only among both Jesus' sedentary and itinerant disciples, but even among the core group of Twelve. Jesus' discipleship community in Luke's narrative, like the *koinonia* community Luke describes later in Acts, is a mixed group made up of men and women, adults and children, working together to bring about God's Kingdom on Earth.

NOTES

1. Although discipleship has never been understood as limited to those who partook in this Last Supper (see Acts 1:21), it will be later argued that the presence and participation of children together with Jesus even at this pivotal event in his ministry should not be precluded.

2. This program for discipleship is then further fleshed out in Jesus' parable of the sower (Lk 8:1–15), which describes four kinds of people, affirming those who both hear and respond to the word of God as those who follow the will of Jesus.

3. See chapters 1 and 2 on the inclusion and restoration of children in Jesus' ministry for a detailed support of this claim.

4. This last category of "doing" subsumes the more specific instructions of abnegation in Lk 14:25–33, as will be demonstrated later on.

5. As will be seen in the analyses that follow, even the Twelve fall short of the demands of discipleship by the end of the Lukan gospel (see Lk 22:54–62); nevertheless, by the beginning of Acts this term is picked up again as a designation of all except Judas Iscariot (Acts 6:1; see also Acts 1:15–26).

6. BDAG, 609.

7. Lk 6:13, 17; 7:11; 9:14; and 19:37.

8. Lk 6:20; 9:18, 43; 10:22–23; 11:1; 12:1, 22; 16:1; 17:1, 22; 20:45; and 22:39, 45.

9. Esther deBoer, "The Lukan Mary Magdalene and the Other Women Following Jesus" in *Feminist Companion to Luke*, ed. Amy-Jill Levine and Marianne Blickenstaff (Cleveland: Pilgrim Press, 2002) 145. The initial ambiguity of 9:18–22 has been attributed to the literary device of prolepsis—waiting to reveal information until later in the narrative for dramatic effect. However, in light of my understanding of Luke 8.1–3 as a summary statement, described below, I suggest that it is more likely that a specific reference would have been unnecessary, since from Luke 8.1–3 on Mary and Joanna would have been assumed to be with this group.

10. Lk 7:11; 8:9, 22–40; 9:14–16, 18, 37–45; 12:1–13, 41; 14:25–33; 18:15; 19:37–40; 20:45.

11. Rosalie Ryan, "The Women From Galilee and Discipleship in Luke" in *Biblical Theology Bulletin*, 15:2 (1985) 57.

12. See Brown, cited in Ryan, 57.

13. Barbara Reid, *Salty Wives, Spirited Mothers, and Savvy Widows: Capable Women of Purpose and Persistence in Luke's Gospel* (Grand Rapids: William Eerdmans, 2012) 38.

14. Contemporary Lutheran baptismal liturgies assume such participation when the assembly greets the newly baptized, including infants, with the words, "We welcome you into the body of Christ and into the mission we share" (Evangelical Lutheran Church in America, *Evangelical Lutheran Worship* [Minneapolis: Augsburg Fortress, 2006] 231).

15. See chapter 2 for a detailed support of these conclusions.

16. Cornelia B. Horn and John W. Martens, *"Let the little children come to me": Childhood and Early Christianity* (Washington, D.C.: Catholic University of America Press, 2009) 266.

17. BDAG, 881.
18. François Bovon, *Luke 2*, translated by Donald S. Deer (Minneapolis: Fortress Press, 2013) 558.
19. *NIB*, 1861–1862.
20. Matthew and Mark both use a form of the word προσκαλέω in connection with Jesus' calling to himself and subsequently naming and sending the twelve disciples/apostles (Matt 10:1; Mk 3:13), where Luke uses προσφωνέω in 6:13. However, given the function of each verb more in terms of summons than vocation—a meaning that is nowhere specifically attached to either verb in the gospel accounts—such use serves neither to add or detract from the argument that the Lukan author portrays Jesus in Lk 18:15–17 as inviting young children into his presence.
21. A gap which, for at least some of Luke's audience may have been/be filled by intertextual knowledge of Mark's account, which states, "And he [Jesus] took them [the children] up in his arms, laid his hands on them, and blessed them" (Mk 10:16) or similarly, Matthew 19:15: "And he [Jesus] laid his hands on them [the children] and went on his way." Notably, however, the fact that Luke does not send Jesus immediately away from the children following this incident suggests a stronger picture of child accompaniment than does its Matthean parallel, despite Matthew's more direct reference to Jesus touching the children.
22. This represents a shift from the use of the term βρέφη in Lk 18:15. As noted in chapter 1, βρέφη is an age-specific term that, while primarily culturally determined, reaches its upward limit in the literature around the age of four (around the age that most children would be expected to have been weaned). As such, despite the best contemporary English translation as "infants," this is misleading in the sense that many of these "infants" need not be pictured as babes in arms, unable to approach Jesus of their own volition, but could just as easily have been toddlers or even small children more than able to walk and respond for themselves. Nevertheless, the lower limit of this age category (actually extending to children within the womb, e.g. Lk 1:41, 44) does present some difficulty in a reading that assumes child led action. Here sensitivity toward the specific physical action of movement toward Jesus must be tempered with Luke's literary notion of the ability of even such young infants to respond to Jesus (Lk 1:39–45) alongside of findings among contemporary child psychologists that increasingly place the age of volition and even moral reasoning at the very start of life (Paul Bloom, "The Moral Life of Babies," in *New York Times*, 5 May 2010).
23. Bovon's lengthy analysis of the verbs in Luke's text illustrate this point: "The verb 'let' (ἄφετε) blows a wind of freedom that excludes any constraint. 'Come to me' is an expression rooted in sapiential literature that Luke had already applied to Jesus (6:47). 'Come to him' or 'go to him' is a personalized manner of approaching God, turning away from one's egocentric way of living, subscribing to the Word, and practicing repentance/conversion (μετάνοια). Obedience here means the path of following: 'principles' are ruled out in favor of relations of person ('you') to person ('me'). Life is understood as a walk; religion, as a movement" (*Luke 2*, 559).
24. Bovon, *Luke 2*, 395.
25. Similarly, see Warren Carter on the significance of this passage in Matthew, although in Luke the language of call is omitted in favor of Jesus' direct action

of embracing a child assumed already to be among the group. Carter writes: "The instruction about discipleship begins when the audience is told that Jesus 'called' a child to him. The verb προσκαλέω is employed in 10:1 in the call of the twelve disciples (so also 15.32; 20:25). The context of the call (the question about being the greatest in the kingdom) explicitly links the child, discipleship, and the kingdom; in responding to Jesus' call, the child represents the starting point for all discipleship" (Warren Carter, *Households and Discipleship: A Study of Matthew 19*–20 [Sheffield: Sheffield Academic Press, 1994] 96).

26. Bovon, *Luke 2*, 494.

27. Adriana Destro and Mauro Pesce, "Fathers and Householders in the Jesus Movement: The Perspective of the Gospel of Luke," *Biblical Interpretation* (January 2003).

28. Destro and Pesce, 226.

29. Destro and Pesce, 232. Nevertheless, following their initial dismissal of the role of young children and adolescents in Jesus' discipleship movement, Destro and Pesce retain this sedentary role of hospitality for householders—the *pater familias*—as representatives of the older generation (234). Having already addressed these authors' too easy dismissal of the youngest generation as a part of Jesus' movement, I posit that the integral roles which youth and children played in the host structure of antiquity, albeit not as the head, nevertheless contributed to the successful reception of Jesus, his itinerant disciples, and the poor. Were children—slave and free—and, for that matter, women and younger generations of men to have resisted this transformation of the system by not welcoming and providing for Jesus, his itinerant disciples, and the poor, the entire enterprise would have failed to succeed. Take for example, again, the parable of the restoration of the two sons to their father (Lk 15:11–32)—it is the servants (some likely children) who actually arrange the welcome that the father commands. Moreover, even when he shows initial resistance, the father continues, against expectations, to beckon the eldest son to participate in the celebration—in the welcoming of the younger son and subsequent transformation of the host structure. In this way, the place of children as disciples of Jesus within the sedentary household is also being transformed.

30. Destro and Pesce, 230.

31. Acts 10:24–48; 16:14, 32; see also 1 Cor 1:16–18; 16:15–16; cf. Joachim Jeremias, *Infant Baptism in the First Four Centuries*, trans. David Cairns (Philadelphia: Westminster Press, 1960).

32. On the "cultural challenging" attributed to the boy Jesus in the *Infancy Gospel of Thomas*, see Reidar Aasgaard, *The Childhood of Jesus: Decoding the Apocryphal Infancy Gospel of Thomas* (Eugene, OR: Cascade Books, 2009) 79–84.

33. To this end, I concur with A. James Murphy's assessment that Luke's challenge to the marginal status of children must be read together with "the special challenges for non-adult children presented by respective characterizations of children against sayings relativizing family ties and the lifestyle indicative of the radical call to discipleship of the broader Synoptic narratives" (A. James Murphy, *Kids and Kingdom: The Precarious Presence of Children in the Synoptic Gospels* [Eugene, OR: Pickwick Publications, 2013] 33). It is not enough simply to paint a rhetorically pleasing picture of Jesus blessing the children without examining the lived experience that such children would have necessarily had in light of the Jesus movement.

Murphy's monograph addresses this lacuna across the three synoptic narratives, concluding that, despite their eschatological portrait of child inclusion, the reality of such children, when brought out of the shadows of the text, suggests a much more precarious reception. In this section, I accept Murphy's challenge to take "seriously the plight of 'real' children in the temporal world of the text" and "deliberately separate the plight of temporal families from the eschatological promises of the authors"—refusing "to sacrifice real children for eschatological or metaphorical ones in the narrative" (135).

34. Murphy, 103.

35. Consider the lives of such early Christian martyrs as Perpetua, Felicitas, and Melania the Elder.

36. Destro and Pesce's review of Luke's household structure, detailed below, confirms a general understanding of the terms "sons and daughters" within Greco-Roman society in which such filial terms describe each generation beneath the *pater familias*—including both physiological children and their grown parents when, quite typically, a grandfather remains alive.

37. Destro and Pesce, 221–222.

38. Horn and Martens, 265.

39. "Clearly the discouragement of family connections applied also to children who followed Jesus, not just to adults who turned from their families" (Horn & Martens, 266).

40. Murphy, 102.

41. Murphy, 114.

42. John M. G. Barclay, "The Family as the Bearer of Religion in Judaism and Early Christianity." In *Constructing Early Christian Families: Family as Social Reality and Metaphor*, edited by Halvor Moxnes (London: Routledge, 1997) 73.

43. Horn and Martens, 181.

44. Horn and Martens, 181.

45. See also Lk 21:16–19.

46. Judith M. Gundry, "Children in the Gospel of Mark, with Special Attention to Jesus' Blessing of the Children (Mark 10:13–16) and the Purpose of Mark," in *The Child in the Bible*, edited by Marcia Bunge, Terence Fretheim, and Beverly Roberts Gaventa (Grand Rapids: William B. Eerdmans, 2008) 160.

47. Beryl Rawson, "Adult-Child Relationships in Roman Society," in *Marriage, Divorce, and Children in Ancient Rome*, edited by Beryl Rawson (Oxford: Oxford University Press, 1991) 26.

48. Rawson, "Adult-Child Relationships," 26.

49. For a sampling of Jesus' teachings that employ the setting or characters of the household, see: Lk 5:33–39; 9:57–62; 10:38–42; 11:10–13; 12:13–21, 42–48, 49–53; 13:10–17, 34–35; 14:1–6; 25–33; 15:8–10, 11–32; 16:1–13, 18; 17:7–10, 22–37; 18:18–30; 19:1–10, 11–27; 20:9–18, 27–40.

50. In the Jewish community, one sign of participation in this community became circumcision (cf. Gen 17:1–27; 34:13). In his depiction of the community of Jesus' followers, particularly after his ascension, Luke emphasizes more generally the prescription to hear (understand) and do the word of God than any particular action (see Acts 15:1–29).

51. Stephen Barton, in his essay, "The Relativisation of Family Ties in the Jewish and Greco-Roman Traditions," in *Construction Early Christian Families: Family as Social Reality and Metaphor*, ed. Halvor Moxnes (New York: Routledge, 1997), persuasively shows that the demand to place religious loyalties above loyalties to household and kin "was not unprecedented in the traditions and practices of either Judaism or of the Greco-Roman world as a whole" (81). Nevertheless, the magnitude with which this relativization was felt within the Jesus movement due to the demands of itinerancy can still be said to have placed the issue of this conflict at the fore in a way that Greco-Roman and Jewish religious practices did not typically demand.

52. See Matt 12:46-50; Mk 3:31-35. While none of the synoptic accounts specifically exclude Jesus' mother, brothers, and even sisters (cf. diverging manuscript traditions of Mk 3:32), arguably, Luke, by omitting Jesus' direct indication of those around him, to the exclusion of the family members waiting outside, offers the most inclusive reading when it comes to locating Jesus' biological family within the new household of disciples.

53. Turid Karlsen Seim, *The Double Message: Patterns of Gender in Luke-Acts* (Nashville: Abingdon, 1994) 207.

54. Karlsen Seim, *The Double Message*, 207.

55. Murphy, 103: ". . . the inclusiveness of children among the disciples and in the kingdom of God by the Synoptic authors is tempered by images of household division and alienation of children as a consequence of Jesus' eschatological gathering of followers."

56. See F. Scott Spencer, "A Woman's Right to Choose? Mother Mary as Spirited Agent and Actor (Lk 1–2) in *Salty Wives, Spirited Mothers, and Savvy Widows: Capable Women of Purpose and Persistence in Luke's Gospel* (Grand Rapids: Wm. B. Eerdmans, 2012) 55–100.

57. Talvikki Mattila, "Naming the Nameless: Gender and Discipleship in Matthew's Passion Narrative," in *Characterization in the Gospels: Reconceiving Narrative Criticism*, ed. David Rhoads and Kari Syreeni (Sheffield: Sheffield Academic Press, 1999) 168.

58. Note that although they define the intermediate adult male as the "typical disciple," Destro and Pesce allow for other conceptions of the disciples, specifically with regard to the women of Lk 8:1–3 (220).

59. Destro and Pesce, 221.

60. Destro and Pesce, while acknowledging that the "typical disciple" is not representative of the entire community of disciples, nevertheless maintain that among Jesus' *itinerant* disciples—the group following him from Galilee—all of the disciples seem to be drawn from this intermediate generation. Their rationale for dismissing the itinerancy of the older "householder" generation is more detailed and moreover, not of immediate pertinence to this argument; however, their rationale for dismissing the presence of the younger—child—generation among Jesus' itinerant disciples is worth addressing. They simply assert that none of Jesus' itinerant disciples are νεανίσκοι or παῖδες (Destro and Pesce, 217). This claim, however, is followed up on only with a brief reference to the son of the widow of Nain about whom they conclude, "the young man does not show any desire to follow [Jesus], nor does Jesus ask him to" (Destro and

Pesce, 219). However, it should be noted that in both instances Destro and Pesce qualify their conclusions with the term "it seems," finding no substantive evidence of the absence of children among Jesus' itinerant disciples in Luke's gospel itself. Moreover, a review of the recorded healings in Luke's gospel yields the conclusion that Jesus *never* asks someone whom he has just healed to join with his group of disciples (in fact, in Lk 8:39–40 he expressly commands the man—clearly here an adult given the length of time he had lived among the tombs (v. 27)—from whom he had just cast many demons to return instead to his home after he begs to follow Jesus). Nevertheless, Lk 8:2 makes it clear that many people "who had been cured of evil spirits and infirmities" did, indeed, join the group of Jesus' itinerant followers. Although many explanations have been given for this, in particular with reference to the Gerasene demoniac and his status as a foreigner, it may be that this gap in Luke's portrayal of the discipleship of those whom Jesus heals is intended more to emphasize the nature of God's caring relationship with God's children as not requiring or expecting any response in return, in contrast to the more contractual and compensatory relationships of the Roman household of that day. In any case, Luke portrays many people following Jesus whose exact moment of response is left untold; therefore, one should not exclude the possibility that the youth and his mother followed Jesus after Luke's account of their restoration—the intended focus of the narrative—in Nain. Regardless of how a reader chooses to fill in the details of this particular experience, however, it is dangerous to take the case of one youth as demonstrative of the role of all youth and children in Jesus' ministry. Indeed, as demonstrated above, the evidence points, to the contrary, of the presence and participation of such youth and children among the community of disciples.

61. Although, as noted in chapter 3, the possibility remains that this child may have, in fact, been the boy from whom Jesus had previously cast a demon out of in Lk 9:37–45 (cf. Johnson, 186). If this is the case, it raises the question of whether this boy and his father may have joined with Jesus' disciples following this incident; in any case, the context of Jesus' address directly to his disciples at this point in the narrative remains clear (9:43b).

62. See Sharon Betsworth, *Children in Early Christian Narratives*. London: Bloomsbury T&T Clark, 2015) 123–124; James L. Bailey, "Experiencing the Kingdom as a Little Child: A Rereading of Mark 10:13–16," in *Word and World* 15:1 (Winter 1995) 63.

63. Carter, *Households and Discipleship,* 90.

64. James Francis, *Adults as Children: Images of Childhood in the Ancient World and the New Testament* (Oxford: Peter Lang, 2006) 84–85.

65. Here it is worth noting that, unfortunately, while the literary portrayal of children as models for discipleship suggests something unique, this does not seem to have played out historically in a significantly different treatment of young children among early Christians in relation to their Jewish and Roman counterparts. Francis writes, "The welcome by Jesus of children in the Synoptic Gospel stories and the image of the child associated with receiving and entering the kingdom did not themselves necessarily change or raise the profile of children in the early Church. On the other hand the metaphorical meaning of the child in Jesus' teaching is strong in contributing to a particular perspective in the proclamation of the Kingdom of God, and which

took root in strengthening discipleship in the early Church in a valuing of the least" (*Adults as Children*, 22).

66. Gundry, 152.
67. Carter, *Households and Discipleship*, 114.
68. Francis, *Adults as Children*, 78.
69. For a more thorough, albeit somewhat differently nuanced vision of this structure as a "transformation of the values of patriarchy" that traces across the entire New Testament, see Francis, *Adults as Children*, 80–84:
    1. Jesus' sonship => affirmation and transformation of family obligations; proclaiming both a subordination of family ties to the mission of the kingdom (presaged in Lk 2:41–51)
    2. Roles of subordinates always mentioned first (Lk 22:26: Let the greatest among you become as the youngest)
    3. 1 Cor 7:12ff – Children already part of the covenantal purpose of God (cf 2 Tim 3:15)
    4. Distinction between childhood and adulthood continues to exist, but is no longer controlled by social convention but by experience of faith (1 Cor 13:11 and Gal 4:1ff)
    5. Paul supports the *paterfamilias* notion, metaphorically father to his churches, but expands this metaphor to include mother and wet nurse as well (1 Cor 3:1–2; 1 Thess 2:7; Gal 4:19; cf. 2 Cor 11:2, 12:14); Paul's language sometimes corresponds to the gospel sayings of Jesus which reverse contemporary values by calling the least greatest (cf Mk 10:42–45 with 1 Cor 9:19; 2 Cor 1:24, 4:5) . . . thus *paterfamilias* may not be wholly adequate to the way in which Paul explores the nature of authority in the metaphorical use of childhood and parenthood
    6. In infant baptism, child was made, for its own sake, a member of the community
70. See chapter 3.
71. See chapter 1.
72. In the former two cases the pairs (James/Alphaeus and Judas/James) are connected with the genitive only. Literally it would read, "James of Alphaeus" and "Judas of James" and could thus imply the reverse relationship, that James is the father of Alphaeus and Judas the father of James. If read in this way, it raises interesting questions regarding why the sons of these men are mentioned and may suggest that these boys are themselves also a part of Jesus' discipleship community. This is a plausible reading and one, in light of the childist lens employed here, worth further exploration at another point. However, here I retain the traditional reading because my focus is on James and John who are clearly identified in the filial role in Lk 5:10 as well as the textual variant of 6:15 present in *codex Sinaiticus Syriacus*, which identifies them again specifically as the *sons* (τοὺς υἱούς) of Zebedee. Moreover, this use of the genitive in v. 15 prior to the identification of the remaining two genitive pairs supports the reading of James and Judas as sons of Alphaeus and James and rather than the other way around.
73. For Jesus as Son of Joseph see Lk 3:23, 30; and 4:22. For Jesus as Son of God see Lk 1:32, 35; 4:3, 9, 41; 8:28; and 22:69.

74. This contrasts with Destro and Pesce who maintain that James and John are members of the intermediate generation in relation to their father (218). However, not only is this argument based on the Markan narrative and thus not directly applicable to the Lukan adaptation, but their rationale is based on their (flawed) assumption that what they perceive as a failure of the young man in Nain to join in as one of Jesus' disciples precludes youth and children from participation in Jesus' discipleship community. This assumption has been questioned at length in my treatment of the Nain story in chapter 2. In any case, what Destro and Pesce are really stating is that it is clear that James and John are *not* householders since their father is still alive, and Destro and Pesce dismissively assume that no one would begin to consider these disciples among the youngest generation. In this much, I concur with the first assessment and will seek in what follows to question what seems too hasty a generalization in the second.

75. K. C. Hanson, "The Galilean Fishing Economy and the Jesus Tradition, " in *Biblical Theology Bulletin* (1997) 103.

76. Hanson, 105.

77. Hanson, 105–106. Cf. Mark 1:16–20 in which James and John are described as in the company of Zebedee in the boat, along with hired workers [τῶν μισθωτῶν]. Given what has already been established around the work habits of children, it is reasonable to assume that these workers may have been adults or children (Horn and Martens, 176). Moreover, in terms of status within the cooperative, if inferences can be drawn from the working relationships in agricultural cooperatives, the non-adult children of boat owners would logically work closely with the paid laborers.

78. Hanson, 100.

79. Tønnes Bekker-Nielsen, "Fishing in the Roman World," cited in *Ancient Nets and Fishing Gear: Proceedings of the International Workshop on 'Nets and Fishing Gear in Classical Antiquity: A First Approach,'* edited by Tønnes Bekker-Nielsen and Dario Bernal Casasola (Cadiz: 15–17 November, 2007).

80. Bekker-Nielsen, "Fishing in the Roman World," 191, 193.

81. Destro and Pesce, 219.

82. In chapters 1 and 3 I have established, in conjunction with Destro and Pesce, the place of νεανίσκοι among the broader concept of "child" as the Lukan narrative constructs it.

83. Aelian, *On the Nature of Animals,* 15.5. Translation mine.

84. Bekker-Nielsen, 191.

85. LSJ 1163.

86. See Fitzmyer, *Luke I–IX*, 567: "In the miracle-story of vv. 4–9a the technical term for partners (*metochoi*) is used; contrast the more generic 'companion' (*koinonoi*) of v. 10, where the Marcan story is resumed."

87. For the application of this analogy see Wilhelm Wuellner, *The Meaning of "Fisher's of Men,"* (Philadelphia: Westminster Press, 1967) 23–24.

88. Horn & Martens, 264–265.

Chapter 5

Child Disciples as Hearers and Doers of God's Word

Having established the assumed presence of children in the world of Luke's narrative, the next step is to determine the role that such children play as characters in the plot progression. Even when child characters are not specifically named, a dynamic understanding of childhood undergirds their presence in Luke's narrative and actively influences the way in which one reads and understands the story to unfold. This chapter examines how a reading attuned to the presence of children as disciples of Jesus can influence one's understanding of Lukan discipleship.

Such a reading depends upon an understanding of child characters *as* children. Child characters, when understood within the constructs of childhood in their time, should not be read simply as miniature, more vulnerable, adults. Contrary to Philippe Ariès' thesis that childhood is solely a construct of modernity, the field of Childhood Studies and its related disciplines have made a compelling case for childhood, or more properly childhoods, as unique, though far from static, categories across history.[1] In addition to drawing out the presence of children assumed within biblical narratives, childist biblical criticism seeks to understand their unique contributions as children within the biblical narrative.

To this end, I draw upon Luke's use of the concept of childhood as a metaphoric device, alongside similar uses by the other Synoptics and Paul, to (re)construct a view childhood as a unique social category within the communities to which Luke writes.[2] The experience of such constructions of childhood influences individual children as well as the communities and environments that surround them. In their new sociology of childhood, Alan Prout and Allison James observe, "Children are and must be seen as active in the construction and determination of their own social lives, the lives of those around them and of the societies in which they live."[3] Hence, upon acknowledging children as a part of the Lukan concept of discipleship (chapter 4), their concomitant influence upon this concept comes to light.

Such influence spreads across Luke's entire gospel account, which is permeated with the presence of child disciples. To account for the influence that children have on the concept of discipleship requires a re-reading. As a starting place, this chapter applies a childist lens to Luke's two standards of discipleship: hearing and doing the Word of God. These two components are introduced by the Lukan Jesus in the parable of the sower (Lk 8:4–15), made explicit immediately following the parable through identification of his true family as those who "hear the word of God and do it" (Lk 8:21), and repeated again in 11:28.[4] In the world of the narrative, Karlsen Seim explains, "Those who hear God's Word and do it, become Jesus' family, the new family of God, and even those biological family relationships that do continue to exist, are integrated in the fictive family and are subordinated to it."[5] The discipleship community, then, read from a childist perspective does not shun family, but rather, re-imagines it. This chapter treats each characteristic in turn to consider how children in Luke's community of disciples participated in and helped to shape this re-imagination of the whole.

Discipleship as Learning from Jesus (Hearing the Word, 8:19-21; 11:27–28)

A childist reading calls for a re-examination of what it means for disciples to hear the word of God. Engaging in this sort of re-examination, Keith White suggests, "As a corrective to the idea that children play no part in the crowds that follow Jesus we should note that there is good reason to suppose that they eagerly followed him, listened to his stories, and rejoiced in the signs that he did."[6] In this context and, indeed, in the context of discipleship more broadly, hearing refers to an internalized response. In a culture more sensitized to the dangers of ableism, "hearing" can feel exclusionary as a description of discipleship; and yet, even for those with the physical ability to "hear," with the admonition, "Let anyone with ears to hear listen!" Luke's Jesus implies something deeper is at stake (cf. Lk 8:8; 14:35). The verb in Luke's usage says less about auditory reception and more about a movement towards understanding—*learning* what is meant by the word of God. Esther de Boer maintains, on the basis of Lk 24.6–10, "that not only the men but also the women following Jesus did so first and foremost to learn from him."[7] Such is the etymology of the term *disciple* itself. After admonishing his disciples to "listen," Jesus goes on in both instances to *teach* them. In this context, hearing refers to an understanding or reception of the parable distinct from any auditory prowess or lack thereof.

To hear the word of God in Luke's gospel account means to *learn* from Jesus as demonstrated above. While contemporary advertising campaigns, community colleges, and Christian Education programs push for a more complete and accurate understanding of learning as a lifelong enterprise, such activity has been traditionally associated with childhood.[8] Reflecting this understanding of the term in antiquity Plato writes, "Education (*paideia*) is the drawing or leading of children to the right principles as enunciated by the law and confirmed by the experience of the oldest and most worthy.'"[9] Education begins in childhood as a part of each child's socialization—what Plato and other ancient authors understood as the taming of the child's spirit.[10] Similarly, in the apocryphal *Infancy Gospel of Thomas*, following a description of several missteps by the boy Jesus bringing him to the attention of adults in his village, a teacher named Zacchaeus entreats Joseph, "Come, give him [to me], brother, so that he can be taught letters, and so that he can have all understanding, learn to have affection for those his own age, and respect the old and please elders, and so that he can in his turn teach them to have a wish to become like children in the same way" (IGT 6:1–2). Indeed, despite the portrayal of the child Jesus' atrocious behavior towards his teachers, his father Joseph seeks to have the boy educated on three separate occasions (IGT 6:1–8:2; 13:1–3; 14:1–4).

This second-century early Christian text, while written later than Luke's account, illustrates a correspondence between classical Greek conceptions of education and early Christian communities in the Mediterranean world, which Luke—although probably unfamiliar with either text—would have shared as a part of the social milieu. Education was understood in these early communities as a means of acculturation and social formation. To the extent that disciples were to "hear the word of God," they were to internalize Jesus' teachings in such a way as to allow themselves to be shaped by them. Such shaping, while possible and present throughout the entirety of one's life, was most frequently associated with the upbringing and socialization of children.[11]

Consequently, even if the sole (or even primary) audience of the Lukan parables may not have been children, the process of instruction itself tacitly puts the disciples in the place of children (see Lk 18:17). Moreover, as already established, when Jesus proclaims the word of God to the crowds and his disciples, actual children ought to be assumed to have been a part of both groups. Thus, the instruction of disciples as "hearers" of the word of God simultaneously addresses literal children as disciples and places adult disciples into the metaphorical role of children. To the extent that the latter theme has received more attention in previous metaphorical treatments of children, this chapter will focus on the literal experience of children as hearers of God's word in Luke's story and how such an experience might together reshape the reader's understanding of child disciples and subsequent metaphorical applications to adult discipleship.

Discipleship as Serving Jesus (Doing God's Will, 8:19–21; 11:27–28)

A childist reading also calls for a re-examination of what it means for disciples to obey the word of God. Again, obedience, while not reserved to the domain of childhood, certainly has its origins there.[12] Returning to the *Infancy Gospel of Thomas*, this is one of the goals that Zacchaeus has in mind when he offers to instruct the boy Jesus (IGT 6:2). This fits with Beryl Rawson's description of the aim of Roman education, with "its emphasis on precedent, tradition, rank, and the role of the great families [which] reinforced principles which underpinned much of Roman society."[13] The actions of hearing and doing went hand in hand for children, who were taught with the expectation that they would obediently perform the cultural roles that they acquired. Children in the ancient Mediterranean world were expected to do as they were told and this theme carries over among the early Christian authors. Consequently, Aasgaard labels as "striking" the boy Jesus' disobedience toward his parents in the *Infancy Gospel of Thomas*.[14] In contrast, Luke's account depicts the twelve-year-old Jesus, despite his initial lingering in the Temple, returning with his parents to Nazareth, after which point "he was obedient to them" (Lk 2:51). While not painted as perfect in Luke's narrative, childhood obedience is nevertheless treated as the norm and the ideal.

Such a norm is also assumed by the author of 1 Peter, who readily likens ideal disciples in that community to "obedient children" (1 Pt 1:14) as a category he expects his audience to readily accept and in the household codes of Colossians and Ephesians that exhort children to obedience (Eph 6:1; Col 3:20). Thus obedience, while held up as an ideal among biblical authors, is not romanticized as a flawless virtue of childhood. Indeed, it occasionally requires exhortation to effect. Rather, within the strictures of the ancient household, such obedience can be thought of as a common and necessary adaptation. Given the vulnerable state of children, to do the will of the *pater familias* would have been, in a very real sense, equivalent to preserving one's precarious existence within a system of security and support. Children, particularly the young and the infants, would have had little need to be exhorted to assume the roles (obedient, subordinate) that sustained their very lives.[15]

In this context, the "child like" response upon hearing God's word is to obediently *do* the will of the Father—to act on the Word of God. What it means to act according to the Word of God, however, is not static in Luke's narrative. The gospel and its interpretation of this word leaves room for both sedentary and itinerant disciples. Likewise, the different roles of the female and male disciples described in Luke 8:1–3 indicate that the Lukan mandate to disinvest in material belongings (14:33; 18:22) may take on different forms within the dynamic discipleship community as a whole.[16] In this context there remains room for children to also emerge in the twin roles of exemplars of child disciples and models for their adult counterparts.

HEARERS OF THE WORD OF GOD

Within Early Christian writings more generally and Luke's narrative specifically, the character of the ideal child is held up largely as an exemplar and desired end. With regards to the real children in his community, Luke presents a more tempered picture in such references as the boy Jesus in the Temple and children playing in the marketplace; however, Luke continues to hold children up as ideal disciples (18:15–17). While scholars continue to debate qualities such as innocence, humility, and the like applied to children, children remain indisputably students. Even if they receive no formal education, from birth humans necessarily acquire a large amount of information—from basic skills (e.g., how to sit, stand, and walk) to more complex learning (such as language, culture, and so forth). Children absorb information through the use of language and observation of the environment around them. They are natural students.[17] As a result, child disciples can be expected to "hear" the word of God presented in Luke's narrative, absorbing the Gospel message as students of all that is around them.

Moreover, within the Lukan construction of childhood, such young disciples present a unique way of hearing and understanding the Word that is proclaimed. Child disciples, as demonstrated previously, by virtue of their discipleship, share with their adult counterparts an experience of God's grace through welcome, nurture, and healing in the kingdom of God; however, by virtue of their youth they participate in this community (kingdom) in particular ways. Children, present as a part of Luke's community of believers, are generally relegated to the background and rarely given voice. In their silence, however, they continue to do what children do very well—observe the world around them and, indeed, observe Jesus' proclamation of the world to come. More adaptable than their adult counterparts, since their maps of their world have not fully formed, child disciples present for the Christian community, as Luke presents it, a decidedly more open world view—one in which the coming Kingdom of God is understood as real possibility in all its complexity.

Although such children are present among all of God's children who have received God's grace through welcome, nurture, and healing, they are also named, on account of their youth, among the "least" in society's eyes. Typical of Lukan reversal, they are as such lifted up as representatives of Jesus and treasured for their own sake.[18] To them, Luke tells us, uniquely, belongs the Kingdom of heaven (Lk 18:16). Luke's Jesus demonstrates this unique reception himself as a child student in the Temple (2:46–49) and later acknowledges it in prayer to God the Father (10:21) and in praise of the disciple, Mary (10:38–42). The following childist reading of these texts approaches each student in turn in order to re-imagine Lukan discipleship through the incorporation of the unique perspectives of young children.

(Re)membering the Boy Jesus (2:46–49)

When he is found with the teachers in the Temple, Jesus is still a child. That this is Luke's intention is made clear by the placement of this story within the infancy narrative, as is established through the parallel narration of Jesus' growth in stature and divine favor (compare Lk 2:40, 52) and Mary's response to Jesus (compare Lk 2:19, 51) in both the Temple and birth accounts. The repetition of Luke's narrative in the later *Infancy Gospel of Thomas* further supports this conclusion. Bovon writes,

> The view that the child became a 'son of the Law' . . . at the festival at twelve years of age cannot yet be attested in this era. Unlike a girl, a twelve-year-old boy is not completely grown, but is indeed at least a παῖς. Whoever places Jesus here at the stage of adulthood misses precisely the point: even as a child, Jesus possesses the wisdom of the great ones.[19]

Both in physical years—Luke references Jesus' age specifically only in the birth narrative—and in cultural perception, the Jesus of this account remains a child. He attends the Passover celebration in Jerusalem not as a matter of covenantal obligation, but out of routine piety, as the reader can assume he has done previously together with his parents.[20]

Agreeing that Jesus is not yet understood by the Lukan author as an adult in this story, commentators range from seeing in this text a parallel to contemporary *puer senex* stories about the extraordinary childhoods of great men to reading the relatively tame portrait of the young Jesus in this story as Luke's attempt to tame such inventions as the *Infancy Gospel of Thomas* illustrates.[21] In either case, most commentators tend to focus on Jesus' precocity and the astonishment of his parents and the teachers at his wisdom.[22] However, while a sense of understanding and wisdom is clear within the text, Fitzmyer sees Jesus' wisdom as primarily that of a student and not a teacher in this scene.

> Though Luke later on, in the Gospel proper, portrays Jesus seated as a teacher (5:3), it is scarcely likely that this is meant here. Jesus is rather depicted as a

pupil, "a genuine learner" (J.M. Creed, *The Gospel*, 45). That this detail foreshadows his own teaching in the Temple in the latter part of the Gospel, in his Jerusalem ministry, is possible. But he is not yet so depicted here, *pace* G. Schneider (*Evangelicum nach Lukas*, 75) and others.[23]

Indeed, in this episode, Luke portrays Jesus as an ideal student. The boy Jesus serves as the epitome of the kind of discipleship that Jesus the teacher later describes.

From the first time that Jesus' character speaks as a child in the Temple (Lk 2:49) to his adult self's dying breath on the cross (Lk 23:46), Jesus professes obedience to the will of God. This obedience is emphasized in this childhood account, in which Jesus is himself the subject (as opposed to the object of his parents' actions) including: his *remaining* behind in Jerusalem (2:43), *sitting* among the teachers (2:46), *listening* to them (2:46), and *asking* questions (2:46). The first of these, remaining, in and of itself is implicit in a child's relationship with a tutor in antiquity, but, as it is done without Jesus' parents' foreknowledge, represents disobedience in this case.

Beyond this, however, each verb directly reflects the proper disposition of a child toward a teacher in antiquity. A student of antiquity describes his day: entering the school, greeting the teacher, taking his seat, copying models, making recitations, asking for dictation, writing, sitting again, and studying his books.[24] Likewise, in Plato's Praetorium, Hippias is described as "sitting on an imposing chair as he gives a lecture surrounded by his pupils sitting on benches."[25] Such, it seems, are the basic activities of students engaged in learning—to show submission, attention, and respect.

Moreover, that the teachers are "amazed at his understanding and answers" (Lk 2:47) suggests that Jesus demonstrates learning—another expected and appropriate quality of an attentive student. The more parents invested in their child's education, which in antiquity could be a great amount, the more understanding they expected the student to exhibit as a result. Libanius describes the questioning of students by their parents at dinner, during which time parents expected astute answers.[26] Thus, Jesus the great teacher first takes action in Luke's telling as a great student.

Luke's depiction of Jesus in this account exemplifies the actions of a good student in antiquity. This is seen in the contrast between Luke's Jesus here and the apocryphal Jesus of the *Infancy Gospel of Thomas*. In the first teacher account of IGT, Zacchaeus actively tries to engage Jesus as a pupil, "but the child did not answer him" (IGT 6:8). Contrast Jesus' answers in Luke 2:47. When Jesus later expresses his understanding to Zacchaeus, he baffles his teacher and puts him to shame (IGT 6:8–7:4). Then, in the next two teacher accounts the child Jesus shows even more impatience with his teachers, failing even to listen to them, instead offering instruction of his own (13:2; 14:2). While Jesus poses questions of two of his teachers in IGT (6:9, 13:2), it is not in the calm and respectful manner that one infers from the relative calm in which Jesus' parents find him *seated* among the teachers in the Temple. To emphasize this, the author of IGT clarifies Luke's description of Jesus asking questions in his account of the same scene, adding, "'he examined (ἀπεστομάτιζεν) the elders and explained the main points of the law and the riddles and the parables of the prophets.'"[27] IGT's depiction of Jesus in the Temple fits with the portrait of Jesus as a student throughout the account—an intractable and hot-headed divinity who will not be taught because he already knows it all.

In contrast, while Luke portrays the child Jesus as a precocious and sophisticated student who inspires amazement, he remains a *student*.[28] Fitzmyer notes that Jesus "listened and posed questions . . . as a pupil would." [29] At this point in the narrative, Luke portrays Jesus with all of the normal dependencies one would expect from a child of his age. When Luke describes Jesus' birth, the newborn needs his mother to wrap him in swaddling clothes (Lk 2:7), as an infant he must be carried (2:22), and as an adolescent Jesus must also be taught (2:46). Fitzmyer appropriately interprets the scene as "emphasizing the training of the young Jewish male."[30] Although there is no historical evidence that such training took place in the Temple, in the world of Luke's narrative the Temple serves as a central location for teaching about the Kingdom of God (see also Lk 19:47; 20:1; 21:37; Acts 5:21, 25, 42). Writing after the destruction of the Temple, it is likely that Luke conflates the Temple location with local synagogue practice for the purpose of the story. While the Temple is by no means the only *locus* of learning, Luke's audience must accept that throughout the narrative real instruction does occur at the Temple.

Moreover, the reaction of the teachers to the understanding that Jesus shows is markedly different between Jesus as a child in Lk 2:46 and as an adult in Lk 19:47. That the teachers seem pleasantly amazed in the first account and "kept looking for a way to kill him" in the second account indicates a drastic change in relationship. The chief priests and leaders at this latter moment in the story are upset because Jesus threatens to usurp their role. To assume that Jesus as a child is already acting as the teacher, as he does when he returns to the Temple, is thus discontinuous with the respective reactions of the Temple leaders that Luke describes. While the ambiguity in the text leaves open multiple options, the simplest reading of the text therefore suggests that Jesus is listening to and answering the teachers as a student—a role quite familiar, either formally or informally, to children across the centuries.

In the character of Jesus, Luke therefore demonstrates the first trait of discipleship: listening to the word of God. While the adult Jesus has moved beyond this point of quiet reception to teaching and reproach within the Temple walls, Luke's dynamic portrait of his maturation highlights the unique contribution of Jesus' twelve-year-old self to a Lukan understanding of discipleship. While learning occurs throughout the entirety of one's life, children are uniquely suited to it. The amount of information that they must acquire in a relatively short span of time would be overwhelming for the average adult. This is due to what developmental psychologist Alison Gopnik describes as "the evolutionary imperative," which "for babies is to learn as much as they can as quickly as possible."[31] As a result, children tend towards a natural receptivity and attention.[32] This is the "work" that God the Father has given the child Jesus to do (2:49).[33] Only when the reader can appreciate listening and learning as a child does can one fully understand what is meant by the adult Jesus' insistence that disciples *listen* to the word of God.

Child disciples are not only better disposed to hear Jesus' message, they also listen in a decidedly unique way that contributes to the overall picture of discipleship as it is practiced together by children and adults alike. While adults and older youth generally are capable of higher-level thinking and reasoning skills that foster the growth and functioning of the Christian community, infants and young children are likewise more capable of attentive listening and reception at the core of developing the community according to Christ's vision in the first place. This is due to a trait that Gopnik calls "lantern consciousness," seen in infants and children, as well as in highly trained spiritual individuals who engage in rigorous meditation.[34] She explains that people in such consciousness, "are immersed in the almost unbearably bright and exciting novelty of walls, shadows, voices."[35] With little to no preconceived notions of what the world is "supposed" to be like, infants and young children are uniquely receptive to a new picture of what the world *can* be like, as revealed through Jesus' proclamation of the Kingdom of God. In this way, young disciples perform a vital function in the work of discipleship and the up building of the Kingdom of God.

Revelation to Infants (10:21)

Luke puts praise of this unique perspective into the mouth of Jesus himself in Luke 10:21. Offering thanksgiving to God the Father, Jesus prays: "I thank you, Father, Lord of heaven and earth, because you have hidden these things from the wise and intelligent and have revealed them to infants; yes, Father, for such was your gracious will" (Lk 10:21). In this way, children, specifically infants (νηπίοις), are described as literally possessing something that their "wiser" adult counterparts lack. John Carroll equates this unique revelation with knowledge of the spirit active in Jesus' ministry.[36] This is supported by the description of Jesus as rejoicing "in the Holy Spirit" ([ἐν] τῷ πνεύματι τῷ ἁγίῳ); however, such a general revelation does not specifically clarify what activity of the Spirit Jesus celebrates as having been revealed to νηπίοις. Literally, this term refers to human babies—infants before they are weaned. Joseph Fitzmyer translates accordingly: "persons incapable of proper human speech."[37] Biologically speaking, then, the νηπίοις of Luke 10:21 represent the most vulnerable—and, as a result, the most attentive of all life stages.

Luke's connection of this prayer to the return of the Seventy (Lk 10:17–20) "at that same hour" (Lk 10:21) offers further insight. Bovon suggests, "By linking the prayer to the vision of the fall of Satan (v. 18), Luke not only displayed evidence of literary finesse . . . it is also certain that Luke wished to make a thematic connection at this point. What he had in mind here was emphasizing the change of persons who receive God's revelation."[38] Worldly wisdom—that knowledge that comes only from lived experiences, often encounters with the evil of this world—is displaced by the advent of the Kingdom. Satan falls down from his throne and the "wise" no longer hold a monopoly of experience over their younger, less initiated counterparts. Instead, Jesus celebrates that it is the *infants*—those with the least worldly experience imaginable—to whom God has given a new revelation.

The context in Luke's narrative makes clear that Jesus' revelation is not reserved only for infants in the literal sense. The apostles who returned in the previous verses, while depicted as one segment of a larger mixed group of children and adults, did not include these smallest among them. Infants would have been unable to perform the commissioned functions of walking and talking. However, the generational mix of disciples continues throughout Luke's gospel account and Acts. To assume that this saying does not address actual infants at all too quickly bypasses the unique contribution that infant disciples *can* make.[39] François Bovon characterizes the little ones in Lk 18 "by their dependence, their ability to listen, and their welcoming attitude," concluding that in both the literal and metaphorical senses as "Children and believers, these 'little ones,' have their own identity and their relational reality."[40] While Bovon speaks from the point of view of a historical critic and with an uncorroborated certainty, his premise—when the agency is shifted from Jesus to the Lukan author—is well founded. As previously demonstrated, technical definitions of childhood are both plentiful and gratuitous to the identities of actual children in Luke's narrative. Luke's use of the term νηπίοις should no more be dictated by literary conventions of metaphor and analogy than it should by biology.

For the reader of Luke, νηπίοις must be interpreted within the broader context in which it is employed. In Luke's gospel account, real children, while not always at the fore, are just under the surface and present in the assumed context that it presents. Infants and children have been seen to be present among the followers of Jesus in households, public places, and among the crowds; Jesus signals the importance of an actual child (Lk 9:47–50); and Jesus even beckons βρέφοις (small babies) to himself as models of discipleship and inheritors of the Kingdom of God (Lk 18:15–17). Such a pattern suggests a reading of Luke 10:21 that first treats the referents of Jesus' speech as actual infants and then, through them, considers those adults who model themselves accordingly. Horn and Martens thus conclude that it is not enough for adults seeking to follow Jesus' instructions to model themselves off of particular assumed characteristics of childhood in a removed or metaphorical sense. Rather, "children themselves, as actual members of the community, were the models for how the community had to receive God and the kingdom."[41] The Lukan author has no problem targeting God's revelation to the youngest members of the community.

If God reveals God's self to infants, though, is it fair to imagine that infants can receive this revelation? It is actually at this phase of development that humans are most attuned to our environment than at any other point in our lives. Alison Gopnik explains that, while babies and young children may lack the same sophistication in their mental processing as adults, "they may be better at picking up incidental information" because ". . . rather than determining what to look at in the world, babies seem to let the world determine what they look at. And rather than deciding where to focus attention and where to inhibit distractions, babies seem to be conscious of much more of the world at once."[42] In short, infants are expert listeners. This posture of listening—of absorbing God's revelation because it has been given to us and not because of any power we've demonstrated on our own (Lk 10:20)—is at the same time the gift that infants bring uniquely into their communities and the model they set for adults and older children.

Such a model fits within the Lukan theme of reversal.[43] Luke begins his account with Zechariah prophesying that John will "turn the hearts of parents to their children . . . to make ready a people prepared for the Lord" (Lk 1:17; see also Mal 4:6; Sir 48:10). In Luke 10:21, Jesus broadens this prophecy even as he declares its fulfillment, turning the hearts and minds of adults towards infants as they seek to receive the revelation of God. Although infants are not the only followers of Jesus to receive a revelation from God in Luke's narrative,[44] Jesus' prayer in 10:21 celebrates their unique experience of *this* revelation. Namely, due to their profound capacity to listen to and absorb all that surrounds them, God's Spirit is revealed to infants.

Such a heightened capacity for learning in infants, of course, does not mean that adults cannot learn.[45] Such an assertion would run counter to the basic premise of Luke's narrative—instruction of disciples about Jesus' revelation of God's Kingdom (Lk 1:1). Nevertheless, that which comes easily to young disciples—namely, the observation of and consequent response to the world—is commended to their adult counterparts (Lk 18:17). Bovon notes,

"They [the disciples] have been eyewitnesses to the Son's unique revelation: his preaching, his activity, his personal impact on human beings, and now of his relation to the Father."[46] With children witnessing this impact together with adults, as has been previously demonstrated, it would be inappropriate to assume that it is left only to the adults to respond.

Because babies are more attuned to everything around them in their effort to make sense of the world, Gopnik reasons that they are also more readily able to adjust to a new sense, or map, of the world. She summarizes, "This [difference in brain function] lets babies and children construct new maps, and change their old ones, much more quickly and easily than adults do."[47] Such change in one's perception of the world is precisely what is demanded by Jesus' announcement of the Kingdom of God. As such, the infants and young children, through their experiences in relation to Jesus, albeit not necessarily through any work of their own merit (see Lk 10:20), absorb the message of the Kingdom and model for their elders how to receive such a revelation for themselves.

(Re)imagining Mary and Jesus' Exchange (10:38–42)

Luke highlights the profound listening and learning capacities of the child characters in Luke 2:46–49 and 10:21 respectively as dynamic (as in the case of the child Jesus) and flat (as in the case of the generic νηπίοις).[48] Since such listening is a key characteristic of discipleship in Luke's gospel (Lk 8:21), children in Luke's narrative become a model for how all disciples are to receive the Kingdom (Lk 18:17). The hearts (and minds) of parents are turned to their children. The character of Mary in Luke 10:38–42 offers another example of this reversal of expectations, as she, through her listening, is said to model "the better part" (10:42).

Mary's age is never specified in the gospel account. It is generally assumed and plausible that Luke envisioned her as a fully mature adult sitting at the feet of Jesus, the great teacher. Precedence for this is set as the woman (γυνὴ) who kneels at Jesus' feet and washes them with expensive ointment and her own tears is almost certainly an adult (Lk 7:37–39). However, it is also plausible that Luke envisioned Mary as a child or young adolescent, sitting at the foot of a teacher in her sister's home. In this case, her posture might be read as relating more closely to that of the children who come to Jesus in Luke 18:15–17 and the boy Jesus seated among the elders (Lk 2:46) rather than the woman in the former account.[49]

Careful attention to the treatment of Mary in the text extends the possibility that her character is not yet an adult. Although female characters in general are infrequently given speaking and acting roles in Luke's narrative, the centrality of children—particularly, girls—in the text is even more rare. In light of Luke's reticence to put words in the mouth of children, the subordination of Mary's character despite the central role of her activity in the narrative begins to make sense. Reading Mary as a child fits neatly into the pattern established by Luke of talking *about* children without giving them voice, as seen with Jairus' daughter (Lk 8:40–56).[50]

The social expectations of Luke's audience are that children are to learn and not teach; therefore, when presented as characters among elders in the story, they remain largely silent. Alexander elaborates further on Luke's semantic patterns:

> These patterns serve to foreground Martha as the active partner with Jesus in the scene. Mary is a background character, of whom are told (in a relative clause) only the bare minimum necessary to explain the dialogue that forms the culmination of the scene . . . What we have, then, is not a three-cornered-scene but, as so often in the gospels, a dialogue between two characters, Jesus and Martha; Mary's actions provoke the dialogue, but she does not herself speak or appear on stage.[51]

If one were to attempt to reconstruct a historical scene from this narrative, Mary would almost certainly regain direct action and speech. Most notably, emphasis may shift to Mary's conscious choice to sit at Jesus' feet and the dialogue with or silent resistance to Martha that might have precipitated this scene. Yet, within the world of the story, these things fade into the background. Instead, Thimmes notes, "Luke's choice of silence for Mary renders her character and her 'position' defenseless and powerless in a world of 'speech.'"[52] Thimmes reads this as a literary act to undercut Mary's authority as a disciple by placing in her in a position of subordination in relation to Jesus.

However, reading Mary's character as a subordinate child from the start shifts the relationship of power. Instead, Mary, whose oral speech may never have held the same power or privilege in her sister's house, speaks through the language of posture—positioning herself in the posture of discipleship at the feet of Jesus. This posture is then validated and affirmed when Jesus speaks in favor of Mary in response to her sister's critique. Such affirmation has the effect of potentially empowering Mary in whatever future speech she takes on—oral or physical—as she continues to live into the discipleship she has chosen; and certainly, of empowering child readers to claim their place alongside Jesus, even, when necessary, in resistance to whatever competing claims their adult guardians might make upon them.

Such a reading of Mary as child is further supported by a closer comparison between the text in question and its closest parallels in Luke's narrative. Although typical adultist interpretations might presume a closer parallel between Mary and the woman who pours oil on Jesus' feet in Lk 7:37, several key differences suggest the alternate possibility of favoring Paul's reference to his relationship with Gamaliel in Acts 22:3.

Focusing first on the differences between the two texts involving females, it is worth noting the purpose that each person shows in sitting at the feet of Jesus. In Mary's case it is to learn, while her unnamed counterpart in 7:37 takes on a posture of service. Given their respective acts of service and common identification as γυνή, the unnamed woman actually shares more in common with Mary's sister Martha than with the character of Mary herself. Second, Mary is identified in the story only as the sister (ἀδελφή) of Martha (10:39). Martha, on the other hand, is described as a woman (γυνή) and the owner of the house (10:38). The term γυνή suggests Martha's adulthood in contrast to the more juvenile identifiers of girl (παιδίσκην; κοράσιον)[53] or even young woman (παρθένος).[54] In contrast, nothing is said of Mary. Third, Martha holds the position of householder,[55] whereas Mary is not identified as such. Mentioned first in the text, Martha seems to have acquired this position either through marriage or inheritance (each representing different adult roles respectively). Textual variants in Luke 10:38 specify that Martha received Jesus *into her home* using the first person singular pronoun.[56] Thus, Luke portrays the two sisters as different not only in their tasks and response to Jesus but also in their parts or roles in the household.[57] Martha is the responsible householder who receives Jesus. Mary also receives Jesus, but as a subordinate in her sister's house.

Such subordination does not exclude Mary from participation in Jesus' ministry together with Martha, just as Luke does not exclude other subordinate members of large households from participation in the ministry of Jesus elsewhere in Luke-Acts.[58] Hence, I concur with Warren Carter's assessment that "Mary, like Martha, is among those who receive Jesus. This response suggests that the term 'sister' points beyond a relation of kinship with Martha to denote their joint participation in the community of the disciples of Jesus."[59] However, while Carter goes onto identify Mary and Martha as "partners in this leadership and its tasks,"[60] a childist reading cannot ignore the different status accorded to each sister by the evangelist.

While Luke's Jesus may declare Mary to have chosen the better part, the narrative constructs Martha's character as possessing the position of power and status in the household. For this reason, many feminist interpreters have lamented this text as an example of Luke's androcentric tendency to limit the leadership of women by preferencing Mary's passive response to Martha's more active role.[61] A childist reading complicates the relationship between Martha and Mary with the acknowledgment of another social marker—namely, age.

By so doing, I do not seek to ignore or downplay the injustices perpetrated against women as a result of androcentric readings of this text. Rather, I hope that this complication is read as another step in Schüssler Fiorenza's call for "sociopolitical contextualizations" to reframe how the text is heard today.[62] Just as re-imagining Mary in a lower social class in which the audacity to sit idle from work has a liberating effect,[63] so too can re-imagining Mary as a youth empowered to pursue discipleship by her sister's ministry and Jesus' teaching provide a liberative alternative to the androcentric narrative of passivity in which the text has historically been read.[64]

The text leaves open this possibility of reading Mary as a youth by placing her at the feet of Jesus. The closest parallels to this usage occur in the account of the Gerasene demoniac (Lk 8:35) and Paul's autobiography (Acts 22:3). Luke uses the term "at the feet" in several other accounts,[65] but these are the only two in which Luke describes one person "at the feet" of another for the purpose of *learning*. While the Gerasene demoniac is clearly described as an adult male, Paul refers in Acts 22:3 to having been "brought up" (ἀνατεθραμμένος) at the feet of Gamaliel. This term, which also can mean to nourish or educate, is used elsewhere by Luke only in Acts 7:20, 21 with reference to Moses as a young child.

Moreover, Luke 2:46 describes Jesus as a child sitting among the elders for the purpose of learning (see chapter 4 on Discipleship), but it does not specify that he is sitting at the teachers' feet. Pervo and Johnson speculate that this distinction occurs because Jesus is presumed equal to the teachers in the Temple, while the term "at the feet" implies subordination to authority.[66] Given the use of substantive chairs to represent the authority of a teacher in antiquity,[67] this would be the inevitable posture of students when not standing before their school master. This posture was still maintained in small Middle Eastern schools into the nineteenth century.[68] Nevertheless, as noted in chapter 4 on children as companions of Jesus, such a reading of Luke 2:46 unnecessarily presumes a level of maturity on the boy Jesus that need not be assumed by the text. If this text is then taken as third parallel to Mary, two of the three other mentions of learning at the feet of a teacher in Luke involve youthful characters—Paul and Jesus. Mary then, if read as a child, would fall into the majority usage of this theme.

Although the elevation of passive learning can be understood as oppressive to the active participation of an adult woman, it is more in fitting with the traditional role of a child as discussed above. Moreover, considering Mary's story from a child's perspective opens up the experience of learning from an entirely different point of view. To assume that learning needs to be a passive enterprise is already to engage in an adult centric understanding of learning akin to Paulo Freire's description of oppressive education. Such an assumption fails to acknowledge the engaged and active role of the learner. On the other hand, children, in their primal quest to discover the "how" and "why" behind the information they receive are naturally drawn to more relational and experiential learning that engages them in this way. To this end, the word learner itself needs to be problematized in so much as it implies what Freire describes as a "fundamentally *narrative* character."[69] Such narrative learning assumes "a narrating Subject (the teacher) and patient, listening objects (the students)" wherein "the contents . . . tend in the process of being narrated to become lifeless and petrified."[70] Given the active and exuberant engagement with which children naturally come to the task of cultural interpretation, when not otherwise hindered by oppressive pedagogies, such narrative teaching is to be avoided.

This is particularly true of the oral culture in which Luke's account was produced, which knew little of the narrative kind of education predominant in Western education today. In oral cultures learning occurs through a dynamic interchange of ideas involving both the teacher and the student. Scholar of orality Tex Sample posits, "traditional/oral people do not learn by 'study,' but through apprenticeship."[71] Relationship and experience dictate meaning in an oral culture rather than critical evaluation. Biblical storyteller and performance critic Thomas E. Boomershine thus concludes,

> In the medium of performance, the meaning of the story did not consist, as it often does today, in the critical assessment of the . . . text as a source of referential information about the actual historical events it purports to record and of a highly nuanced set of theological ideas. The hearing of the story is an experience more analogous to watching a great film . . . Indeed, it is an experience of suspense and anticipation of events, of hope and disbelief, of closeness to or alienation from the characters rather than an experience of contemplation of a set of theological ideas or an evaluation of historical reports. Thus, the alternative to "meaning as reference" can be called "meaning as experience." And "meaning as experience is dependent on the willingness of audiences to enter fully into the story and identify with the characters of the story.[72]

Given the experiential meaning production typical of such oral cultures, Mary's character understood as a learner—whether adult or child—need not be read as passively receiving from Jesus. Rather, in such a pedagogical interchange, Mary is actively engaging in meaning production as she experiences Jesus' teaching.

In modern pedagogical discourse Freire describes this type of interchange as "dialogics."[73] Speaking to his contextual aim of political liberation, Freire insists, "It is to the reality which mediates men [sic.], and to the perception of that reality held by educators and people, that we must go to find the program content of education."[74] In short, for learning to truly occur, as Jesus seems to insist that it does with Mary in Luke's narrative, the subject must be relevant to those to whom it is proclaimed—an audience which is frequently teeming with children, and in Mary's case, may well have been an audience of one.

Moreover, for the learner, in this case, Mary, to internalize this message and commit herself to the Word as the call to discipleship clearly demands, she must receive God's Word in a "transformative process"[75] in which both learner and teacher are "actors in intercommunication"—actively in dialogue with one another, reflecting and acting on the realized needs of their context.[76] To this end, contemporary disciples have much to learn not only from the character of Mary as she participates in such an interchange within her oral culture, but also, from all young children who in their pre- and nascent literacy, tend naturally to engage much more dynamically in the production of knowledge.

Historically, Israelite tradition understood learning and listening in this more active sense as well. The commandment to "hear and obey the word of the Lord" (1 Sam 4:9–10), akin to Luke's definition of discipleship, was understood as one in the same action. Freire's action-reflection axis bears echoes of this. This is captured by Bovon's vivid description of Mary: "Seated at the feet of the Master, she takes on the role of a disciple; with her whole being, she listens to what is being said by Jesus, who quotes and comments on God's word."[77] While feminist scholars are right to resist the passivity that some contemporary churches have demanded from women on account of their reading of this text, Mary's action of listening at the feet of Jesus need not be so defined.[78] Indeed, while such a passive reception of Mary's learning is perilously possible, a reading that uplifts Mary and Jesus as engaged in an intercommunicative dialogue not only removes Mary from the role of a passive vessel, but suggests the positive influence and unique contribution that children are capable of bringing to the Jesus movement as a whole.

As such, I prefer what Schüssler Fiorenza labels as "the apologetic feminist interpretation," which "celebrates Mary's role as a rabbinical student or disciple, seated at the feet of Jesus the rabbi" in opposition to what Jane Schaberg labels the "extremely dangerous" in her appropriately cautionary, but overly passive interpretation of women in Luke's text.[79] Schüssler Fiorenza critiques residual polarities between Mary and Martha in such an apologetic interpretation, while later feminists, notably Loveday Alexander, point to the important role that Martha, for her part, continues to play.[80] However, by shifting the focus from the interchange between Mary and Martha to that between Mary and Jesus, the revolutionary character of their dialogue can be discerned. In addition, by noting the status differences between Mary and Martha rendered by age, a childist reading challenges the ability to treat Mary and Martha simply as polar opposite depictions of a woman's role, when it is possible to conceive of Mary as not yet a woman. Such a reading of Luke's account allows each person's discipleship to stand on its own merit.

Although it is true that Jesus holds up Mary's actions in the particular moment of the text as preferred, this does not necessitate that he is dismissing the importance of Martha's discipleship. Carter notes that in the context of the narrative as a whole,

> [Martha] appears as a model disciple in contrast to those in the previous verses who do not receive Jesus' message (Lk 9.52–53; 10.10). Moreover, what is appropriate to Martha at this point is shown in Lk 10.39 to be applicable also to Mary. She is presented as 'listening' to Jesus' teaching. The verb used to denote her listening (ἤκουεν, 10.39) appears in Lk 10.16 as an antonym for 'rejecting' the disciples, Jesus, and God, and hence, as a synonym for 'receiving' them. It also appears in Lk 10.23–24 in Jesus' blessing of disciples who 'see' and 'hear.'[81]

Both sisters are to be understood as model disciples in the sense that they receive Jesus. However, Jesus draws particular attention to Mary's posture of listening, after it is critiqued by Martha from her superior status as an adult householder. Read as such, this encounter between Jesus and the two sisters foreshadows the encounter between Jesus, his adult disciples, and the children being brought to him in Luke 18:15–17. In each instance, all involved appear to be held up by Luke as disciples of Jesus—followers who receive both him and his Word. The adults—Martha in Lk 9 and an unnamed grouping in Lk 18—attempt to prevent the gathering of children around Jesus. Similarly, Jesus lifts up children, or a child as in Mary's case, as model disciples in each text. The adults are not dismissed but are encouraged to turn their hearts and their minds toward children.

Much speculation has been made with regards to Luke 18:15–17 on what it means to receive God's Kingdom like a little child. I have argued previously that such modeling cannot and should not be reduced to any one characteristic. Nor should Mary's part be reduced to simple listening, as critiques of the text's value of passivity seem to do. Rather, Bovon describes an active listening that simultaneously internalizes and engages what is being said. For a child, this is the difference between simply acquiring information and acquiring a trade—the latter of which was the goal of all but the most elite of educational programs in the first century. Just as Paul learns to be a Pharisee at the feet of Gamaliel, Mary learns to be a disciple at the feet of Jesus.

Within the structure of the story, it can be assumed that Mary *will* engage in the other tasks of discipleship soon enough. Carter notes, "Mary's listening is appropriate to the specific moment, and it is good as far as it goes, but there is no commendation of her as a perpetual listener. Listening requires that she also do, or keep, the word."[82] This is the active, embodied nature of hearing *and* obeying God's word as it is modeled throughout Luke's account (Lk 8:15, 21; 11:28).[83]

According to Luke, hearing is only good insofar as it inspires obedience to (and thus action with regard to) God's Word. This is the relationship outlined in the parable of the sower earlier in Luke's account (Lk 8:4–15). As such, Bovon rhetorically asks, "Once trained, was she [Mary] not going to share her knowledge of the good news with others? Did her 'part' not also involve assuming responsibilities, a ministry of the word, just as Martha felt herself to be charged with a ministry of service?"[84] The merit of such an interpretation is that it opens up the role that Jesus commends in Mary as entailing much more than mere attention and passivity. While the interpreters of the story, and perhaps even Luke as author himself, may have used this account to ascribe submission to women in the church, Bovon helpfully proposes an alternative in which Mary's role in the story remains pointedly more open.

Nevertheless, even this "ministry of service" as Bovon describes it remains ethically problematic. It is worth celebrating the participation of women and children in the early church. However, if their roles are limited to attention, obedience, and service, then little has been done to liberate such characters (and those in Luke's audience who identify with them) from the hegemonic power of an adultist patriarchy. Rather, in Mary's "obedience" to the Word of God spoken to her in her sister's house, a childist reading brings out the potential for Mary's full participation in the proclamation and promulgation of the Kingdom that Jesus' Word proclaims—a ministry in which she engages *as a child*. Neither Mary nor Martha is expected to dutifully listen or serve for the duration of their ministry; nor are they expected to minister in the same way. Unique to their status, age, and individuality, Mary and Martha are each called to respond to God's Word and engage creatively and constructively in the up-building of God's Kingdom. Such engagement, for the Lukan Jesus, exemplifies obedience far more than a rigid observance of a hierarchical order set by any individual or set of authorities.[85]

Moreover, for Luke, such true obedience can only come *after* one hears the Word of God—as Mary does, seated here at Jesus' feet. Bovon continues, "Jesus was not anxious to punish Martha.... All he did was propose a doctrinal hierarchy of values and actions. Priority should be given to listening to the word of God, to taking time out, to the act of sitting down; it consists in not wishing to precede the Lord, in accepting to be served before serving."[86] This is the natural progression for infants and children who learn primarily through observation. Children acquire language only after it is repeated to them over a period of time. They learn to perform a task, like fastening a button or unrolling a rug, by observing someone else do it first. A childist reading of Mary's encounter with Jesus suggests the same—that Mary learns discipleship, the task of sharing the good news of God's Kingdom, by first allowing Jesus to pass the same good news onto her.

However, one cannot simply stop here. For while Bovon's generous reading of Jesus' praise helpfully suggests room for more expansive response to God's Word than any one action or sensibility would entail, he nevertheless retains the adultist, patriarchal hierarchy that suggests women and children must sit and listen before an adult male. To do so undermines the power of acknowledging the agential participation and embodied proclamation of those children who have emerged from the shadows of Luke's text. Just as the infant John responds in a free and uninhibited manner when he encounters the Christ, so too should Mary and all children who would learn from her, be given such opportunity. Therefore, while acknowledging the clear merits of a reading that emphasizes Mary's posture of learning before Jesus, a childist reading must at the same time resist such a posture as the only or primary attribute of the interchange that Luke describes.

Consequently, for the sake of the liberation of children from beneath adultist hierarchies of order, I invite childist readers to consider the mutuality inherent in this interchange. In pursuit of such mutuality, one must interrogate: How did Mary come to be positioned at the feet of Jesus to begin with? How did Jesus respond? Was there an invitation by Jesus for this child to engage in the stories with him? Or, as children can be prone to do, did Mary scoot her way forward on the rug until eager and enthusiastic, she was inches from Jesus' face, her very presence demanding both that his teaching continue and that it do so in a lively and engaging manner? Did Mary demand a story of Jesus—or "just one more"? Did her presence influence the topic of his teaching? Did her response dictate his manner and his tone? The fantastic work that has been done recently in gospel performance criticism suggests that such audience response and engagement would not only have been a possibility but would have been par for the course. David Rhoads offers, "Meaning is negotiated between the performer, the composition, and the audience. We cannot separate audience from performance. They are in an interwoven, symbiotic relationship."[87] At the feet of Jesus, therefore, Mary does not merely listen to the Word that Jesus proclaims—she helps to shape it.

Moreover, reading Mary's interaction with Jesus in this way shifts what could be taken as a narrative portraying a subservient woman or child powerfully into a dynamic illustration of the mutuality and interdependence inherent to the Kingdom of God. Mary's interchange with Jesus, particularly in light of Martha's request that she help work instead, takes on a liberative quality of its very own. Koperski notes, "Calmly sitting and relaxing in the company of a guest can be viewed as a creative choice, particularly while someone else who is possibly in a superior position is anxious."[88] Children in the first century were rarely granted the privilege to sit and listen in the presence of a guest. They certainly would not have possessed the same free range of play typical of twenty-first century Western children while their parents tend to tasks of hospitality at home. Martha is thus within her place both socially and culturally to demand that Mary help. Mary's character instead remains at the feet of Jesus—(presumably) by her own choice—and is defended by Jesus. Re-imagining the interaction in this light turns a stale and oppressive call for women to sit silently into a liberative encouragement for children to exercise their autonomy and to participate in the life of discipleship—learning from and engaging with the performance of the master himself.

Young Children as Students of God's Word

Luke represents children as learners through the character of Jesus himself at the Temple, the generic infants of Jesus' prayer, and the characterization of Mary as silent but affirmed at the feet of Jesus. In typical Lukan fashion, such representations carry on a great Hebrew Bible tradition, in this case, of understanding a primary role of children as that of learning (as expressed particularly in Proverbs and the Psalms, see above). However, such a role is not only characteristic of children across the centuries, but in fact is uniquely suited to them.

Because of the unique way in which children are known *to learn*, attentive to new possibilities and actively engaging and responding to what they hear, these young students serve an important role in Luke's narrative. They bring together Jesus' call for disciples to hear and obey the word of God, modeling proper response for their adult counterparts, and interjecting into the discipleship community their unique mode of reception and response through which they inhabit the coming Kingdom of God in the present as possessors (Lk 18:17) in a way that is difficult for the adult learner to easily replicate or even comprehend.

Such a reception not only proliferates Jesus' message to a wider audience, but through the interaction with it, actually helps to shape the message and Jesus' presentation of it as well. In this way, the presence of children at the feet of Jesus, their ability, enthusiasm, and commitment to hearing the Word of God not only shapes their own experience of the Kingdom but that of the entire community through Jesus' response and adaptation as a performer with children in his midst.

DOERS OF THE WORD OF GOD

While children are fantastic learners and such learning has the powerful potential to shape the broader education of the whole Christian community, the role of children as disciples does not end in the (Sunday) school room—at least not in Luke's narrative. In the ancient world, learning typically had a clear purpose.

This would have been particularly true for the lower-class audience to whom Luke addresses himself. Moreover, as discussed above, listening to the word of God implicitly assumes obedience to the word of God (see Jer 22:21). To receive Jesus' proclamation of the Kingdom without becoming a part of the proclamation would be to miss the point and hence not to have received it at all. As such, Luke's narrative contains not only references to children as present among those whom Jesus taught, listening and receiving his Word as disciples, but also children who actively engage in the act of proclamation themselves.

Luke portrays different children engaging the task of proclamation differently throughout his gospel narrative. Beginning in his infancy narrative with Gabriel's prophecy and John's response to the unborn Jesus in utero (1:17, 39–55), Luke portrays children as embodied agents of proclamation. At the same time, despite the infrequency with which they are given actual voice within the text, children in Luke's narrative emerge as implied agents of vocal proclamation as well. This is seen through listening to the roles of children omitted from Luke's direct text, and yet retained in both the narration of their remembered speech and the proclamation of groups of collective characters of which children were a part.

Children as Agents of Embodied Proclamation

Throughout Luke's gospel account, God's Kingdom is proclaimed in both word and deed (8:1–3; 9:3, 11; 10:1–9; 18:16). Child characters are no exception to this practice. Drawing from Malachi's prophecy (Mal 4:6), the Lukan author situates John the Baptist as one who will "turn the hearts of parents to their children," implicitly realizing the Kingdom through the action of turning that such children incite. Moreover, even before his birth, John embodies a proclamation of God's Kingdom, celebrating the presence of the unborn Jesus by leaping in his mother Elizabeth's womb.

Infants Inspiring Response (1:17)

Luke's gospel narrative hinges on the theme of reversal, or turning. Mary's Magnificat, or Canticle of the Turning,[89] celebrates God's preference of the lowly and anticipates a reversal of power as early as 1:46–55. While this prophecy may be better known, the theme of reversal actually begins earlier in the angel's canticle to Zechariah in verse 17. Anticipating what is to follow, the angel prophesies about Zechariah's soon-to-be-born son: "With the spirit and power of Elijah he will go before [the Lord], to turn the hearts of parents to their children, and the disobedient to the wisdom of the righteous, to make ready a people prepared for the Lord." Contrary to conventional wisdom about wise parents and disobedient children,[90] Luke's parallelism connects parents with the disobedient and children with the wisdom of the righteous. Both of the latter appear in the "a" position of the prophecy and the former in the "b" position. This anticipates Luke 10:21 in which a preference is expressed for children over and against adults, traditionally considered by society to be wise. The roles of parents and children are hence reversed.

Children occupy the seat of wisdom (σοφία). This is further confirmed by Luke's description of Jesus' maturation, in which he states of the infant Jesus that he "grew and became strong, filled with wisdom" (Lk 2:40) and of the twelve-year-old Jesus that he "increased in wisdom and in years" (Lk 2:52). This is the same wisdom that Jesus promises that he will give to his disciples in preparation for the last day so that they may make their defense before those who persecute them (Lk 2:12–15). Moreover, every time that the term wisdom is used by Luke in Acts it is in support of the act of proclamation (Acts 6:3, 10; 7:10, 22). Consequently, to connect children to wisdom is to connect them with proclamation. Wisdom in God's Kingdom, as Luke employs it, supports one's ability to proclaim the Kingdom.

Hence, while the angel's prophecy does not explicitly describe children in the act of proclamation, it implicitly points to such a role. In this way the angel anticipates both the action of Luke 18:15, in which parents, with their hearts turned toward their children, bring their children to Jesus that he might touch them and Jesus' response that it is to such children to whom the Kingdom itself belongs (Lk 18:16). Children then, without ever speaking a word in either of these texts, embody such proclamation through the wisdom and possession with which they receive the Kingdom of God.

Already in Luke 1:17 the infant John, who will later go "into all the region around the Jordan, proclaiming a baptism of repentance for the forgiveness of sins" (Lk 3:3), inspires the beginning of this proclamation in the mouth of an angel of the Lord. The angel's prophecy is in direct response to the conception of John (see Lk 1:13 "your prayer has been heard," εἰσηκούσθη in the aorist passive, completed past). John brings about this act of proclamation while still in utero due to the anticipation of his birth.

Even for parents who do not receive an angelic visitor and whose child is not destined to prepare the way for the Messiah "with the spirit and power of Elijah" (Lk 1:17), the birth of a child is often a highly anticipated event. It inspires action, preparation, reflection, and, indeed, at times, proclamation. This is experienced in contemporary society (even when such actions are not always celebratory in nature) and testified to in the Hebrew Bible. Take for example the response of Hannah when she learns that her prayer has been answered and she will bear a son (1 Sam 1:19ff). Children, through their very existence, then, can embody a proclamation of the Kingdom through their ability to inspire such positive response.

The ability of young children to inspire such a response is further emphasized by a comparison of this prophecy with its Septuagint parallel. In typical Lukan fashion, the angel's words are actually a quotation of a Hebrew prophet—in this case, Malachi 4:6. Notably missing from Luke's version, however, is the latter half of the angel's prophesy, that Elijah will return to "turn the hearts of parents to their children *and the hearts of children to their parents*" (Mal 4:6a, emphasis added). Instead, Luke more closely parallels the apocryphal prophecy that Elijah will return "to turn the hearts of parents to their children, and to restore the tribes of Jacob" (Sir 48:10). Without speaking a word, children are expected to bring about change in their parents. This is an act of embodied proclamation.[91]

John Leaping in his Mother's Womb (1:39–55)

Such embodied proclamation of the very young continues even more explicitly as Luke's telling of John's birth and infancy progresses. When John's mother, Elizabeth, was in her sixth month of pregnancy, Luke narrates a visit by her cousin Mary and her unborn son, Jesus. He writes: "When Elizabeth heard Mary's greeting, the child leaped in her womb. And Elizabeth was filled with the Holy Spirit" (1:41).

The verb "leap" (σκιρτάω) literally refers to an "exuberant springing motion."[92] It is associated with the excited movement of young animals.[93] It is used three times in the New Testament, all by Luke. The first two instances occur in this episode, with the final use in Luke's beatitudes. In each other use the verb is paired with a sense of celebration. First, Elizabeth declares, "For as soon as I heard the sound of your greeting, the child in my womb leaped for joy [ἐσκίρτησεν ἐν ἀγαλλιάσει, lit. leaped with gladness]" (Lk 1:44). Then, Jesus commands those listening to "Rejoice!" (χάρητε) and "Leap!" (σκιρτήσατε), translated by the NRSV: "Rejoice in that day and leap for joy, for surely your reward is great in heaven" (Lk 6:23a). Throughout Luke's usage σκιρτάω takes on a meaning of celebratory exuberance.

The verb σκιρτάω also appears seven times in the Septuagint. The first use, in Gen 25:22 (LXX), refers to the movement of Jacob and Esau in Rachel's womb. Every other use reflects celebratory movement, with five of the six remaining usages referring to celebration on the eschatological Day of the Lord.[94] Following Septuagint patterns, Luke's usage further reflects a celebration of the advent of God's Kingdom. Luke Timothy Johnson calls this "eschatological recognition," concluding that John, at this young age, "is thus shown to be a prophet in accord with the angel's prediction."[95] Luke narrates John leaping in utero at the arrival of Mary and Jesus in order to prefigure his later role as a prophet preparing the way for the coming of Jesus the Lord. Within the context of the story, however, such a prefiguration accepts as normative the movement of infants in utero (for John and, by allusion, Jacob and Esau[96]) as acceptable means of celebrating and proclaiming the coming Kingdom of God.

John's action is itself an embodied proclamation of the incarnate Christ in Mary's womb and also the source of two further moments of proclamation. These latter two moments are similar in tone to the proclamation of the angel that Luke has already attributed to John's conception in Lk 1:17.[97] Since the latter type of proclamation has already been addressed in the previous section, this section focuses on John's initial moment of proclamation—his physical leap as an unborn child in Elizabeth's womb.

Language consists of much more than spoken word. Science has shown that "Nonverbal communication forms a social language that is in many ways richer and more fundamental than our words."[98] For example, in one study participants were able to detect the basic emotions of actors based on nonverbal cues alone.[99] To proclaim the good news of Jesus Christ, likewise, does not always require verbalization. Citing predictions made in antiquity about children based on circumstances surrounding their birth (such as a young infant smiling before the fortieth day), Bovon affirms: "God makes use not only of words but also of body language." [100]

Such embodied speech is what Luke uses to portray John's proclamation of the joy of Christ's presence. As an infant within his mother's womb, John first attests to this truth with a celebratory leap. Luke then narrates how Elizabeth is empowered to interpret this speech act as a gift of the Holy Spirit, which Elizabeth finally vocalizes for Mary and the readers. John's action, therefore, serves as the impetus for the subsequent dialogue,[101] including Mary's Magnificat, thus anticipating the central theme of reversal in the Lukan narrative. Given Mary's initially reserved response to the angel's proclamation (Lk 1:32, 38), it is possible even to say that her encounter with John in this youthful exuberance even influences her to take on his joy in an almost contagious way, as she in turn proclaims to both John and Elizabeth a newly celebratory response (Lk 1:46–55).

Accordingly, John serves as Jesus' precursor and, more immediately, an agent for the proclamation of Jesus and the coming Kingdom of God already from within his mother's womb. Most commentators who attend to John at all within this episode acknowledge this role.[102] However, while traditional scholarship acknowledges the prefiguration of John's role in relation to the rest of the narrative, they do not linger on the active role of John already as an infant in his mother's womb. Consequently, Bovon writes, "But when John leaps in his mother's womb, showing himself already to be a prophet and a precursor, the narrative turns toward Mary."[103] Not only does the narrative turn quickly to Mary, however, but commentators turn equally if not more rapidly to Mary's proclamation, ignoring John's contribution as a result.

Fitzmyer points to Mary's proclamation in the Magnificat as a demonstration of Luke's intention to portray her as a disciple from the beginning of his account;[104] however, the same inference could easily be drawn about John himself. In his context, amidst emerging feminist interpretations of Scripture, Fitzmyer's reading of Mary as a disciple was and remains an important one. Nevertheless, liberating readings of Scripture cannot end with women. Mary's individual discipleship opens the possibility of other female disciples within Luke's narrative world. So too does the embodied proclamation of John here open up possibilities for other young disciples both within and outside of the text, as reflected by Luke's narrative world.

Moreover, to the extent that John's proclamation influences Mary's Magnificat, this childist reading illustrates the potential for child proclamation to stir and encourage joy and praise in their audience.[105] Since the hesitation and doubt that characterizes Mary's initial response to the angel is often attributed to over intellectualization characteristic of older youths and adults in contemporary parlance, the pure joy expressed by John in utero represents a marked contribution that is uniquely, albeit not exclusively, fitted to infants.[106] The uninhibited way with which John shares such joy, unaware of or unconcerned about external responses it might elicit, allows the sheer experience of emotion to overtake Mary and to move her further in her discipleship journey, even as John continues to move forward in his.

Children as Agents of Verbal Proclamation

Children also serve as agents of *verbal* proclamation in Luke's gospel account. This precedent for children as verbal agents of God's Word is later elaborated in the apocryphal *Acts of Peter* with the miraculous account of an infant, only seven months old, being "compelled by God to speak" prophetically (*Acts of Peter*, 15). Although such overt proclamation is not so easily recognized in Luke's account, it demonstrates a familiarity with the possibility of proclamation from the mouths of children in the early Christian communities. Moreover, the speech of the children in Luke's gospel account is perhaps even more astounding than this apocryphal text due to the power such children's speech exerts even in the limited capacities in which Luke conveys it. Despite the already limited roles of children in Luke's gospel account and even more limited speech, when children *are* given voice, proclamation often results.

The direct speech of a specific child is only recorded three times in Luke's narrative: the boy Jesus at the Temple (Lk 2:46–51); the resurrected youth at Nain (7:15); and the servant girl in Caiphas' courtyard (22:56). In the first two cases, the majority (or entirety) of each child's speech is described, but not recorded, leaving the possibility for the reader to infer, within the context, that some or all of the speech contains proclamation. However, as members of larger group characters among the shepherds, disciples, and crowds, children participate in proclamation of God's Kingdom throughout Luke's account.

In addition to these direct references, Luke's Jesus employs the speech of children in his teachings three additional times: comparing the current generation to children calling out (7:31–32), comparing the disciples' prayers to children asking of their parents (11:10–13), and in the parable of the prodigal son (15:11–32). Each of these instances illustrates the accepted role of child's speech within Luke's community. While perhaps not valued at the level of an adult's speech, the speech of children was both heard and remembered in such a way that it can be called upon as an example. Moreover, in so much as Jesus uses this speech to further his own proclamation, it is put to service in favor of the Kingdom in its own right.

Drawing on this acknowledgment of the existence and knowledge of child speech, this section (re)members the proclamation of children in Luke's narrative world that has been hidden over the course of centuries through authorial elision of content and behind collective characters respectively. To do so I first return to the characters of the boy Jesus and the youth at Nain, discussed earlier, in order to re-imagine the proclamative nature of their speech. Next, I return to the category of collective characters: considering first those groups of which I have already established that children were a part—the crowds and the disciples; finally, retrieving children from the shadows of the very first human carriers of the gospel message—the shepherds outside Bethlehem.

Jesus in the Temple (2:46–51) and the Youth at Nain (7:15)

The boy Jesus in the Temple and the resurrected youth at Nain, together with the servant girl who briefly identifies Peter at the end of Luke's narrative, are the only remnants of direct speech attributed to child characters in Luke's gospel. Both of these children, although their words are elided, speak in relation to the power and action of God. While Luke considers the content of their speech insignificant enough to skip over (perhaps because they are children), the respective contexts of each episode suggests that their speech could plausibly point to the glory and power of God.

Jesus' speech is narrated at least in part. Specifically, Luke recounts Jesus' response to his parents, asking: "Why were you searching for me? Did you not know that I must be in my Father's house?" (2:49). Here Jesus is proclaiming himself Son of the Father. Irenaeus "claimed that here Jesus had wanted to introduce his rather uninsightful parents to the unknown God."[107] By declaring his place in God's house to his earthly parents, Jesus is identifying his place within God's household and reminding Mary of the good news of his role proclaimed to her already by the angels. This is divine proclamation.

Hearing this proclamation, even though she does not fully understand, Mary thus responds as she has upon receiving previous proclamations—by treasuring all these things in her heart (2:51; also 1:51; 2:19). In this way she begins to fulfill the prophecy cited by the angel Gabriel that the hearts of parents will be turned to their children (1:17).

Although I have already emphasized Jesus' role in this Temple scene as a student, learning from the teachers, such a role does not preclude the parallel characterizations of teacher and proclaimer of the good news. This was the model of a typical grammar school in antiquity in which "older and more able students also discharge some teaching functions."[108] Due to the expectation that children are continually learning, while also sharing what they learn within the classroom, this overlap is most easily seen among such characters. The ease with which the child Jesus slips between the roles of student and teacher of the Kingdom can serve as a valuable example for contemporary Christians—both youth and adults—living into their roles as disciples.

It is therefore fitting within such a reading to assume that the speech Luke does not narrate—the questions and answers supplied by the boy Jesus while sitting among the teachers—need not be understood as all inquiry or all proclamation. Rather, given the dynamic nature of both learning and proclamation, it is most likely that Luke elides within this exchange some combination of both. That Jesus' speech within this unnarrated exchange can be assumed to include at least some quality of proclamation is further implied by the amazement with which his words are met (2:47).

Likewise, the youth at Nain, while not possessing the divine qualities of the child Jesus, can also be read as proclaiming the good news of God in at least a portion of his unnarrated speech. Luke tells us, simply, that the young man "sat up and began to speak" (7:14). In response to all that they have witnessed, the crowd then "glorified God, saying, 'A great prophet has risen among us!' and 'God has looked favorably on his peoples!'" (7:16). While Luke does not reveal the content of the boy's speech, the narrative leaves room for several reasonable inferences.

The boy's speech represents a literary gap between these two moments—Jesus' resuscitation of him on the funeral bier and the crowd's proclamation of God's power. This gap is otherwise filled only with Jesus' return of the boy to his mother in 7:15. Based upon this action of returning the boy to his mother, chapter 3 suggests that part of this gap might be filled with this youth's frightened and disoriented cry for his mother. The crowd's response that follows, however, leaves room for at least one more plausible response—that the boy himself gives glory to God upon having experienced this miracle.

Such a response of glorification or praise is in keeping with typical Lukan responses by those who receive Jesus' healing.[109] That such a response occurs immediately upon receiving Jesus' healing is demonstrated in such episodes as the bent over woman in Lk 13:12, who "immediately stood up straight and began praising God" (13:13). Within the geographic and cultural context, with mourners identified and no special note otherwise, Luke seems to understand the youth at Nain as within the Israelite faith, as with the bent over woman. For the youth to immediately connect his miraculous recovery to God's work, then, would have been a typical if not expected response. So the Psalm says of the faithful, "The Lord sustains them on their sickbed, in their illness you heal all their infirmities" (Ps 41:3).

Thus, in both the case of Jesus in the Temple and the youth at Nain, the unidentified content of their speech can plausibly and legitimately be assigned (at least in part) to the category of proclamation. Moreover, in the case of the boy Jesus in the Temple, Luke directly attributes to him the act of proclamation in his encounter with Mary and Joseph. In terms of consistency with this proclamation and with other responses to Jesus' acts of healing throughout the gospels, and with an eye toward lifting up contributions of children as disciples who both hear and *do* the word of God in Luke's gospel account, it is therefore worthwhile to (re)member the speech of these children in terms of their proclamative value.

Children in the Crowds and Among the Disciples

In a generic sense, Luke's gospel account is full of words of proclamation from the mouths of children. It is necessary only to peel past the adultist layers of interpretation that have obscured children from these acts in order to hear them. Recalling all that has been said up to this point to establish the presence of children within the crowds and disciples whom Luke describes, it must suffice at this point to note that, unless the context or the text point otherwise, children are to be assumed in such gatherings.

Upon assuming children among Luke's crowds and disciples, their frequent participation in proclaiming the good news of Jesus Christ and God's Kingdom is reclaimed. The crowds gathered around Jesus frequently participated in the act of proclaiming God's Kingdom in response to Jesus' good works and miracles. This is seen, among other instances, in the crowds' response to the resuscitation of the youth at Nain cited above (7:16). Such responses, however, begin after Luke first records Jesus working miracles in Capernaum (4:37) and continue throughout Luke's narrative.[110] The crowds consistently perform the narrative function of spreading word about Jesus throughout the countryside, often also glorifying God because of what Jesus has done.[111]

More explicitly, as participants within the group identified as Jesus' disciples, children also can be seen to engage in proclamative speech throughout Luke's narrative. This can be read into such summative descriptions as Luke

5:10–11 and 8:1–3; however, in as much as dwelling on such episodes merely employs a tautology in demonstrating the unique contribution of children as disciples of Jesus, I will not dwell on such episodes here.

Instead, it is worth noting that when Luke ascribes such acts of proclamation to the collective characters of the crowd and Jesus' disciples, one should not assume that it is only certain individuals (perhaps only the adults) who engage in such acts. Rather, Luke makes clear that public acknowledgment of Jesus is a prerequisite for *all* among those who follow Jesus: "And I tell you, *everyone* who acknowledges me before others, the Son of Man also will acknowledge before the angels of God; but *whoever* denies me before others will be denied before the angels of God" (Lk 12:8–9, emphasis added). With the stakes so high, to assume that the description of a group act excludes members of that group without explicit acknowledgment is not only presumptuous, but destructive. Hence, in as far as children are a part of the crowds and disciples and in so far as the crowds and disciples glorify God and proclaim Jesus, children ought be assumed to engage in these roles.

Child Shepherds (2:8–20)

Finally, reading Luke's gospel with an eye towards the roles and participation of children in everyday life reveals a third collective character group in which children can be assumed to have taken part, if not, in fact, dominated in this case. This group is the shepherds—the very first people in Luke's account to proclaim the good news of Jesus' birth after the angels proclaim it to them.

The connection of children with the shepherds is different from that described above with relation to the crowds and the disciples. Children are connected with shepherds in Luke's narrative not as a result of collective communal participation, but due to their social and physical roles and through the application of biblical tradition. Child labor was a routine part of existence in the first century world. Indeed, it remains a routine part of childhood in many places across the world today. While many children in the first century Mediterranean world would have at least worked within their homes, children who belonged to agricultural families—either as offspring or as slaves—were often given the task of caring for smaller livestock, like sheep, goats, and swine[112] who did not require significant herding.[113]

Affirming the early age at which slave children in particular were put to work in the first centuries of the Mediterranean world, Hanne Sigismund-Nielsen cites Varro, noting that among other farm jobs, "Both boys and girls could also be employed as shepherds, Varro informs us (*RR* 2.10.1). These children, just like Daphnis and Chole in Longus' novel, must have been quite young. Young men would be responsible for the bigger cattle that grazed on the pastures away from the farm, while boys and girls would look after the smaller ones that were taken in every night."[114] Similarly, in the centuries immediately following Luke's gospel account, John Moschus describes shepherd boys "'playing Eucharist . . . after their midday meal' (*Prat. Spir.* 196)."[115] In traditions akin to the 'boy who called wolf' in modern literature, child shepherds seem to have been a part of the culture of the time. Such evidence from both agricultural practice and early Christian literature points to children serving as shepherds in the time and context within which Luke was writing.

Moreover, slaves were not the only children who served as shepherds. Jack Vancil notes that within the biblical tradition, "The work [of shepherding] might be delegated to the owner's children; Rachel looked after Laban's sheep (Gen 29:6), and David, though the youngest of Jesse's sons, was given this responsibility (1 Sam 16:11; 17:15)."[116] Such ancient Israelite precedents seem not to have changed much in the centuries intervening the two testaments, as Lena Larsson Loven and Agneta Stromberg conclude that in the first century BCE "many poor Roman families relied on their children for agricultural work."[117]

Luke and/or his audience would thereby likely have assumed and accepted the presence of children among the shepherds outside of Bethlehem in the infancy narrative. Such an assumption is further supported when one considers Luke's concern for connections with the biblical tradition—a tradition that includes, as noted above, young David the shepherd boy. Commentators agree that neither the setting of Jesus' birth nor the occupation of the first people to greet him are coincidence in Luke's telling. Fitzmyer elaborates, "In the background of the story is the association of David as a boy with his father's sheep in a district near Bethlehem (1 Sam 17:15)."[118] Since the setting outside of Bethlehem, the city of David, recalls the story of David the shepherd boy, an acceptance and understanding of shepherding as a child's task is written into Luke's narrative.

Contemporary readers often miss this connection between shepherding and children both because of a forced blindness toward child labor in much of the academy and because scholarship has, over the centuries, painted Luke's shepherds in a harsher, adult light that is difficult to resonate with children. This comes from certain rabbinic writings, mostly from the Babylonian Talmud, that speak of shepherding as a shameful profession. However, most recent scholars acknowledge, "The rabbinic texts critical of shepherds are not weighty enough to cancel out the positive evaluation of shepherds in biblical literature."[119] Following the same logic, it is difficult to disconnect the positive evaluation of shepherds in biblical literature from the role of children in shepherding that the same literature also presents.

Luke's description of the shepherds' actions further supports the assumption of children among them, behaving in ways typically ascribed to children.

The shepherds' initial terror (Lk 2:9), while perhaps not unexpected from children or a group of mixed children and adults, does not weigh either for or against any assessment of their age, given the shared fear exhibited by both Zechariah (in his old age) and Mary (in her relative youth) when the angel Gabriel first visits them. However, following the angelic message, the shepherds exhibit unquestioned trust, saying among themselves, "Let us go now to Bethlehem and see this thing that has taken place" (2:15), in sharp contrast to the initial disbelief of Zechariah and even, to a lesser extent, Mary.

The function of the shepherds, Bovon notes, "is showing the spontaneous trust in the heavenly message, which results in their hastening to the child. It is an example of the kind of spontaneous faith of which the Lucan Gospel is full."[120] Such trust is typical of that which is commonly ascribed, albeit not always to be assumed, with relation to children. If one reads this early episode in Luke's gospel as a demonstration of the lived faith of a group of children, Jesus' later exhortation in Lk 18:17 to "receive the Kingdom as a little child" takes on a greater depth of meaning.

Most immediately, however, as it concerns the place of children as disciples, it is noteworthy that the shepherds represent the first human messengers of the good news of Jesus' birth. Not only do they respond to the angels' message in faith and relay this message to Mary and Joseph, but also upon seeing the Christ child, "The shepherds returned, glorifying and praising God for all they had heard and seen, as it had been told them" (Lk 2:20). To this end, Tannehill describes the shepherds as "earthly messengers of the heavenly messengers."[121] When read with children at the forefront, this episode becomes not only the first instance of children as proclaimers of God's Kingdom, but easily the most powerful proclamation attributed to children in Luke's account.

Young Children as Evangelists

Luke's gospel can and should be read to include children as present among Jesus' disciples. However, a childist reading of Luke's narrative must go further than this. Children ought not be treated as mere passive observers of the work of God's Kingdom. Their role was not, nor should it be, one of simple absorption of information. Rather, careful attention to child characters both explicit and implicit in Luke's text illuminates the role of children as active disciples, both receiving and proclaiming the word of God's Kingdom.

Such participation begins in the infancy narrative through the embodied acts of John in Elizabeth's womb and the faith-led verb proclamations of the Bethlehem shepherds, including those children among them, upon Jesus' birth. By (re)membering children in the crowds and among the disciples, the proclamation of children continues to permeate Luke's account. This proclamation comes to a head when one child notes the speech of another, even when Luke deems the content of their words (perhaps because of their age) not worth recording.

CONCLUSION

A childist reading serves to reclaim and (re)member the presence of children among the disciples in Luke's gospel account. It shows both the feasibility and value of reading Luke's gospel account in such a way as to take note of and learn from such children. Lukan discipleship is defined by hearing and doing, and both of these actions are not only engaged in by child characters in Luke's account, but also influenced by child performances of them.

From Jesus sitting among the teachers and Mary sitting at Jesus' feet, readers learn to treat listening and learning as an active rather than a passive task. It is the task of the disciple not merely to hear the words of the Gospel but to engage with them. Again from the child Jesus, but also from the shepherds who proclaimed his birth, readers learn to respond to God's word with faith and trust. While from Gabriel's prophecy as it is lived out in intergenerational acts of proclamation, ranging from Elizabeth's response to John's leap in her womb, to shared acts of proclamation and glorification among the crowds and disciples, the reader learns the importance of interdependent collaboration among the generations.

In Luke 18:17 Jesus instructs his disciples to receive the Kingdom as a child. Throughout the rest of Luke's narrative, both before and after, Luke narrates the dynamic ways in which child disciples engage in the work of the Kingdom. Unfortunately, adult readers have too frequently either overlooked or metaphorized the role of children in these episodes. In order to reclaim the richness with which children themselves can and should participate in the Kingdom and all that they have to contribute to their adult counterparts in the process, it is necessary to reclaim their part

NOTES

1. Contrast Philippe Ariès, *Centuries of Childhood: A Social History of Family Life,* translated by Robert Baldick (New York: Vintage Books, 1962) and Allison James and Alan Prout, ed., *Constructing and Reconstructing Childhood* (New York: Routledge Falmer, 1997).

2. On the use of children metaphorically in Paul's letters, see James Francis, *Adults as Children: Images of Childhood in the Ancient World and the New Testament* (Oxford: Peter Lang, 2006) 24.

3. Allison James and Alan Prout, "A New Paradigm for the Sociology of Childhood?" in *Constructing and Reconstructing Childhood: Contemporary Issues in the Sociological Study of Childhood*, edited by Allison James and Alan Prout (Basingtoke: Falmer Press, 1990) 8.

4. This distancing of the character of Jesus from his mother and siblings has been read as evidence, however circumstantial, of the complete dissolution of families in synoptic portraits of the Jesus movement (cf. E. E. Ellis, *The Gospel of Luke* [London: Nelson, 1966] 127; to a lesser extent, J. M. Creed, *The Gospel According to St. Luke* [London: MacMillan, 1930] 118; etc.). Such separation could be read to impact young children negatively. However, Luke, more so than any of the other synoptics, takes pains to see that this is not the case. In Luke's portrait of the Jesus movement, biology may no longer be the standard, but family—even among members of Jesus' biological family—continues to thrive. For example, Jane Schaberg argues: "Mary the mother of Jesus is often considered Luke's model of obedient, contemplative discipleship.... She is not defined by her biological motherhood but blessed for her belief, as are all who 'hear the word of God and obey it'" ("Luke" in *The Women's Bible Commentary*, ed. Carol A. Newsom and Sharon Ringe [Louisville: Westminster John Knox, 1992] 279).

5. Turid Karlsen Seim, *The Double Message: Patterns of Gender in Luke-Acts* (Nashville: Abingdon, 1994) 253.

6. Keith J. White, "He Placed a Little Child in the Midst," in *The Child in the Bible*, ed. Marica J. Bunge, Terence Fretheim, and Beverly Roberts Gaventa (Grand Rapids: Eerdmann's, 2008) 362.

7. Esther de Boer, "The Lukan Mary Magdalene and the Other Women Following Jesus," in *Feminist Companion to Luke*, edited by Amy-Jill Levine and Marianne Blickenstaff (Cleveland: Pilgrim Press, 2002) 145.

8. See Francis, *Adults as Children*, 23.

9. Plato, *Laws,* 2.659d.

10. Given the purpose of education to tame passions and the continual experience of passions throughout life, Plato understood education to be a lifelong goal—albeit begun and with its greatest emphasis in childhood. See Cynthia B. Patterson, "Education in Plato's Laws," in *Childhood and Education in the Classical World*, ed. Judith Evan Grubbs and Tim Parkin (Oxford: Oxford University Press, 2013) 378–379.

11. See Prov 22:6, "Train children in the right way, and when old they will not stray."

12. Here it is worth noting that the role of "obedience" in the ancient world was also expected of adult children in relation to the *pater familias*, and even more strictly, of household slaves.

13. Beryl Rawson, "Adult-Child Relationships in Roman Society," in *Marriage, Divorce, and Children in Ancient Rome*, edited by Beryl Rawson (Oxford: Oxford University Press, 1991) 20.

14. Reidar Aasgaard, *The Childhood of Jesus: Decoding the Apocryphal Infancy Gospel of Thomas* (Eugene, OR: Cascade Books, 2009) 79.

15. See Sir 7:23: "Do you have children? Discipline them, and make them obedient from their youth"; 1 Pet 1:14: "Like obedient children, do not be conformed to the desires that you formerly had in ignorance"; Clemens Alexandrinus, *Stromata* 3.18.110.2.1.

16. This is counter to Schaberg's understanding that the provision of the women out of their wealth necessarily excludes them from the community of disciples (287). See chapter 4 on sedentary discipleship for a more thorough explanation of this.

17. While borne out more recently in scientific and sociological research on the development and plasticity of a child's brain (see Alison Gopnik, *The Philosophical Baby: What Children's Minds Tell Us About Truth, Love, and the Meaning of Life* [New York: Picador, 2009] 120), an implicit knowledge of the child as natural student can be seen throughout the Hebrew Bible in its treatment of children as recipients of teaching. See Deut 4:10; 11:19; Ps 34:11; 78:5; Prov 1:8; 3:1; 6:20; Isa 54:13; Sir 4:11.

18. There is little doubt that childhood was a difficult time in antiquity, both because of a greater susceptibility to disease and because of a lower, subservient status; however, recent research has shown that children were nevertheless valued within the sentimentalities and infrastructures of their time.

19. Bovon, *Luke 1*, translated by Christine Thomas (Minneapolis: Fortress Press, 2002) 110–111.

20. See chapter 2.

21. IGT 17:2.

22. See Bradley Billings, "'At the Age of 12': The Boy Jesus in the Temple (Luke 2:41–52), The Emperor Augustus and the Social Setting of the Third Gospel," in *Journal of Theological Studies* 60:1 (April 2009) 70–89; Bovon, *Luke 1*, 108–115; John T. Carroll, "'What Then Will This Child Become?': Perspectives on Children in the Gospel of Luke," in *The Child in the Bible*, edited by Marcia Bunge, Terence Fretheim, and Beverly Roberts Gaventa (Grand Rapids: Wm. B. Eerdman's, 2008) 185; Karen Chakoian, "Luke 2:41–52" in *Interpretation* (April 1998) 185–190; Luke Timothy Johnson, *The Gospel of Luke* (Collegeville, MN: Liturgical Press, 1991) 60–62; and Valdir Steuernagel, "Doing Theology Together with Mary," in *Journal of Latin American Theology* 8:2 (2013) 239–269.

23. Joseph A. Fitzmyer, *The Gospel According to Luke I–IX* (New York: Doubleday, 1970) 442.

24. Rafaella Cribiore, *Gymnastics of the Mind: Greek Education in Hellenistic and Roman Egypt* (Princeton: Princeton University Press, 2001) 15. Such a description is typical of vignettes found in the *Hermeneumata*; thus, written evidence suggests that students sat during the work of their lessons (likely a pragmatic need). Nevertheless, it is striking that in artistic portrayals of the school scene "teachers are always portrayed as sitting, while their pupils—boys and girls—are standing" (Cribiore, 31). In these scenes, it seems, the primary goal is to portray the power of the seated teacher over and against the standing student, often waiting to receive the teacher's correction. Nevertheless, descriptions of the actual passing of knowledge—specifically in lecture and symposium form—continues to occur while the student is seated (albeit in less formidable ways).

25. Cribiore, 31 fn 67. Cf. Plato *Prt.* 315c.

26. Cribiore, 109–1110.

27. Aasgaard, 115–116.

28. This interpretation contrasts with the view that Jesus' presence among, rather than at the feet of, the teachers places him at equal rank to them (Bovon, *Luke 1*, 112).

While it is certainly possible and legitimate to read Luke's text in this way, I prefer Fitzmyer's interpretation for what it has to offer in understanding Luke's potential portrait of childhood more generally through the teacher/student relationship. Moreover, while Bovon contrasts the communal posture of Lk 2:46 with Luke's portrait of Paul as a student at the feet of his tutor (Acts 22:3), this reading does not fit with the use of the term "among" (ἐν μέσῳ) throughout the rest of Luke. Rather, Luke's use of ἐν μέσῳ reflects a general locative sense, meaning in the same location, with enough variety to leave room for the individual located among the others to be of equal, lesser, or greater rank with the others (see Lk 8:7; 10:3; 22:27; 24:36; Acts 1:15; 2:22; 17:22; 27:21). The term is used both to describe Jesus acting as a servant as he washes his disciples feet (Lk 22:27) and, on the other hand, of Peter and Paul as teachers in Acts. Likewise, in Lk 9:47, Jesus places a child "by his side" (παρ' ἑαυτῷ) not to imply equality of stature or that the child (or he) have nothing left to learn, but instead, to connote community—the child is *with* him, accompanying him in his service.

29. Fitzmyer, *Luke I–IX*, 442.
30. Fitzmyer, *Luke I–IX*, 438.
31. Gopnik, 123.
32. See Lise Eliot, *What's Going On in There?: How the Brain and Mind Develop in the First Five Years of Life* (New York: Bantam Books, 1999): ". . . hardware improvements [in the brain at around the age of six] explain why children, for all their lack of cognitive sophistication, are so much better at learning than most adults. What grown-ups can catch on to the latest computer game or memorize the words to a new song after just a few tries? Children's brains are programmed to learn, and when you add their plasticity to their steady improvement in neural speed and efficiency, it's a little less surprising (though no less wonderful) to discover that your twelve- or fifteen-year-old can speak a foreign language, do calculus, or solve a Sunday crossword puzzle" (416).
33. A difficult phrase to translate, τοῖς τοῦ πατρός μου literally means "the things of my father," but is often translated as "my father's house" (NRSV, NASB) or "my father's business" (NKJV). I translate it as "work" above to reflect both the shared quality of purposeful activity across generations, while highlighting the unique activities at which children are most suited to work. For more on the activities of childhood as work, see Maria Montessori, *Discovery of the Child*, trans. by M. Joseph Costelloe (New York: Ballantine Books, 1967).
34. Gopnik, 129–130.
35. Gopnik, 129–130.
36. Luke's "world of stunning reversals is well captured in 10:21, where Jesus thanks God for disclosing strange wisdom (i.e., concerning the Spirit active in Jesus' ministry not to those who are already wise but to infants (*nepioi*) instead" (Carroll, 190).
37. Joseph A. Fitzmyer, *The Gospel According to Luke X–XXIV* (New York: Doubleday, 1983) 873.
38. François Bovon, *Luke 2*, translated by Donald S. Deer (Minneapolis: Fortress Press, 2013) 42.
39. This is in contrast to the typical adultist leap made by most exegetes to immediately metaphorize the term "infants" to mean that Jesus' adult disciples are to be

understood as "lowly and simple" (Johnson, 170; cf. Bovon, *Luke 2*, 41; Fitzmyer, *Luke X–XXIV*, 873). Such a move insults both the adult and infant disciples alike by diminishing the particular group of adults described in the gospel as necessarily possessing these characteristics, diminishing all infants in the same way, and finally, ignoring the presence of actual infants and children among the diverse group of disciples who follow Jesus in Luke's account. Moreover, it is a small step from such interpretations that oppose the entirety of Jesus' disciples to the entirety of the Jewish wisdom tradition to a supercessionist reading that dangerously declares the Christian experience of revelation to be superior to that of our Jewish siblings (Fitzmyer, *Luke X–XXIV*, 869).

40. Bovon, *Luke 2*, 42.
41. Horn & Martens, 260–261.
42. Gopnik, 119.
43. Bovon, *Luke 2*, 42; Johnson, 170.
44. See Lk 2:26, 32; 8:12–15; 10:22; 12:3; Acts 2.
45. Studies have shown that certain basic functions, such as language acquisition, are markedly easier for infants and young children for adults; however, adults *can* learn them: "Soliciting responses from 2.3 million immigrants from Spanish and Chinese backgrounds, [Professors Kenji Hakuta of Stanford University and Professors Ellen Bialystok and Edward Wiley, both of York University in Toronto, Canada] asked whether the age of immigration made any difference in the ability to master the English language. They found that across all ages, immigrants who arrived in the United States earlier had better language proficiency than those who arrived later. Yet they report that there is no 'critical' age after which the new language *cannot* be learned" (Kathy Hirsh-Pasek and Roberta Michnick Golinkoff, *Einstein Never Used Flash Cards: How Our Children REALLY Learn and Why They Need to Play More and Memorize Less* [Emmaus, PA: Rodale Inc., 2003] 31).
46. Fitzmyer, *Luke X–XXIV*, 869.
47. Gopnik, 119.
48. There are always exceptions to such generalizations and this statement is intended as a classification of Luke's literary treatment of children, not a description of all children in reality. However, it is worth noting that even children who are diagnosed in our contemporary society with extreme learning disabilities absorb and learn at a lightning-fast rate compared to later adult acquisition of language and knowledge in a conventional way.
49. See chapter 4 on Discipleship for a childist reading of 2:46 that takes seriously the typical aspects of childhood portrayed in this scene despite Jesus' acknowledged divinity.
50. See also Lk 9:41–43, 46–48; 18:15–17 and elsewhere.
51. Loveday C. Alexander, "Sisters in Adversity: Retelling Martha's Story," in *Feminist Companion to Luke*, ed. Amy-Jill Levine and Marianne Blickenstaff (London: Sheffield, 2002) 206.
52. Pamela Thimmes, "The Language of Community: A Cautionary Tale (Luke 10:38–42)," in *A Feminist Companion to Luke*, ed. Amy-Jill Levine and Marianne Blickenstaff (London: Sheffield Press, 2002) 239.

53. The latter, being a term more typical of Mark, never appears in Luke's writing; however, the former term appears four times in Luke-Acts (Lk 12:45; 22:56; Acts 12:13; 16:16), often translated as "slave-girl or maiden."

54. Lk 1:27; Acts 21:9.

55. That Martha, a woman, would hold such a position would likely have been accepted by Luke's audience. Thimmes notes, "In Lukan narratives, women householders are not an unusual phenomenon since Luke also rooted the origin of the Philippian community in Lydia's house (Acts 15:11–40)" (236).

56. Reid persuasively makes the case that these variants are original due to both a common sense reading of the text (without which it seems abruptly incomplete) and in light of later redactions to blur the role of women as heads of house churches (Barbara E. Reid, *Choosing the Better Part? Women in the Gospel of Luke* (Collegeville, MN: Liturgical Press, 1996) 149–154, summarized in Veronica Koperski, "Women and Discipleship in Luke 10:38–42 and Acts 6.1–7: the Literary Context of Luke-Acts," in *A Feminist Companion to Luke*, ed. Amy-Jill Levine and Marianne Blickenstaff (London: Sheffield Academic Press, 2002) 184. See also Bovon, *Luke 2*, 71.

57. This is in contrast to D'Angelo's thesis that Mary and Martha represent an equal partnership, preferring instead the traditional hierarchy (though in a different light) with which the sisters are commonly portrayed in other accounts. (Cf. Mary Rose D'Angelo, "Reconstructing 'Real' Women from Gospel Literature: The Case of Mary Magdalene, in *Women and Christian Origins,* ed. by Ross S. Kraemer and Mary Rose D'Angelo [Oxford: Oxford University Press, 1999], 107–108.).

58. The participation of women and children disciples is discussed at greater length in previous chapters of this work and confirmed by the baptisms of whole households in Acts.

59. Warren Carter, "Getting Martha Out of the Kitchen: Luke 10.38–42 Again," in *Feminist Companion to Luke*, ed. Amy-Jill Levine and Marianne Blickenstaff (Cleveland: Pilgrim Press, 2002) 218.

60. Carter, "Getting Martha Out of the Kitchen," 222.

61. See Elisabeth Schüssler Fiorenza, *But She Said: Feminist Practices of Biblical Interpretation* (Boston: Beacon Press, 1992), 54–76, esp. 66: "Luke plays down the ministry of those women leaders of the early Church whom he has to mention because they were known to his audience. Martha and Mary are a case in point."

62. Veronica Koperski, "Luke 10.38–40 and Acts 6.1–7: The Literary Context of Luke-Acts" in *Feminist Companion to Luke*, ed. Amy-Jill Levine and Marianne Blickenstaff (London: Sheffield Academic Press, 2002) 173.

63. Koperski, 173.

64. For a discussion of such androcentric interpretations see Alexander, "Sisters in Adversity," 200.

65. See Lk 7:38; 8:41; 17:16; Acts 4:35; 5:2, 10.

66. Richard I. Pervo, *Acts* (Minneapolis: Fortress Press, 2009) 563, fn 35: "Lit. 'at the feet of,' an indication of subordination. See Luke 7:38; 8:35, 41 (*v.l.* in 10:39); 17:16; Acts 4:35; 5:2, 10. Note also *Act. Paul* 3.10." Also, Johnson, 173: "Throughout Luke-Acts sitting at the feet indicates acknowledgment of authority (7:38; 8:35, 41; 17:16; Acts 4:35, 37; 5:2; 22:3)."

67. Cribiore, 28–34.
68. See Cribiore, 66 fn 10.
69. Paulo Freire, *Pedagogy of the Oppressed*, translated by Myra Bergman (New York: Continuum, 1970) 71.
70. Paulo Freire, *Pedagogy of the Oppressed*, translated by Myra Bergman (New York: Continuum, 1970) 71.
71. Tex Sample, *Ministry in an Oral Culture: Living With Will Rogers, Uncle Remus, & Minnie Pearl* (Louisville: Westminster John Knox, 1994) 14.
72. Thomas E. Boomershine, *The Messiah of Peace: A Perfomrance-Criticism Commentary on Mark's Passion-Resurrection Narrative* (Eugene, OR: Cascade Books, 2015) 12.
73. See Freire, 125.
74. Freire, 96.
75. Freire, 126.
76. Freire, 129.
77. Bovon, *Luke 2*, 70; See also Alexander, "Sisters in Adversity," 198.
78. This is counter to Koperski, 192: "Whether Martha's διακονία involves preaching or practical hospitality, there remains a strong sense that Lk 10:38–42 in the literary context of Luke-Acts validates a passive role for women rather than an active role, even if the passive role is an apparently sublime one."
79. Elisabeth Schüssler Fiorenza, 'A Feminist Critical Interpretation,' 28, summarized in Paula Thimmes, "The Language of Community: A Cautionary Tale (Luke 10:38–42)," in *A Feminist Companion to Luke*, ed. Amy-Jill Levine and Marianne Blickenstaff (London: Sheffield Press, 2002) 235; Schaberg, 275.
80. Alexander, "Sisters in Adversity."
81. Carter, "Getting Martha Out of the Kitchen," 218.
82. Carter, "Getting Martha Out of the Kitchen," 230.
83. See Fitzmyer, *Luke X–XXIV,* 892.
84. Bovon, *Luke 2,* 75.
85. For examples of such creative response to God's word in Luke's account, see Jesus' praise for the woman who creatively and elaborately anoints him with oil as an embodied expression of her love (Lk 7:36–50), Stephen's great deeds and preaching despite his appointment by the apostles to a far more limited role (Acts 6:5–10), and Jesus' exhortation that in preparation for the coming Kingdom sheer obedience is not sufficient (Lk 17:7–10).
86. Bovon, *Luke 2,* 77.
87. David Rhoads, "Performance Criticism: An Emerging Methodology in Biblical Studies—Part I," in *Biblical Theology Bulletin* 36:3 (2006) 11.
88. Koperski, 195.
89. Rory Cooney, "Canticle of the Turning," GIA Publications: 1990.
90. On the wisdom gained with years, see Ps 90:12; on disobedience, cf. the biblical theme of Israel as disobedient child of God.
91. This role of children (even unborn children) inspiring proclamation through their embodied presence is present in Luke's gospel account; however, it is not at the forefront of the text. Rather, this role must be recovered from the more ostensibly adult centric

narrative that the Lukan author crafts. As a sign of such a narrative, it is worth noting, for example, that, by omitting the latter half of Malachi's prophecy, Luke misses an opportunity to make children the *subject*, rather than solely the objects, of the prophetic action. Surely, as the prophecy indicates, children in Luke's Jewish context, as adults, would have been understood as both subject and object of such Messianic prophecies. The Messiah—Jesus—comes for everyone, adult and child, and *everyone* responds.

92. BDAG, 930.

93. Ps 114:4, 6. See Gottfried Fitzer, "σκιρτάω," *TDNT* 7 (1971) 401–2.

94. See Ps 114:4, 6; Wis 17:18; Joel 1:17; Mal 3:20 (LXX). The remaining reference comes from Jer 27:11 and refers to the celebration of the prophet's adversaries in the past tense.

95. Johnson, 40; see also Bovon, *Luke 1*, 58–59 and Robert C. Tannehill, *Luke* (Nashville, Abingdon Press, 1996) 52.

96. See Fitzmyer, *Luke I–IX*, 358. For further parallels between John/Jesus and Jacob/Esau see Esther M. Menn, "Child Characters in Biblical Narratives: The Young David (1 Samuel 16–17) and the Little Israelite Servant Girl (2 Kings 5:1–19)," in *The Child in the Bible,* ed. Marica J. Bunge, Terence Fretheim, and Beverly Roberts Gaventa (Grand Rapids: Eerdmann's, 2008), 330: "The deference of John the Baptist to his younger relative Jesus, from the womb (Luke 1:39–45) to the baptismal scene at the Jordan (Matt 2:1–17; Mark 1:1–11; Luke 3:15–22; John 1:19–36), is an adaptation of this same pattern [of the ascendancy of the younger son]."

97. This is to say nothing of the very explicit proclamation of Mary in Lk 1:46ff., who is described in 1:27 as a παρθένος, or young maiden—little more than a young girl herself. I omit Mary's role as a disciple here and elsewhere, while acknowledging its significance, due to the fact that she is pregnant when this role begins in Luke's narrative. As highlighted in chapter 1, it is difficult if not impossible to peg down exact ages as to when first century (or twenty-first century!) childhood might be understood to end or begin; however, there are certain milestone moments that mark such transitions. While child and teenage pregnancy are real and societal concerns in the twenty-first century, in the first century, whatever age one might have been, pregnancy was one of the social markers of entry into adulthood.

98. Leonard Mlodinow, "How We Communicate Through Body Language," in *Psychology Today* 29 May 2012. https://www.psychologytoday.com/blog/subliminal/201205/how-we-communicate-through-body-language.

99. Mlodinow.

100. Bovon, *Luke 1*, 58.

101. In contrast, by focusing on the dialogue (in particular, the Magnificat) with little or no attention paid to the act of the infant, commentators can unwittingly dismiss the role of one of "the least" for whom Mary proclaims that through Jesus God is now lifting up.

102. See Bovon, *Luke 1*, 55; Fitzmyer, *Luke I–IX*, 358; Tannehill, *Luke*, 52.

103. Bovon, *Luke 1*, 55.

104. Fitzmyer, *Luke I–IX*, 358.

105. Not all childist interpreters understand the character of Mary as an adult (see Betsworth, 101–106); however, given the operative social definition of age presented

in chapter one of this work, I read Mary's character as interacting at the level of an adult at this point in the narrative given the fact of her pregnancy.

106. This is not to suggest, as have previous interpreters, that all infants are characteristically joyful. Indeed, anyone who has spent anytime with a hungry infant knows this not to be the case. Nevertheless, joy is one among many traits of infanthood broadly conceived and one from which adult disciples might do well to learn.

107. *Adv. Haer.* 1.20.2, cited in Bovon, *Luke 1*, 113.

108. Cribiore, 42.

109. See Lk 5:12–15, 25; 8:38–39, 47; 13:12; 17:15–19; 18:43.

110. See Lk 5:26; 7:17; 8:34; 9:11, 19; 13:17; 18:43; 19:36–39; 23:27, 48.

111. It is worth noting that this changes after Jesus' arrest. Here, too, children must be assumed to be a part of the crowds, but no longer are they glorifying God because of Jesus, now they are engaged in public outcry condemning Jesus (see Lk 23:1, 18). Although there is strong historical evidence to suggest that it was only a small group of leaders who sought Jesus' arrest and crucifixion, Luke's narrative presents this guilt in a communal quality. The point is not to condemn any one subsection of the population, either Jews or adults, but rather to acknowledge a communal complicity among Jesus' disciples. Although all (adults and children) glorify God because of Jesus earlier in the narrative, all (adults and children) also ultimately fall short. Theologically, it is only with such recognition that contemporary disciples can move forward in efforts to continue to proclaim the Gospel despite our own shortcomings (including ageist discrimination that continues to occur in our churches).

112. See Lk 8:34; 15:15–16. Following the suggestion made in chapter 3 that swineherds fall into this same category of simple pastoral workers among whom children would have been prevalent, the role of the foreign swineherds in spreading the news of the exorcism performed by Jesus in 8:34 may also fall into the category of children engaging in proclamation about the Kingdom—doing the work of discipleship.

113. Anecdotally, while staying with a family on a communal farm in Northern Namibia in the winter of 2002, I experienced this reality still at work first hand. During my stay, one of my tasks was to assist (rather ineptly, compared to his prowess) four-year-old Gneo in his daily tasks of herding and milking the family's goats.

114. Hanne Sigismund-Nielsen, "Slave and Lower-Class Roman Children," in *The Oxford Handbook of Childhood and Education in the Classical World*, edited by Judith Grubbs, Tim Parkin, and Roslynne Bell (Oxford: Oxford University Press, 2013) 290.

115. Blake Leyerle, "Children and 'The Child' in Early Christianity," in *The Oxford Handbook of Childhood and Education in the Classical World*, ed. Judith Evans Grubbs, et. al. (Oxford: Oxford University Press, 2013) 562.

116. Jack W. Vancil, "Sheep, Shepherd," in *ABD* 1187.

117. Lena Larsson Lovén and Agnet Strömberg, "Economy," in *A Cultural History of Childhood and Family in Antiquity,* edited by Mary Harlow and Ray Laurence (London: Bloomsbury, 2010) 56.

118. Fitzmyer, *Luke I–IX*, 408–409. Cf. Bovon, *Luke 1,* 87; Johnson, 52; Vancil, 1190.

119. Bovon, *Luke 1,* 86. Cf. Brown, 673; Fitzmyer, *Luke I–IX,* 396; Tannehill, 65.

120. Fitzmyer, *Luke I–IX,* 397.

121. Tannehill, 67.

Chapter 6

(Re)Membering Children, and Through Them, Christ's Church

This project has been one of *remembering*—of looking again at familiar texts and reimagining their meaning(s) through a childist lens. Through a literary critical reading of Luke's gospel account, I have sought to bring out of the shadows children too often forgotten both by contemporary biblical interpreters and perhaps by the Lukan author himself. Grounded in socio-cultural evidence from the first century Mediterranean world, I have demonstrated the prominent place of children both within Greco-Roman households, cities, and agricultural farms and within a Jewish understanding of the household of God. Thus reclaiming a subject-oriented biblical childhood, I have traced the presence of children in Luke's description of Jesus' ministry of restoration, among Jesus' disciples, and finally as disciples themselves. Such remembrance serves to bring children into the light of interpretive study.

Yet, in another, more profound sense, this project has also been one of *membering*—giving flesh and blood to children within, behind, and in front of Luke's gospel account. Through such (re)membering this reading seeks to hear these children back into existence, or perhaps into existence for the first time, as embodied members of the discipleship community that Luke describes and toward which his gospel account points.

This combined act of (re)membering falls within the Christian liturgical tradition of *anamnesis*. Used to describe the liturgical remembering of Christ's death, resurrection, and return, *anamnesis* comes from the Greek noun ἀνάμνησις, which connotes an embodied kind of remembering. The word is used only three times in the New Testament—in Luke's description of the Last Supper, during which Jesus breaks and distributes the bread saying, "This is my body, which is given for you. Do this in remembrance of me [εἰς τὴν ἐμὴν ἀνάμνησιν]" (Lk 22:19); in Paul's description of the same act (1 Cor 11:23–25); and in the book of Hebrews with reference to the material "reminder [ἀνάμνησις] of sin" performed through the act of sacrifice (Heb 10:3). With regards to the Eucharist, *anamnesis* is the way in which Christians across time and place actively engage in and become a part of Christ's body offered and received. Such (re)membrance is an active, embodied response in which an entire person and, indeed, an entire community is engaged. It is the process by which worshipping Christians *become* community.

To (re)member children in Luke's account, therefore, cannot remain a static academic exercise concerned only with children as characters within Luke's text. It must, at the same time, give flesh and bone to the real children behind and in front of these characters. Such an objective must broaden the lens to the (re)member children within the broader Christian community that Paul calls the "Body of Christ" (Rom 12:4–5; 1 Cor 12:12–31) and, through them, the discipleship community as a whole.

(RE)MEMBERING CHILDREN AS A PART OF THE BODY OF CHRIST

Children were not merely *present* in Luke's description of Jesus' early disciples and those for whom he practiced a ministry of restoration—children were a vital part of the singular body that these followers evolved into over the first two generations of Christian witness. Celsus, the first pagan author to write about Christianity, confirms this with his scornful account of Christianity as a religion. Toward the beginning of the second century he writes that Christianity was only attractive to "the foolish, dishonorable and stupid, and only slaves, women, and little children."[1] What Celsus takes as a point of reproach, Paul uplifts a century earlier as a point of distinction. Exhorting the Corinthian congregation against competition among themselves, Paul writes,

> For just as the body is one and has many members, and all the members of the body, though many, are one body, so it is with Christ. . . . Indeed, the body does not consist of one member but of many . . . the members of the body that seem to be weaker are indispensable, and those members of the body that we think less honorable we clothe with greater honor, and our less respectable members are treated with greater respect, whereas our more respectable members do not need this. But God has so arranged the body, giving the greater honor to the inferior member, that there may be no dissension within the body, but the members may have the same care for one another (1 Cor 12:12–25).

This is what it means to practice mutual love. Children, though they held varying degrees of inferior status within the Roman household system, are lifted up among the disciples of Jesus as those treated with equal—even greater—respect and honor as their free male heads.

Luke does not use the same "body" language that Paul does; however, he expresses this relationship of interdependence in the language of "Kingdom" (βασιλεία), or more specifically, the Kingdom of God. Youngmo Cho observes, expressions for the proclamation of God's Kingdom ". . . are used only by Luke among the other New Testament writers and occupy up to one quarter of the total references to the kingdom of God in Luke-Acts. Its proclamation by Jesus and the disciples is the means by which the kingdom of God becomes a present reality."[2] In Luke's gospel, Jesus and his disciples proclaim a Kingdom whose proximity is not primarily a physical reality to be experienced at a later date, but rather is revealed in the present through the Spirit. Jesus explains, "For in fact, the kingdom of God is among you [*entos humon estin*]" (Lk 17:21). Like Luke's metaphor of the body, the Kingdom of God as Luke understands it is relational. It is the living out of the prophetic proclamation of good news for the poor and the restoration of parents to their children. It is manifested in Jesus' concrete ministries of restoration, as seen in the preceding discussion of the lives of the children whom Jesus touched.[3]

At the same time, however, such elevation and restoration is not expressed in Luke's gospel as the mythical "level playing field" of contemporary American culture. To do this would be to obscure all of the ways in which children and other marginalized people in the first century Mediterranean world required support and protection, as well as all of the unique gifts that children bring to the Christian community *as children*. The characters of Mary, John the Baptist, James, and John demonstrate some of the possibilities for such contribution.

True restoration occurs through relationship—the interdependent living of people alongside one another. To this end, Jesus grants children, along with all the marginalized poor, the greatest honor imaginable in his fledgling eschatological movement as Luke describes it—declaring, "it is to such as these that the Kingdom of God belongs" (Lk 18:16; see also 6:20). Children are not only *a* part of the body of Christ—or, in Luke's words, God's Kingdom—children are an *integral* part of it. A childist reading of Luke's gospel opens up the ways in which an awareness of and sensitivity towards children changes the ways in which the community interacts, learns, receives God's word, and expresses praise. Such a reading adds to the growing body of child-centered interpretations of biblical texts demonstrating the weight and value of children in the biblical world and, concomitantly, in contemporary understandings of biblical texts. In the context of Luke's gospel account, children introduce a dialogical and enthusiastic reception of the Kingdom that catapults adults from faith-paralyzing intellectualization and encourages instead active and exuberant *response* to the Word of God—and through it, to one another.

Given the reconstructed place of children within the community that Luke describes for which this project argues, it is worthwhile to (re)member such children not only as characters in a story but also as the physical, embodied people to whom Luke addresses his gospel. Although Luke's gospel has had many diverse audiences across the centuries, I focus for the sake of clarity upon the real children implied by the text who would have been a part of Luke's first century ideal audience and the twenty-first century children whom the gospel continues to address.

Young Children in Luke's Ideal Audience

Up to this point this project has treated the children in Luke's gospel account purely as literary characters. I have sought to reclaim them as characters from adultist interpretations that have read these child characters as static and one-dimensional. Such interpretations find children in Luke's text useful primarily by way of analogy or simply as background or objects to move the story along. In contrast, I argue that both the children mentioned directly and inferred beneath the surface of Luke's text are dynamic characters. These children receive and respond to Jesus' preaching and restoration in dynamic ways. Moreover, they live together with and as disciples both among those sedentary in households and those itinerant disciples who follow Jesus on his way to the cross.

These characters, however, were crafted to speak to a real audience. While such an audience cannot be deciphered from the text, nor assumed to be a solitary unity, it is possible to mine Luke's writing for clues about the intended community or communities that his "most excellent Theophilus" represents (Lk 1:3). Given the widespread presence and acceptance of children in most all corners of life—including the religious—argued for previously, it is hard to imagine that their presence would not also have been assumed in Luke's ideal audience.[4] Even if Luke did not write specifically with children in mind, he would have almost certainly expected that children would, together with their caregivers, receive his account. However, in light of Luke's message of double reversal and use of specialized language and categories of childhood, it is likely that Luke intentionally authored his gospel account with children in mind—at least as a segment of his audience together with adults.

Double Reversal as Attractive to Young Children

Luke's gospel bears a message of hope to those at the margins of society, who, as I have argued, include children. The core of this message is contained in Luke's repeated use of the theme of double reversal. John York, in his book *The Last Shall Be First*, argues persuasively that Luke's narrative is characterized by a succession of bi-polar (double) reversals.[5] Thomas Hoyt points to the Lukan form of the Beatitudes as illustrative of this on account of "antithetical parallelism between blessings and woes (6:24–26) which are unique to Luke: poor/rich; hunger/full; weep/laugh [double reversal]," concluding, "eschatological reversal is more dominant in Luke: Jesus' message was a message of hope for the downtrodden."[6]

Such reversals set up a divine value system in opposition to that of the world, in which the poor and disabled (shamed or shameless) are honored—the first reversal—and those who seek self-aggrandizement are put to shame—the second reversal. Such reversals are first anticipated in Mary's Magnificat (1:46–55),[7] but they continue throughout the narrative.

Within this system of values, York sees Luke's healing narratives as *chronos* enactments of the *kairos* reversals both anticipated and being lived into in Jesus' inauguration of God's Kingdom.[8] Unfortunately, York fails to see the rejection of Jesus' disciples' dismissal in favor of the reception of children in Luke 18:15–17 as a double reversal. However, he does draw out the theme of reversal implicit in Luke's allusion to children in Luke 9, noting that the need to rely upon God for salvation is "solidified by use of the child metaphor" in Luke 9.[9] While I would stretch York's resistance to move beyond the child as metaphor in these texts, what is clear is that both the paradigmatic child stories of Luke 9 and 18, framed as they are within a larger narrative of poverty and wealth, are intertwined in Luke's theme of double reversal.

Furthermore, York's perceptive link between the theme of double reversal and Luke's healing narratives further solidifies the place of children on the positive end of this theme. As already demonstrated, children are enmeshed in Luke's narratives of healing and restoration, and thus are portrayed as already living into the promise of reversal. This, together with the established marginal status of children within the household implicitly connects them with the honor side of Luke's reversals. The Magnificat, referencing the continuity of God's mercy across the generations, assumes such inclusion (1:50).

The inclusion of children on the honored end of Luke's double reversals is seen even earlier in the text when Gabriel announces John's vocation "to turn the hearts of parents to their children" (Lk 1:17). Luke uses the verb ἐπιστρέψαι, meaning literally "to turn, return, or reverse." Moreover, by leaving out the latter half of Malachi's prophecy that "the hearts of children" will also be turned "to their parents" (Mal 4:6), Luke turns what Malachi intends as a single reversal—a leveling of playing fields, in effect—into a *double* reversal in which children are honored by the attention of their parents, while parents are put to shame by the failure to require similar attention from their children in return.

Looking towards the up-building of the entire Kingdom of God, inclusive of all members, however, the end of such reversal for adult disciples cannot simply be to experience shame. I propose that the reversal occurs, rather, in the place of privilege given to each side of the adult/child dyad. In terms of their ability to contribute to the meaning and character of the community, adults must therefore listen seriously to children. Pam Moore, a Christian educator who works closely with children, has chosen to engage in this reversal with regard to what it means to educate all Christians—young and old. As such, she writes of the need to "listen to God with children."[10] She reflects, "When we are attentive to children . . . we see that they take us right to the core truths of the Christian faith. Even though adults are the ones who make the initial proclamation, children get right to what is most essential. The result is mutual blessing."[11] Although Moore's affirmation, written for the sake of her adult audience in this context, falls short in continuing to assume that there are certain immutable truths of the Christian faith—presumably determined by adults—she gets right the truth of the richness of children in their own faith, perception, and interpretation. Such insights are the unique gifts that they bring to their adult counterparts in Christian community when such mutual interaction is permitted to flourish and thrive.

Through liberative readings of Luke's gospel account that take seriously such reversals and begin to imagine how to embody and live them out in God's in-breaking Kingdom, there is sufficient cause for hope. Nevertheless, multiple feminist scholars rightly caution against a naïve application of such hope that assumes the Lukan author always (or even frequently) had such noble intentions in mind.

Illustrating this point with reference to Luke's presumed reversal of the roles of women, Turid Karlsen Seim counters, "Even if Jesus makes a reversal of established value in [the woe to mothers expressed in] 23:28ff . . . this is not determined positively by the relationship to the word or by the all-consuming dominance of discipleship, but by the fact that the turbulence and horror of the coming time of tribulation render normal life impossible."[12] In pronouncing woe on mothers, Luke's Jesus is thus not so much reversing societal expectations and norms that attach status—and even freedom—with childbirth. Rather, he is lamenting for these mothers and for their children as what Karlsen Seim describes as "victims of the catastrophe."[13]

This is an important critique because it cautions against associating contemporary idealist hopes for a message of liberation in Luke's gospel account with the author's likely intent within the confines of his ancient cultural context. François Bovon similarly reminds, "The New Testament itself, by virtue of the meager place it allots children, is a witness to those ancient times that neglected boys and girls and did not think of them except as a mass to shape into their adult state through education and the inculcation of obedience."[14] While I have earlier taken issue with the one-dimensional portrait of ancient treatment of children that Bovon assumes, his overall point, that the New Testament *by itself* is insufficient for the liberation of children, is an important one. Karlsen Seim's analysis also bears out this sense of the necessity of mindful interpretation both with regard to women and, implicitly, their children.

Fortunately, as in any interpretive act, it is impossible to take the New Testament texts *by themselves*. Texts are by their very nature always read, and, as such, interpreted. Moreover, such interpretation is conducted, whether or not the interpreter acknowledges it, with a particular audience and a particular interpretive agenda in mind. Consequently, Karlsen Seim, reading at a time of crucial liberation of (primarily white) women in both the home and the workplace, laments that Luke's Jesus does not separate women from the expectation of childbirth and motherhood in 23:28–31. On the other hand, reading in hope of a nascent liberation of children and childhood in the United States, I read the same text through a different lens.

I concur with Karlsen Seim's assessment that Lk 23:29 does not represent a de facto rejection of child bearing and nursing, but rather a lament of the pain of caring for such vulnerable lives in the midst of crisis and calamity. We differ, however, in that for me such a lament bears a cautious word of hope. The present world, like the first century world before it, wrongly oppresses, marginalizes, and demeans many people for many reasons, including women and children in all their intersectionalities. This is a fact of life; one with which Jesus, on the road to his crucifixion, was painfully aware. This is not news for children, or women, who continue to fall victim to such realities. However, Jesus' lament for, and consequently his naming of such victimization, is a kernel of hope in the midst of the horror.

The first century Roman order celebrated and rewarded the bearing of citizen children as a means of growing and institutionalizing their cultures and value. Jesus, on the other hand, anticipates and shares in their lament of such procreation. Significantly, Jesus is not merely speaking generally in terms of the merits of procreation, but rather addresses himself specifically to the weeping "daughters of Jerusalem" (Lk 23:28)—his own followers, the ones whose children would have presumably similarly built up and institutionalized his teachings. In so doing, he effectively reverses the Roman expectations of mothers and children as cogs in an imperialist machine, acknowledging them instead as hurting persons—victims of that same imperialism.

Was such overt critique of empire intended by the original Lukan author? Did Luke's original audience recognize the content of such critique? These are questions worth pondering; yet, more significantly, it is undeniable that critique of Empire is present in the text. Was Luke specifically thinking about children when he crafted a message of double reversal? Would he have immediately applied emphatic and consistent liberation to children in his own community even if he was? Again, these questions can be debated in perpetuity. Nevertheless, the evidence of children teeming among those at the margins in Luke's context and that of his audience, as well as the links to their consistent up-building throughout Luke's text, suggest that such possibilities should not be ignored. Such interpretations are both plausible and legitimate within Luke's context and lend themselves favorably to an embodied reading of the lives and personhood of children and all people in the communities Luke addresses.

Language and Categories of Childhood

Within such uncertainties, moreover, the narrative structure of Luke's gospel account gives further pause for the consideration of children as an original audience implicitly assumed by the text itself. Luke uses language, characterization, and narrative structure to draw out multiple layers of childhood that might both have appealed to an ancient child audience and have lent complexity to child characters in his account.

Luke uses six independent terms for child or children, in addition to more generic terms such as υἱός (son) and τῶν μικρῶν τούτων (these little ones, Lk 17:2).[15] The richness of this vocabulary, paying attention to particular developmental stages of childhood, suggests that Luke may have had at least a rudimentary sense of the diverse and various moments of childhood and perhaps even the richness and diversity among children themselves. To treat child characters akin to objects, important only in so far as how they cause the other more "developed" characters of the story to respond does not require such sophistication. Rather, Luke's attention to the diverse vocabulary of childhood, while often obscured in English translation, suggests a vibrant and dynamic engagement with children as characters within the account.

Furthermore, while oftentimes child characters in Luke's account may be concealed in the background or treated ostensibly as vehicles to move along the plot, at least several children explicitly emerge as active and dynamic characters. Although children, even more so than women, fall victim to the Lukan author's patriarchal tendency to deprive them of names and speech in the gospel account, a closer look at their characterization reveals dramatic changes and shifts in their characters as a response to Jesus. Such shifts are seen most clearly in the individual children whom Luke describes receiving Jesus' ministries of healing and restoration, discussed in depth in chapter 3.

Perhaps the most dramatic examples are the two children whom Luke describes responding to Jesus' call back to life (Lk 7:11–17; 8:40–56). In response to Jesus' call for them to "get up" (ἐγέρθητι in 7:14; ἔγειρε in 8:54), the status of these children shifts not only in relationship to the narrative but also in relationship both to God and their communities. They are actively restored to participation and included in the family of God. They morph from inactive, unable even to request help for themselves, to active, responding *immediately* to the call and command of Jesus. Similarly, after Jesus' healing of a young slave (7:1–10) and expulsion of a demon from a boy (9:37–45), both these children are restored to and reaffirmed in their place in God's Kingdom.

The parable of two brothers and their experience of forgiveness (15:11–32), however, is the most dynamic example of the characterization of children in Luke's gospel account. Within this short story, Luke utilizes both static and dynamic child characters—the former in the case of the slave child who relays message of the father's actions and the latter in the case of the two brothers. The younger brother who is, together with his father, one of the two primary actors in this parable, begins as an entitled and demanding son (15:12). Through his experiences of both surplus and hardship, he shifts first to a disposition of repentance (15:13–19). Finally, following his unexpectedly warm restoration by his father, the boy's character shifts again to an experience of full restoration in his father's household (15:24). The elder brother's change and subsequent restoration to relationship remains a gap for the reader to choose whether or not to fill in (15:31–32).

This dynamism, centered on the two brothers, is in sharp contrast to the static role of the father as a loving and forgiving constant in the story. God does not change in God's relationship to humanity. However, in response to God's entry into humanity and restorative healings, blessings, and reversals through Jesus, God calls humanity to change and return to God. This is the consequence of the in-breaking of God's Kingdom in Luke's gospel account, and it is experienced as profoundly by Luke's child characters as it is by the adults. Through these characters, children in Luke's audience are being called, together with adults, to respond to Jesus.

Finally, the narrative structure, particularly of Luke's prologue, suggests at least some possible attention to children in an ideal audience. Scholars have noted similarities between the Lukan prologue and ancient biographies or hero stories. The Lukan prologue shares with this genre a concern for noble origins of a respected figure; however, it is here that the similarities end. In contrast to such biographies, more similar in this regard to the non-canonical account of Jesus' childhood recorded in *The Infancy Gospel of Thomas*, the child Jesus in Luke's prologue does not perform any miraculous deeds.[16]

Tony Chartrand-Burke contends that in ancient biographies, "The primary purpose behind childhood tales of great men (common throughout the world) is to foreshadow the adult career of their protagonist."[17] To this end, child characters in ancient biography, whose intended audience seems to be primarily adults concerned with the enduring character of great figures in history, are relatively static. In contrast, Luke describes both the child Jesus and the child John as growing and gaining in strength of spirit, wisdom, and divine and human favor respectively (Lk 1:80; 2:40; 2:52).

Although Luke recognizes the special character of these children as distinct from ordinary children, he does not portray them as simply miniaturized versions of the men that the narrative knows them to have become. Rather, as these children grow in years and physical capacity, this is matched by shifts in their spirit, wisdom, and relationships. Neither does Luke portray John and Jesus in their childhoods as embryonic forms of the same men later in the narrative, patiently developing until they reach a point that they can fulfill their divine potential.

Both children are celebrated *already* as bringing God's promises to fulfillment both in utero and when they are newly born.[18] However, the way in which they fulfill God's promise as children in Luke's account is *distinct* from the ways in which they continue to fulfill the same promises as adults. This change—I avoid the word development in order not to assume that one moment of Jesus' ministry is superior to another—in Jesus' character over the course of his lifetime is reflected in his ministry with relation to the Temple.

As an infant, Jesus acts to bring about the fulfillment of God's promise in the Temple through receiving the embrace of Simeon and Anna (Lk 2:25–38). Jesus' ministry at this moment in Luke's narrative is one of presence, granting peace in a way that cradled infants are uniquely able to do. As an adolescent child, when Jesus returns to the Temple his ministry is one of listening, answering, and being listened to. He engages in a two-way dialogue with the teachers at the Temple that is mutually beneficial and reveals in a new way the in breaking of the Kingdom of God (2:41–51). Lastly, as an adult, Jesus enters the Temple with a new sense of authority, driving out those who were selling things there and proclaiming God's Kingdom (19:45–48).

In antiquity, there was no sharp distinction between adult and child audiences. Reidar Aasgaard explains, "The generations lived closely together and cultural traditions were handed over in multi-age settings, in which stories would float back and forth being transformed in the process."[19] Nevertheless, Aasgaard argues persuasively that within this context there were certain tales exchanged with the interests of children in the audience particularly in mind—much as families have engaged in the telling of fairy tales in more recent times. In light of this tradition, Aasgaard suggests that the *Infancy Gospel of Thomas* "can offer a special glimpse into ancient child pedagogy, and in particular into how early Christian communities communicated religious beliefs to their children."[20] Aasgaard bases this claim on a number of literary elements in the *Infancy Gospel of Thomas* that correspond to ancient stories directed at children. These include, among others, content, chronology, characters, and theology expressed in the text.

Although I concur with Aasgaard that the *Infancy Gospel of Thomas* contains more content and form directed explicitly at children, applying some of his same criteria can suggest at least a peripheral attention to children in the audience of Luke's gospel account as well. Theologically, this already begins to occur through Luke's emphasis on double reversal, with a preference for the poor and marginalized—including children. The focus of content, chronology, and characterization can be seen particularly in chapters 1 and 2 of Luke's gospel account—the materials typically identified as the prologue, but which I have argued are integral to the narrative as a whole.

First, with regard to content, Luke's prologue pays attention to the child heroes it portrays *as* children. Although Luke's account moves on from the childhoods of John and Jesus to narrate their adult lives and ministries, it does so not in the sense of a traditional *puer senex* novella that portrays these characters as static throughout their development, but rather with attention to the unique characteristics of each character as a child, as illustrated above. Through Luke's attention to the unique moments of childhood and to the lived experience of the heroes of his narrative account *as children* rather than miniature adults, his account may well have been uniquely appealing to children from among the canonical gospels. By thus presenting the two main characters of his narrative in ways that are, over the course of the story, relatable to both children and adults, Luke seems to assume a broad audience that includes both groups.

Similarly, Luke's attention to the development of these two characters in particular shows an astute regard for chronology that adheres well to general ancient concepts of the socialization and growth of children. The narrative begins with John described in utero as τὸ βρέφος (the infant, Lk 1:41, 44); this same term is used to describe Jesus when he is first born (Lk 2:12, 16). Shortly after birth, following each child's official acceptance into his respective father's family, the language shifts from that of neonate to child (τὸ παιδίον).

For John, this acceptance is first voiced by the narrator and his father Zechariah on the eighth day after his birth in conjunction with his ritual naming and circumcision (Lk 1:59, 66, 76), thus following Jewish custom. For Jesus, this custom is broken by the narrator who describes Jesus as τὸ παιδίον shortly after his birth, connecting this developmental shift not with his circumcision (an earthly rite), but rather with the shepherds' confirmation of the divine inclusion of Jesus as the heavenly child proclaimed to them by the angels—messengers of his heavenly father (Lk 2:17; see also 1:32). The same language is then applied consistently with regard to both characters throughout the prologue, finally with reference to their childhood growth (Lk 1:80; 2:40), until Luke resumes narration with them as adults.

Likewise, Luke applies similar vocabulary to babies and young children whom Jesus encounters in his adult ministry. Although Luke does not use the intermediary terms (such as νεανίσκος) to describe the stage between young childhood and adulthood with relation to Jesus or John, he does so with regard to youth whom Jesus encounters in his ministry. Such attention to the nuances of childhood suggests both an awareness by the Lukan author of real children as well as an application of this awareness to his narrative in such a way that would be likely to resonate with children across the developmental spectrum described.

Next, with regard to characters, Luke's gospel concedes a steady presence of children both implicitly and explicitly throughout the narrative. Such a presence, while bolstered by Luke's unique attention to the childhoods of John and Jesus, does not end there. Rather, Luke's Jesus receives, addresses, and heals children throughout the narrative account. Even when the pace of the narrative picks up and the scope narrows as Jesus approaches the cross, Luke describes Jesus pausing before the women of Jerusalem, lamenting with them the turmoil that remains for them and for their children (23:28).

Luke's picture of discipleship is not always an easy one for children to be involved in, but it remains consistently inclusive of them nonetheless. Indeed, children in antiquity were not afforded the luxury of protection from the harsh realities of life. As such, an expectation that discipleship must be easy for children is as misplaced as is the assumption that discipleship must be easy for adults. Rather, the focus, for good and for ill, is on the mutual inclusion of all members of God's family as a part of the body of Christ that comes to be known as the Christian Church.

Young Children in Luke's Contemporary Audience

Adults and children in the first century Mediterranean world make up only a small portion of the gospel's audience when one considers that Luke's account has been passed on as Scripture in Christian communities ever since. Regardless of whether or not one accepts the presence of children in Luke's first ideal audience, since their initial reception of the text (if it was ever received as such), this gospel account has been passed across continents and centuries. As such, it has come to reach a diversity of audiences beyond what its original author could have wildly imagined. This audience, of which contemporary Christians are a part, continues to receive and appropriate the gospel narrative according to our cultures, circumstances, and ethical dispositions.

In light of the place of children among Jesus' first disciples, I contend that contemporary children are also, or at least *should be*, a part of this expanded audience. Moreover, returning to chapter 1's discussion of the broad language for and various definitions of children and childhood both in ancient and contemporary terms, I contend that *all* contemporary children—including infants and the very young—ought to be treated as a part of this gospel audience.

The fact that children are not, and have not been, universally assumed to be a part of Luke's contemporary audience can be seen in trends such as "children's bibles" and "children's church," which began with the invention of the printing press and have proliferated throughout modernity.[21] While the purposes of these practices and publications are multitudinous, they represent, at least in part, a general anxiety among Christian adults that the text (both written and spoken) of canonical Scripture should not be received directly by children. As such, a question that must be answered before proposing an audience of contemporary children for Luke's gospel account is, "Can Luke's gospel account speak directly to children today?"

The practice of recording simplified versions of favorite Bible stories as devotional literature for "the young and simple" dates back to before the Protestant Reformation.[22] These texts have shaped the religious imagination of generations of Christians, often serving in the not so distant past as both a religious and secular grammar, as children learned to read and write from their pages. Their appeal exists both in their narrative simplicity and in their engaging illustrations. However, as reception critic Ruth Bottigheimer astutely notes, whereas the meaning in Bible stories remain "'open' texts," subject to interpretation, Children's Bibles and similar devotional literature, in both their text and illustrations, involve "choice and affirmation of particular interpretations of an inherently polysemic text."[23] Such texts do the work of interpretation for their audience.

In contrast, recent work on the religious capacity and vocations of children suggests that children are both capable of and benefited by engaging in their own interpretations of polysemic biblical texts. Although there may be certain portions of the narratives better reserved for devotional focus until particular moments in a child's development, exposure to narratives within the biblical texts themselves, with all their meaning potential, allow children to engage with the texts most deeply. Sofia Cavalletti's international catechesis program, developed for children from age 3 to 12 based entirely on her translations of the Greek and Hebrew scriptures, gives children the space to hear and respond to actual biblical texts. She contends that such a presentation of Scripture together with the space and respect for the child's own interpretation responds "to the child's silent request: 'Help me to come closer to God by myself.'"[24]

Cavalletti's religious education program titled *Catechesis of the Good Shepherd* is aimed at cultivating wonder and excitement in the youngest child as he or she experiences God. Selected Bible stories are explicitly "presented" rather than "taught" with the goal of giving each child the space to creatively interact with God, through the biblical text and accompanying devotional materials, and to ponder God's presence in their lives. Such an encounter necessarily relies on adults, or older children, as presenters in order to pass on the communal stories and faith that younger children have not yet had the opportunity to hear. However, at the same time, it encourages children to ask their own questions and come to their own realizations about God and their spirituality—to develop in children the capacity for what Paulo Freire calls "moral courage,"[25] the ability to critically assess and respond to a situation from one's own being in contrast to acting according to a pre-defined moral compass.

Consequently, it is not only possible to conceive of contemporary children as an audience of Luke's gospel account, but to do otherwise would be to deprive children of a great encounter with God as God reveals God's self through their reading of the text as Scripture. One catechist of young children describes the process of hearing and internalizing the words of the ancient Scriptures for a young child as "learning our church's secret handshake"—an exercise of inclusion in which many young children across a variety of contexts are eager to engage.[26] Adults are not the only ones revealing secrets in this exchange, though. Through the multifaceted experiences and emotions that children uniquely bring to these texts, like Mary at the feet of Jesus, they alter the conversation entirely, bringing new insights to the adults who present the stories and helping adults to learn the stories anew. Sometimes exchange brings about entirely new revelation, sometimes it changes the character of the reading, sometimes it stirs a new way of thinking, and sometimes, as described again by Moore in another experience engaging in dialogic learning with primary grade children, a child may simply ask the adult, "Can we read more?"[27] This quest for more—this hunger and passion for that which nourishes us together in community—is but one of the many gifts that such mutual relationship entails.

Given the power of such dynamic interchange when adults and children together engage in mutual learning of Christian sacred texts, I am convinced that explicitly child-centered materials should not replace the primary role of Scripture, including Luke's gospel account, as a proclamation of the Word of God for all Christians—adults and children—to hear and do.[28] Marcia J. Bunge, editor of both *The Child in the Bible* and *The Child in Christian Thought* summarizes this theological perspective: "Christian understandings of children . . . could all be strengthened by . . . developing theological conceptions of children that acknowledge: their strengths and gifts as well as their vulnerabilities and needs; their full humanity as well as their need for guidance; and their spiritual wisdom as well as their growing moral capacities."[29]

Moreover, given the experiential quality of liberative education, to deprive children from encountering these texts and communally lived expressions of them in Christian worship is equally dangerous. To this end, Cavalletti's pedagogy is set up to present Scriptural texts alongside liturgical action in the Christian Education environment. However, in order to follow Freire's proposal for freedom, even this does not go far enough. Children learn what it is to be the community of Christ—and indeed, adults learn it too—by *being* this community together in all the aspects that such community entails. This means that there is something unique about experiencing the words of Luke's gospel read in a communal worship setting among children that does not exist when all of the community's children are sent away to the nursery or a separate children's church (and that, likewise, would not exist for children in such settings apart from adults). Such accommodation may require in many contemporary churches substantial revisioning and reworking of how such worship is engaged; however, to do so is necessary in order to take seriously the mutually interdependent relationship disciples enter into with one another.

Such changes are important and ethically necessary because to exclude children from the reception of Luke's gospel account as a core piece of our faith heritage in these ways fails to take seriously their full humanity and, indeed, their full participation in the divinity revealed to the Christian community through Scripture. To exclude children from the liturgical service of the same community based on these Scriptures is equally, if not more, dangerous. Such exclusions effectively dismember them from the body of Christ. By taking seriously the place and role of children both as disciples in these Scripture texts and as disciples receiving these texts, a childist reading presents the possibility of (re)membering children into this body as Luke's narrative clearly places them as possessors of the Kingdom of God.

(RE)MEMBERING THE BODY OF CHRIST IN LIGHT OF CHILDREN

Childist interpretation, alongside other ideological approaches to the biblical texts, carries the concomitant goal of the liberation of the oppressed and through them the oppressor. In the case of childist readings, this means that the liberation of children through a close reading of their presence and participation in the text opens up space for the liberation of all wo/men to be freed from the oppressive structures of adultism that limit the understanding and implementation of discipleship. The preceding reading of Luke's gospel account only holds value in so much as it is able to accomplish both tasks. Having established the presence of children and adults together in Luke's audience(s) both in antiquity and present day, the final turn considers the impact of a childist reading on the larger Kingdom communities embodied in

Christ. Such communities, when understood through a child-centered reading of Luke's gospel account, embody a certain interdependence, which, while perhaps more necessary in an ancient Mediterranean context, remains valuable for a reconceptualization of the contemporary Christian family.

Young Children as Interdependent Agents

The first inclination of a liberative reading for any minoritized group is often to assert the independence and self-agency of the members in that group. Children are unique in this regard in that they (particularly at the youngest end of the spectrum) are often incapable of fully exercising this independence on their own. As a result, the United Nations' *Convention on the Rights of the Child* affirms the protection of basic human rights for children alongside rights of protection from abuse and exploitation.[30] To this end, John Wall observes, "The task of transforming social norms through the lens of children's experience 'is already under way'. . . . The clearest example can be found in studies of children's citizenship, where some now argue for a 'children-sized citizenship' based on the idea of broad human interdependence instead of on the idea of adult autonomy."[31] Children are at the same time intensely independent and capable of acting for themselves from a very young age and intensely dependent and in need of protection. Wall and others engaged in Childhood Studies and the vocation of childhood, however, argue that such a dual relation with the world is not a hindrance, but rather a great asset that children bring to intergenerational communities.

The unique characteristics of childhood open children up to a unique experience of the world—one from which both children and the adults who engage with them can benefit immensely. Quoting theologian of childhood David Jensen's definition of vulnerability as living "on the edge, open to the world's profound beauty and its threatening violence,"[32] Bonnie Miller McLemore contends, "In a sense, children and aging adults both 'live on the edge' of life, more exposed than others to its precariousness and perils."[33] Such exposure opens children up to vulnerability but also to beauty. It requires of the adult both protective diligence and respectful attentiveness.

As such, when considering what it means to liberate children, Duanne advocates for a position of *inter*dependence. She posits, "Rather than arguing for moving children over to the empowered side of the equation, childhood studies offers new ways of engaging interdependence as a social reality and offers new frameworks for thinking about how to negotiate the obligations incurred across the very real gaps of power that do, and will, exist."[34] Children are in need of the respect of both their self-agency and their vulnerability.

Indeed, this is characteristic of *all* humans—it is simply most intensely witnessed in the persons of the very young. Duanne further explains:

> Foucault's now-classic assertion that subjects are created through power acting on and through them and Judith Butler's argument that identity—particularly gendered identity—is created through performance are just two of the revolutions in thought that reveal the extent to which we are all humans-in-the-making, perpetually in flux, continually responding to authoritative forces beyond our own minds and bodies. There's arguably no better way to understand this form of subjectivity than through the child, a term often used uncritically as a placeholder for the dependence and malleability we still seek to partition off from adult autonomy. Rather than denying the child's fragility, we insist that bringing a critical eye to childhood will teach us to better conceive of a realistic human subject.[35]

It is at this point of constant malleability that stage theories of development fall short.

Theorists of child development such as Jean Piaget or of child spiritual development like James Fowler present helpful paradigms to identify moments and types of engagement in a child's life. However, by naming these moments as stages they create the illusion of a linear progressive model of human and, specifically, Christian life that does not match up completely with lived experience, and even less with such experience as lived in the Christian notion of *kairos* time.[36] Miller-McLemore laments, "Stage theory tends to value where one is headed more than what one leaves behind. One result of this Christian inheritance today is a continued struggle to regard children as active participants in and contributors to the Christian life, a problem that resurfaces when we start talking about vocation."[37]

In contrast, Miller-McLemore suggests "a Christian view of childhood" that is not bound to the constraints of *chronos* time. She writes, "Children have a vocation grounded in God's own childhood that is as essential to Christian life, if not more so, than our purpose as adults. Their task or 'claim upon us all' that we must help the child perform is to help us become the children we began to be in our own childhood, again *not* metaphorically but in reality. For in childhood, our 'first intimations of God are attained.'"[38] Such attainment involves not only the reclamation of the liminal, "edge" existence that Jensen describes, but indeed, a rebalancing of both power and relationships in line with the *interdependence* that full life in God's Kingdom entails.

Duanne observes, "By engaging the liminality of childhood, we are pushed to a more nuanced understanding of and engagement with dependence and the way such dependence can generate unequal distributions of power."[39] Instead of seeing children as deficient adults, waiting to reach an imagined nadir point of full humanity, a childist reading of Luke's text demands respect for the full humanity of both children and adults at *whatever* moment or context of life they might find themselves. To do this, however, means encountering the uncomfortable power dynamic that accompanies typical adult-child relationships in contemporary Western culture, whereby typical adults believe that by pandering to children as lesser humans we are doing them a charitable service when, in fact, such actions are often more honestly concerned with exerting adult power over children.

Such power dynamics have existed across history, and to some extent are necessitated by the vulnerability and dependency of children named previously. Nevertheless, they have become more dangerous in contemporary Western cultures such as the United States, which to date remains the only member nation of the United Nations to refuse to pass the *UN Convention on the Rights of the Child*. Social commentator Karen Attiah suggests that the United States' reluctance to pass this international convention is in part due to an adult-centered desire to protect parents and legal guardians against perceived violations of their dogged control of the children in their care.[40] To (re)member children and their rights within the context of such an individualistic culture threatens individualism at its core. To own the unnamed oppression of children in the midst of a society that celebrates its protections of freedoms is to call into question both what it means to be free and what it means to be human. It is to acknowledge, against the grain of American individualist culture, that freedom can exist within relationships of mutual dependency and that all humans are, to some degree, interdependent and in relationship with one another.

Interdependence in the Ancient and Contemporary Family

The ancient Mediterranean family, while it was heavily entrenched in uneven power dynamics brought on by the structures of the Roman household, nevertheless understood human interdependency in a way that Western history too easily forgets. Susan Dixon suggests, "The evidence surely indicates that [early Roman] children were indeed viewed as different from adults and valued for these differences, as well as for the functions they could perform within the family in maintaining the name, the religious rites, the general concept of community, the family property, and so on."[41] Marilou Ibita and Reimund Bieringer label this an "intergenerational interdependent cycle."[42] Similarly, writing on the ancient Hebrew family, with whom it has been previously established that first century Palestinians retained many similar ties, Laurel Koepf-Taylor concludes, "The ancient family would have been far more likely to be interdependent, with each member of the ancient family depending upon the subsistence activities of the others. This familial interdependence lies behind the motivations described in the ancestral and other narratives, as well as the exilic and postexilic rhetoric of (in)fertility."[43] In short, given the realities of ancient subsistence, agricultural, and even small town environments, families *needed* one another across the generations in ways that are foreign to the typical 1¼ generation families in America and parts of Western Europe today.

To compensate for this shift in perceived need for children, families in the industrialized world pride themselves, almost to a fault, on the degree of care shown to children. Nonetheless, the same families rarely take seriously the contribution that such children make to the family themselves. While such behavior may seem consistent with generationally isolated families in the West, even contemporary Eastern families, which do better at honoring the elder generation too often fail to celebrate the contributions of young children to the well-being of the household. A typical Japanese family living with three generations under their roof is more likely to uplift the contribution of the elder grandparents in caring for the non-adult children while their parents work, but still frequently misses the gifts that this youngest generation themselves bring to the household. By failing to acknowledge (or give place for) the contributions of children in the household, contemporary parents and caregivers often portray their roles as sacrificial. Feminist theologian Christine E. Gudorf warns that such a portrait of family life ultimately "serves as ideological support for patriarchy . . . by pedestalizing women and children as innocent and good and therefore in need of protection by husbands and fathers."[44] Freedom is only freedom for those whom the ideology recognizes as fully human and thus, deserving such freedom. While protections, especially for children, remain necessary and valid, the role of children in the contemporary family need not be as the object of protection alone. Within contemporary Christian households in particular, a childist reading of Luke's gospel account reveals not only the opportunity, but the imperative, to take seriously children as independent proprietors of the Kingdom of God. From a religious perspective, and, I would argue a great number of other perspectives as well, children bring their own power and resources to bear in the economy of the household.

When the contributions of children are overlooked, the loss, moreover, is not just for children and women alone, but for all people. While a child's rights are the ones most immediately violated, an adult, by centering their purpose solely internally with disregard for their child as "other" misses valuable opportunities for both growth and connection. To this end, Gudorf a mother of three, two of whom are developmentally disabled, reflects on the disjunction between the perceived sacrificial nature of parenting and the fact that "so many people universally desire it and find it a joyful and life-enriching experience," concluding that parenting brings with it its own rewards.[45] Miller-McLemore adds, "Children form adults in countless ways . . . They compel us to move at a difference pace . . . remind adults about life's limits and mortality . . . they remind us of the significance of bodily care . . . Children also form people in larger communities."[46]

Children are not simply the next generation whom society is obliged to propel forward and protect, they are a part of *this* generation, moving and being in a world and in communities in which they are vitally a part. (Re)membering children in Luke's community thus opens the possibility not only of envisioning an ancient body of people differently than scholarship has tended to depict them in the past, but also of *embodying* a different way of life for contemporary families and communities that takes seriously the bodies of *all* persons in our midst.

Adults (Re)membered Through Interdependency with Children

The gains for children in such a practice of (re)membering by this point might seem obvious; however, what is the experience for everyone else? Although Luke sets the stakes for discipleship high and elevates the position of the marginalized within the Kingdom through a series of double reversals, the gospel account continues to paint God's Kingdom as an expansive and inclusive place. Luke's Jesus says, "What is impossible for mortals is possible for God" (Lk 18:29). As a result, although the Kingdom *belongs* to those who are poor and who are children, there remains a place in Luke's conception of it even for rich adults, although to claim their place requires reconfiguring their relationship with the world and one another—the content, I suggest, that lies behind Luke's unique series of woes (Lk 6:24–26).

At the core of this reconfiguration is acceptance of the reality that everyone in God's Kingdom is interdependent. Whether or not it was ever a historical actuality, this is the concept that lies behind the idealized community of common goods that the Lukan author describes in Acts 2:43–47. However, where this community is often misinterpreted is in the assumption that, because they "had all things in common" (Acts 2:44), these early Christians engaged in a community of complete equality whereby the same expectations and protections were assumed of everyone. Reading Luke's texts through the lens of children shines light on the deficiency of such a model.

Commenting on Jesus' exhortation to be like little children in Matthew's Gospel, Warren Carter affirms, "As children, disciples participate in an egalitarian, not hierarchical, way of life. . . . Disciples are called to a permanently transitional existence of dependency on God the Father until Jesus returns."[47] Carter thus notes, importantly, the shift in the power differential in the synoptic picture of the emerging church as "family." Within this fictive household, the role of patriarch does not fall upon any single member but rather upon God. Such an organizational shift, indeed, rebalances the power differentials in this new household.

However, the consideration of actual children (παιδίας) among the broader body of children (τέκνα) of whom God is Father does not allow a purely even distribution of power and control. A childist reading also compels Christians to take seriously the whole community as siblings, even across generational and other differences as they intersect. In light of the dependence that such realities demand of brothers and sisters, particularly the youngest, the way in which the Body of Christ lives out such relationship in the contemporary world often means relying on communities of support—such as the family, or new "fictive family" that the Christian community provides, which must thus be re-visioned.

(Re)membering children into the body of Christ makes clear the insufficiency of terms like "egalitarian" in defining Christian existence. Rather, Christians are called to care for one another in the midst of our diversity. Carter begins to acknowledge this shift when he concludes, "This metaphor [of disciples as children] views dependence differently. Over against the societal emphasis that urges children to leave behind their dependency and weakness to become adults, this metaphor creates an anti-structure existence in which dependency is a norm for disciples."[48] (Re)membering children into the body means reconsidering the entire way adults have tended to think about the body—and, indeed, ourselves.

In families, the workload and return on it are rarely distributed equally. Neither, however, at least in a well-functioning family, do certain members give over their rights in favor of the absolute power of another. This would be a sign of unhealthy codependency. Rather, there is a time and a season for each person's participation in the family life. This is what the apostle Paul describes through the metaphor of the body: "For as in one body we have many members, and not all the members have the same function, so we, who are many, are one body in Christ, and individually we are members one of another" (Rom 12:4–5). This is the interdependency that a childist reading draws out of Luke's gospel account. As members of one body—citizens of one Kingdom—Christians, indeed all of humanity, need one another.

Appropriately, it is those to whom the Kingdom belongs—those who are children and those who are impoverished—who help us to notice and live into this reality of interdependence. John Wall observes, "Childism suggests that there are flaws in contemporary conceptualizations of ethical love . . . children require a certain superabundant regard which . . . contains a fundamental element of decentering self-excess . . . [but] children are not merely recipients, but active givers of love themselves."[49] By living into the decentering that regard for children necessarily entails, such a reading not only (re)members the place of children within the larger body, but, in fact, makes the body whole. By extension, (re)membering the children in their midst makes each adult whole as an individual member of the collective body. By including children in their understanding of discipleship, adult disciples can come to experience power and relationships in a more holistic form.

J. M. Francis writes, "The literal and metaphorical role of children and childhood in the New Testament has much to tell us of the role of power in this particular context where so much of who we are is shaped and fashioned, and where our imaging of the divine is also formed."[50] Reading through a childist lens, all power—even God's power—is transformed to be seen no longer as a privilege to be exerted over another, but rather as a tool to be used for the care of one another. Living into such a norm requires a radical restructuring of expectations but offers the radical promise of liberation to all wo/men who take seriously the full humanity of one another—regardless of any physical, mental, or emotional distinctions, including chronological age.

CONCLUSION: AN INVITATION TO (RE)IMAGINATION

Childist readings of Scripture in general illustrated by a childist reading of Luke's gospel in particular, hold great potential for (re)membering both children and adults into God's Kingdom, calling followers of Jesus to accept and affirm the full humanity of all of God's children. To holistically embody God's Kingdom in the way that such a reading demands is both an exciting and daunting prospect. It involves not only a new way of *reading* written texts, such as Luke, but a new way of *living into* the multiple texts and contexts that define us and our identities as disciples of Christ. A project such as this one is only a small beginning to such a radical reorientation of both Christian and family life. The (re)membering of the Church cannot happen through one, or even several, new readings of scripture. It takes time and requires an openness to both (re)imagine our relationships with and engagement with one another as "other" and yet, as intimately, intertwined.

Appropriately, while *(re)imagination* is the final step in Schüssler Fiorenza's rhetorical emancipatory paradigm, *imagination* is one of the most celebrated characteristics of childhood in contemporary Western culture. A (re)imagining of how to live into God's Kingdom in light of a childist reading of Luke's gospel, therefore, invites adult scholars to make room for children in this process. Adult readers must take seriously the generative energy, engagement, and creativity with which children of all ages approach Luke's text. Adults must accept their invitation for us to listen and, at the same time, invite children into our conversations.

Unfortunately, such dynamic engagement with the full expression of the Church as Christian body has not been possible in the confines of this project, which has necessarily engaged largely in a setting of the scene. The obvious pitfalls of any such interpretive endeavor, such as childist criticism, is the compulsion both to continually defend its own existence and, as a result, to engage in sweeping, generalized overviews in order to trace larger trends. Such justification is the first step towards a holistic engagement together as a (re)membered Kingdom body, but it cannot be the last.

By engaging Luke's gospel account in its particularities, I have sought to both refine and narrow the scope of my project. Nevertheless, I am aware that the length of Luke's gospel itself and the range of child characters within it still require much generalization. As such, it remains to delve deeper, taking into account more explicitly the diversity of childhoods, both ancient and modern—particularly among the most marginalized, such as slave children. I am confident that such explorations will yield even more specific applications for children across the contemporary world who continue to be marginalized and oppressed. I therefore call upon the academy to widen the table to invite such voices into the conversation.

In the meantime, the preceeding reading of Luke's gospel invites (re) imagination. Through engagement with child characters in Luke's account and a vision for these characters within the broader discipleship and Kingdom community, this project sets forth an agenda of promise and hope both lived out in Luke's narrative world and the contemporary Christian world into which it is now received. Acknowledging the value, both for children and adults, of engaging God's Kingdom with an awareness of our shared humanity, fully embodied from the youngest to the oldest amongst us, I invite us to be vulnerable to one another. Such vulnerability, in the way of a child, ought not be forced or feigned. It is, rather, a true acknowledgment of the ways in which human beings continually rely upon, indeed *depend,* upon one another in ways we rarely admit or often notice.

To take seriously the place of a child in our midst and, indeed, our own place as children in the Kingdom of God, "complicates," as Duanne notes, "how we process knowledge about the human subject."[51] It means acknowledging that, while children may require adults to write critical essays on the role of children in the Bible, adults also require children to engage our minds and imaginations to consider hitherto unthought-of ways of reading both the texts of the Bible and the texts of our lives. It means inviting children into the fabric of our lives, not only in a personal sense of love and affection, but in the full sense of giving power over to another in order to learn from them.

In her list of "best practices" for doing theology for and with children, Bunge incisively suggests, "The more we can keep in mind and hold in tension the many paradoxical strengths and vulnerabilities of children expressed in the Bible and the Christian tradition, the more likely we are to learn from children, to carry out our many obligations to them, and to enrich our understanding of children and of child-adult relationships."[52] In this way, through my survey of the inclusion, participation, and power of children witnessed to in Luke's gospel account, I conclude with an invitation to listen—to reorient adult-child relationships in families, religious communities, and, more broadly, to take seriously the interdependence of adults and children upon one another both as human beings and disciples in a common *koinonia*.

Sharon Warkentin Short observes, "The greatest test for a fully humanized society is the degree to which it welcomes the innovative participation of the least within it."[53] When contemporary Christians begin to live into such reversals of power, (re)imagining relationships with one another through the eyes and experiences of those children in our midst, God's Kingdom reveals itself among us. In the words of Jesus as he dined at the table with his disciples—the young and the old, our Christian celebration of community commands us: "Do this in remembrance of me" (Lk 22:19; 1 Cor 11:24).

NOTES

1. Cited in Wayne A. Meeks, *The First Urban Christians: The Social World of the Apostle Paul* (New Haven: Yale University Press, 1983) 53.
2. Youngmo Cho, *Spirit and Kingdom in the Writings of Luke and Paul* (Waynesboro, GA: Paternoster, 2005) 171.
3. See chapter 3.
4. See chapter 2.
5. Contra Joel B. Green, *The Gospel of Luke* (Grand Rapids, MI: Eerdmans, 1997) 59–60; 650.
6. Thomas Hoyt Jr., "The Poor/Rich Theme in the Beatitudes" in *Journal Of Religious Thought* 37:1 (March 1, 1980) 31–41.
7. See Green, *Gospel of Luke,* 59–60.
8. John O. York, *The Last Shall Be First: The Rhetoric of Reversal in Luke* (Sheffield: Sheffield Academic, 1991) 166.
9. York, 154–155. See also York, 102; 170; 171 fn 3; 185 fn 2.
10. Pam Moore, *Taste and See: Savoring the Child's Wisdom* (Chicago: Liturgy Training Publications, 2011) 1.
11. Moore, 1.
12. Turid Karlsen Seim, *The Double Message: Patterns of Gender in Luke-Acts* (Nashville: Abingdon, 1994) 206.
13. Karlsen Seim, *The Double Message,* 207.

14. François Bovon, *Luke 2*, translated by Donald S. Deer (Minneapolis: Fortress Press, 2013) 559.

15. See chapter 1 for a more thorough discussion of Luke's vocabulary for childhood including: βρέφος, παιδίον, παιδίος, νεανίσκος, τέκνον, and παρθένος.

16. Tony [Chartrand] Burke argues that *IGT* should be considered a part of the ancient biography genre of literature on this account (Tony Burke, "'Social Viewing' of Children in the Childhood Stories of Jesus," in *Children in late ancient Christianity*, Cornelia Horn and Robert Phenix, ed. [Tübingen: Mohr Siebeck, 2009] 29–43); however, I find Reidar Aasgaard's conclusion that *IGT* represents a unique genre not so easily collapsible into the categories of ancient biography more persuasive (Reidar Aasgaard, *The Childhood of Jesus: Decoding the Apocryphal Infancy Gospel of Thomas* [Eugene, OR: Cascade Books, 2009] 49–50).

17. Tony Chartrand-Burke, "The Infancy Gospel of Thomas," in *Non-canonical Gospels* (London: T&T Clark, 2008) 134. Cf. also Childhood and Personality in Greek Literature, in *Characterization and Individuality in Greek Literature* (Oxford: Clarendon Press, 1990) 235–240.

18. See Lk 1:15–17; 24–25, 42–45, 46–55, 67–79; 2:10–14; 2:28–32.

19. Aasgaard, 196.

20. Aasgaard, 212.

21. Ruth Bottigheimer traces the origins of collections of Bible stories written specifically for children to the beginnings of the printing press, with Peter Comestor's *Historia Scholastica* (fifteenth century) and Martin Luther's *Passional* (sixteenth century). See Ruth Bottigheimer, *The Bible for Children: From the Age of Guttenberg to the Present* (New Haven: Yale University Press, 1996) 14–37.

22. Bottigheimer, 12.

23. Bottigheimer, 57.

24. Sofia Cavalletti, *The Religious Potential of the Child*, trans. Patricia M. Coulter and Julie M. Coulter (Chicago: Catechesis of the Good Shepherd Publications, 1992) 45.

25. Paulo Freire, *Pedagogy of the Oppressed: 30th Anniversary Edition*, trans. Myra Bergman Ramos (New York: Continuum, 2010).

26. Joanna Williams, *Catechesis of the Good Shepherd Level I Formation Seminar*, St George Episcopal Church (Nashville, TN) November 2012.

27. Moore, 59.

28. There is, of course, a place for additional devotional literature and practices directed at children, just as there is for such materials and practices for adults, but true and mutual inclusion in the Christian community demands that as our primary source all disciples begin with the sacred texts.

29. Marcia J. Bunge, "Biblical and Theological Perspectives and Best Practices" in *Understanding Children's Spirituality: Theology, Research, and Practice*, ed Kevin E. Lawson (Eugene, OR: Cascade Books, 2012) 6.

30. United Nations, *Convention on the Rights of the Child*, 20 November 1989.

31. John Wall, "Childism: The Challenge of Childhood to Ethics and the Humanities." In *The Children's Table: Childhood Studies and the Humanities*, edited by Anna Mae Duanne (Athens, GA: University of Georgia Press, 2013) 70.

32. David Jensen, *Graced Vulnerability: A Theology of Childhood* (Cleveland: Pilgrim, 2005) 47.

33. Bonnie Miller-McLemore, "Childhood: The (Often Hidden Yet Lively) Vocational Life of Children," in Kathleen Cahalan and Bonnie J. Miller-McLemore, eds., *Calling All Years Good: Christian Vocation across the Lifespan* (Grand Rapids: Eerdmans, forthcoming 2017) 16–17.

34. Anna Mae Duanne, "Introduction," in *The Children's Table: Childhood Studies and the Humanities*, edited by Anna Mae Duanne (Athens, GA: University of Georgia Press, 2013) 7.

35. Duanne, 6–7.

36. Laurel Koepf-Taylor explains, "Indeed, contrary to assumptions of cognitive deficiency, children and youth are adept at learning new technologies, and children acquire physical and linguistic competencies much more quickly than adults do, but are still seen as lacking" (*Give Me Children or I Shall Die: Children and Communal Survival in Biblical Literature* [Minneapolis: Augsburg, 2013] 11).

37. Miller-McLemore, "The Vocational Life of Children," 6; Cf. Bonnie J. Miller-McLemore, "Whither the Children? Childhood in Religious Education," *Journal of Religion* 86, no. 4 (October 2006): 635–657.

38. Bonnie Miller-McLemore, "Childhood: The (Often Hidden Yet Lively) Vocational Life of Children," in *Calling All Years Good: Christian Vocation across the Lifespan*, edited by Kathleen Cahalan and Bonnie J. Miller-McLemore (Grand Rapids: Eerdmans, 2017) 48, 50.

39. Duanne, 7–8.

40. See Karen Attiah, "Why Won't the US Ratify the UN's Child Rights Treaty?" in *Washington Post* (21 November 2014) https://www.washingtonpost.com/blogs/post-partisan/wp/2014/11/21/why-wont-the-u-s-ratify-the-u-n-s-child-rights-treaty/.

41. Suzanne Dixon, *The Roman Mother* (Norman, OK: Oklahoma University Press, 1989) 102.

42. Marilou Ibita and Reimund Bieringer, "The Beloved Child: The Presentation of Jesus as a Child in the Second Testament," in *Children's Voices: Children's Perspectives in Ethics, Theology, and Religious Education*, edited by Annemie Dillen and Didier Pollefeyt (Walpole, MA: Uitgeverij Peeters, 2010) 12.

43. Koepf-Taylor, 126.

44. Christine E. Gudorf, "Sacrificial and Parental Spiritualities," in *Religion, Feminism, and the Family*, edited by Ann Carr and Mary Stewart Van Leeuwen (Louisville: Westminster John Knox, 1996) 300.

45. Christine E. Gudorf, "Parenting, Mutual Love, and Sacrifice" in *Women's Conciousness and Women's Conscience: A Reader in Feminist Ethics*, edited by Barbara Hilkert Andolsen, Christine E. Gudorf, and Mary D. Pellauer (New York: Harper and Row, 1985) 299.

46. Miller-McLemore, "The Vocational Life of Children," 29–30.

47. Carter, *Households and Discipleship*, 91.

48. Carter, *Households and Discipleship*, 114.

49. John Wall, "Childism and the Ethics of Responsibility," in *Children's Voices: Children's Perspectives in Ethics, Theology, and Religious Education*, edited by Annemie Dillen and Didier Pollefeyt (Walpole, MA: Uitgeverij Peeters, 2010) 258.

50. James Francis, *Adults as Children: Images of Childhood in the Ancient World and the New Testament* (Oxford: Peter Lang, 2006) 85.

51. Duanne, 2.

52. Marcia J. Bunge, "Biblical and Theological Perspectives and Best Practices," in *Understanding Children's Spirituality: Theology, Research, and Practice*, edited by Kevin E. Lawson. Eugene, OR: Cascade Books, 2012) 6.

53. Sharon Warkentin Short, "The Story that Grew: The Metanarrative of Scripture as Recounted by Storytellers in the Bible," in *Understanding Children's Spirituality: Theology, Research, and Practice*, edited by Kevin E. Lawson (Eugene, OR: Cascade Books, 2012) 258.

Bibliography

Aasgaard, Reidar. *The Childhood of Jesus: Decoding the Apocryphal Infancy Gospel of Thomas*. Eugene, OR: Cascade Books, 2009.
Alexander, Loveday. "Luke's Political Vision." *Interpretation* 66:3 (July 2012): 283–294.
———. "Sisters in Adversity: Retelling Martha's Story." In *Feminist Companion to Luke*, edited by Amy–Jill Levine and Marianne Blickenstaff. 197–213. London: Sheffield, 2002.
Archard, David. *Children: Rights and Childhood*. London: Routledge, 1993.
Ariès, Philippe. *Centuries of Childhood: A Social History of Family Life*. Translated by Robert Baldick. New York: Vintage Books, 1962.
Attiah, Karen. "Why Won't the US Ratify the UN's Child Rights Treaty?" in *Washington Post* (21 November 2014). https://www.washingtonpost.com/blogs/post-partisan/wp/2014/11/21/why-wont-the-u–s–ratify-the-u–n–s–child–rights–treaty/.
Bailey, James L. "Experiencing the Kingdom as a Little Child: A Rereading of Mark 10:13–16." *Word and World* 15:1 (Winter 1995): 58–67.
Balch, David and Carolyn Osiek. *Families in the New Testament World: Households and House Churches*. Louisville: Westminster John Knox, 1997.
Balla, Peter. *The Child–Parent Relationship in the New Testament and Its Environment*. Tübingen: Mohr Siebeck, 2003.
Barclay, John M. G. "The Family as the Bearer of Religion in Judaism and Early Christianity." In *Constructing Early Christian Families: Family as Social Reality and Metaphor*, edited by Halvor Moxnes, 66–80. London: Routledge, 1997.
Barton, Stephen. "The Relativisation of Family Ties in the Jewish and Graeco–Roman Traditions." In *Construction Early Christian Families: Family as Social Reality and Metaphor*, edited by Halvor Moxnes, 81–102. New York: Routledge, 1997.
Bauman–Martin, Betsy J. "Women on the Edge: New Perspectives on Women in the Petrine Haustafel." *Journal of Biblical Literature* 123:2 (2004).
Bekker–Nielsen, Tønnes. "Fishing in the Roman World." Cited in *Ancient Nets and Fishing Gear: Proceedings of the International Workshop on 'Nets and Fishing*

Gear in Classical Antiquity: A First Approach,' edited by Tønnes Bekker–Nielsen and Dario Bernal Casasola (Cadiz: 15–17 November, 2007).

Betsworth, Sharon. *Children in Early Christian Narratives.* London: Bloomsbury T&T Clark, 2015.

Billings, Bradley. "'At the Age of 12': The Boy Jesus in the Temple (Luke 2:41–52), The Emperor Augustus and the Social Setting of the Third Gospel." *Journal of Theological Studies* 60:1 (April 2009) 70–89.

Bloom, Paul. "The Moral Life of Babies." *New York Times.* 5 May 2010.

Boomershine, Thomas E. *The Messiah of Peace: A Performance–Critical Commentary on Mark's Passion–Resurrection Narrative.* Eugene, OR: Cascade Books, 2015.

Bottigheimer, Ruth. *The Bible for Children: From the Age of Guttenberg to the Present.* New Haven: Yale University Press, 1996.

Bovon, François. *Luke 1*, translated by Christine Thomas. Minneapolis: Fortress Press, 2002.

———. *Luke 2*, translated by Donald S. Deer. Minneapolis: Fortress Press, 2013.

Bradley, Keith R.. *Discovering the Roman Family: Studies in Roman Social History.* Oxford: Oxford University Press, 1991.

———. "Wet–nursing at Rome: a Study in Social Relations." In *The Family in Ancient Rome*, edited by Beryl Rawson. New York: Cornell, 1986.

Bradner, Lester. "The Kingdom and the Child." *Anglican Theological Review* 3:1 (May 1920).

Bunge, Marcia J. "Biblical and Theological Perspectives and Best Practices." In *Understanding Children's Spirituality: Theology, Research, and Practice,* edited by Kevin E. Lawson. Eugene, OR: Cascade Books, 2012.

———. "Introduction." In *The Child in the Bible,* edited by Marcia Bunge, Terence Fretheim, and Beverly Roberts Gaventa. Grand Rapids: Wm. B. Eerdman's, 2008.

———, ed. *The Child in Christian Thought.* Grand Rapids: Wm Eerdmann's, 2001.

———, Terence Fretheim, and Beverly Roberts Gaventa, eds.. *The Child in the Bible.* Grand Rapids: Wm Eerdmann's, 2008.

Burke, Tony. "'Social Viewing' of Children in the Childhood Stories of Jesus." In *Children in Late Ancient Christianity*, edited by Cornelia Horn and Robert Phenix. Tübingen: Mohr Siebeck, 2009.

Busse, Ulrich. *Die Wunder des Propheten Jesus: Die Rezeption, Komposition, und Interpretation der Wundertradition im Evangelium des Lukas.* Stuttgart: Katholisches Bibelwerk, 1977.

Carroll, John T. "'What Then Will This Child Become?': Perspectives on Children in the Gospel of Luke." In *The Child in the Bible*, edited by Marcia Bunge, Terence Fretheim, and Beverly Roberts Gaventa, 177–194. Grand Rapids: Wm. B. Eerdman's, 2008.

Carter, Warren. "Getting Martha Out of the Kitchen: Luke 10.38–42 Again." In *Feminist Companion to Luke*, edited by Amy–Jill Levine and Marianne Blickenstaff. 214–231. Cleveland: Pilgrim Press, 2002.

———. *Households and Discipleship: A Study of Matthew 19–20.* Sheffield: Sheffield Academic Press, 1994.

Cavalletti, Sofia. *The Religious Potential of the Child*, translated by Patricia M. Coulter and Julie M. Coulter. Chicago: Catechesis of the Good Shepherd Publications, 1992.

Chakoian, Karen. "Luke 2:41–52." *Interpretation* (April 1998): 185–190.
Chartrand–Burke, Tony. "The Infancy Gospel of Thomas." In *Non–canonical Gospels*. London: T&T Clark, 2008.
Cho, Youngmo. *Spirit and Kingdom in the Writings of Luke and Paul.* Waynesboro, GA: Paternoster, 2005.
Clark, Ronald R. "Kingdoms, Kids, and Kindness: A New Context for Luke 18:15–17." *Stone–Campbell Journal* 5 (Fall 2002): 235–248.
Coecke van Aelst, Pieter. *Scenes from the Life of the Prodigal*. 1530. Pen and brown ink and gray wash, over traces of black chalk 19.2x51.4cm. The J. Paul Getty Museum, Los Angeles.
Cohen, Shaye, ed. *The Jewish Family in Antiquity*. Atlanta: Scholar's Press, 1993.
Cooney, Rory. "Canticle of the Turning." GIA Publications: 1990.
Creed, J. M. *The Gospel According to St. Luke*. London: MacMillan, 1930.
Cribiore, Rafaella. *Gymnastics of the Mind: Greek Education in Hellenistic and Roman Egypt*. Princeton: Princeton University Press, 2001.
Crossan, John Dominic. "A Kingdom of Nobodies." In *The Historical Jesus: The Life of a Mediterranean Jewish Peasant*. New York: Harper Collins, 1991.
D'Ambra, Eve. *Roman Women*. Cambridge: Cambridge University Press, 2007.
D'Angelo, Mary Rose. "Reconstructing 'Real' Women from Gospel Literature: The Case of Mary Magdalene." In *Women and Christian Origins*, edited by Ross S. Kraemer and Mary Rose D'Angelo. Oxford: Oxford University Press, 1999.
Day, Peggy L. "From the Child is Born the Woman: The Story of Jephthah's Daughter." In *Gender and Difference in Ancient Israel*, edited by Peggy L. Day. Minneapolis: Augsburg Fortress, 1989.
Dean–Jones, Lesley. "The Child Patient of the Hippocratics: Early Pediatrics?" In *The Oxford Handbook of Childhood and Education in the Classical World*, edited by Judith Evan Grubbs and Tim Parkin, 108–124. Oxford: Oxford University Press, 2013.
de Boer, Esther. "The Lukan Mary Magdalene and the Other Women Following Jesus." In *Feminist Companion to Luke*, edited by Amy–Jill Levine and Marianne Blickenstaff, 140–160. Cleveland: Pilgrim Press, 2002.
Destro, Adriana and Mauro Pesce. "Fathers and Householders in the Jesus Movement: The Perspective of the Gospel of Luke." *Biblical Interpretation* (January 2003).
Dillen, Annemie and Didier Pollefeyt. *Children's Voices: Children's Perspectives in Ethics, Theology, and Religious Education*. Walpole, MA: Uitgeverij Peeters, 2010.
Dixon, Suzanne. *The Roman Mother*. Norman, OK: Oklahoma University Press, 1989.
Duanne, Anna Mae, ed. *The Children's Table: Childhood Studies and the Humanities*. Athens, GA: University of Georgia Press, 2013.
Eliot, Lise. *What's Going On in There?: How the Brain and Mind Develop in the First Five Years of Life*. New York: Bantam Books, 1999.
Ellis, E. E. *The Gospel of Luke*. London: Nelson, 1966.
Evangelical Lutheran Church in America. *Evangelical Lutheran Worship*. Minneapolis: Augsburg Fortress, 2006.
Farley, Lawrence R.. *The Gospel of Luke: Good News for the Poor*. Chesterton, IN: Conciliar Press, 2011.
Fitzer, Gottfried. "σκιρτάω." *TDNT* 7 (1971)
Fitzmyer, Joseph A. *The Gospel According to Luke I–IX*. New York: Doubleday, 1970.

———. *The Gospel According to Luke X–XXIV*. New York: Doubleday, 1983.
Fleishman, Joseph. "The Age of Legal Maturity in Biblical Law." *Journal of the Ancient Near Eastern Society* 21 (1992).
Foucault, Michel. *The Archaeology of Knowledge*. London: Tavistock, 1974.
Francis, James. *Adults as Children: Images of Childhood in the Ancient World and the New Testament*. Oxford: Peter Lang, 2006.
———. "Children and Childhood in the New Testament." In *The Family in Theological Perspective*, edited by Stephen Barton. Edinburgh: T&T Clark, 1996.
Freire, Paulo. *Pedagogy of the Oppressed: 30th Anniversary Edition*, translated by Myra Bergman Ramos. New York: Continuum, 2010.
French, Valerie. "Children in Antiquity." In *Children in Historical and Comparative Perspective: An International Handbook and Research Guide*, edited by Joseph M. Hawes and N. Ray Hiner, 13–21. New York: Greenwood Press, 1991.
Garland, Robert. "Children in Athenian Religion." In *The Oxford Handbook of Childhood and Education in the Classical World*, edited by Judith Evans Grubbs, Tim Parkin, and Roslynne Bell, 207–226. Oxford: Oxford University Press, 2013.
Garroway, Kristine. *Children in the Ancient Near Eastern Household*. Winona Lake, IN: Eisenbrauns, 2014.
Gopnik, Alison. *The Philosophical Baby: What Children's Minds Tell Us About Truth, Love, and the Meaning of Life*. New York: Picador, 2009.
Green, Joel B. "Good News to Whom? Jesus and the 'Poor' in the Gospel of Luke." In *Jesus of Nazareth: Lord and Christ. Essays on the Historical Jesus and New Testament Christology*, edited by Joel B. Green and Max Turner, 59–74. Grand Rapids, MI: Eerdmans, 1994.
———. *The Gospel of Luke*. Grand Rapids, MI: Eerdmans, 1997.
Grenholm, Cristina. *Motherhood and Love: Beyond Gendered Stereotypes of Theology*, translated by Marie Tåqvist. Grand Rapids, MI: Wm. B Eerdmann's, 2011.
Gudorf, Christine E. "Parenting, Mutual Love, and Sacrifice." In *Women's Conciousness and Women's Conscience: A Reader in Feminist Ethics*, edited by Barbara Hilkert Andolsen, Christine E. Gudorf, and Mary D. Pellauer, 294–309. New York: Harper and Row, 1985.
———. "Sacrificial and Parental Spiritualities." In *Religion, Feminism, and the Family*, edited by Ann Carr and Mary Stewart Van Leeuwen. Louisville: Westminster John Knox, 1996.
Guijarro, Santiago. "The Family in First–century Galilee." In *Constructing Early Christian Families: Family as Social Reality and Metaphor*, edited by Halvor Moxnes, 42–65. London: Routledge, 1997.
Gundry, Judith M.. "Children in the Gospel of Mark, with Special Attention to Jesus' Blessing of the Children (Mark 10:13–16) and the Purpose of Mark." In *The Child in the Bible*, edited by Marcia Bunge, Terence Fretheim, and Beverly Roberts Gaventa. Grand Rapids: William B. Eerdmans, 2008.
Hanson, K. C. "The Galilean Fishing Economy and the Jesus Tradition." *Biblical Theology Bulletin* (1997).
Harlow, Mary. "Family Relationships." In *A Cultural History of Childhood and Family in Antiquity*, vol. 1. Oxford: Berg Press, 2010.

———. "Toys, Dolls, and the Material Culture of Childhood." In *The Oxford Handbook of Childhood and Education in the Classical World*, ed. by Judith Evans Grubbs, Tim Parkin, and Roslynne Bell. Oxford: Oxford University Press, 2013.

———.,and Ray Laurence. *Growing Up and Growing Old in Ancient Rome: A Life Course Approach.* London: Routledge, 2002.

Higonnet, Anne. *Pictures of Innocence: The History and Crisis of Ideal Childhood.* New York: Thames and Hudson, 1998.

Hirsh–Pasek, Kathy and Roberta Michnick Golinkoff. *Einstein Never Used Flash Cards: How Our Children REALLY Learn and Why They Need to Play More and Memorize Less.* Emmaus, PA: Rodale Inc., 2003.

Horn, Cornelia B. and John W. Martens. *"Let the little children come to me": Childhood and Early Christianity.* Washington, D.C.: Catholic University of America Press, 2009.

Ibita, Marilou and Reimund Bieringer. "The Beloved Child: The Presentation of Jesus as a Child in the Second Testament." In *Children's Voices: Children's Perspectives in Ethics, Theology, and Religious Education*, edited by Annemie Dillen and Didier Pollefeyt. Walpole, MA: Uitgeverij Peeters, 2010.

———. "(Stifled) Voices of the Future: Learning about Children in the Bible." In *Children's Voices: Children's Perspectives in Ethics, Theology, and Religious Education* edited by Annemie Dillen and Didier Pollefeyt. Walpole, MA: Uitgeverij Peeters, 2010.

James, Allison and Alan Prout, eds.. *Constructing and Reconstructing Childhood*, 2nd ed. New York: Routledge Falmer, 1997.

———. "A New Paradigm for the Sociology of Childhood? Provenance, Promise, and Problems." In *Constructing and Reconstructing Childhood: Contemporary Issues in the Sociological Study of Childhood*, edited by Allison James and Alan Prout. Baskingtoke: Falmer Press, 1990.

Janssen, Claudia and Regene Lamb. "Gospel of Luke: The Humbled Will Be Lifted Up." In *Feminist Biblical Interpretation: A Compendium of Critical Commentary on the Books of the Bible and Related Literature*, edited by Luise Schottroff and Marie–Theres Wacker. Grand Rapids: Wm. B. Eerdmann's, 2012.

Jenks, Chris. *Childhood.* London: Routledge, 1996.

Jensen, David. *Graced Vulnerability: A Theology of Childhood.* Cleveland: Pilgrim, 2005.

Jeremias, Joachim. *Infant Baptism in the First Four Centuries*, translated by David Cairns. Philadelphia: Westminster Press, 1960.

Johnson, Luke Timothy. *The Gospel of Luke.* Collegeville, MN: Liturgical Press, 1991.

Karlsen Seim, Turid. *The Double Message: Patterns of Gender in Luke–Acts.* Nashville: Abingdon, 1994.

———. "The Gospel of Luke." In *Searching the Scriptures: A Feminist Commentary*, edited by Elisabeth Schüssler. New York: Crossroad, 1994.

Kartzow, Marianne Bjelland. "Slave Children in the First–Century Jesus Movement." In *Childhood in History: Perceptions of Children in the Ancient and Medieval Worlds*, edited by Reidar Aasgaard, Cornelia Horn, and Oana Maria Cojocaru. London: Routledge, 2017.

Kiambi, Julius. *Postcolonial 'Redaction' of Social–economic parables in Luke's Gospel: Bible and Making of the poor in Kenya.* Saarbrücken, Germany: LAP Lambert Academic, 2011.

Knapp, Robert. *Invisible Romans*. London: Profile Books, 2011.
Koepf–Taylor, Laurel. *Give Me Children or I Shall Die: Children and Communal Survival in Biblical Literature*. Minneapolis: Augsburg, 2013.
Koperski, Veronica. "Luke 10.38–40 and Acts 6.1–7: The Literary Context of Luke–Acts." In *Feminist Companion to Luke*, edited by Amy–Jill Levine and Marianne Blickenstaff. 161–196. London: Sheffield Academic Press, 2002.
Kraemer, Ross. "Typical and Atypical Jewish Family Dynamics: The Cases of Babatha and Bernice." In *Early Christian Families in Context: An Interdisciplinary Dialogue*, edited by David Balch and Carolyn Osiek, 130–156. Grand Rapids: Wm. Eerdmann's, 2003.
Laes, Christian. "Desperately Different? *Delicia* Children in the Roman Household." In *Early Christian Families in Context: An Interdisciplinary Dialogue*, edited by David Balch and Carolyn Osiek. Grand Rapids: Wm. Eerdmann's, 2003.
Larsson Lovén, Lena. "Children and Childhood in Roman Commemorative Art." In *The Oxford Handbook of Childhood and Education in the Classical World*, edited by Judith Evans Grubbs, Tim Parkin, and Roslynne Bell, 302–321. Oxford: Oxford University Press, 2013.
———and Agnet Strömberg. "Economy." In *A Cultural History of Childhood and Family in Antiquity,* edited by Mary Harlow and Ray Laurence, 45–60. London: Bloomsbury, 2010.
Lassen, Eva Marie. "The Roman Family: Ideal and Metaphor." In *Constructing Early Christian Families: Family as Social Reality and Metaphor*, edited by Halvor Moxnes, 103–120. London: Routledge, 1997.
Laurence, Ray. "Community." In *A Cultural History of Childhood and Family in Antiquity,* edited by Mary Harlow and Ray Laurence, 31–44. London: Bloomsbury, 2010.
Levine, Lee I. *The Ancient Synagogue: The First Thousand Years.* New Haven: Yale University Press, 2000.
Leyerle, Blake. "Children and 'The Child' in Early Christianity." In *The Oxford Handbook of Childhood and Education in the Classical World*, edited by Judith Evans Grubbs, Tim Parkin, and Roslynne Bell, 559–579. Oxford: Oxford University Press, 2013.
Lindeman Allen, Amy. "Reading for Inclusion: The Girl from Galilee (Luke 8:40–56)." *Journal of Childhood and Religion* Vol 7(2017), 1–17.
López Rodriguez, D. O. *The Liberating Mission of Jesus: The Message of the Gospel of Luke*. Eugene, OR: Pickwick Publications, 2012.
MacDonald, Margaret. *The Power of Children: Construction of Christian Families in the Greco–Roman World.* Waco, TX: Baylor University Press, 2014.
Mattila, Talvikki. "Naming the Nameless: Gender and Discipleship in Matthew's Passion Narrative." In *Characterization in the Gospels: Reconceiving Narrative Criticism,* edited by David Rhoads and Kari Syreeni. Sheffield: Sheffield Academic Press, 1999.
McGinn, Thomas A. J. "Roman Children and the Law." In *The Oxford Handbook of Childhood and Education in the Classical World*, edited by Judith Grubbs, Tim Parkin, and Roslynne Bell, 341–364. Oxford: Oxford University Press, 2013.

McWilliam, Janette. "The Socialization of Roman Children," in *The Oxford Handbook of Childhood and Education in the Classical World,* edited by Judith Grubbs, Tim Parkin, and Roslynne Bell, 264–285. Oxford: Oxford University Press, 2013.

Meeks, Wayne A. *The First Urban Christians: The Social World of the Apostle Paul.* New Haven: Yale University Press, 1983.

Menn, Esther M. "Child Characters in Biblical Narratives: The Young David (1 Samuel 16–17) and the Little Israelite Servant Girl (2 Kings 5:1–19)." In *The Child in the Bible,* edited by Marcia Bunge, Terence Fretheim, and Beverly Roberts Gaventa. Grand Rapids: Wm. B. Eerdman's, 2008.

Meyer, Marvin W. "The Youth in the *Secret Gospel of Mark.*" *Semeia* (Jan 1990).

Miller–McLemore, Bonnie. *Also a Mother: Work and Family as Theological Dilemma.* Nashville: Abingdon Press, 1994.

———. "Childhood: The (Often Hidden Yet Lively) Vocational Life of Children." In *Calling All Years Good: Christian Vocation across the Lifespan,* edited by Kathleen Cahalan and Bonnie J. Miller–McLemore. Grand Rapids: Eerdmans, 2017.

———. "Jesus Loves the Little Children?: An Exercise in the Use of Scripture." *Journal of Childhood and Religion* 1:7 (October 2010).

———. *Let the Children Come: Reimagining Childhood from a Christian Perspective.* San Francisco: Jossey–Bass, 2003.

———. "Whither the Children? Childhood in Religious Education," *Journal of Religion* 86, no. 4 (October 2006): 635–657.

Mlodinow, Leonard. "How We Communicate Through Body Language." *Psychology Today.* 29 May 2012. https://www.psychologytoday.com/blog/subliminal/201205/how-we-communicate-through-body-language.

Moore, Pam. *Taste and See: Savoring the Child's Wisdom.* Chicago: Liturgy Training Publications, 2011.

Montessori, Maria. *Discovery of the Child,* translated by M. Joseph Costelloe. New York: Ballantine Books, 1967.

Moxnes, Halvor. "What is Family? Problems in Constructing Early Christian Families." In *Constructing Early Christian Families: Family as Social Reality and Metaphor,* edited by Halvor Moxnes, 13–41. London: Routledge, 1997.

Murphy, A. James. *Kids and Kingdom: The Precarious Presence of Children in the Synoptic Gospels.* Eugene, OR: Pickwick Publications, 2013.

O'Day, Gail R. "Singing Woman's Song: A Hermeneutic of Liberation." *Currents In Theology And Mission* 12:4 (August 1, 1985): 203–210

Parker, Julie Faith. *Valuable and Vulnerable: Children in the Hebrew Bible, Especially the Elijah Cycle.* Atlanta: Society of Biblical Literature, 2013.

Parkin, Tim. "The Demographics of Infancy and Early Childhood in the Ancient World." In *The Oxford Handbook of Childhood and Education in the Classical World,* edited by Judith Evans Grubbs, Tim Parkin, and Roslynne Bell, 40–61. Oxford: Oxford University Press, 2013.

———. "Life Cycle." In *A Cultural History of Childhood and Family in Antiquity,* edited by Mary Harlow and Ray Laurence, 97–114. London: Bloomsbury, 2010.

Patte, Daniel. "Jesus' Pronouncement about Entering the Kingdom Like a Child: A Structural Exegesis." *Semeia* 29 (1983).

Patterson, Cynthia B.. "Education in Plato's Laws." In *Childhood and Education in the Classical World*, edited by Judith Evans Grubbs, Tim Parkin, and Roslynne Bell, 365–380. Oxford: Oxford University Press, 2013.

Pervo, Richard I. *Acts*. Minneapolis: Fortress Press, 2009.

Piaget, Jean. *The Moral Judgment of the Child*, translated by Marjorie Gabin. Edinburgh: Edinburgh Press, 1932.

Pomeroy, Sarah. *Goddesses, Whores, Wives, and Slaves: Women in Classical Antiquity*. New York: Schocken Books, 1995.

Price, Robert M.. *The Widow Traditions in Luke–Acts: A Feminist Critical Scrutiny*. Atlanta: Scholar's Press, 1997.

Rawson, Beryl. "Adult–Child Relationships in Roman Society." In *Marriage, Divorce, and Children in Ancient Rome*, edited by Beryl Rawson. Oxford: Oxford University Press, 1991.

———. *Children and Childhood in Roman Italy*. Oxford: Oxford University Press, 2003.

———. "Children in the Roman *Familia*." In *The Family in Ancient Rome*, edited by Beryl Rawson. Ithaca, NY: Cornell University Press, 1986.

Reid, Barbara. *Salty Wives, Spirited Mothers, and Savvy Widows: Capable Women of Purpose and Persistence in Luke's Gospel*. Grand Rapids: William Eerdmans, 2012.

Rhoads, David. "Performance Criticism: An Emerging Methodology in Biblical Studies—Part I." *Biblical Theology Bulletin* 36:3 (2006):1–16.

Roberts Gaventa, Beverly. *Our Mother Saint Paul*. Louisville: Westminster John Knox, 2007.

Ryan, Rosalie. "The Women From Galilee and Discipleship in Luke." *Biblical Theology Bulletin*, 15:2 (1985).

Sample, Tex. *Ministry in an Oral Culture: Living With Will Rogers, Uncle Remus, & Minnie Pearl*. Louisville: Westminster John Knox, 1994.

Schaberg, Jane. "Luke." In *The Women's Bible Commentary*, edited by Carol A. Newsom and Sharon Ringe. Louisville: Westminster John Knox, 1992.

Schersten LaHurd, Carol. "Re–viewing Luke 15 with Arab Christian Women." In *A Feminist Companion to Luke*, edited by Amy–Jill Levine and Marianne Blickenstaff, 246–268. London: Sheffield Academic Press, 2002.

Schilling, Frederick A. "What Means the Saying about Receiving the Kingdom of God as a Little Child." *Expository Times* 77:2 (Nov 1965).

Schüssler Fiorenza, Elisabeth. *But She Said: Feminist Practices of Biblical Interpretation*. Boston: Beacon Press, 1992.

Shing Chung Kwong, Ivan. *The Word Order of the Gospel of Luke*. London: T&T Clark, 2006.

Sigismund–Nielsen, Hanne. "Slave and Lower–Class Roman Children." In *The Oxford Handbook of Childhood and Education in the Classical World*, edited by Judith Grubbs, Tim Parkin, and Roslynne Bell, 286–301. Oxford: Oxford University Press, 2013.

Sivan, Hagith. "Pictorial *Paideia*: Children in the Synagogue." In *The Oxford Handbook of Childhood and Education in the Classical World*, edited by Judith Evans Grubbs, Tim Parkin, and Roslynne Bell, 532–558. Oxford: Oxford University Press, 2013.

Spada, Leonello. *The Return of the Prodigal Son*, 1608. Oil on canvas, 160x119cm. The Louvre, Paris.

Spencer, F. Scott. "A Woman's Right to Choose? Mother Mary as Spirited Agent and Actor (Luke 1–2)." In *Salty Wives, Spirited Mothers, and Savvy Widows: Capable Women of Purpose and Persistence in Luke's Gospel*. Grand Rapids: Wm. B. Eerdmans, 2012.

St. Clair, Stanley J. *Most Comprehensive Origins of Clichés, Proverbs, and Figurative Expressions*. Minnville, TN: St Clair Publications, 2013.

Steuernagel, Valdir. "Doing Theology Together with Mary." *Journal of Latin American Theology* 8:2 (2013): 239–269.

Strange, William. *Children in the Early Church*. Cumbria, UK: Pater Noster, 1996.

Tannehill, Robert C. *Luke*. Nashville, Abingdon Press, 1996.

Thimmes, Pamela. "The Language of Community: A Cautionary Tale (Luke 10:38–42)." In *A Feminist Companion to Luke*, edited by Amy–Jill Levine and Marianne Blickenstaff. 232–245. London: Sheffield Press, 2002.

Tropper, Amram. "Children and Childhood in Light of the Demographics of the Jewish Family in Late Antiquity." *Journal for the Study of Judaism* 37:3 (2006).

United Nations. *Convention on the Rights of the Child*. 20 November 1989.

Vancil, Jack W. "Sheep, Shepherd." In *ABD*.

Wall, John. "Childism and the Ethics of Responsibility." In *Children's Voices: Children's Perspectives in Ethics, Theology, and Religious Education*, edited by Annemie Dillen and Didier Pollefeyt. Walpole, MA: Uitgeverij Peeters, 2010.

———. "Childism: The Challenge of Childhood to Ethics and the Humanities." In *The Children's Table: Childhood Studies and the Humanities,* edited by Anna Mae Duanne. Athens, GA: University of Georgia Press, 2013.

Warkentin Short, Sharon. "The Story that Grew: The Metanarrative of Scripture as Recounted by Storytellers in the Bible." In *Understanding Children's Spirituality: Theology, Research, and Practice*, edited by Kevin E. Lawson. Eugene, OR: Cascade Books, 2012.

Weaver, P. R. C. "Children of Freedmen (and Freedwomen)." In *Marriage, Divorce, and Children in Ancient Rome*, edited by Beryl Rawson. Oxford: Oxford University Press, 1991.

Weber, Hans–Ruedi. *Jesus and the Children: Biblical Resources for Study and Preaching*. Atlanta: John Knox Press, 1979.

Williams, Joanna. *Catechesis of the Good Shepherd Level I Formation Seminar*. St George Episcopal Church (Nashville, TN) November 2012.

Williams, Margaret. "The Jewish Family in Judaea from Pompey to Hadrian—the Limits of Romanization." In *The Roman Family in the Empire: Rome, Italy, and Beyond*, edited by Michael George (Oxford: Oxford University Press, 2001).

Wolff, Hans. *Anthropology of the Old Testament*, translated by Margaret Kohl. Philadelphia: Fortress Press, 1974.

Wuellner, Wilhelm. *The Meaning of "Fisher's of Men."* Philadelphia: Westminster Press, 1967.

York, John O. *The Last Shall Be First: The Rhetoric of Reversal in Luke*. Sheffield: Sheffield Academic, 1991.

Topical Index

abandonment, 23, 25, 76, 135–36, 140, 142–43, 145, 150, 156n51, 55
acculturation. *See* cultural transmission
adolescents/ce, 3–8, 52, 76, 80–81, 104–7, 117n47, 120n106, 147–49, 154n29, 168, 172, 212
adultism, xiv, xx, 10, 12, 15, 24–25, 40, 78, 84, 92, 103, 134, 147, 173, 179–80, 189, 196n39, 206, 217, 220
agency, 36, 39, 56–57, 71n114, 80–81, 85–86, 91–92, 94, 98, 111, 130–31, 135–36, 138, 140, 145, 151, 153n22, 161, 170, 180, 182–92, 211, 218–20
analogy. *See* metaphor
anamnesis, 203–204
apostles, 46, 48–49, 63, 67n34, 124, 126, 131, 199n85;
Twelve, xxi, 33, 48–49, 66n33, 67n34, 100, 102, 123–29, 141–142, 146–51, 152n5, 153n20, 153n25;
Seventy, 48, 170
Aries, Philippe, xvi, xxii, 16, 73n124, 161, 193n1
autonomy, 18n24, 72, 136, 138, 140, 181, 218–19
audience, xxi, 6, 11, 32–33, 38, 47–48, 55, 58–59, 63, 69n60, 72n115, 73n122, 75, 79, 81, 89, 96, 101, 103, 106–10, 130, 146, 148–49, 153n21,

154n25, 163–64, 168, 173, 176–82, 186, 191, 198nn55–61, 206–17

Betsworth, Sharon, xviii, 36
Bieringer, Reimund, xxi, 10, 103, 220
Body of Christ, 123, 152n15, 203–26
Bradner, Lester, xvii, xxiii, 68
breastfeeding, 24–25, 38, 44, 47, 62–63, 65n6, 140, 153n22, 158n69, 170, 209
Βρέφος. *See* infants
brother(s), xx, 16, 24, 51, 75–76, 102–12, 119n93, 120n106, 124, 127, 133, 135, 137, 139, 142–43, 147, 151, 156n52, 211, 223
Bunge, Marcia J., xvii, 216, 226

call to discipleship, 38–39, 67n34, 88, 93–94, 101, 125, 128–30, 132, 135–136, 138, 141, 143, 147, 153n20, 153nn23–33, 154n25, 177, 179, 181, 211
Carroll, John T., xvii–xviii, 36–38, 111, 114n18, 169, 196n36
Childist Biblical Criticism, xviii–xix, 9, 15, 36–37, 75–78, 95, 99, 103, 146, 151, 161, 180, 192–93, 203, 205, 217, 219–20, 224–25
Childhood Studies, xvi, 161, 218
children's bibles, 215–16, 227n21, 28

chronological age, 2–4, 9, 14–16, 146–47, 150, 166, 219, 224
citizenship, 2–5, 20n61, 26, 30, 84, 89, 115n24, 209, 218, 223
civic service. *See* work
Coecke van Aelst, Pieter, 104
compassion, 34, 60, 79, 84–85, 98–99, 102, 111
covenant, 27, 30–31, 37, 40–43, 45, 53, 62, 94, 96, 155n50, 158n69, 166
crowd(s), 54–63, 87–88, 97–98, 100–103, 108, 117n49, 124, 126, 127, 141, 162–63, 170, 187, 189–90, 192, 201n111
cultural transmission, 47, 51–53, 56, 128, 131–32, 134, 144, 163–64, 208–209, 212–16
cultural interpretation, 176

David (son of Jesse), 20n65, 78, 191
Day of the Lord. *See* end times
demographics, 48–49, 55–57, 100
demon(s). *See* spirit(s); exorcisim
dependence, xix, 10, 23, 37, 56, 69n54, 81–82, 84–85, 87, 92, 95, 99, 106–7, 110, 115n24, 116n39, 133, 135–36, 143–45, 168, 170, 218–25
disciple(s), 33–39, 44, 49, 66n33, 67n34, 68n54, 69nn60–64, 95, 97–103, 118n66, 119nn84–88, 123–59, 161–193, 196n39, 200n97, 201nn106–11, 203, 205, 207, 217, 223–224;
  Twelve disciples. *See* apostles
discipleship, 35–36, 69n64, 85, 102, 118n60, 121n127, 124–45, 151, 152nn1–5, 154n25, 157n65, 161–62, 167–69, 173, 175, 193, 194n4, 201n112, 203–204, 208, 214, 217, 222, 224–25;
  accompaniment, 123–51, 153n21, 196n28;
  itinerant, 132–38, 146, 151, 156n60, 164, 205;
  sedentary, 132–34, 151, 154n29, 164, 205;
  related to the Word of God, 140–41, 152nn2–4, 155n50, 161–93, 194n4, 205–206
disease, xxiin12, 26, 82, 97–98, 118n70, 195n18.
  See also healing

education, 30, 47, 51–53, 71n93, 86, 137, 162–68, 175–81, 188, 194n10, 195n24, 197nn45–48, 208–209, 212, 215–17, 222, 228n36
  See also storytelling; students; work, teachers
Elizabeth (mother of John), 41–42, 182, 184–86
end times, 32, 39–40, 58–63, 72n118, 91, 137, 139, 141–42, 155n33, 156n55, 165, 183–84, 190, 205–208
eschaton. *See* end times
eternal life. *See* end times
equality, xv, 32, 103, 138, 145, 150, 175, 195n28, 198n57, 205, 219, 222–23
exorcism, 96, 112, 118n70, 201n112

faith, 76, 78–79, 90, 92–94, 98–99, 101, 117n51, 137, 141, 144, 158n69, 189, 192–93, 205, 208, 216–17
family. *See* household
fatherhood, 3, 6, 24, 26, 49, 57, 60–62, 115n24, 121n125, 124, 137, 143, 150, 158n72, 159n74, 191, 213, 221
  of boy with demon in Galilee, 95–102, 118n64, 139, 157n61;
  God as father, 37, 107–11, 143–45, 164, 166, 169, 172, 187, 196n33, 211, 213, 222–223;
  Jairus (father of girl from Galilee), 89–95, 107, 113n1, 117nn48–59, 139, 173;
  Joseph (father of Jesus), 4, 41–46, 54, 147, 158n73, 163, 189, 192;

Topical Index 243

in parable of two sons, xx, xxiin3, 24, 102–112, 119n93, 120n103, 121n125, 133, 145, 154n29, 211–13;
pater familias, xiv, 5–6, 12, 18n24, 23–24, 26, 31, 34, 105–6, 133–34, 136, 148, 154n29, 155n36, 158n69, 164, 194n12;
Zebedee (father of James and John), 147–151, 158n72, 159n74;
Zechariah (father of John), 14, 41–42, 112, 147, 171, 182, 192, 213
forgiveness, 60, 75, 104–8, 111, 145, 183, 211
Francis, James, xvii, 144–46

grace, 39, 60–63, 72n118, 75, 89–98, 101–3, 107–13, 113n3, 165, 207
Gundry, Judith M., xvii–xviii, 36–38, 144–45

Haustafel (household code), 107–8, 145, 164.
See also household
healing, 48–52, 54, 58, 63, 75–102, 112, 113nn3–6, 114nn15–18, 117nn49–51, 118n70, 124, 139, 157n60, 165, 188–89, 207, 210–11, 214
heaven. *See* end times
Holy Spirit. *See* Spirit
home. *See* household
Horn, Cornelia B., xvii, 6–7, 19n31, 36, 75–76, 94, 104, 108, 113, 113nn3–6, 128, 135–37, 151, 155n39, 159n77, 171
hospitality, 39, 132–33, 136, 154n29, 199n78
household, 4, 7–8, 60–62, 64n1, 65n2–15, 70n79, 76, 90, 95, 99, 107, 127–28, 139, 142, 156n51;
acceptance into, 94, 110–11, 211, 213;
celebrations, 27, 44–45, 83–84, 109, 112, 133;
conversion, 51, 133;

economics, 24–25, 28, 49, 77, 85, 87, 105, 221;
of God, 23–31, 34, 37–40, 85, 92, 108, 112, 121n127, 124, 132–33, 137–42, 144–45, 156n52, 162, 187, 203, 211, 218, 223;
locus for ministry, 47–50, 51–52, 63, 79, 93–94, 109, 127, 132–36, 139, 173–74, 198nn55, 56;
protection, 23, 25, 37, 72, 110–112, 132–33, 137–38, 145, 164, 221–22;
roles within, 14–15, 17n2, 23, 27–28, 31, 35, 46–50, 55, 70n80, 76–78, 81–82, 90–91, 95–96, 100, 104–112, 116n34, 127–28, 133–38, 147–48, 154n29, 157n60, 159n74, 170, 174, 178, 198nn55, 56, 203–205;
structure, 11–12, 25, 28, 106, 121n125, 132, 155n36, 164;
value of children, 23, 26–28, 35–36, 40, 64, 68n44, 77, 90, 96, 99–100, 104–106, 113, 138, 144, 207, 220–21.
See also pater familias; Haustafel
Houston McNeel, Jennifer, xvii

Ibita, Marilou, xxi, xxiii, 10, 103, 220, 228n42
impurity. *See* purity
independence, 82, 85, 110, 116n39, 218
individual(ism), xiv, 25, 29, 33, 45, 49, 57, 66n31, 80, 94, 102, 112, 123, 161, 179, 220, 223–24
Infancy Gospel of Thomas, 8, 20n55, 73n122, 154n32, 163–64, 166–68, 212–13, 227n16
infants, 41–47, 58, 63, 67n35, 68n54, 76, 147, 164, 168–169, 179–186, 197n39, 200n106, 214–15;
baptism, 67n41, 133, 152n14, 158n69, 198n58, 200n97;
Βρέφος, xiv, 9–10, 25, 32, 36, 38–40, 42, 52, 129, 153n22, 171, 213;

infans, 8;
  mortality, 48–49, 55, 82–83;
  νηπίοις, 52, 169–72, 197n36;
  revelation to, 169–72
interdependence, xix–xx, 31, 69n54,
  72n117, 82, 86–87, 135, 145–46,
  180, 193, 205, 217–24

Jacob and Esau, 184–85, 200n96
James (son of Zebedee), 117n49, 125,
  129, 146–51, 158n72, 159n74,
  159n77, 205
Joanna, 126, 152n9
John (son of Zechariah and Elizabeth),
  xiii–xv, xix, 11, 14, 32, 40–42, 46,
  54–55, 58, 83, 87–88, 112, 125, 147,
  171, 180–86, 192–193, 200n96, 205,
  207, 212–14
John (son of Zebedee), 117n49, 125,
  129, 146–51, 158n72, 158n74,
  159n77, 205
Jonah, 58–60, 101
judgment, 24, 60–63, 72n118, 80, 101,
  111, 121n127;
  See also end times

Kingdom of God, xiv, xix, 23, 32–42,
  48, 53–54, 58, 63, 67n41, 69n60, 75,
  79, 84–92, 96, 102, 108, 110–112,
  123–124, 130, 133, 137–44, 151,
  154n25, 156n55, 157n65, 158n69,
  165, 178–89, 192–93, 199n85,
  201n112, 205–208, 211–12, 217–26
knowing child, 110–11
koinonia, xx–xxi, 128, 132, 137, 150–
  51, 159n86, 226

lament, 55, 62, 101, 112, 208–209, 214,
  219
liberation, xv, xx, xxiii n16, 38, 134,
  175–76, 179–81, 186, 208–10,
  216–18, 224
liminality, 5–6, 13, 80–83, 103–104,
  117n47, 134, 166, 219
Lot, 61–62, 101

marriage, 4–5, 17n16, 18n19, 27, 41,
  48–49, 61, 80, 83–85, 89–90, 95,
  104–108, 116n34, 117n47, 135–137,
  148, 174
Martens, John W., xvii, 6–7, 19n31, 36,
  75–76, 94, 104, 108, 113, 113nn3–6,
  128, 135–37, 151, 155n39, 159n77,
  171
Mary (mother of Jesus), xiv–xv, xxiin3,
  4, 12, 14, 20n65, 31, 42–46, 98, 127,
  139–41, 156n52, 166, 168, 182–89,
  192, 194n4, 200nn97–105, 207
Mary (sister of Martha), xxiin3, 49, 166,
  172–181, 193, 198nn57–61, 205, 216
Mary Magdalene, 126, 152n9
μειράκιον, 3
mercy. *See* grace
metaphor, xiv–xix, 14, 33, 35–37, 40,
  66n31, 68n54, 80, 108, 134, 144–45,
  155n33, 157n65, 158n69, 159n87,
  161, 163–64, 170–71, 193, 193n2,
  197n39, 205–207, 219, 223–24
μικρός, 15–16, 57, 59, 62, 131, 210
Moses, 175
mother of youth at Nain, 81–89, 99,
  107, 116n39, 135, 139, 149, 157n60,
  188–189
motherhood, 24, 44–45, 47–48, 62–63,
  71n94, 72n119, 104, 115n23, 124,
  139–143, 148, 151, 156n52, 158n69,
  194n4, 208–209, 221–22
  See also Elizabeth (mother of John);
  Mary (mother of Jesus); mother of
  youth at Nain
Murphy, A. James, xviii, 23–24,
  73n123, 135–36, 154n33, 156n55
mutuality, 87, 89, 116n39, 142, 180,
  204–205, 208, 212–217, 220, 227

νεανίσκος, 3, 12–14, 57, 73n120, 79–84,
  115n20, 147–50, 156n60, 159n82,
  214
νέος, 15–16

Noah, 60–62, 101

nursing of infants. *See* breastfeeding; child care
obedience, 12, 19n52, 27, 31, 43, 70n89, 86, 94, 140, 153n23, 164, 167, 177–82, 194nn4–12, 199nn85–90, 209
occupation. *See* work
οἶκος. *See* household

παιδίον. *See* παῖς
παῖς, 10–13, 20n55, 20n65, 25, 30–38, 43, 57–58, 76–82, 90, 95, 100, 108–109, 114n6, 118n64, 121n118, 128–35, 142–43, 156–157n60, 168, 213, 223
parable, 75–77, 102–112, 132–133, 136, 145, 152n2, 162, 168, 187, 211
parental affection, 27–28, 35–36, 104, 111–12, 142–43
 See also father(s); mother(s); household
Parker, Julie Faith, xviii–xix, xxiiin16, 9, 21n74, 73n119, 87, 115n23
pater familias. See father(s)
physical maturity, 2–5, 8, 10, 12–13, 30–31, 43, 61, 72n119, 73n120, 82, 95–96, 115n24, 117n51, 120n106, 147, 149
Piaget, Jean, xvi, 219
play, 32, 54–58, 71n107, 81, 136–137, 146, 165, 181
power, 5, 12, 15, 18n16, 23, 31, 38–39, 46, 71n107, 75, 79, 86, 88–91, 94–102, 112–113, 117n51, 119n88, 128, 131, 134, 140, 145, 148, 171–175, 179–188, 192, 195n24, 216, 218,
pregnancy, 41, 62, 73n119, 87–89, 98, 116n34, 140, 153n22, 163, 182–86, 200nn97–105, 209
proclamation, xiv, 48, 54, 60, 63, 88–89, 123–28, 157n65, 165, 169, 172, 179–192, 199nn91–97, 201n112, 205, 208, 212, 216–26

prophecy, 41, 54, 58–59, 80, 112, 171, 182–84, 188, 193, 199n91, 207
prostitution. *See* work, sexual
puberty. *See* physical maturity
puer senex, 166, 211–13, 227n16
purity, 79, 88, 94–97, 110, 118n62

Rachel, 191
reconciliation, 75, 112
Reign of God. *See* Kingdom of God
repentance, 60, 153, 183, 211
religious ceremonies. *See* ritual
restoration, xx, 76, 86, 89–91, 97–113, 199n93, 121n127, 124–25, 133, 145, 154n29, 157n60, 203–211
revelation, 58, 169–72, 197n30
reversal, xiv–xv, 54, 95, 98, 131–32, 166, 171–73, 182, 185, 196n36, 206–13, 222, 226
rites. *See* ritual
ritual, 2, 26, 29–30, 89, 94, 203–204, 216–17;
 baptism. 200n96; *See also* infants;
 burial, 80, 83–84, 86–88, 115n32, 117n49, 189;
 celebration, 40–41, 44, 52;
 circumcision, 27, 40, 42, 45, 155n50, 213;
 child participation, 30–31, 53–54, 57, 59, 64, 72n117, 88, 109, 123, 152n14;
 dedication, 42;
 fasting, 57, 59–60, 72n117;
 lustratio, 27;
 naming, 41–42, 213;
 Passover, 40–46, 50, 166;
 prayer, 30, 46, 52, 54, 166, 170–71, 181, 183, 187;
 presentation, 42;
 purification, 42, 44, 46;
 sacrifice, 30, 52, 61, 117n47, 142, 204;
 synagogues, 30–31, 48, 50–54, 63, 70n89, 168;

Temple, 31, 42–44, 46, 49, 50–54, 63, 164–69, 175, 181, 186–89, 212.
See also anamnesis
salvation, 80, 87, 89–95, 117n51, 118n62, 207
servant(s). *See* slavery
sexual maturity. *See* physical maturity
sin, 13, 62, 92–93, 96, 111, 131, 183, 204
sister(s), xxiin3, 24, 49, 85, 124, 143, 156n52, 172–79, 198n57, 223
slavery, 6, 8, 11–12, 23, 25–26, 28–29, 47–48, 56–57, 70n75, 70n80, 75–79, 80, 104, 107–109, 111–12, 115n23; 118n64, 120n106, 121n118, 133–34, 154n29, 190–91, 194n12, 196n28, 198n53, 204, 211, 225;
delicia, 77–78, 114n12, 120n106;
δοῦλος, 11, 76, 78, 109, 112, 121n118;
vernae, 77–78
slaves. *See* slavery
social age, 2–3, 8, 10, 16, 80–82, 84, 89, 95–96, 104–107, 147–48, 158n69, 166, 200n97
socialization. *See* cultural transmission
solidarity, 33, 143–44
Spada, Leonello, 104
Spirit, 85, 126–27, 143, 169–71, 184–85, 196n36, 205
spirit(s), 91, 96–98, 102, 118n70, 139, 157n60, 163, 169, 182–83, 211
state celebrations. *See* ritual
storytelling, 47, 103, 119n96, 162, 176, 180–81, 212–13
See also cultural transmission; education
student(s), 165–68, 175–77, 181, 188, 195nn17–28
sui iuris, 6, 13, 83

Tabitha, 126
teacher(s), see work

τέκνον, xiii, 14–15, 20n65, 25, 57–58, 62–63, 111, 142, 223
θυγάτηρ, 14–15
toys, 29, 55, 117n47
trust, 36, 89, 144, 192–93

υἱός, 9, 14–15, 81, 98, 100, 118n64, 135, 139, 143, 158n72, 210
vulnerability, xxiin12, 23–26, 31, 91, 135, 161, 170, 195n18, 209, 216–20, 225–226

weaning. *See* breastfeeding
work, 6–9, 18n29, 28–29, 47, 56–57, 95, 99, 136, 190–91, 196n33, 221;
agricultural, 7, 19n31, 28, 56, 71n114, 104, 107–9, 112, 120n103, 148, 190–91;
apprenticeship, 7, 56, 176, 178;
child care, 8, 25;
civic service, 5–6, 20n62, 77, 89, 104;
entertainers, 137;
fishing, 148–150, 159n77;
household chores, 8, 28, 46, 48, 51, 55–56, 70n75, 77, 109, 133, 180–81, 190;
laborers, 57, 80, 104, 112, 148, 159n77;
merchants, 50, 54, 56;
messengers, 57, 80, 118n59, 192;
religious, 8;
sailors, 57;
sexual, 57, 61, 77–78, 120n106;
shepherding, 8, 187, 190–92, 201n113, 213;
swineherding, 71n114, 110, 190, 201n112;
teaching, 43, 46–52, 54, 57, 71n93, 151, 163, 166–68, 172, 175–77, 188, 193, 195nn24, 28, 196n28, 212.
See also slavery

youth. *See* νεανίσκος

Scripture Index

Genesis
6:1–4, 61
6:5, 61
6:6, 61
6:7, 61
7:1, 60
7:7, 60
7:23, 61
9:18, 60
9:24–27, 60
17:1–27, 155n50
17:10–14, 27
19:4, 62, 73n120
19:7–8, 61
19:8, 61
19:11, 62
19:12, 62
19:15–16, 61
19:24–25, 62
19:30–38, 73n119
21:8, 115n23
24:2, 121n119
25:22, 184
29:6, 191
34:13, 155n50
37:2, 115n23
37:2–28, 106
37:30, 81–82, 115n23

41:42, 106
42:22, 115n23

Exodus
2:3–10, 115n23
12:42, 45
12:43–50, 45
21:22, 115n23
30:13–14, 20n62
38:26, 20n62

Leviticus
12:3, 27
23:37–38, 44
27:1–8, 8

Numbers
1:2–3, 20n62
1:18, 20n62
1:22, 20n62
4:3, 20n62
4:23, 20n62
8:24, 20n62

Deuteronomy
1:39, 13
4:10, 195n17
6:2, 30

6:7, 30
11:19, 52, 195n17
14:1, 139

1 Chronicles
23:24, 20n62
23:27, 20n62
27:23, 20n62

2 Chronicles
25:5, 20n62

1 Kings
3:25, 115n23
17:17–24, 81

2 Kings
4:18–37, 81, 87, 115n23
4:20, 115n23
4:31, 118n66
4:37, 115n23

1 Samuel
1:19, 183
4:9–10, 177
16:11, 191
17:15, 191

Scripture Index

2 Samuel
12:15, 115n23

Ezra
3:8, 20n62

Psalms
34:11, 195n17
41:3, 189
73:23, 92
78:5, 195n17
90:12, 199n90
114:4, 200nn93–94
114:6, 200n93–94
127:3, 41

Proverbs
1:8, 195n17
3:1, 195n17
6:20, 195n17
22:6, 194n11

Jonah
3:5, 59
3:5–9, 59–60, 101

Ruth
4:16, 115n23

Daniel
1:4, 115n23

Isaiah
9:6, 115n23
41:13, 92
42:6, 92
52:13, 12
54:13, 195n17

Jeremiah
22:21, 182
27:11, 200n94

Zechariah
8:5, 115n23

Joel
1:17, 200n94
2:28, 80
3:3, 115n23

Malachi
3:20, 200n94
4:6, 171, 182, 184,
 199n91, 207

Wisdom
17:18, 200n94

Sirach
4:11, 195n17
7:23, 195n15
19:11, 10
33:19–23, 105
48:10, 171, 184

Tobit
1:1–6:18, 106
6:3, 81–82
8:19–21, 105

1 Maccabees
1:61, 10

2 Maccabees
6:10, 10

3 Maccabees
5:49, 10

Matthew
2:1–17, 200n96
2:16, 11
3:13–4:11, 19n52
4:3, 12
8:5–13, 113n6
8:6, 114n6
8:8, 114n6
10:1, 153n20
12:46–50, 156n52
14:21, 58, 141
15:21–28, 114n6
15:38, 141
17:19–20, 99
17:22, 100
18:2–3, 33
18:4, 19n52, 33
18:5, 36
19:13–15, 144
19:15, 130, 153n21
20:20–23, 151
27:56, 151

Mark
1:1, 12
1:1–11, 200n96
1:16–20, 159n77
3:13, 153n20
3:31–35, 156n52
3:32, 156n52
5:36, 93
7:24–31, 114n6
9:23–24, 99
9:30, 100
9:35, 33
9:36, 33
9:37, 33–34, 100
10:14, 129
10:16, 130, 153n21
10:42–45, 158n69
15:40, 151

Luke
1–2, 41–46
1:1, 146–147
1:3, 206
1:5, 15
1:7, 14
1:11–17, 32
1:13, 14, 183
1:13–14, 41
1:15–17, 227n18
1:17, xiii, 32, 112, 171,
 182–85, 188, 207
1:19, 41
1:22, 41

Scripture Index

1:24–25, 227n18
1:25,41, 97
1:26–2:5, 4
1:27, 200n97
1:32, 185, 213
1:35, 12
1:38, 185
1:39–45, 153n22, 200n96
1:39–55, 182, 184–86
1:41, 10, 68n54, 153n22, 184, 213
1:41–44, xiv
1:42, 141
1:42–45, 227n18
1:44, 10, 68n54, 153n22, 184, 213
1:45, 141
1:46, 200n97
1:46–55, xiv, 31, 182, 185, 207, 227n18
1:48, 98
1:50, 207
1:51, 188
1:57–80, 147
1:58, 41
1:59, 11, 42, 213
1:59–63, 41
1:66, 11, 213
1:67–79, 227n18
1:69, 20n65
1:76, 11, 213
1:80, 11, 212–13
2:7, 14, 168
2:8–20, 190–92
2:9, 192
2:10–14, 227n18
2:12, 68n44, 213
2:12–15, 183
2:15, 192
2:16, 68n44, 213
2:16–21, 10
2:17, 213
2:19, 166, 188
2:20, 192
2:21, 42

2:22, 168
2:22–23, 42
2:25–38, 212
2:26, 197n44
2:28, 42
2:28–32, 227n18
2:29, 114n13
2:32, 197n34
2:36, 15
2:40, 11, 43, 166, 183, 212–13
2:40–43, 10
2:41, 42, 45
2:41–51, 158n69, 212
2:42, 147, 150
2:43, 45, 95, 167
2:44, 45, 150
2:46, 49–50, 167–68, 172, 175, 196n28, 197n49
2:46–49, 166–69, 172
2:46–51, 187–89
2:47, 43, 50, 167, 188
2:48, 20n65, 43
2:49, xiii, 167, 169, 188, 196n33
2:51, 43, 83, 164, 166, 188
2:52, 43, 83, 166, 183, 212
3:2, 147
3:3, 183
3:3–21, 71n114
3:15–22, 200n96
3:21, 58
3:23, 14, 146, 147, 158n73
3:30, 158n73
4:3, 158n73
4:9, 158n73
4:14, 58
4:15, 51
4:16–20, 54
4:18–19, 88
4:22, 54

4:31–37, 51
4:37, 189
4:38, 48, 148
4:39–41, 48
4:40, 48, 117n52
4:40–41, 112
4:43–44, 51
5:1, 57
5:1–3, 71n114
5:1–11, 125
5:3, 148, 166
5:4–9, 159n86
5:7, 150
5:10, 129–30, 136, 147–48, 150, 158n72, 159n86
5:10–11, 190
5:11, 125, 129–30
5:12–15, 201n109
5:15, 71n114
5:17, 118n70
5:17–19, 51
5:17–26, 117n52
5:18–19, 50
5:25, 201n109
5:26, 201n110
5:27, 129–30
5:28, 130
5:30, 125
5:33, 125
5:33–39, 155n49
5:37, 15–16
6:1, 125–26
6:6, 51
6:8–10, 117n52
6:12–16, 126
6:13, 67n34, 124, 152n7, 153n20
6:15, 147, 158n72
6:15–16, 136, 158n72
6:16, 147
6:17, 57, 124, 139, 152n7
6:17–7:1, 71n114
6:18–19, 118n70

6:20, 152n8, 205
6:23, 184
6:24–26, 207, 222
6:35, 139
6:47, 153n23
7:1–10, 71n114, 75–79, 108–109, 113n6, 117n52, 211
7:2, 75, 77
7:2–3, 109, 114n13
7:7, 75, 109, 114n6, 118n70, 121n118
7:8, 78, 114n13
7:10, 75, 109, 114n13
7:11, 83, 87–88, 152n7, 10
7:11–17, 71n114, 75, 79–89, 95, 106, 115n18, 117n52, 149–50, 156n60, 159n74, 210
7:12, 79, 81, 90
7:13, 84–85, 87
7:14, 79, 85, 88, 188, 210
7:15, 79, 82, 84, 99, 186–89
7:16, 188–89
7:17, 201n110
7:18, 87–88
7:18–35, 71n114
7:21, 117n52
7:22, 88
7:23, 58
7:29, 58
7:31–32, 55, 81, 187
7:31–35, 32, 146
7:32, xxiin3, 58
7:35, 58
7:36–50, 199n85
7:37, 173–174
7:37–39, 172
7:38, 93, 198n65, 198n66, 198n66
7:44–46, 39

7:50, 92–93
7:57, 93
8:1–3, 67n34, 126, 142, 149, 151, 152n9, 156n58, 165, 182, 190
8:1–15, 152n2
8:1–21, 71n114
8:2, 157n60
8:3, 142
8:4–15, 139, 162, 179
8:7, 196n28
8:8, 162
8:9, 152n10
8:11, 93
8:12–15, 197n44
8:15, 93, 178
8:19–21, 132, 162–65
8:20–21, 140
8:20, 139
8:21, 124, 139, 141, 162, 172, 178
8:22–40, 152n10
8:26–39, 71n114, 110, 117n52
8:27, 96–97, 157n60
8:28, 127, 158n73
8:34, 201nn110, 112, 201n112
8:34–36, 71n114
8:35, 175, 198n66
8:38–39, 201n109
8:39, 48
8:39–40, 157n60
8:40–56, 71n114, 75, 89–95, 106, 173, 210
8:41, 90, 198n65, 198n66
8:42, 15, 89–90, 117n49, 146
8:43, 97
8:44, 91, 93
8:47, 118n70, 201n109
8:48, 92–93
8:49, 90
8:50, 92

8:51, 90, 117n49
8:52–53, 93
8:54, 90–91, 93, 210
8:54–55, 91
8:55, 86, 93
9:1–6, 48
9:1–7, 58
9:1–50, 67n34
9:2, 118n70
9:3, 182
9:4, 48
9:6, 71n114
9:10–17, 71n114
9:11, 118n70, 182, 201n110
9:14, 152n7
9:14–16, 152n10
9:18, 126–127, 152nn8–10
9:18–22, 152n9
9:18–27, 67n34, 126
9:19, 201n110
9:22, 100
9:37, 98, 100
9:37–45, 75, 95–102, 152n10, 157n61, 210
9:37–43, 71n114, 100, 124
9:37–50, 100
9:38, 118n64
9:39, 96
9:41, 96, 98, 100–102
9:41–42, 100
9:41–43, 197n50
9:42, 11, 95–102
9:43, 33, 100–101, 152n8, 157n61
9:43–45, 100–101, 124
9:43–49, 143–44
9:44, 102
9:45, 59, 100
9:45–46, 119n85
9:46, 33, 100, 130
9:46–48, 98, 197n50

9;46–50, 100–101, 207
9:47, 11, 33, 95, 102, 118n78, 143, 196n28
9:47–50, 32–34, 35, 40, 67n34, 75, 170
9:48, 15, 23, 3–33, 110, 128, 130–31
9:48–49, 34
9:52–53, 178
9:57–62, 155n49
9:58, 39
9:60, 139
10:1, 154n25
10:1–9, 182
10:1–20, 48
10:3, 196n28
10:5–6, 48
10:10, 178
10:16, 178
10:17, 34
10:17–20, 170
10:18, 170
10:20, 171–72
10:21, 169–72, 183, 196n36
10:21–22, 33
10:22, 197n44
10:22–23, 152n8
10:23, 126
10:23–24, 178
10:38, 49, 174
10:38–42, 49, 155n49, 172–81, 199n78
10:39, 174, 178, 198n66
10:42, 172
11:1, 126, 142, 152n8
11:1–13, 142, 145
11:5–7, 47
11:5–8, 142
11:6, 142
11:7, 143
11:10–13, 155n49, 187
11:11–12, 143
11:11–13, 143

11:14–28, 71n114
11:27, 140–141
11:27–28, 132, 141, 162–65
11:28, 124, 140, 162, 178
11:29–30, 59
11:29–32, 58, 101
11:29–36, 71n114
12:1, 126, 152n8
12:1–13, 152n10
12:1–13:9, 71n114
12:3, 197n44
12:8–9, 190
12:13–21, 155n49
12:22, 152n8
12:37, 114n13
12:41, 152n10
12:42–48, 155n49
12:43, 114n13
12:45, 76, 198n53
12:45–47, 114n13
12:48, 86
12:49–53, 134–36, 155n49
12:52, 143
13:10, 51
13:10–13, 117n52
13:10–17, 155n49
13:12, 189, 201n109
13:13, 189
13:17, 201n110
13:22–45, 71n114
13:34–35, 155n49
14:1–6, 117n52, 155n49
14:4, 118n70
14:7–14, 39
14:8, 77
14:15–24, 40
14:17, 114n13
14:21–23, 114n13
14:25–26, 124, 134–136
14:25–33, 138, 152n4, 152n10, 155n49
14:25–15:32, 71n114

14:26, 23–24, 143
14:26–33, 67n34
14:27, 124
14:33, 124, 165
14:35, 162
15:1–7, 107
15:8–10, 107, 155n49
15:11–32, xxiin3, 24, 71n114, 75, 102–112, 121n127, 133, 145, 154n29, 155n49, 187, 211
15:12, 16, 105, 110, 211
15:13, 106, 110–11, 120n106
15:13–19, 211
15:15–16, 201n112
15:17, 110–12
15:18–19, 110
15:20, 111
15:22, 110, 114n13, 121n118
15:22–23, 105
15:24, 106, 110, 211
15:25, 104
15:26, 76–78, 108–109, 121n118
15:27, 112
15:28–30, 111
15:29, 104
15:30, 120n106
15:31, 111
15:31–32, 211
15:32, 110, 154n25
16:1, 152n8
16:1–13, 155n49
16:18, 155n49
17:1, 152n8
17:2, 15, 59, 131, 210
17:7, 114n13
17:7–10, 155n49, 199n85
17:9–10, 114n13
17:15, 118n70
17:15–19, 201n109

17:16, 129, 198n65, 198n66
17:19, 92
17:21, 205
17:22, 152n8
17:22–37, 155n49
17:25, 101
17:26, 60
17:27, 60
17:27–30, 60
17:28–31, 61
18:14, 38
18:15, 10, 38, 42, 69n54, 152n10, 153n22, 183
18:15–17, xiv, 11, 24, 32, 35–40, 58, 60, 63, 69n60, 75, 111, 128–31, 134–35, 143–45, 153n20, 165, 171–72, 178, 197n50, 207
18:16, 33, 37–39, 130, 166, 182–83, 205
18:17, 36, 42, 110, 130–31, 163, 171–72, 181, 192–93
18:18–24, 138
18:18–30, 155n49
18:22, 141, 165
18:28, 141
18:28–30, 135
18:29, 142, 222
18:29–30, 137, 142
18:35–42, 71n114
18:43, 201nn109, 110
19:1–10, 49, 155n49
19:1–27, 71n114
19:11–27, 155n49
19:13, 114n13
19:13–15, 86
19:15, 114n13
19:17, 114n13
19:22, 114n13
19:29, 124

19:36–39, 201n110
19:36–44, 71n114
19:37, 67n34, 124, 126, 152n7
19:37–40, 152n10
19:44, 62
19:45, 50
19:45–48, 212
19:47, 168
20:1, 50, 168
20:9–18, 155n49
20:10–11, 114n13
20:25, 154n25
20:27–40, 155n49
20:45, 152n8, 152n10
20:46–47, 85
21:8, 34
21:12, 34
21:16–19, 155n45
21:17, 34
21:23–24, 62
21:34–35, 32
21:35, 62
21:37, 168
21:37–38, 51
22:19, 123, 203, 226
22:26, 158n69
22:27, 196n28, 196n28
22:31–34, 124
22:39, 126, 152n8
22:45, 126, 152n8
22:47–23:49, 71n114
22:50, 114n13
22:51, 118n70
22:54–62, 124, 142n5
22:56, xiii, 127, 186, 198n53
22:69, 158n73
23:1, 201n111
23:18, 201n111
23:27, 44, 201n110
23:27–29, 63
23:28, 208, 210, 214
23:28–31, 209

23:29, 209
23:46, 167
23:48, 201n110
23:49, 44, 126
23:55, 126, 151
24:6–8, 67n34, 126
24:6–10, 162
24:9, 126
24:9–11, 71n114
24:10, 139–40, 151
24:13–35, 71n114
24:22, 126
24:29–31, 49
24:33, 126
24:36, 196n28
24:40–41, 86
24:45–53, 32
24:46–47, 107

John
1:19–36, 200n96
1:34, 12
4:46–54, 113n6
6:9, 58
11:1–44, 85

Acts
1:2, 126
1:14, 127, 139
1:15, 127, 196n28
1:15–26, 152n5
1:16–17, 127
1:21, 126, 152n1
2, 197n44
2:1, 127
2:1–17, 31
2:5–36, 44
2:17, 80
2:17–18, 44
2:18, 114n13
2:22, 196n28
2:38, 34
2:39, 44
2:41, 127

2:42, 150
2:43–47, 25, 222
2:44, 150, 222
2:44–45, 85
2:46, 51
3:6, 34
3:13, 78
3:16, 34
3:26, 12, 78
4:7, 34
4:10, 34
4:12, 34
4:17–18, 34
4:25, 78
4:27, 78
4:29, 114n13
4:30, 34, 78
4:32–35, 25
4:35, 198n65, 198n66
4:37, 198n66
5:2, 198n65, 198n66
5:10, 80, 198nn65–66
5:14, 127
5:21, 168
5:25, 168
5:28, 34
5:40, 34
5:42, 168
6:1, 152n5
6:1–2, 127
6:1–6, 85
6:2, 124
6:3, 183
6:5–10, 199n85
6:7, 124
6:10, 183
7:6, 79
7:9, 78
7:10, 183
7:19, 68n54
7:20, 175
7:21, 175
7:22, 183
8:10, 15, 59

8:12, 34
8:16, 34
9:14, 34
9:16, 34
9:26, 127
9:27, 34
9:28, 34
9:34, 118n70
9:36, 126
10:24–48, 154n31
10:38, 118n70
10:43, 34
10:48, 34
12:13, 198n53
14:21, 124
15:1–29, 155n50
15:10, 127
15:11–40, 198n55
16:14, 154n31
16:16, 198n53
16:17, 114n13
16:18, 34
16:32, 154n31
17:22, 196n28
19:1, 127
19:5, 34
19:8, 127
21:9, 198n54
21:16, 127
22:3, 174–175, 196n28, 198n66
22:16, 34
23:17, 80
23:22, 80
26:9, 34
26:22, 59
27:21, 196n28
28:8, 118n70

Romans
2:20, 52
12:3–8, 123
12:4–5, 204, 223

1 Corinthians
1:16–18, 154n31
3:1–2, 158n69
7:12, 158n69
9:19, 158n69
11:23–25, 203
11:24, 226
12, 123
12:12–31, 204
12:12–25, 204
13:11, 158n69
16:15–16, 154n31

2 Corinthians
1:24, 158n69
4:5, 158n69
11:2, 158n69
12:14, 158n69

1 Thessalonians
2:7, 158n69

Galatians
4:1, 158n69
4:19, 158n69

1 Peter
1:14, 164, 195n15

Coloissians
3:20, 164

Ephesians
6:1, 164

2 Timothy
3:15, 10, 158n69

James
2:3, 98

Hebrews
10:3, 204

Infancy Gospel of Thomas
6:1–2, 163
6:1–8:2, 163
6:2, 164
6:8, 167
6:8–7:4, 167
6:9, 168
10:1–2, 19n38
13:1–3, 163
13:2, 167–68
14:1–4, 163
14:2, 167
17:2, 195n21

Protoevangelium of James
8:3, 117n51

Acts of Andrew and Matthew
6:1, 57
7:10, 57
18:5, 57
22:8, 57
43:1, 57

Acts of Paul and Thecla
2:2, 57
22:1, 57
23:2, 57
23:3, 57
23:4, 57
23:5, 57

Acts of Peter
15, 186

Acts of Peter and Andrew
2:1, 57
16:1, 57

Acts of Philip
4:2, 57
5:3, 57
29:1, 57
143:2, 57

Acts of Thomas
5:6–9:3, 137
154:11, 57

Acts of John
19:7, 57
47:1–3, 57
48:2, 57
49:1, 57
50:3, 57
53:1, 57
54:2–5, 57
71:1, 57
73:1, 57
75:1–2, 57
76:3, 57
79:3, 57
86:1, 57
88:3–89:2, 147
88:4, 57
89:2, 147
111:3–6, 57
113:1, 147

About the Author

Amy Lindeman Allen is assistant professor of New Testament at Christian Theological Seminary. She earned her PhD in New Testament from Vanderbilt University and has previously taught at Truckee Meadows Community College and Columbia Theological Seminary. She is an ordained minister in the Evangelical Lutheran Church in America and has served congregations in Ohio, Pennsylvania and Nevada. Together with her spouse Erik, she is the proud parent of three children: Rebecca (11), Joanna (7), and William (4).

www.ingramcontent.com/pod-product-compliance
Lightning Source LLC
Chambersburg PA
CBHW021847300426
44115CB00005B/52